WORLD
WAR I

WORLD
WAR I

H. P. WILLMOTT

LONDON, NEW YORK, MELBOURNE,
MUNICH AND DELHI

Senior Designer Caroline Hill
Designers Joern Kroeger, Mark Stevens,
Colin Goody, Jerry Udall, Mabel Chan,
Alison Gardner, Paul Jackson
Additional design assistance Nicola Liddiard,
Caroline Quiroga
Senior Editors Ferdie McDonald, Jane Edmonds
Editorial Contributors Neil Grant,
Margaret Mulvihill
Editors Jane Oliver-Jedrzejak, Jannet King,
Elizabeth Wyse, Sam Atkinson, Lee Johnson
Picture Researcher Anne-Marie Ehrlich
Special Photography Gary Ombler
Digital maps created by Advanced Illustration,
Encompass Graphics
Project Cartographers Iowerth Watkins,
Rob Stokes
DTP John Goldsmid
Production Wendy Penn
Index Caroline Wilding

Editorial Direction Andrew Heritage
Art Direction Bryn Walls
Managing Editor Debra Clapson
Managing Art Editor Louise Dick

First published in Great Britain as First World War
in 2003 by Dorling Kindersley Limited
80 Strand, London WC2R ORL
Copyright © 2003
Dorling Kindersley Limited
A Penguin Company

A CIP catalogue record for this book is
available from the British Library

ISBN 1-4053-1263-7

Colour reproduction by GRB, Italy
Printed and bound in China by L.Rex Printing Co. Ltd.

For our complete catalogue visit
www.dk.com

A British trench, 1918
Much of a front-line soldier's duty was simply to watch
and wait. These British troops are manning an observation
post in a forward sap at Givenchy.

CONTENTS

INTRODUCTION

~

THE FIRST WORLD WAR has a good claim to be the most decisive event of the modern age, changing the world in ways not even the French Revolution could achieve. When war broke out early in August 1914, no one could have predicted just what a cataclysm it would be. After four years of the most costly war in human history, no one could be in any doubt. The political map of the world was transformed, the long period of 19th-century peace was destroyed, and growing confidence in the progressive power of liberal values and modern capitalism eroded. The principal legacy of the First World War was an atmosphere of hatred and resentment, between nations, between classes and between races, whose consequences were to be felt in the bitter political struggles of the 1920s and 1930s, and the eventual slide into a second, even more destructive, war 20 years after the end of the first.

At the start of the war, most of the world was ruled by sprawling dynastic empires. By 1920 most of them were gone. The great European empires – the Habsburg, the Russian and the German – disappeared, to be replaced by modern republics. The Ottoman Empire was defeated and dismembered; a nationalist dictatorship took its place in what is now modern-day Turkey. A necklace of new states emerged from the Baltic to the Persian Gulf on the basis of national "self-determination". The old Europe of great monarchies, dominated by aristocracy and army, was in decline well before 1914, but the war accelerated and distorted its fall. The Europe of the 1920s is recognizably the Europe of today.

The war brought other changes in the international arena. The USA entered the war late, and began its long ascent to superpower status. The desire to put an end to war once and for all in 1918 bore fruit in the League of Nations, founded in 1920. For all its many weaknesses, the League laid the foundation for international collaboration on issues that have become the key concerns of the post-1945 United Nations. The Russian Revolution of October 1917, which brought communists to power, ushered in the confrontation between capitalism and communism that blighted the international system for 70 years and produced the Cold War of 1945–89.

The war also changed the nature of the modern state. No European state had ever been asked to organize armies in millions. The mobilization of the home front to cope with provisioning the army brought the state to the point where whole economies had to be controlled in the name of the war effort. Everywhere states organized rationing on a national scale, expanded welfare services, encouraged scientific research, collected statistics and engaged in home front propaganda. In the 1920s states kept on many of these responsibilities. The war taught modern states how to police, mobilize and persuade their populations in ways previously unheard of.

The one thing the First World War did not do was to transform the hardware with which war was fought. The war was larger in scale than any before it, but for most of its duration conventional warships, artillery, machine-guns, rifles and horses dominated combat. Aircraft were in their infancy; submarines were used sparingly, as were tanks, the one major new invention for land warfare. The potential of these new weapons would not be realized until the next war. As a result, much of the war, especially on the Western Front, became a stalemate, as both sides searched desperately for new weapons or ways of fighting which might break through the enemy's lines of trenches and barbed wire.

The terrible cost of the war gave rise to a widespread pessimism, a morbid fear of decline. In the 1920s thousands of angry young men rejected the principles of the older generation that had sent them to the front and hankered for revenge on those they blamed for the disastrous conflict. In Italy and Germany, former veterans Mussolini and Hitler used a thirst for political violence to build up new radical nationalist movements that swept to power, first in Italy in 1922, then Germany in 1933. Rejecting the liberal west, the new dictators saw the war as the harbinger of a new age of empire and war-making.

If the First World War had never happened the world would almost certainly have been spared the horrors of civil war, political terrorism, a second total war and genocide in the 1930s and 1940s. While the outcome of the war laid the foundation of much of the modern world, the uncertainties that went with it created a deeply disturbed Europe, whose darker side opened the way to Stalingrad and Auschwitz.

Richard Overy
June 2003

Mark V tanks in action 1918
From July 1918 Allied forces advanced across France and Belgium, driving the Germans back from their lines of trenches. Tanks played only a small part in the advance.

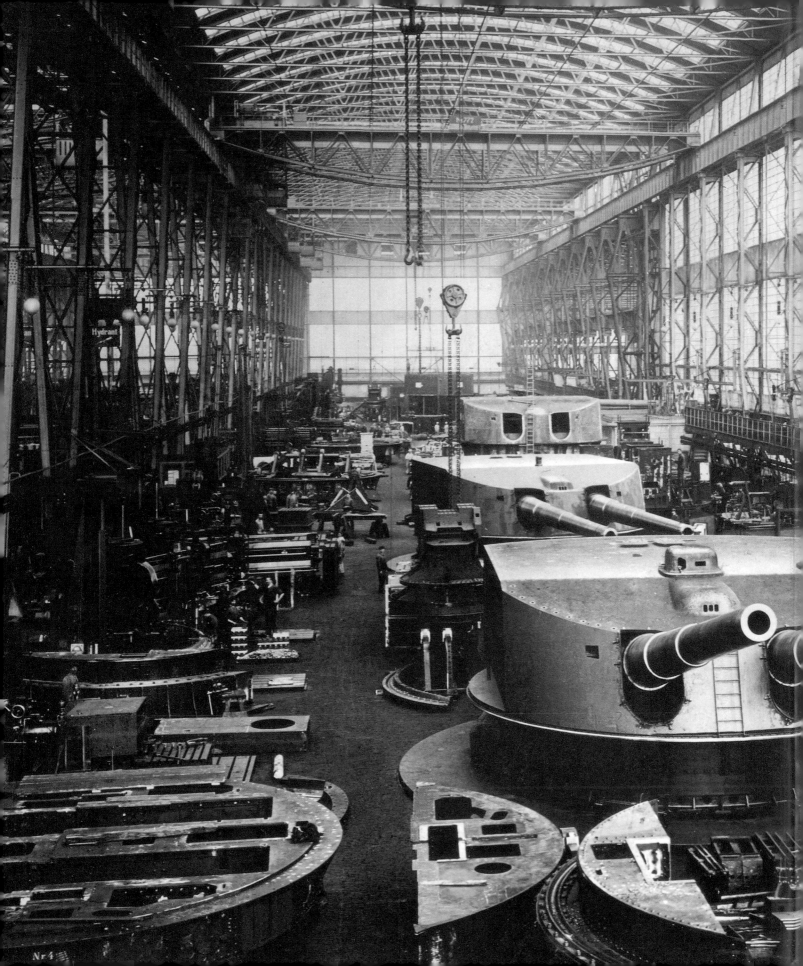

THE ROAD TO WAR

1878–1914

~

ON THE SURFACE, THE YEARS LEADING UP TO THE FIRST WORLD WAR WERE A PERIOD OF PEACE AND PROSPERITY IN EUROPE. WHENEVER THE THREAT OF WAR AROSE, A DIPLOMATIC COMPROMISE WAS FOUND TO AVERT IT. THE GREAT POWERS, HOWEVER, ACTED ON THE ASSUMPTION THAT ONE DAY THERE WOULD BE A WAR. FACTORIES PRODUCED NEW SHIPS, GUNS AND RIFLES, HUGE STANDING ARMIES WERE RAISED AND WAR PLANS WERE PREPARED. YET, WHEN THE SPARK CAME THAT LIT THE POWDER-KEG IN 1914, THE SCALE OF THE CONFLAGRATION WAS GREATER THAN ANY OF THE COMBATANTS HAD IMAGINED.

~

The Krupp steel works, Essen
For 20 years before the First World War Europe armed itself in anticipation of a major conflict. The Krupp works produced Germany's heavy artillery. These naval guns are destined for the ships of Germany's brand new fleet, constructed between 1898 and 1914.

THE CULTIVATION OF HATRED

THE OUTBREAK OF THE FIRST WORLD WAR WAS TRIGGERED BY THE ASSASSINATION

OF THE AUSTRIAN ARCHDUKE FERDINAND AND HIS WIFE BY A SERB NATIONALIST IN

SARAJEVO, THE CAPITAL OF BOSNIA-HERZEGOVINA. THIS ONE EVENT, HOWEVER, WAS NOT

A BASIC CAUSE OF THE WAR. FEW WOULD DISAGREE THAT A COMPLEX INTERPLAY OF

POLITICAL, ECONOMIC AND SOCIAL FACTORS THAT HAD DEVELOPED SINCE THE 1870S

WAS TO BE RESPONSIBLE FOR SHATTERING THE PEACE OF EUROPE IN 1914.

THE FIRST WORLD WAR is commonly seen as a watershed between two distinct periods of history, in many ways marking the end of the 19th century and the beginning of the 20th. It was certainly the first war of the 20th century in terms of its scale and the lethal power of the weaponry involved. At the same time, however, it had very real links with the 19th century, none more obvious than the ideas and beliefs that shaped national and social attitudes and contributed to a climate of mutual hostility between the Great Powers of Europe. The 19th century witnessed the cultivation of that hostility, the 20th century the reaping.

GREAT POWER RELATIONSHIPS

The states of Europe moved to war in 1914 not simply because of immediate political issues and events, but as the result of profound economic and social changes in Europe in the previous four decades. The most significant of these was in the relationship between the Great Powers, where a balance of power had been created that had resulted in instability. Perhaps surprisingly, a balance of power need not produce stability, any more than an imbalance of power need produce war. Given the prevailing circumstances, either may preserve peace or initiate conflict.

For almost 20 years after France's defeat and the creation of a united Germany in the Franco-Prussian War of 1870–71, Bismarck, the German chancellor, sought to ensure peace within Europe by maintaining an imbalance of power. He did so by checking Austria-Hungary and Russia in their dealings with each other – restraining both by holding the power of decision between them – and by ensuring that France remained diplomatically isolated, with no allies, and so unable to challenge German military superiority.

Bismarck's policy, however, barely survived his departure from office in March 1890. The balance created by the existence of two rival alliance systems – the Triple Alliance of Germany, Austria-Hungary and Italy and the Franco-Russian Entente (see map page 15) after 1891 – was one of the major causes of war. One important factor was that the various members of these alliances in 1914 considered themselves obliged to support their ally (or allies); they assumed that failure to do so would result in their being repudiated by the ally, and that the arrangements on which they relied for their security would be destroyed as a consequence.

The end of the Bismarckian diplomatic system was accompanied by further changes that added to the uncertainties of the rival alliance systems. One of these was the uneven spread of industrialization.

THE EFFECTS OF INDUSTRIALIZATION

Britain had taken the lead in embarking on an "industrial revolution", and by the mid-19th century it was known as "the workshop of the world". From the 1830s, however, the other states of northwest Europe had also begun to industrialize, though at different rates. From the 1870s, Germany in particular had increased its production of coal, iron and steel at an incredible pace, to replace Britain as the leading industrial power in Europe by 1913. (It could not, however, challenge the position held by the USA since the end of the 19th century as the world's leading industrial power.) As other states in Europe struggled to keep up with the pace of industrialization in Germany, an imbalance of power developed, with far-reaching implications.

GREAT POWER STATUS

By 1914 there were most definitely two grades of "Great Power" in Europe: Britain, France and Germany; and Austria-Hungary, Italy and Russia.

The German kaiser watching manoeuvres
Wilhelm II took a keen interest in military tactics and the latest developments in weaponry. Distrust of his motives was one factor in the militarization of Europe in the years before the First World War.

"Recklessness and weakness will plunge the world into the most horrible war aimed to destroy Germany. For there can no longer be any doubts: England, France and Russia have conspired… to wage a war of annihilation against us."

KAISER WILHELM II, MEMO SENT ON LEARNING
OF RUSSIAN MOBILIZATION ON 30 JULY 1914

Arguably, there were more than two groupings. Britain and Germany were certainly Great Powers of the first rank, on account of their industrial and economic power. France might be included with the other two, but more for historical reasons than any other, because in terms of industrial power and manpower resources it was now overshadowed by Germany. Austria-Hungary and Russia were increasingly hard-pressed to sustain themselves in the first rank, while Italy's status as a Great Power was solely honorary and nothing to do with its power, armed strength or military capability. The Turkish Ottoman Empire, which had for a long time resisted modernization and the benefits of industrial and economic change and was referred to as "the sick man of Europe", was no longer one of this select group of states. An element of instability arose in the wake of Europe's industrialization because France and Russia, both of which had failed to keep up with Germany in terms of economic power, formed an alliance to create a balance between themselves on the one hand and Germany and Austria-Hungary on the other.

THE POWER OF THE STATE

Alongside this redefinition of Great Power status and the balance between Europe's rival alliances were two significant developments. The first was the fact that between the 1870s and 1914 the state effectively defeated all challenges to itself. Separatist and nationalist movements threatened the unity and stability of Austria-Hungary and Germany, and religious-based differences plagued France and, to a lesser extent, the various states of Germany. There was also the political challenge to the state posed by socialist and Marxist ideologies, and the emergence of anarchist and syndicalist splinter-groups. In 1905 a revolution in Russia almost overthrew the tsar and his government; only the loyalty of the imperialist army saved him. By 1907 the revolutionary tendencies within Russian society had been suppressed, although they would resurface again during the First World War. In 1914 it seemed that the state was still the primary focus of allegiance of the vast majority of people throughout Europe.

The second development was the extraordinary growth in state power. By the 1870s the state had acquired unprecedented power over its own population and unparalleled capacity to wage war. The two were related. The Franco-Prussian War of 1870–71 spelt out the need for all states, unless they were prepared to accept German military hegemony, to ensure their security by raising armies through conscription. In doing so, the major European powers acquired the ability to mobilize across hundreds of kilometres of front by raising armies that were no longer numbered in hundreds of thousands, but in millions, of men.

A CLIMATE OF HATE

Mobilization on this scale was only possible because of the willingness of societies to bear the financial burden of the new armies and an equal willingness to allow their young men to be conscripted. This acceptance of the possible sacrifice of men's lives was very much an active one, which developed partly in response to the increasing tendency of governments to view, and refer to, all neighbours as potential enemies. This tendency was accompanied

Kaiser Wilhelm II and the Prince of Wales
The Kaiser entertains his cousin, the future King George V of England, on board his yacht in 1907. Both men were grandsons of Queen Victoria, as was Tsar Nicholas II of Russia. Royal family ties proved no insurance against war.

by a general intellectual change that was the legacy of the British naturalist Charles Darwin and the philosopher Herbert Spencer. Darwin, in his epoch-making *On the Origin of Species by Means of Natural Selection* (published in 1859) had described the theory of evolution, while Spencer had applied the theory to people in society. The twin Darwinian notions of the "struggle for existence" and "the survival of the fittest" came to be widely accepted throughout Europe, and in debased form provided the basis of an increasingly strident and assertive nationalism. Inferior racial qualities and national characteristics were attributed to potential enemies, often by a popular press that pandered to the worst elements of intolerance and hatred in society.

The war that broke out in 1914 was not, as is sometimes claimed, the product of a scurrilous press promoting a mixture of nationalism and militarism. However, the fervent nationalism that

Austro-Hungarian dreadnought, SMS *Viribus Unitis*
In the years preceding the First World War all the major European powers built up their navies, even those such as Austria-Hungary that lacked a strong maritime tradition.

greeted the outbreak of war was largely the product of years of demonizing and ridiculing foreigners and the acceptance of ideas of national and racial superiority throughout European societies.

THE EVE OF WAR

Such were the more important general factors at work in shaping the course of events that led to the outbreak of war in Europe in 1914. The instability created by the balance of power within Europe, combined with the sense of apprehension produced by successive crises – notably those in the Balkans in 1908–9 and 1912–13 – were the basic factors that led to the crisis triggered by the assassination of Archduke Ferdinand in June 1914 and the outbreak of war. Compounding these matters, however, were public attitudes, shaped by states that had little difficulty in justifying their actions to their peoples.

The process of industrialization was crucial in that it made possible the raising, organization and arming of unprecedented numbers of fighting men. The armed forces were transformed from those of 1870, most obviously the navies, which underwent fundamental changes in types of warship and their systems of firing and communications. Armies were less obviously affected in that they retained their three main branches – artillery, infantry and cavalry – and horses were still the main means of moving weapons and supplies. Communications had, however, undergone massive changes since the 1870s, with the refinement of the electric telegraph and the invention of the telephone and the wireless. Meanwhile, in the air a whole new dimension of war had appeared during the Balkan Wars of 1912–13.

The changes that affected armies and navies after 1914 would overshadow those of the previous period. Even so, it is alarming how little the military high commands of the various powers had understood the implications of the changes that had taken place. This would have major repercussions for the way in which they would conduct the war that was about to unfold.

"At first there will be increased slaughter on so terrible a scale as to render it impossible to get troops to push the battle to a decisive issue…Everybody will be entrenched in the next war; the spade will be as indispensable to the soldier as his rifle."

JAN (IVAN) BLOCH, POLISH RAILWAY MAGNATE AND AUTHOR,
FROM *WAR IN THE FUTURE*, 1897

The Years of Plenty

AFTER THE DEFEAT OF NAPOLEON in 1815, 19th-century Europe experienced just six wars between major powers, of which three involved Russia and the Ottoman Empire (Turkey). The former sought greater influence in the Balkans and access to the eastern Mediterranean from the Black Sea. The latter ruled over large areas of the Balkans, but was struggling to retain control in the face of increasing nationalism in the region.

After the Russo-Turkish war of 1877–78, the victorious Russians imposed the Treaty of San Stefano on the defeated Turks. The Balkan states of

The Congress of Berlin 1878
The conference marked the highpoint of the career of German chancellor Bismarck. The decisions made there overruled the terms of the Treaty of San Stefano, concluded by Russia and Turkey earlier in the year.

The Suez Canal
Though built by the French, the Suez Canal became a symbol of British maritime and imperial power when Britain acquired a controlling interest in the company after occupying Egypt in 1882.

Serbia, Montenegro and Romania were granted full independence from Turkish control, while a large, new autonomous Bulgarian principality was created. Russian influence in the Balkans was greatly increased as a result, raising alarm bells in the rest of Europe. Austria-Hungary was, in particular, anxious not to encourage nationalism among its own Balkan territories, and considered Russia a rival in the region. The British had already supported the Turks against Russia in the Crimean War of 1853–56, and they were aware that if the Ottoman Empire were to fall to the Russians it would threaten British interests in India, and the vital sea route through the Suez Canal.

THE CONGRESS OF BERLIN
At the invitation of Austria-Hungary, a congress was convened in Berlin in June 1878, presided over by the German chancellor, Bismarck. All the major European powers – Austria-Hungary, Britain, France, Germany, Italy, Russia and the Ottoman

Empire sent their representatives. It was agreed that the fate of Turkish territories in the Balkans should be decided jointly by all the powers, and the Treaty of San Stefano was set aside. Austria-Hungary was allowed to occupy Bosnia-Herzegovina (although not formally to annex it), and Russia gained Bessarabia on its border with Romania, which exchanged its coastline north of the Danube for the Dobruja, the coastal region to the south. Turkey was given back Eastern Rumelia and Macedonia, which the Russians had granted to Bulgaria. The new smaller Bulgaria was autonomous, but still nominally part of the Ottoman Empire. Serbia, Montenegro and Romania had their independence confirmed.

NEW ALLIANCES

The immediate problem that arose from the Congress of Berlin was Russian resentment. Having defeated the Turks, Russia had seen the treaty it had dictated torn up, and it blamed Germany for having sided with Austria-Hungary. The latter comprised the Austrian Empire and self-governing Hungary, both ruled by the Habsburg dynasty as a "Dual Monarchy". Germany, which had attempted to mediate between its eastern neighbours at the congress, did now conclude an alliance with Austria-Hungary. The alliance was intended to forestall a clash between the Habsburgs and the rulers of Russia, the Romanovs. It presented Russia with having to face the might of Germany should it attack Austria-Hungary, while at the same time making it clear to Austria-Hungary that Germany would not support any aggression against Russia.

The balance of power came under increasing threat, however. During the 1880s, Russia realized that its freedom of action in the Balkans depended on France maintaining its status as a rival power to Germany. Although Germany professed not to oppose Russian designs on Constantinople, Russia knew that it could never gain control of the Straits (the straits linking the Mediterranean and the Black Sea) without provoking a war with Austria-Hungary, and hence with Germany. In 1882 these two allies formed a Triple Alliance with Italy, which itself had territorial ambitions in the Balkans.

British satirical map of 1877

Russia is depicted as an octopus with designs on the outstretched form of Turkey. Many saw Russian territorial ambitions in the Balkans, the Middle East and Central Asia as the greatest threat to continuing stability in Europe.

EUROPEAN ALLIANCES
1878 –1914

◆ Austro-German alliance
1878–1918
◆ Three Emperors' alliance
1881–87
◆ Austro-Serbian alliance
1881–95
◆ Triple alliance
1882–1915
◆ Austro-German–Romanian alliance
1883–1916
◆ Franco-Russian alliance
1894–1917
◆ Russo-Bulgarian military convention
1902–13
◆ Anglo-French Entente
1904–
◆ Anglo-Russian Entente
1907–1917
ALLIANCES DURING FIRST WORLD WAR 1914–18
The Allies (and allied states)
Central Powers (and allied states)
Neutral states

Balance of power

The two key alliances were those between France and Russia and between Germany and Austria-Hungary.

In 1887 a crisis developed after Bulgaria refused to obey Russian demands that it discourage the people of Eastern Rumelia from revolting against their Turkish rulers and uniting with Bulgaria. This intervention by Russia caused Britain to associate itself with the Triple Alliance in its attempt to maintain the status quo in the Balkans. As a result Russia strengthened its ties with France in an alliance that would play an important role in the events leading to the First World War.

THE FRANCO-RUSSIAN ALLIANCE

Such an alliance seriously disturbed the delicate balance of power in Europe by presenting Germany with a threat on two fronts. A preliminary agreement between Russia and France in 1891 was

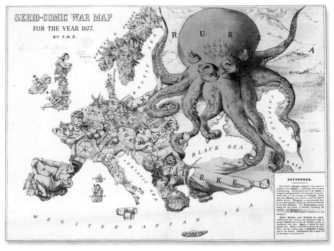

strengthened by military conventions in 1892 and 1894. The need for secrecy meant that it was not possible for the alliance to be discussed by the French parliament, and it was therefore ratified by an exchange of letters early in 1894, and subsequently confirmed and consolidated in 1899 and 1912. For many years it was a disappointment to both parties. Russia refused to regard it as the means whereby France could recover Alsace and Lorraine, which had been lost to the Germans in 1871, and France felt in no way bound to support tsarist ambitions in the Balkans.

EXPANDING EMPIRES

In the world beyond Europe the Great Powers often came to understandings that cut across the alliances made within Europe. In April 1895 Germany, France and Russia co-operated to relieve the Japanese of gains they had exacted from China after their recent war, and in 1900 the powers jointly suppressed the anti-imperialist Boxer Rebellion, which threatened their interests in China. With almost all the nations of Africa and Asia unable to resist the military technology of the Western powers, imperialism reached its peak around the turn of the century. A number of newcomers – Germany, Italy, Japan and the United States – joined the traditional imperial powers in acquiring overseas possessions.

All the powers exercised restraint with respect to one another's ambitions. Even occasional crises during the "Scramble for Africa", as the powers divided up the continent after 1885, were resolved. No country wanted to risk complications within Europe for the sake of its non-European interests.

Blohm und Voss shipyard, Hamburg 1910
Around the turn of the century, German shipyards began to rival British ones. This steamer is being built for the Hamburg–America Line (HAPAG).

CHANGES IN EUROPE

The Europe of 1914 was very different from that of the mid-19th century, when only Britain and Belgium could be considered industrialized states, in which manufacture and trade were the mainstay of the economy. By 1914 this was true of almost all of northern Europe.

Hand in hand with industrialization went a marked population increase in the region as a whole. This had started in the 18th century, and had been caused by a number of factors, including improved food supplies. Technological developments in agriculture had led to an increase in food production, and improvements in transport systems enabled food to be moved around more easily. Better-nourished people lived longer and had more children who survived into into adulthood.

In the second half of the 19th century the populations of European states continued to grow rapidly alongside the rapid spread of industrialization. The exception was France, which, until 1871, was the most

Berlin–Baghdad railway
The railway was instrumental in Germany gaining economic and military influence in the Ottoman Empire. A German consortium won the contract for building the railway in 1888, but it was not completed by 1914.

populous state in Europe, apart from Russia. The newly unified Germany took over that position, and increased its population by more than 50 per cent over the next 40 years, while that of France remained static. By 1914, with the exception of Italy, it was the least populous of the powers.

Britain was also overtaken by Germany, and not just in terms of population. For more than 100 years it had been the leading manufacturing nation,

Ford factory 1914
Workers fit a Model-T engine on a Ford assembly line. The methods of production introduced by Ford helped make America the world's leading economic power.

but, within 40 years of unification in 1871, Germany had taken the lead. (Neither country could, however, compete with America, which had, by 1900, emerged as the greatest manufacturing nation in the world.)

AN IMBALANCE DEVELOPS

The industrialization of Europe after the mid-19th century was very different from the earlier stages of the Industrial Revolution, which had primarily been concerned with iron-working, steam power, textiles and potteries. Chemical industries started to produce a wide range of new substances, from synthetic dyes to powerful new explosives. The year 1889 saw the Eiffel Tower built in Paris; it was also the year when cheap, mass-produced, high-grade steel was used for the first time used in battleship construction. Other developments in the late 19th century included electrification and the internal combustion engine. These new technologies led to profound economic and social changes in the industrializing countries, but eastern and southern Europe were left behind in the process.

A PERIOD OF PEACE

Growing prosperity, advancing living standards and increasingly enlightened social legislation played their part in the easing of internal social tensions in most European states. Vast class differences still remained, but social welfare and parliamentary representation did much to draw the sting of class warfare, though in Russia there remained a social militancy that, for most of this period was not apparent in the rest of Europe.

With increasing literacy and slowly improving social conditions, this was an era of hope. Between 1871 and 1914 much of Europe enjoyed as long a period of peace as any in its history, but paradoxically it was also a period when the states of Europe were preparing themselves for war by maintaining massive armies and filling their arsenals with all the latest weaponry.

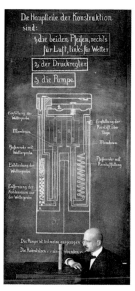

Fritz Haber (1868–1934)

Brilliant scientists such as Haber, Nobel prize winner for chemistry (1918), made great contributions to German industrial growth. Here Haber shows his design for a firedamp whistle to save the lives of coalminers. During the war his method of synthesizing ammonia helped make up for Germany's shortage of nitrates for fertilizer, and he also worked on the gas warfare programme.

Industrialization, the gathering pace of technical change, and the rapid population increase in certain countries were major factors in the militarization of Europe. The invention of the electric telegraph, of the humble typewriter and steel filing cabinet, and later of the telephone, combined with ever-expanding railway networks and police forces, provided European states with unprecedented means of controlling their populations. One of the most obvious uses to which these powers were put was conscription.

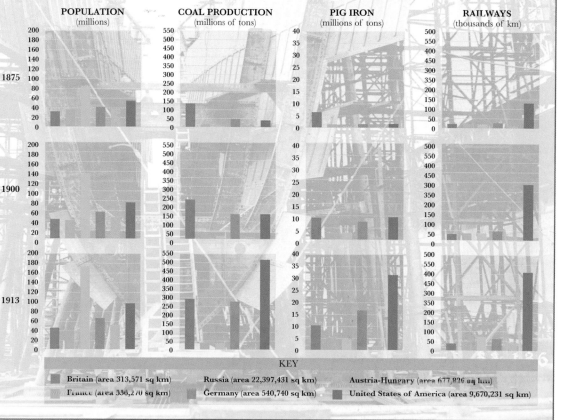

INDUSTRIAL GROWTH OF THE GREAT POWERS 1875–1913

EUROPE'S LEADING industrial powers were Britain, which had been the first country to experience an industrial revolution, and Germany, which rapidly made up for lost time following unification in 1871. Both in old, established industries and, in particular, in the new precision and petro-chemical industries Germany had, by 1910, established itself as the leading state in Europe. By 1914 it was the leading trading partner of virtually every other nation in Europe, including Britain, which had become increasingly dependent upon Germany for finished goods.

France, with its limited coal and iron resources, lagged a little way behind Germany and Britain. Austria-Hungary and Russia had been late starters and still had a long way to catch up. In the USA economic growth in the late 19th century was far more spectacular than that in any of the European states, but most of its production was as yet for its vast home market

POPULATION (millions)

COAL PRODUCTION (millions of tons)

PIG IRON (millions of tons)

RAILWAYS (thousands of km)

1875

1900

1913

KEY

Britain (area 313,571 sq km)

Russia (area 22,397,431 sq km)

Austria-Hungary (area 677,926 sq km)

France (area 536,270 sq km)

Germany (area 540,740 sq km)

United States of America (area 9,670,231 sq km)

THE EVOLUTION OF THE MACHINE-GUN

VARIOUS INVENTORS OVER THE CENTURIES had experimented with rapid-firing guns, but it was not until the third quarter of the 19th century that the first "machine-guns" were developed. The two that enjoyed most success were the Gatling, produced in the USA in 1862, and the French *mitrailleuse*, also developed in the 1860s. Rate of fire was achieved by the the number of barrels: in the Gatling ten and in some *mitrailleuses* as many as 37. Neither was a true machine-gun; both depended on how fast the operator turned the crank handle to fire the next barrel; they did not automatically harness the energy of the gun's recoil to load and fire the next round. This system was developed by the American Hiram Maxim (1840–1916), who acquired the patent for such a gun in 1882 and made the first in 1884. The Maxim gun underwent

extensive trials with all the major European armies in 1887 and in the USA in 1888. The various countries subsequently produced their own national weapons, though machine-guns continued to follow the basic Maxim concept. From the start there were three basic problems: a reliable loading and ejection mechanism, dependable cartridges and overheating (hence need to cool the single barrel). The Hotchkiss, produced in France, worked on slightly different principles, using the gases emitted from each bullet rather than the recoil to reload the gun and dispensing with the water-cooled jacket. Only one nation, Germany, thoroughly integrated machine-guns into its military organization. In 1914 the German armies had about 12,000 machine-guns with between six and twelve guns per regiment. Machine-guns at this point were too large and heavy to be used by individuals: the standard German Maschinengewehr 08 weighed 24.66 kg (58.31 lb), but with water and sledge weighed 32 kg (70.5 lb).

Gravity-feed magazine, refilled directly from box of cartridges

Gardner single barrel
The American Gardner, which also came in a twin-barrel version, was used by the British Navy from 1880, installed on fixed mountings on ships.

Hand-operated firing crank

Tripod mounting

Montigny mitrailleuse
A Belgian invention, this 37-barrel gun was taken up by the French army in 1869. A 25-barrel version, said to be capable of 300 rounds a minute, was used in the Franco-Prussian War.

Magazines – each contained 37 rounds – one for each barrel

Heavy mounting provides stability but makes the gun practically immobile

Machine-gunners in the Balkans Wars
A Bulgarian unit, dug in with a Maxim gun, gives a foretaste of the trench warfare of 1914–18.

Rear ranging sight

Steam generated by heat of barrel drained off, condensed, cooled and reused

Toggle-lock trigger – fire continues as long as trigger is pressed and held

Foreward sight

Water-cooled barrel-jacket to help prevent overheating and jamming

Belt-fed with 250-round fabric belts

Cold water for cooling the barrel fed into jacket through valve

Elevation wheel and lock

.303-in calibre capable of firing up to 600 rounds per minute

Tripod mounting for stability. Collapses for easy transport

British .303-in Maxim Mark 3
This was the standard British medium machine-gun of the prewar era. Adopted by the British Army in 1889, the Maxim was replaced in 1912 by the Vickers. This, however, used the same basic principles of the Maxim as did German, Austrian and Russian machine-guns.

Gravity feed magazine – a variety of magazine capacities were available ranging from 30 to over 100 rounds

Hand-operated firing crank – the rate of fire is increased or decreased by turning faster or slower

Ten rotating barrels enable high rates of fire – up to 1,000 rounds per minute in later models

Locking mechanism to prevent too much movement during firing

Wheeled gun-carriage made moving the heavy gun easier – the wheels could be locked or removed to provide a stable firing platform

US Gatling Gun
The Gatling saw action in the Civil War, but was not officially adopted by the US Army until 1866. It was subsequently used by many European countries, including Britain and Russia.

Conscription

Compulsory military service in the late 19th century had a clear political and social purpose. The army became "the school of the nation", introducing young men to the responsibilities of citizenship and prevailing patriotic ideals. The German armies owed their victory against the French in 1870–71 to superior organization, the product of the general staff system, and superior numbers – the result of conscription. After 1871 France and most of the other powers followed suit. The result was that, by 1914, Europe was armed on a scale that would have been unthinkable in 1870. In 1914 Germany succeeded in mobilizing an army of 3,500,000 regulars, conscripts and reservists, which enabled it to match Russian numbers.

The exception to the rule was Britain, where the notion of conscription was politically unacceptable. Its small professional army was largely designed for the purpose of subduing uprisings in the empire, for example in the Sudan (1896–98) and in South Africa (1899–1902). The country could rely on its navy for defence.

Maintaining such vast armies obviously inflated military budgets. States found that increased expenditure could only be justified to elected legislatures by comparing their armed forces with the armies of potential enemies. The constant monitoring of their neighbours' military strength contributed little to the harmony of Europe.

Technology and the Arms Race

The peace of Europe was rendered ever more fragile by the pace of technological progress. This now necessitated the re-equipment of armies every 18 to 20 years, and of navies once a decade. Industrialization generated an arms race that broke down the existing balance between the powers.

The most important changes resulting from industrialization to be seen in the First World War were in the way armies fought. While railways could transport ever greater numbers of men to the battlefield, changes in weaponry, brought about by developments in metallurgy and chemistry, gave armies far greater firepower. Breech-loader, quick-firing weapons and high-explosive shells combined to bring to the battlefield a heavier volume of accurate, long-range fire that ensured that the defence could break up an attack before the latter could get close enough to represent a threat. The firepower that halted emerged as stronger than the firepower that advanced.

In terms of mobility, larger armies equipped with new weaponry created increasing logistic demands. Supply columns had to double in length. Whereas in 1870 a German corps was supplied by 457 wagons, the number had risen to 1,168 by 1914. In 1870 it was reckoned that an army could operate to ranges of 160 km (100 miles) from its nearest railhead; by 1914 this figure had halved.

A question frequently asked about the First World War is why the effect of such changes was so little appreciated by the generals who had spent decades preparing for war. There was evidence available to suggest that a future conflict might turn into prolonged trench warfare because clear-cut victory in the field proved elusive. In the American Civil War (1861–65) the siege of Petersburg had proved an accurate forecast of the trenches of the First World War. The Russo-Turkish War (1877–78) had been the first European war in which "the spade had been more important than the rifle", and more recently the Russo-Japanese War (1904–05) had witnessed scenes in which hundreds of thousands of men had fought from fieldworks in battles that sometimes lasted weeks.

These wars were, however, far removed in terms of distance and time from the Europe of 1914, where the evidence of the Balkan Wars of 1912–13 suggested that wars could be decided in a matter of weeks. In both conflicts, a heavy concentration of troops and offensive action had led to a speedy outcome before such mundane matters as logistics intervened. Despite the evidence that firepower killed, the belief prevailed that victory would be won as a result of the willingness of infantry to move forwards into fire. The French considered the bayonet an instrument of moral will. The conventional wisdom was still that any war would be short, characterized by offensive action – and won, of course, by the armies.

The South African War
Britain's experience in the South African War (1899–1902) was no preparation for the First World War. The Boers' guerrilla tactics were at first very successful against the professional British army. One major change introduced by the British as a result was the khaki uniform.

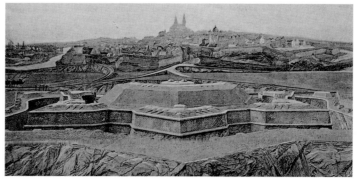

Fortifications
In the 19th century the powers of continental Europe fortified their strategically important cities and towns. The French town of Verdun *(left)*, for example, was ringed by 20 forts and 40 redoubts. In the years leading up to 1914, however, many of these forts were neglected; some were still armed with old iron cannons.

BRITISH AND GERMAN SEA POWER

For Britain, arguably the most prestigious of the powers, victory would not be won by its armies. In every war it had fought over the previous 250 years it had emerged, if not triumphant, then intact and undefeated as a result of its command of the sea.

The 19th century had seen rapid developments in ship design. Wooden hulls and rows of muzzle-loading cannon had been replaced by ironclad battleships. By 1914 they were sheathed in armour, powered by oil-burning engines that produced speeds in excess of 25 knots, and had massive guns that could fire distances of 20 km (12 miles). Other developments, namely the electric telegraph and then radio, provided admiralties with direct control over even their most distant commands. The second half of the 19th century also saw the development of mines, while the technology that provided the torpedo with reliable depth-keeping qualities – the horizontal rudder and ballast tanks – also made the submarine a practical proposition.

In the Russo-Japanese War of 1904–05, mines claimed three battleships, five cruisers, four destroyers and four other warships. The mine and the torpedo together now made the close blockade of an enemy coastline extremely hazardous. This danger was recognized by the British admiralty, which decided to impose a distant, rather than a close, blockade upon Germany in the event of war.

The growth of Germany's political power, and its increasing industrial pre-eminence, were accompanied by a new assertiveness that did not bode well for the peace of Europe. The first

The siege of Port Arthur, 1904

In the Russo-Japanese War, Port Arthur was shelled by land-based artillery and Japanese warships. The Russian cruiser *Pallada*, seen here in the harbour, was wrecked in December 1904. The Russians surrendered on January 2, 1905.

A new power in the east

Yokohama celebrates Japan's victory over Russia in the war of 1904–05. Japan's defeat of Europe's largest, most populous empire heralded the end of the old world order.

manifestations of this were the German naval laws of 1898 and 1900. These committed Germany to building a fleet powerful enough to threaten Britain's naval supremacy. Germany calculated that problems in various parts of the British Empire, and general hostility to Britain in continental Europe, would oblige the latter to make concessions to Germany's territorial ambitions. Attempts in 1898 and 1901 to negotiate an Anglo-German alliance foundered when Britain refused to give Germany a free hand in Europe. After the conclusion of the South African War in 1902, Britain felt better able to resist German pressure.

THE ANGLO-FRENCH ENTENTE

In an attempt to reduce its problems outside Europe, Britain entered into an alliance with Japan in January 1902 and an entente with France in April 1904. The agreement with France was intended to eliminate a number of imperial issues that had bedevilled Anglo-French relations. In return for Britain's support for French territorial ambitions in Morocco, the French agreed to let Britain have a free hand in its dealings with Egypt.

Germany, convinced that the British and French were still essentially rivals, decided in 1905 to put the new Anglo-French understanding to the test. Choosing a time when Russia was still reeling from the shock of its defeat by Japan, Germany provoked a major crisis when the kaiser, on a visit to Tangier, in Morocco, declared support for the sultan as an independent sovereign.

Britain responded with active diplomatic support for France, and an important consequence of the crisis was that Anglo-French relations were, if anything, strengthened. Britain became ever more convinced that maintaining France as a great power to offset Germany's increasing military strength was essential to Britain's own security.

GROWING OPPOSITION TO GERMANY

Russia's defeat by Japan in 1904–05 cleared the way for the Anglo-Russian Entente of August 1907, aimed at settling the two countries' disputes outside Europe. It also allowed Russia to redirect its attention to the Balkans and its support for the Serbs. In 1908 a *coup d'état* in Turkey by a group known as the Young Turks led the Ottoman Empire to attempt to reassert its sovereignty in Bulgaria (which resisted such interference), and in Bosnia-Herzegovina. The latter had been under Austro-Hungarian administration since the Congress of Berlin in 1878, but Austria-Hungary now announced that it would formally annex it. Neighbouring Serbia felt Bosnia-Herzegovina, with its majority Serb population, should become part of an enlarged Serbia, and Russia was expected to support it in this objective.

At first, Russia considered agreeing to acquiesce in this matter if Austria-Hungary would support its long-held aim of obtaining right of passage for its warships through the Bosphorus and Dardanelles (while the navies of all other powers were denied access to the Black Sea). However, the Austrians pre-empted the conclusion of negotiations and proceeded with the annexation. In March 1909, in the face of a veiled threat of war from Germany, Russia was given no option but to endorse the move.

THE BRITISH NAVY

~

A T THE OUTBREAK OF WAR the British Navy could match – at least in terms of modern dreadnoughts and battlecruisers – any two of its rivals. It had 22 dreadnoughts and nine battlecruisers, compared with Germany's 15 dreadnoughts and five battlecruisers and America's ten dreadnoughts. In terms of pre-dreadnought battleships, cruisers, destroyers and submarines the British also enjoyed a clear margin of superiority over other navies.

In the two decades prior to 1914, navies underwent fundamental change as submarines, airships and aircraft, and radio came into service. As torpedoes acquired increased range and bigger warheads, the destroyer was developed as the counter to the torpedo-boat. Mines were used extensively and to telling effect during the Russo-Japanese War of 1904–05, so were likely to play an important role in any future conflict. In Britain's plans for a distant blockade of Germany, mines would be laid in the southern part of the North Sea, in the Strait of Dover and around home ports, but British mines proved inferior to Germany's and did little damage.

These developments went hand in hand with another fundamental change: the reduction of Britain's worldwide commitments, and the concentration of the fleet in home waters. An arrangement with France led to a major reduction of British naval forces in the Mediterranean, which, in the 100 years following Nelson's victory at the Nile in 1798, had effectively been a British lake.

Minelaying
During the war Britain called on its vast merchant navy to assist with tasks such as minelaying. Here, mines attached to nets are being laid from a British drifter. This was the kind of mine barrage used to block the Strait of Dover.

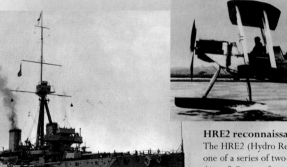

HRE2 reconnaissance seaplane
The HRE2 (Hydro Reconnaissance Experimental 2) was one of a series of two-seater aeroplanes built by the Royal Aircraft Factory from 1914. Other versions of the plane were used for reconnaissance work on land.

HMS *Dreadnought*, launched 1906
The revolutionary 18,110-ton ship with her ten 12-in (305-mm) guns, steam turbines and top speed of 21 knots gave her name to a new class of battleship. Earlier battleships were thereafter dismissively termed "pre-dreadnoughts".

British submarine *C3*
In 1914 the British Navy had 73 submarines, compared with Germany's 31. In 1918, the elderly *C3*, packed with high explosive, was used to ram a viaduct at Zeebrugge in a raid designed to trap German U-boats in their bases.

Britain and France took exception to Germany's militant threats, which were repeated in 1911, when French troops occupied Fez in Morocco. This second Moroccan crisis was settled with a minor exchange of colonial territories between France and Germany, but only after Britain supported France.

Even as late as 1907 the circle of alliances around Germany had by no means been firm, but following the crises of 1908–09 and 1911, solidarity between the Entente powers – Britain, France, and Russia – was far more robust. In the Balkans, Austria-Hungary's annexation of Bosnia-Herzegovina, designed to forestall Serbian claims on the territory, succeeded in humiliating its neighbour, but failed to curb Serbian nationalism.

ITALIAN ASPIRATIONS

The 1887 treaty that bound Germany, Austria-Hungary, and Italy in alliance had been concluded only after Austria-Hungary conceded that Italy had an equal interest in the Balkans. The least of the powers, and by 1909 little more than a nominal member of the Triple Alliance, Italy emerged from the 1908–09 Bosnian crisis in a familiar situation – with nothing. By 1911, however, it was determined to secure territory. At various times all the powers had endorsed Italy's claims to the Turkish provinces of Tripolitania and Cyrenaica in North Africa, but none supported its declaration of war on Turkey in

Italian troops in North Africa 1911
The Italians defeated the Turks in 1911–12 and took control of the Libyan coastline, but had great difficulty subduing the local Arab and Berber populations.

1911. The Italians occupied the coastal towns of Tripoli and Benghazi, but the campaign proved more difficult than anticipated, and in 1912 they turned their attention to the Aegean, and occupied Rhodes and the Dodecanese. In the Treaty of Lausanne of October 1912 Turkey conceded its rights over Tripoli and Cyrenaica to Italy.

THE BALKAN WARS

Meanwhile, Turkey was to suffer further territorial losses in the Balkans. In March 1912 Bulgaria and Serbia concluded a pact that provided for the division of Macedonia between them. In May a further pact between Bulgaria and Greece brought

into being the Balkan League, which was united in its opposition to Turkish rule in the region. Throughout the summer of 1912 the Great Powers sought to defuse the crisis in the Balkans, but by the time they agreed in October to act in order to maintain the status quo, the First Balkan War had begun, following a declaration of war on Turkey by independent Montenegro. By the time an armistice was concluded on December 3, Turkish armies had suffered a series of defeats and the Bulgarians were within sight of Constantinople.

Complicated negotiations followed, involving the Balkan League, the Great Powers, and Turkey, but after a flareup of Turkish resistance in February and March 1913, peace was eventually concluded on May 30, 1913. The Treaty of London created an independent Albania, an arrangement demanded by Austria-Hungary and Italy as the means of denying Serbia access to the sea. Serbia sought compensation in eastern Macedonia at Bulgarian expense. Bulgaria was also in dispute with Greece over Salonika, and, faced with these difficulties, chose to move against its former allies on June 29, 1913, thus starting the Second Balkan War. With the hitherto quiescent Romania and a vengeful Turkey also taking the field against them, the Bulgarians were defeated within a month. The Treaty of Bucharest of August 13, 1913 established, for the moment, a new set of borders in the Balkans.

Macedonian revolutionaries 1912
In their struggle to throw off Turkish rule in 1912, the Macedonians were supported by Bulgaria, Greece, Serbia, and Montenegro.

STRATIFIED SOCIETIES

~

FOR ALL THE ECONOMIC SHIFTS and technological advances of the previous 50 years, the Europe that went to war in 1914 was still a network of societies divided along starkly traditional lines. Even in relatively modern Britain, the largest single occupation on the eve of the war was domestic service.

Like Britain and France, Germany had an elected parliament, the Reichstag, with deputies representing the interests of various sections of the male population. But government ministers were not directly accountable to the Reichstag. The German Reich was a federation of states dominated by Prussia. The Prussian king was also the kaiser and Prussian nobles, the Junkers, formed Germany's ruling elite. In Germany, as in Britain and Austria-Hungary, the landowning aristocracies maintained their status as "high society", with a calendar of balls, horse races and country house weekends.

The persistence of the old order was most obvious in autocratic Russia. Answerable only to God, the czar appointed the commanders of the army and the fleet, the ministers and provincial governors. Despite Russia's rapid industrialization, which caused the urban population to double in the 40 years before 1914, well over 80 per cent of the people lived in rural areas. When Revolution came in 1917, it was hardly a surprise that so many chose to support the new order rather than the old.

Porters on the Volga
Although serfdom had been abolished in 1867, there had been little change in the lives of the vast majority of the Russian peasantry. A seemingly unbridgeable gulf still separated them from their former owners.

Russian ball 1914
The extravagant lifestyle of the aristocracy shocked foreign visitors to imperial Russia. The war made little difference. Sir Samuel Hoare, British intelligence officer in Petrograd, commented that: "The wealth and the lavish use they made of it dazzled me after the austere conditions of wartime life in England."

THE EVE OF WAR

The Balkan Wars had the effect of excluding Turkey from Europe, with the significant exception of Constantinople and the Straits. That this had come about through the actions of the small Balkan states was somewhat surprising. These states had shown themselves able to act in a way that conflicted with the interests of the Great Powers.

For Austria-Hungary, the outcome of these wars was little short of disastrous. Serbia had doubled its territory, and Austria-Hungary had no option but to accept the enlargement of its neighbour. The question of Serbia's strength, and the increase in nationalist feelings in the region, which Austria-Hungary saw as "the south Slav problem", was now pressing. It presented itself at a time when the frequent crises of the previous ten years had given a momentum to events and a general excitement – increasingly strident, militant nationalism – that had reduced resistance to war. This development, moreover, came at a time when those with the power of decision in Berlin and Vienna were aware that their countries stood at the peak of their strength relative to their potential enemies. They were well aware that their advantage would decline with the passing of the years. French military reforms and Russian railroad construction programmes would be completed in or about 1916, increasing the military strength and mobility of these countries. In the crises of 1912 and 1913, Germany and Austria-Hungary had held back, despite being aware that it might be in their interest to induce, rather than to postpone, hostilities. In 1914, when faced with another crisis in the Balkans, they were not to show the same restraint.

Fateful visit of June 28, 1914
Archduke Franz Ferdinand, the heir to the Habsburg thrones, and his wife make their way to their car during their visit to Sarajevo, the capital of Bosnia-Herzegovina.

Hatred and distrust in the Balkans
As new states were created and new borders drawn in the Balkans, no country could rely on the loyalty of its population. Here Bulgarian troops watch the hanging of suspected Turkish spies during the Balkan Wars of 1912–13.

War is Declared

JUNE 28
Archduke Franz Ferdinand and his wife assassinated in Sarajevo

JULY 23
Austro-Hungarian note to Serbia delivered, with demand for reply by July 25

JULY 24
Austria-Hungary notifies powers of note to Serbia

JULY 25
Serbian reply to Austro-Hungarian note delivered

JULY 25
Austria-Hungary severs diplomatic relations with Serbia

JULY 26
Britain seeks agreement for conference to settle Serbian problem: France and Italy indicate acceptance

JULY 26
Austria-Hungary orders partial mobilization against Serbia

JULY 27
Germany indicates refusal to participate at conference

JULY 27
Russia indicates acceptance of proposed conference

JULY 28
Austria-Hungary declares war on Serbia

JULY 29
Britain proposes international mediation to solve crisis. Russia seeks German restraint on Austria-Hungary. Russia orders partial mobilization

JULY 29
Germany refuses to confirm adherence to Belgian neutrality

JULY 30
German warning to Russia to halt mobilization. Germany orders mobilization. Austria-Hungary orders mobilization in Galicia

JULY 31
Russia orders general mobilization

JULY 31
German demand that Russia halt mobilization

AUGUST 1
Belgium and France order general mobilization

AUGUST 1
Germany declares war on Russia

AUGUST 2
German violation of Luxembourg; Germany demands right of transit through Belgium

AUGUST 3
Germany declares war on France. German invasion of Belgium

AUGUST 4
Belgium severs diplomatic relations with Germany. Britain declares war on Germany

AUGUST 4
Germany declares war on Belgium

AUGUST 5
Montenegro declares war on Austria-Hungary

AUGUST 6
Serbia declares war on Germany

AUGUST 6
Austria-Hungary declares war on Russia

AUGUST 7
Landing of first British troops in France

AUGUST 8
Montenegro declares war on Germany

AUGUST 12
Britain and France declare war on Austria-Hungary

KEY

▪ Moves by Entente powers and their allies   ▪ Moves by Central Powers

The arrest of Gavrilo Princip in Sarajevo
The police hold back members of the public as Princip (second from the right) is led away into custody, following his assassination of Archduke Franz Ferdinand and his wife, the Countess Sofia.

THE SUCCESSION OF CRISES in the decade before 1914 had left Britain, France and Russia fearful of German military power. Germany, meanwhile, despite its industrial primacy and increasing economic domination of Europe, was conscious that both Russia and France had plans to increase their military strength. Europe was divided into two camps by a system of alliances, with Britain, France and Russia linked by ententes, and Germany and Austria-Hungary part of an alliance with Italy. Neither side, however, was completely secure in their arrangements. France and Russia were aware that their alliance could not survive continued refusal to support each other militarily, and Germany recognized that it could not refuse to stand by Austria-Hungary in its problems with Balkan nationalism for much longer.

The factors that produced the First World War were long in the making, but in the end war broke out as the result of calculations and miscalculations made in the weeks following an incident in Sarajevo, Bosnia-Herzegovina, on June 28, 1914. Archduke Franz Ferdinand, nephew and heir to the Habsburg Emperor Franz Josef, and his wife, the Countess Sofia, were in the city for the summer manoeuvres of the Austro-Hungarian army. Members of "Young Bosnia", a secret society dedicated to liberating Slav lands from Habsburg rule, had laid plans for their assassination.

The first attempt failed, when a bomb thrown at the archduke's car bounced off, injuring two policemen and a number of bystanders. Later that morning, however, the car pulled up where one of the other members of the gang, Gavrilo Princip, happened to be standing. Seizing this second chance, he fired his pistol into the open-topped car, killing the archduke and his wife.

DIPLOMATIC MANOEUVRES

In itself this incident need not have led to war, but Austria-Hungary, acting on a well-founded but unproven suspicion of Serbian complicity in the murder, saw an opportunity to crush Serbia and thereby solve the south Slav problem once and for all. Accordingly, on July 5–6 the Austrian ambassador in Berlin sought an assurance of German support in eliminating Serbia "as a political factor in the Balkans". This assurance was given by the kaiser and the chancellor, the latter with the observation that if war was to come then it was "better now than in one or two years' time when the Entente will be stronger". The German leadership thus surrendered the power of decision to Austria-Hungary, encouraging its ally to start a war with Serbia even at the risk of provoking a larger, Europe-wide conflict.

The Habsburg monarchy, however, had no wish to become embroiled in a general war. It simply wanted a victory, a military victory rather than a diplomatic one, in order to demonstrate that it was still a power to be reckoned with. In order to achieve this, Hungarian support for what was primarily an Austrian enterprise had to be secured. In the past, Hungary, wary of Austrian aggrandizement, had opposed an aggressive policy in the Balkans and had used German reluctance to support such a policy as the means of checking Austrian ambitions. The German promise of July 5 thus undercut Hungary's resistance to Austrian policy, and on July 14 Hungary endorsed the Austrian position. But it was not until July 23 that an ultimatum was delivered to Serbia, couched in such a way that its demands – tantamount to the

The conspirators
Gavrilo Princip (left) with two of his fellow conspirators. Princip was spared the death penalty because he was only 19, but died of tuberculosis in an Austrian prison in 1918.

destruction of Serbia as a state – would prove unacceptable. The Serbian reply of July 25 was consummately conciliatory and diplomatic in tone, as the situation demanded. It accepted all of Austria-Hungary's demands bar two. These would have given the Austro-Hungarian government power to interfere both in an inquiry into the assassination, and in the internal running of Serbian affairs. Serbia suggested the disputed demands could be subjected to arbitration either by a tribunal in The Hague or by the Great Powers. The Serbian reply could not disguise a diplomatic triumph for Austria-Hungary. Yet, despite this success and the fact that mobilization plans precluded an attack on Serbia before August 12, Austria-Hungary declared war on Serbia on July 28.

From this action all else followed. At first Russia had advised Serbia to comply with Austria-Hungary's demands. Now, however, conscious of the humiliation of 1909 over Austria-Hungary's annexation of Bosnia-Herzegovina, Russia was not prepared to allow Austria-Hungary to destroy Serbia, and thus Russia's prestige and influence in the Balkans. Accordingly, on July 29 Russia ordered a partial mobilization, directed against Austria-Hungary. Given the slowness with which Russia could mobilize, this was a diplomatic rather than a military ploy, designed to demonstrate Russian interest and force Austria-Hungary to back down. But on this day, Germany, aware of the implications of a Russian mobilization for its own war plan, warned Russia to desist. On July 30

> "To try to avoid such a calamity as a European war, I beg you in the name of our old friendship to do what you can to stop your allies from going too far."

Russia, which had never prepared a plan for partial mobilization and faced an all-or-nothing dilemma, ordered general mobilization. Even before they were made aware of this decision, both Germany and Austria-Hungary began their own general mobilization.

GERMAN DEMANDS

On the same day, July 31, Germany presented the French with an ultimatum demanding their neutrality in the present crisis and the surrender of the fortress towns of Toul and Verdun as a guarantee of their intentions. This demand was rejected by France, which ordered a general

Austria-Hungary goes to war
The Emperor announces that a state of war exists with Serbia in the newspapers of July 29 (right). The 97th Infantry Regiment parades in a Trieste square (below) before its departure for the Serbian front.

THE GERMAN ARMIES OF 1914

Identity disc
This was worn round the neck attached to a cotton cord.

THE GERMAN EMPIRE in 1914 consisted of 26 states: four kingdoms, six grand duchies, five duchies, seven principalities, three free cities and the former French provinces of Alsace and Lorraine. It possessed an Imperial Navy but no army. In fact there was no such organization as the German army until after the 1918 armistice. Up until then Germany had four armies, those of the kingdoms of Prussia, Bavaria, Saxony and Württemberg. Before the war these were organized into 217 infantry regiments, of which 166 were Prussian, 24 Bavarian, 17 Saxon and ten Württemberger. The Prussian Guard, the historic bodyguard to the king of Prussia, provided a further 11 regiments. Their activities were co-ordinated by the Greater German General Staff.

The army enjoyed enormous prestige thanks to the kaiser's position as commander-in-chief and his personal enthusiasm for all things military. It was also in many ways independent from control by the civilian government. The general staff's responsibilities covered all military requirements, most obviously the preparation of war plans and mobilization. It possessed powers, for example, to direct railway construction programmes. Six main railway lines stretched across Germany, allowing the rapid transfer of forces between its eastern and western borders. Between 1909 and 1914 the Germans undertook a major construction programme along the borders with Belgium and Luxembourg. Many of the stations there were built with platforms longer than the villages they ostensibly served. Thanks to this planning – and more powerful locomotives and larger rolling stock – Germany was able to mobilize some four times faster in 1914 than in 1870 – some 11,530 men per line per day compared to 2,580 at the time of the Franco-Prussian War.

In 1912 Germany's armies had a peace-time establishment of some 646,000 officers and men. The law of June 1913 made provision for a much larger army of 870,000 with 669 infantry battalions, 550 cavalry squadrons and 633 artillery batteries. This planned increase was to be implemented over three years. In the event, with the use of first-line reservists, Germany was able to put 1,750,000 officers and men into the field in August 1914. Other reservists totalled 1,800,000 officers and men and, in addition, Germany had some 4,250,000 untrained men of military age, a reflection of the fact that before 1912 Germany had conscripted only 53 per cent of eligible manpower.

German weapons and equipment
The standard rifle was the 7.98-mm Mauser "Gewehr" (1898 model) with a magazine of five rounds. The German infantryman was better prepared for the onset of trench warfare than his French or British counterpart.

LUGER PISTOL

GEWEHR (1898)

AMMUNITION CLIP

Readiness for war
Germany's military planning before the war was apparent in the concentration of garrison towns on the borders with France in the west and Russia in the east and in the railways that connected them.

LOCK KNIFE

SPADE

PIONEER'S AXE

Pre-war manoeuvres
Military manoeuvres attended by the kaiser (far left) were an important annual event in imperial Germany. In the foreground Crown Prince William, wearing a flat-topped uhlan helmet stands stroking his chin.

GERMANY 1914
- ■ Army corps headquarters

DIVISIONAL HEADQUARTERS
- Prussian
- Bavarian
- Saxon
- Württemberg
- ---- Major railway

0 km 50 100
0 miles 50 100

BALTIC SEA

DENMARK

PRUSSIAN JÄGER

PRUSSIAN ARTILLERYMAN

Flensburg
Kiel Canal · Kiel
Altona
IX CORPS
Schwerin
II CORPS
Stettin
III CORPS/PRUSSIAN GUARD
BERLIN
X CORPS
Hanover
Magdeburg
Brandenburg
IV CORPS
Halle
Leipzig
XIX CORPS
Erfurt
Chemnitz
Dresden
XII CORPS
VI CORPS
Breslau
Glogau
Neisse

Insterburg
Königsberg
I CORPS
Danzig
XVII CORPS
XX CORPS
Allenstein
Deutsch-Eylau
Bromberg
Thorn
Vistula
WARSAW
Posen
V CORPS
RUSSIAN EMPIRE

NETH.
Münster
VII CORPS
Düsseldorf
Cologne
XI CORPS
Kassel

BEL.
Liège
VIII CORPS
Koblenz
Frankfurt
II BAVARIAN CORPS
Würtzburg

LUX.
LUX.
Trier
XXI CORPS
Saarbrücken
Metz
XVI CORPS
Landau
II BAVARIAN CORPS
XIV CORPS
Karlsruhe
Strassburg
XV CORPS
Colmar
Freiburg
Basel · Zurich

Elbe
Weser
Oder
Rhine

GERMANY

Nuremberg
III BAVARIAN CORPS
Stuttgart
XIII CORPS
Ulm · Augsburg
Munich
I BAVARIAN CORPS

PRAGUE
SAXON CAP

AUSTRIA-HUNGARY

VIENNA
Danube

FRANCE

SWITZ.

WÜRTTEMBERGER INFANTRYMAN

BAVARIAN INFANTRYMAN OF THE RESERVE

1914 uniform

Pickelhaube and cover

Forage cap

Ammunition pouches

Bayonet

Haversack and water bottle

Boots (1866 model)

The uniform shown is that of an Unteroffizier (a rank between corporal and sergeant) in the Prussian infantry. Infantrymen wore the *Pickelhaube* (spiked helmet), with a cloth cover to prevent its gleaming in the sun, until the steel helmet was introduced in 1916.

On their way to Paris

Germany's vast reserve of men answered the call to arms in 1914 with patriotic fervour.

Germany's view of the war

This patriotic postcard from 1914 shows Germany and its solitary ally, Austria-Hungary, surrounded by enemies bent on their destruction.

mobilization on August 1, on which date Germany declared war on Russia and occupied Luxembourg. The German declaration of war on France followed on August 3, the same day that Germany presented an ultimatum to Belgium demanding right of transit through that country. The next day, after learning that its demand that Belgian neutrality be respected had been answered by invasion, Britain declared war on Germany.

Such was the process by which Europe was plunged into war. After July 28, as diplomacy failed, all the powers were carried along by military considerations. Once a country knew or suspected that one of its enemies was mobilizing, it needed to mobilize its own armies, and this had to be done according to a set timetable, dictated by the railway system. The logistics of transporting hundreds of thousands of men and horses to their appointed positions came to be known as "war-by-timetable". The timetables that would dictate the course of the opening weeks of the war were those of the French, the Russians and the Germans.

THE FRENCH WAR PLAN

France's war plan was known as Plan XVII. Its two principal aims were to clear the west bank of the Rhine and to demonstrate to Russia the good faith

of France as an ally through immediate offensive operations. It envisaged the deployment of five armies between Switzerland and the Sambre River on the border with Belgium.

Conceived as a response to an expected German attack through Lorraine and eastern France, the initial French offensive would be on the extreme right in an attempt to secure Mulhouse (Mülhausen) and Colmar in Alsace. Having established the First and Second Armies in Alsace and on the Rhine, the French would then launch a major offensive into Lorraine. The Alsace effort was seen as the first part of an advance down the Rhine valley as far as Koblenz, as well as providing flanking support for the Lorraine offensive. North of Verdun, the French were to deploy three armies, and, depending on German movements, these were to be directed either through the southern Ardennes or into Luxembourg and Belgium.

Belgian neutrality

This British recruiting poster shows the treaty guaranteeing Belgian neutrality, signed by five nations, including Prussia, in 1837. The British made much of the fact that the Germans, in trying to persuade Britain to keep out of the war, dismissed the treaty as a "scrap of paper".

THE LOST PROVINCES

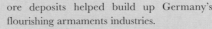

FRANCE'S WAR PLANS were largely determined by *la revanche* (revenge), a burning desire to reclaim the lost provinces of Alsace and Lorraine. After the lightning Franco-Prussian War of 1870–71, Germany had annexed the province of Alsace and the northern part of the province of Lorraine. In the Middle Ages the region had been part of the Holy Roman Empire, but had been French since the 17th century. Part of it had been confirmed as French by the Treaty of Westphalia (1648), the rest had been annexed by Louis XIV in the second half of the century. After the Franco-Prussian War, Bismarck advised the kaiser to give the people of Alsace and Lorraine as much freedom as possible, so that they kept their local identity and would not resent German rule. But his advice went unheeded and the two provinces were ruled as a conquered territory. Especially galling to the French was the fact that Lorraine's vast iron ore deposits helped build up Germany's flourishing armaments industries.

A constitution granting limited "home rule" in 1911 came too late, and anti-German feeling in the region exploded into public anger in 1913, after a German officer attacked a crippled shoemaker. In the same year Hansi, an Alsatian cartoonist, published *Mon Village*, a collection of scenes from village life, poking fun at the German authorities. In 1914 he was sentenced to one year's imprisonment for libelling public officials.

Events such as these kept the lost provinces in France's national consciousness. Politicians and soldiers alike nursed their "sacred anger". Just as the return of the stork, symbol of Alsace, signalled the return of spring, the war signalled a long-awaited opportunity for French rule to be restored.

Arrival of the stork
In this cartoon by Hansi, Alsatian schoolchildren and their teacher gather to greet the stork. A German policeman goose-steps sulkily up and down on the far side of the square.

French propaganda
A French border guard offers a bouquet to a young Alsatian beauty, who accepts it happily. Sentimental images of this kind appeared as posters and in the French press.

The landscape of Alsace
The French have always had a special fondness for the region's picturesque villages and steep hills cloaked in vineyards.

FRANCE'S LOVE OF THE OFFENSIVE

In the Franco-Prussian War of 1870–71, the French had found themselves fighting against a coalition of German states that collectively had a population equal to that of France. However, the population of the new German Empire grew so fast that, by 1914, it had twice as many men of military age as France. With such a massive inferiority of manpower – and an equally serious industrial inferiority – to try to wage war defensively could result only in defeat. A defensive strategy would only prolong, not win, a war against Germany.

The French army had become a very inward-looking institution. Relations between its commanders and the French government had always been difficult, and the army's prestige had suffered badly after it was found to have unjustly accused a Jewish officer, Alfred Dreyfus, of espionage in 1894, and subsequently imprisoned him. In the face of criticism, the army had sought a return to traditional soldierly virtues and a revival of the Napoleonic legend. The shame of France's defeat in the Franco-Prussian War of 1870–71 came to be seen as the result of the army having been false to its traditions of offensive action, and it became accepted that the offensive suited the French national temperament.

The offensive at least offered France some hope of forestalling German plans and the terms of its alliance with Russia reinforced this way of thinking. The alliance naturally brought with it obligations. France could not consider waging a defensive war and leaving Russia with the burden of offensive operations. Given Germany's overwhelming military superiority, both France and Russia were obliged to undertake offensive operations together or risk defeat and destruction separately.

THE RUSSIAN PLAN

Russia's plan, Plan XIX, was put together in 1910, substantially revised in 1912, and further revised after the outbreak of war. In its original form, Plan XIX envisaged the use of four armies to clear East Prussia, on the assumption that Germany would have few forces in the east. After clearing East Prussia, the Russians would then be free to move directly against Berlin.

By 1912 the conventional wisdom in the Russian army had decided that the armies of Austria-Hungary posed a more immediate threat to Russia than those of Germany. Accordingly, two of the armies earmarked for East Prussia would be redeployed to strengthen forces opposite Galicia. This change left the armies opposite East Prussia short of numbers relative to the length of the front, and even in comparison to whatever limited German force might be left to halt a Russian invasion. In August 1914 a final change assigned two Russian armies to the Silesian front in preparation for an invasion of Germany from the southeast. This was the most distant sector of the front and would take much longer to reach than East Prussia or Galicia.

BRITISH INTENTIONS

Britain was not bound by treaty to support France in a war with Germany, but plans for sending a small expeditionary force to assist the French army had been prepared. Britain's more important task was to impose a blockade on Germany, cutting it off from trade with the outside world. The Strait of Dover would be mined and patrolled. The main fleet, based at Scapa Flow in the Orkney Islands off northern Scotland, would patrol the North Sea, stopping and searching merchant ships for arms or anything that might help Germany's war effort, and confiscating the goods.

GERMANY'S PLAN

Ever since France and Russia signed a treaty of friendship in 1891, the German high command had known that it would probably have to fight a war on two fronts. A plan for dealing with this problem began to take shape as early as the 1890s. Its premise was that France would mobilize much more quickly than Russia, so it was essential to have the vast majority of the German forces ready to deal with France, while a small force in the east stood on the defensive to check any Russian offensive. The German general staff under Alfred von Schlieffen calculated that the Russians would need six weeks to have their armies fully mobilized. It was therefore essential to defeat France in this short space of time. The Schlieffen Plan provided the means of achieving this. The right wing of the German armies would invade France through the neutral Netherlands, Belgium and Luxembourg, then sweep round to trap the French armies, which would be wrongly positioned facing Alsace and Lorraine. The plan was worked out in fine detail, pinpointing exactly where each army should be on any particular day. Refinements and adjustments were made to the plan, especially after Helmuth von Moltke succeeded as chief of staff after Schlieffen's retirement in 1906. Moltke's most significant change was the decision not to send any troops through the Netherlands.

RESPONSIBILITY FOR THE WAR

The First World War is usually regarded as one that arose from a dispute between Russia and Austria-Hungary in the Balkans, but, ironically, it was not until August 6 – when Russia received an Austro-Hungarian declaration of war sent through the post – that the powers that were the main parties to the Balkans dispute were at war with one another. The decisions that led to a general war in Europe had already been taken between July 25 and July 28.

It is significant that as early as July 26, the Chief of the German General Staff had prepared the ultimatum to Belgium that was to signal the German invasion of France, and which prompted the involvement of Britain. In the Treaty of Versailles of 1919, the victorious Allied powers placed responsibility for the war solely on Germany, which strongly resisted having to make such an admission of guilt. Although Germany had neither planned nor sought war at that precise moment, however, the conflict that erupted in 1914 in Europe can be seen largely as the result of the Germany quest for "mastery in Europe".

Multiply or be defeated
This pre-war booklet urged France to increase its birthrate as Germany's birthrate exceeded it by five to two.

We got here yesterday at 9.30 and after supper set off for the line of forts. Spirits are high, extraordinarily high, as if we were on manoeuvres... No real news. French and Germans just look at each other. I cannot say any more, or my letter wouldn't get to you.

ALEXANDRE JACQUEAU IN A LETTER
TO HIS WIFE FROM VERDUN, AUGUST 6, 1914

THE SCHLIEFFEN PLAN

THE PLAN EVOLVED when Alfred von Schlieffen was German Chief of Staff between 1891 and 1906. It was designed as an answer to Germany's dilemma should it find itself at war simultaneously with both France and Russia. The plan envisaged an initial effort in the west in an attempt to defeat France between the outbreak of war and the completion of Russian mobilization.

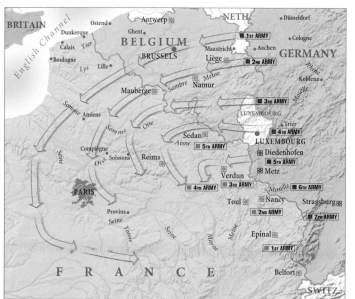

The original plan
Confronted by French fortifications along the common border, German troops would pass through Luxembourg, the Netherlands and Belgium, then advance through northern France around the rear of the main French armies. Having won a great battle of encirclement, German forces would then be despatched by rail to the east to fight the Russians.

THE SCHLIEFFEN PLAN

→ Planned routes of German armies
⊠ German fortified town
⊡ French fortified town
⊡ Belgian fortified town

THE ARMIES ARE MOBILIZED

IN THE FRANTIC FINAL DAYS of July 1914, all of the Continental powers were on the brink of mobilization. First off the mark was Austria-Hungary, which began to mobilize on July 28, bringing chaos to the railways. On July 30, the Tsar of Russia ordered full mobilization, trusting in the "Great Military Programme", which aimed to have all the imperial Russian armies mobilized in 18 days. Fearful that the Russian "steamroller" would reach Berlin before they could defeat the French, on August 1 the Germans began their meticulously planned operation, designed to have 3,500,000 soldiers ready for action within a week. The regular army was swelled by reservists, who hurried to designated depots to be issued with arms and new grey uniforms and taken by precisely scheduled trains to concentration points near the frontiers. Germany's mobilization was the signal for a much less slick operation in France, where about 3 million men were mobilized. The general staff expected the draft evasion rate to be at least 10 per cent. To their surprise, mobilization was greeted by a surge of patriotic support, with evasion at little over 1 per cent.

In all the combatant states departing soldiers were cheered on by enthusiastic crowds, confident that their "boys" would be home for Christmas. British men were not liable for military service and Britain sent a force of just 150,000 men, a "contemptibly small army" in the famously mistranslated words of the kaiser. Within a matter of weeks, however, they were joined by half a million voluntary recruits. As mobilization got under way, individual soldiers had their private fears and doubts, but many shared the sentiments expressed by the Austrian writer Stefan Zweig: "As never before, thousands and hundreds of thousands felt what they should have felt in peacetime, that they belonged together."

Joining up
Volunteers queue to enlist at a London recruiting office in August 1914. Such was the response to the government's appeal for volunteers that 2 million men joined up within a year and Britain did not have to introduce conscription until January 1916.

Opposing views
While the Germans depicted their soldiers as heroes with God on their side *(Gott mit uns)*, the British cartoon from Punch magazine shows "plucky little Belgium" standing up to a bullying Germany.

German reservist leaving for the front

"Off to the war, all linked in death we go.
I wish my sweetheart wouldn't blubber so.

What's wrong with me? I'm glad to leave, I feel.
Now mother's crying. You need a heart of steel.

The good old sunset's up there glowing red.
A fortnight's time and maybe I'll be dead."

VERSES FROM *ABSCHIED* (FAREWELL) BY THE POET ALFRED LICHTENSTEIN, WHO DIED ON THE SOMME ON SEPTEMBER 25, 1914, AGED 25

Algerian tirailleurs leaving for the front
Algerian *tirailleurs* (riflemen), affectionately known as "Turcos", receive a warm send-off at the railway station of Champigny-sur-Marne in August 1914.

Calls to arms
The German order for general mobilization *(right)* was issued on August 1, the French *(above)* later on the same day. The call for volunteers in Britain *(above right)* was launched by Kitchener on August 7, the day after he took office as Secretary of State for War.

THE OUTBREAK OF WAR
1914

~

EUROPE HAD BEEN PREPARING FOR WAR FOR
MORE THAN 20 YEARS, BUT WHEN IT BROKE OUT IN 1914,
IT SOON BECAME CLEAR THAT THE GREAT POWERS HAD
LITTLE IDEA OF WHAT A GENERAL EUROPEAN
WAR WOULD ENTAIL. AUSTRIA-HUNGARY, GERMANY,
FRANCE AND RUSSIA ALL LAUNCHED OFFENSIVES. NOT
ONE SUCCEEDED IN THE WAY THAT HAD BEEN
ANTICIPATED. EVEN AFTER SUFFERING A CRUSHING
DEFEAT AND LOSING HUNDREDS OF THOUSANDS
OF MEN, ARMIES COULD CALL ON SUFFICIENT
RESERVES TO CONTINUE THE WAR.

~

The Russian steamroller
The sheer numbers of men available to its
armies made Russia appear a possibly invincible
enemy. In the event, manpower alone was not
enough, and by 1917, 1,800,000 Russian soldiers
had been killed and nearly five million wounded.

THE PURSUIT OF ILLUSION

IN 1914 THERE WAS A WIDESPREAD EXPECTATION OF RAPID, COMPREHENSIVE

VICTORY. MOST PEOPLE'S CONFIDENCE WAS BASED ON LITTLE MORE THAN CRUDE

STEREOTYPING OF THE MORAL AND PHYSICAL INFERIORITY OF THE ENEMY.

A CENTURY HAD PASSED SINCE EUROPE HAD SEEN CONFLICT ON SUCH A SCALE,

AND VERY FEW PEOPLE HAD ANY IDEA WHAT A GENERAL WAR MIGHT ENTAIL.

IN AUSTRIA-HUNGARY, the country that had set the whole machinery of hatred in motion by declaring war on Serbia, confidence of victory was naturally high. However, in seeking the destruction of Serbia, the Dual Monarchy had envisaged a swift military victory; what it found it had committed itself to was a war for which it was hopelessly ill-prepared. As Russia mobilized more quickly than anyone had imagined, Austria-Hungary changed its plans: one of its armies, deployed initially on the Serbian front, had to be transported north to counter the Russian threat in Galicia. The two armies entrusted with the invasion of Serbia were unequal to the task. Three times between August and December 1914 the Austria-Hungarians tried to crush their neighbour; three times they were beaten back. It was not until the following autumn, assisted by the Germans and Bulgarians, that they were able to punish Serbia for its impudence in refusing to submit to all of the Austro-Hungarian demands in the wake of the assassination of June 1914.

Austria-Hungary was not alone in its expectation of a short, victorious campaign. France and Germany were equally confident of quick success. Why expectant societies were denied their promised victory in 1914 is a difficult question to answer. One explanation is that armies had simply become too big. They had grown to a size that ensured them against total defeat even if they suffered any number of local reverses. They also enjoyed great powers of recuperation through their reserve strengths. At the end of even the most successful campaign, the offensive faced a reconstituted defence drawn from new drafts. This was certainly the case between 1914 and 1916. Towards the end of the war all the European powers had difficulty making good their losses and, by 1918, none of them were able to do so.

PROBLEMS OF MOBILITY

In August–November 1914 the pursuit of victory was an illusion. None of the great powers was in a position to defeat an enemy of similar status in the course of one, short campaigning season. Thanks to their rail networks, most were able to mobilize across their entire area and they could mobilize in depth, but, once deployed, their armies could not move with the speed and effectiveness of armies of 100 years before. If one considers the Grand Army of Napoleon and the 1805 campaign, the speed and scale of operations were astonishing. The French broke camp at Boulogne on September 2 and with some 210,500 men, crossed the Rhine River on September 26 and the Danube River on October 6. Vienna was occupied on November 13; the Battle of Austerlitz was won on December 2. By 1914 an advance of such a distance in such a short time had become impossible. Attacking armies lacked the mobility to advance and clinch victory. They had no means of paralysing an enemy defence which, operating on home soil, could move larger numbers more quickly over greater distances by rail than an advancing army could move on horseback or on foot. Meanwhile, the defenders had numbers and a strength in depth that ensured against defeat.

Explaining the outcome of campaigns in terms of impersonal forces may appear to belittle the

Serbian field artillery
The Serbian armies that drove back the attempted invasions of 1914 were poorly equipped compared to their Austro-Hungarian enemies, but the troops were hardened veterans of the Balkan Wars fighting for the very survival of their nation.

achievements of the commanders and troops who have to fight the battles. Even so, an individual general's successes are diminished and his failures may be excused if the outcome of his campaign has been determined largely by other factors. This was especially true of the Schlieffen Plan, with which Germany's chief of staff, Helmuth von Moltke, went to war. Moltke had made changes to the original plan, the most important being his decision not to violate Dutch territory, but to send the German First Army through Belgium rather than through the Netherlands.

IMPOSSIBLE DEMANDS
With or without Moltke's amendments, the German plan was questionable for two reasons – one political and one military.

First, the Schlieffen plan failed to take account of the political reactions that it would provoke. The German high command justified the violation of Belgium as a "military necessity", a very dubious principle when it results in the loss of trust and goodwill of other neutral states. Second, military plans depend on men for their execution. The Schlieffen Plan set German forces the goal of an advance of some 1,300 km (800 miles), with a series of encounter battles en route, and then fighting – and winning – a battle of encirclement and annihilation in eastern France inside six weeks. How entire armies were to march 32 km (20 miles) a day, brushing aside all resistance as they advanced, every day for six weeks and finally fight and win an enormous battle at the end of a tenuous line of communication defies belief. The advancing armies had no guarantee of being able to capture and use an intact rail system and there was also the problem posed by Paris. The forces committed to the invasion through northern France were insufficient either to occupy the French capital or to "mask" it, that is to deploy enough troops to prevent the garrison from moving against an exposed, unguarded German flank. Much of the criticism subsequently directed against Moltke seems unfair; real criticism should be directed instead against the original plan.

FAILINGS AND STRENGTHS OF THE FRENCH
In accounts of the opening engagements of the First World War, the French army often comes in for harsh criticism: it managed to get things wrong in 1870 and appeared to do so again in 1914. That, of course, is grossly unfair. In the matter of the violation of Belgium neutrality, the French were never guilty of the errors committed by the German high command. The French army asked the political authorities if it would be allowed to enter Belgium and was informed that it could not, and the person who asked was dismissed.

The weakness of the French war plan was that it was conceived by the operations section of the staff with scarcely any reference to the intelligence section. The latter had anticipated that the main German effort would be made through Belgium. In so far as this possibility was considered by those in the operations section who drew up the plan, they reckoned that the fortresses of Liège and Namur could withstand a German attack. Since they did not anticipate the German use of reserve formations in the initial assault, they also assumed that any German deployment of forces in Belgium would involve a weakening of forces in the centre and on the German left in Alsace and Lorraine.

"There is not much to say about our successes compared with those of the Germans, mainly because German victories have been gained at our expense…The enormous weight of the Russian army is thrown upon us."

CONRAD VON HÖTZENDORF,
AUSTRIAN COMMANDER-IN-CHIEF IN A LETTER OF AUGUST 27, 1914

BACK FROM THE BRINK

In their offensives against Alsace and Lorraine, the French First and Second Armies met with disastrous defeat in August 1914, suffering some 250,000 casualties, but managed to recover. With the French armies wrongly positioned to meet the German advance through Belgium, the armies in Alsace and Lorraine nonetheless managed to break contact with the enemy and redeploy formations to counter the emerging threat. The French recovery helped stall the German offensive, though in truth the advance was more or less doomed by the time it reached the Marne. With their lines of communication still intact, the French and British were able to counterattack across the Marne in the second week of September and drive the Germans back to the Aisne. From this point both sides tried and failed to turn the enemy's open flank in a series of actions known as the "Race to the Sea". This culminated in the indecisive battle of Ypres in November and the onset of trench warfare.

THE IMPORTANCE OF RUSSIA

There was one other major factor in the French recovery in the first week of September 1914 – the efforts made by Russia to sustain its ally. In the first month of war Russia mounted two offensives, one against East Prussia, the other against Galicia.

Russian forces defeated those of Austria-Hungary but were defeated in turn by those of Germany. This was to be the pattern of operations over the next 30 months: the Russians were able to defeat the armies of Austria-Hungary, but could not compete with the superior organization and equipment that the Germans brought to the battlefield.

In what remained of 1914 both the Austro-Hungarian and Russian armies demonstrated remarkable spirit in extricating themselves from potential disasters. The Russians thwarted two determined German offensives in Poland and fought the Germans to a standstill in front of the city of Lodz, but their losses in these battles,

The BEF

British troops wheel their bicycles through the town of Rouen in northern France on their way to counter the German advance through Belgium. The BEF would form the left wing of the Allied line alongside the French Fifth Army. Relations between the two did not always run smoothly, but the British were able to play their part in the Battle of the Marne in September.

plus the exposed position of the city, led the Russians to cede Lodz voluntarily in December. The year closed with both the Austro-Hungarian and Russian empires having lost their best trained and equipped field armies, and both now largely dependent on their allies.

A DIFFERENT BATTLEFIELD

One thing that clearly distinguished the Eastern and Western Fronts was the degree of movement. The rail and road systems of northwest Europe were so well developed that it was virtually impossible for either side to gain any significant local advantage of numbers; any threat could easily be countered by the movement of reserves. In the East, however, while Germany had 1.6 km (1 mile) of rail track for every 15 sq km (6 sq miles), Austria-Hungary had 1.6 km (1 mile) for every 50 sq km (20 sq miles) and Russia had just 1.6 km (1 mile) of single track for every 180 sq km (70 sq miles) of its European territories. The scarcity of roads and railways would affect the conduct of the war in the East in many ways, most obviously in the transport of food, raw materials, arms and ammunition. With nearly all the fighting taking place on Russian or Austro-Hungarian soil, local superiority of numbers, sufficient to register local success, could be achieved by both sides. The problem was to sustain an offensive, especially into areas served by an intact rail system of the enemy. In the vastness of the Eastern Front, offensives effectively led nowhere.

"Every effort must be made to attack and drive back the enemy. A soldier who can no longer advance must guard the territory already held, no matter what the cost. He must be killed where he stands rather than draw back."

JOSEPH JOFFRE, FROM HIS ORDER OF SEPTEMBER 5 , ON THE EVE OF THE BATTLE OF THE MARNE.

Road to the Marne
A French unit carries its machine-guns towards the front line. In the background can be seen some of the cars, including the famous "taxis of the Marne", commandeered to ferry fresh troops from Paris to the battlefield.

The Invasion of Belgium and France

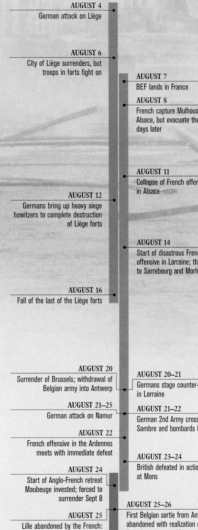

MILITARY OPERATIONS in the West began on August 1 when formations from the German Fourth Army violated and occupied neutral Luxembourg in order to secure the railways needed to complete Germany's mobilization plan. The logic of this act of aggression was not lost on Belgium. When the Germans delivered an ultimatum demanding rights of transit, the Belgian government issued orders for the destruction of bridges and rail installations that the Germans would need and for the concentration of the Belgian army on its eastern borders.

FRENCH REACTIONS

The French high command, although intent on an offensive along the common border with Germany to recover Alsace and Lorraine, had anticipated that the Germans might try to invade France via Belgium. The French Fifth Army was to be raised in the Mézières-Sedan area, covering the border with southern Belgium and with the option of moving to

Belgian resistance

The Belgian army of 117,000 men had no hope of halting the German advance for long, but made use of rivers and canals in holding operations as the troops withdrew to the fortified city of Antwerp.

the Longwy area and undertaking an offensive in the direction of Metz. The initial German moves led the French high command to order this army to move into the Belgian Ardennes, and the Fourth Army and part of the Third Army to conform to this movement. What the French had failed to appreciate was that the main German effort was to be made through central Belgium, not through the Ardennes. This error established the course of events in the first month of the war. The French launched their main offensive into Alsace and Lorraine against forces defensively deployed, while the German offensive fell upon the Belgian army and the open French left flank (see map page 43).

The initial French attacks into Alsace and Lorraine resulted in the capture of Altkirch, Thann and, most importantly, Mulhouse (Mülhausen), but the latter was lost on August 10 as battle was joined along the whole of this front. The French managed to take Mulhouse again on August 19, and also fought fierce battles for Morhange and Sarrebourg (August 14–20). In these two battles the French made modest gains, but at inordinate cost, and it was the confidence that flowed from having halted the French attacks that led to the German decision, on August 17, to move from the defensive to the offensive in this area. From August 20, German forces undertook a series of offensives. These were intended to defeat the French forces in this area and allow the German left wing an active role in the planned battle of encirclement and annihilation. It was only with difficulty that the French Second Army, reeling under its losses, retained possession of Nancy and managed to hold the Germans in front of the Verdun-Nancy-Belfort line of fortresses.

THE INVASION OF BELGIUM

By now, however, more significant events were unfolding to the north. While the German First Army completed its mobilization before its advance into the plains of central Belgium, elements of the German First and Second Armies (the Army of the Meuse) were given the task of capturing Liège, which was protected by a ring of 12 forts.

THE SIEGE OF LIÈGE

After crossing the border on August 4, the Germans took Liège itself on the night of August 5/6. As German columns tried to advance through the gaps between the forts, most were halted by stiff Belgian resistance. However, 14 Brigade, approaching from the east, had better fortune, despite losing its general in confused fighting in the dark. Major-General Ludendorff (soon to make his name on the Eastern Front) assumed command and led a

column of 1,500 men into the thinly defended city. On the 8th the Germans began the systematic bombardment of Liège's forts. On the 12th they reinforced their batteries with two mighty 420-mm siege howitzers and on the 16th the last of the forts surrendered. The Germans, having possibly lost just two days through the Belgian defence of Liège, could now begin to move into central Belgium.

THE GERMAN ADVANCE

The German armies swept rapidly west and on August 20 German forces entered Brussels in readiness for a wheel to the southwest into northeast France. Meanwhile batteries from the German Second Army set about the reduction of the fortified towns of Namur and Charleroi. Having learnt much from the siege of the Liège forts, they brought their heavy artillery into action

THE SIEGE OF THE LIÈGE FORTS

~

WHEN THE CITY OF LIÈGE flew white flags at 2:00 pm on August 6, General Leman, in command of the Belgian defence, was in Fort Loncin. He ordered one division to withdraw and join the retreating Belgian army, but refused to surrender. The battle for the city was over, but the 12 forts that ringed Liège remained. Fort Pontisse could direct its guns at the Meuse where German troops were constructing pontoons, while Fort Loncin commanded the roads into the central Belgian plain. The guns in the other forts also kept firing, but, once their observation posts had been knocked out, they had difficulty locating the German batteries. Heavier and heavier guns were brought up to subdue them, culminating in two 420-mm howitzers that went into action on the 12th. The last fort held out until the 16th. Some forts were shelled into submission, others surrendered because of conditions inside. Poor ventilation and sanitation meant that asphyxiating gases from exploding shells combined with the smell of human waste to make the air unbreathable.

Shattered gun cupola
The unreinforced concrete of the Liège forts could not withstand the German heavy guns. Many of the forts' own guns were soon put out of action.

420-mm high-explosive shell

210-mm high-explosive shell

German siege howitzers
Most of the damage to the Liège forts was inflicted by smaller guns, chiefly 210-mm howitzers. The forts were designed to withstand shells of this calibre back in the 1880s, but modern high-explosive shells could penetrate their defences. The huge 420-mm Mörser, the original "Big Bertha" (right) caused the fall of two of the forts: Pontisse and Loncin.

GERMAN 210-MM AND 420-MM HIGH-EXPLOSIVE SHELLS

A destroyed gun at Fort Loncin
The ruins of Fort Loncin are preserved as a Belgian national monument. The bodies of the 350 men who died when the fort's magazine exploded lie buried beneath the rubble.

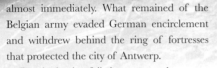

The Anglo-French retreat
A French column passes a pile of horses lying dead in a field. As the British and French retreated south pursued by the Germans in August 1914, casualties among the horses on both sides were high.

almost immediately. What remained of the Belgian army evaded German encirclement and withdrew behind the ring of fortresses that protected the city of Antwerp.

Despite having failed to prevent the escape of the Belgian army, the German armies had secured very considerable advantages of position and numbers. The French Fifth Army was forced to extend its left flank in an attempt to keep abreast of the German deployment through central Belgium. As the German First and Second Armies

"Where are the prisoners? Where are the captured guns"

HELMUTH VON MOLTKE, EXPRESSING HIS DOUBTS ON THE SUCCESS OF THE SCHLIEFFEN PLAN, SEPTEMBER 1914

approached the Belgian–French frontier, they faced only the overstretched Fifth Army, the British Expeditionary Force (with just five infantry divisions) and a few weak French formations protecting the extreme left flank.

THE BATTLE OF MONS

On August 23–24, eight German corps attacked the British Expeditionary Force, which was attempting to hold a line that stretched for 43 km (27 miles) either side of the Belgian town of Mons. To the west the British had dug in hastily along the Canal de Condé, but around the town itself they occupied an exposed salient. This was where the main attack was launched. At first the German infantry advanced in close order and suffered heavy casualties at the hands of British riflemen and machine-gunners. The Germans then started to direct heavy artillery and machine-gun fire at the British, forcing them to abandon their positions. General French, the commander of the BEF, could have chosen to withdraw into the nearby fortified town of Maubeuge, but did not. The town was besieged by the Germans on the 24th, but its garrison held out until September 8, by which time the main invasion force had moved far to the south.

Heavily outnumbered, the British and French forces in northeast France had no alternative but to cede ground and withdraw to the southwest. The British made another day-long stand at Le Cateau on August 26, but then continued their retreat. On the same day the fortified towns of Longwy and Les Ayvelles were occupied by the German Third Army as the Germans developed their offensive along the whole of the front west of Metz. The Allied front, despite the French intention to stand on the Amiens-Laon-Aisne-Verdun line, was in danger of being turned in exactly the way that the Schlieffen Plan had envisaged.

GERMAN ATROCITIES

~

THE VIOLATION OF BELGIAN NEUTRALITY made the Germans ogres in the eyes of the world's press. Determination to crush popular resistance in Belgium, especially the activities of *franc-tireurs* (civilian snipers), resulted in a number of "atrocities" that the Allies exploited for propaganda purposes. Where resistance was suspected, the Germans burned houses, rounded up civilians and picked out groups of them to be executed. There were well-documented incidents at Dinant, where a large number of civilians, including women and children, were executed, and at Louvain, where the university library with its priceless collection of medieval manuscripts was razed to the ground.

US war bond poster
American propaganda, even four years later in 1918, still recalls the "rape" of neutral Belgium.

REMEMBER BELGIUM
Buy Bonds
Fourth
Liberty
Loan

Belgian woman killed by German shelling
The press in Britain and France published many pictures like this, even though they did not show atrocities as such, in order to whip up anti-German feeling.

PROBLEMS OF SUPPLY

In reality the Schlieffen Plan was incapable of implementation and had begun to break down long before German formations reached the Oise. Staff work could not resolve problems of command and resupply that plagued the German armies as they advanced into northern France. With the French jamming German radio signals, the armies that advanced into France were increasingly without direction from superior authority, while behind them chaos mounted as the German logistic system broke down. Without sufficient specialist troops to clear demolitions and return railways to service at a rate that kept pace with the advancing armies, the nearest available railheads for the various armies were on average some 135 km (85 miles) from the lead formations during the last five days of August.

The German Second Army, with support from the First, was able to overcome the resistance of the French Fifth Army around Guise (August 28–29). Although delayed by this action, both German armies continued to advance despite the increasing exhaustion of their troops and horses. That they were able to advance at all was mainly because of captured military supplies and being able to live off the rich countryside. After Mons, the advance involved relatively little fighting, so the troops required less resupply in terms of ammunition.

FALTERING PROGRESS

But the fact remained that the first German horses to die of exhaustion during this campaign died on German soil, and as early as August 11 one German cavalry division had to be withdrawn from operations because of the condition of its mounts. Many German horses were further weakened in the course of the invasion by being fed on green corn. At the same time German troops did themselves no favours by eating unripe fruit picked from the orchards that they passed. Few German infantry formations saw their heavy weapons and supply columns after the German border was crossed, and without motor transport there was no possibility of German formations being supplied much beyond the Aisne. By the time the German forces wheeled inside Paris and came to the Marne in the first week of September, they were spent, and the French high command, after more than two weeks of retreat, was able to consider mounting a counterattack.

German troops waiting to advance
With the French and British armies retreating in front of them, the German troops were faced by very little opposition as they advanced through the French countryside in the brilliant sunshine of August 1914.

Aug 20
Belgian Army withdraws to Antwerp. After heavy bombardment, city finally surrenders on Oct 10

Aug 24
Maubeuge, besieged by Germans, holds out until Sept 8

THE INVASION OF FRANCE
Aug 2–Sept 5, 1914

- German advance (Aug 2–Sept 5)
- German position Sept 5
- French position Sept 5
- Belgian position Sept 5
- British position Sept 5
- German GHQ
- French GHQ
- ⊠ German fortified town
- ⊠ French fortified town
- ⊠ Belgian fortified town
- ⚔ Major battle or siege
- The Allies (and allied states)
- Central Powers (and allied states)
- Neutral states

The march through Belgium into France
The speed of the German invasion was impressive, not far behind the timetable of the Schlieffen Plan, which allowed six weeks to defeat the French before redeploying Germany's armies to face Russia. In the end, exhaustion and failures of command and supply would bring the invasion to a halt on the Marne.

German troops entering Brussels
The occupation of the Belgian capital by the German First Army on August 20, 1914 was unopposed. The Belgian army had retreated north to Antwerp, allowing the Germans to pass unimpeded through central Belgium.

The Eastern and Balkan Fronts

SERBIA, GALICIA AND EAST PRUSSIA
AUGUST – SEPTEMBER 1914

~

On August 12 Austria-Hungary attempted to invade Serbia, but was soon beaten back. The imperial armies enjoyed more success in the opening manoeuvres on the Russian front, but at the end of August suffered a humiliating reverse in eastern Galicia. Russia's fortunes were equally mixed. Victory in the south against the Austro-Hungarians was offset by catastrophic defeat by the Germans at Tannenberg.

~

AUGUST 12
Austria-Hungary invades Serbia

AUGUST 17
Russian 1st and 2nd Armies begin advance on East Prussia; 1st Army crosses border

AUGUST 19
Serbs defeat Austrians on Jadar River

AUGUST 20
Battle of Gumbinnen; Germans retreat. Prittwitz, the German commander in the east, tells his superior Moltke that he may have to withdraw behind the Vistula

AUGUST 21
Austrians driven back across the border by Serbian forces

AUGUST 22
As Russian 2nd Army advances on a wide front, German troops diverted by train to face this threat. Hindenburg and Ludendorff arrive at Marienburg to take command

AUGUST 23
Austrian 1st Army collides with Russian 4th Army at Krasnik

AUGUST 25
Austrians force Russians to retreat at Krasnik

AUGUST 26
Russian 2nd Army pushes on, unaware of threat of encirclement. Start of Battle of Tannenberg

AUGUST 26
Russian 5th Army defeated at Komarov; Start of battle along Gnila Lipa River in eastern Galicia

AUGUST 29
Suicide of Samsonov as the bulk of his 2nd Army is surrounded

AUGUST 29
Start of disorderly Austrian retreat to positions behind Lemberg, pursued by victorious Russian 3rd and 8th Armies

AUGUST 31
Battle of Tannenberg ends with the capture of 125,000 Russians

SEPTEMBER 3
Lemberg occupied by Russians

SEPTEMBER 7
Germans advance in Masurian Lakes region to clear Russian 1st Army from East Prussia

SEPTEMBER 11
Conrad orders Austrian armies in Galicia to fall back behind the San River

SEPTEMBER 8
Second Austrian invasion of Serbia

SEPTEMBER 13
Germans drive Rennenkampf out of East Prussia, but fail to encircle his forces

SEPTEMBER 17
Austrians halted by Serbian counterattacks, but hold on to small gains on border with Bosnia

SEPTEMBER 17
New German 9th Army sent by rail from East Prussia to reinforce Austrians in the south

SEPTEMBER 24
Russians besiege fortress town of Przemysl and attack passes through the Carpathians, aiming to invade northern Hungary

SEPTEMBER 28
Transfer of German 9th Army complete

KEY
- Austrian invasions of Serbia Aug 12–21 & Sept 8–17
- Russian campaign in East Prussia Aug 17–Sept 13
- Galician battles Aug 23–Sept 28

Cossacks advancing through Poland
In 1914 the war on the Eastern Front was far more mobile than in the West. Cavalry was used by both sides for reconnaissance and cavalry skirmishes were common.

AT THE OUTBREAK OF WAR Germany intended to stand on the defensive in East Prussia until victory was won in the West. Both Austria-Hungary and Russia, however, were committed to offensive action. Russia hoped to drive the German forces from East Prussia and the Austro-Hungarians from Galicia in readiness for an advance on Berlin. Austria-Hungary, aware of its long-term military inferiority to Russia, was to attempt a pre-emptive attack in the direction of Warsaw in order to hamper Russia's mobilization. But the first Austro-Hungarian move had to be directed against Serbia – as punishment for the assassinations of June 28. On July 29, before any of the other great powers had entered the war, Austria-Hungary sent gunboats down the Danube to bombard the Serbian capital, Belgrade.

FIRST INVASION OF SERBIA

In the crucial opening days of hostilities, the Austro-Hungarian army, because it also had to counter the Russian threat to Galicia, possessed no appreciable margin of superiority over its Serbian enemy. The latter, aware that the survival of the nation was on the line, concentrated three armies in the north of the country to counter Austrian attacks across the

Sava and Drina rivers (see map page 121). When the Serbian high command realized there would be no major offensive across the Sava, it redeployed the First and Second Armies to support the Third Army, which was threatened by the Austro-Hungarian Fifth Army moving across the Drina. The invading army found its left flank, north of the Jadar, counterattacked by the First Army, while south of the river its right flank was met by the Second Army. The main battle began on August 17 and, with the flanks of the Austrian army unable to support each other, they were defeated separately on August 19 and then driven from Serbian soil.

This first offensive cost the Austro-Hungarians about 40,000 killed and wounded, and provided the Serbs with a useful haul of guns, rifles and ammunition. After a brief Serbian incursion into Bosnia, the Austro-Hungarian Fifth Army again crossed the Drina on the night of September 7–8. In a ten-day battle it secured a number of shallow bridgeheads and the Serbs withdrew to positions in

THE HAZARDS OF RADIO

~

FOLLOWING MARCONI'S EXPERIMENTS in "wireless telegraphy" in the 1890s, the first "radio war" was the Russo-Japanese War of 1904–05. Despite considerable progress made over the following decade, radio was still very much in its infancy in 1914. Equipment was bulky and difficult to transport and the relative slowness of radio transmission meant that all armies were obliged at times to transmit without using code. The Russians were especially negligent in this regard and the Germans often had prior knowledge of their intentions in the early campaigns on the Eastern Front.

Russian radio station
The local inhabitants pose proudly beside a newly erected radio aerial in Russian Poland.

front of the Kolubra River. There the front remained until November 5 when two Austro-Hungarian armies renewed the offensive.

THE EASTERN FRONT

On the Eastern Front, where Russia faced both Germany and Austria-Hungary, events in the northern sector unfolded slightly ahead of those to the south. Reacting immediately to French difficulties as the Germans advanced through Belgium, Russia committed its two best armies against East Prussia (see maps page 49), which was defended by a single German army. The Russian First Army crossed the border on August 17 and cleared the German defensive positions at Gumbinnen on the 20th. The Second Army, crossing the border on August 20, aimed to establish itself on a line to the rear of the German forces so that the Russians could use their superior numbers and position to encircle and annihilate the enemy.

AUSTRO-HUNGARIAN SUCCESS

In the south the first encounters proved to be collisions rather than planned engagements. The main Austro-Hungarian advance was to be made from Galicia northwards into Russian Poland (see map page 50). The First Army, advancing on Lublin between the Vistula and Bug rivers, met and drove back the Russian Fourth Army around Krasnik on August 23. This success led the Habsburg high command to order the Fourth Army forward with its flank supported by part of the Third Army. The Russian high command reacted by ordering the Fifth Army to move against the Austrian First Army. In so doing, however, the Russian army exposed its left flank to the Austrian Fourth Army and became involved in a losing battle around Komarov.

THE TIDE TURNS

The Austrian high command had failed to appreciate that the main Russian offensive was to be made in the direction of Lemberg (Lvov) in eastern Galicia. Here Austro-Hungarian forces had been thinned to meet commitments in Serbia and to

Serbian artillery position
The Serbian army, hardened in the battles of the Balkan Wars and with the advantage of fighting on home soil, was able to halt all Austrian attempts at invasion in 1914.

support the advance of their forces into southern Poland. Despite their initial successes, lack of co-ordination between the individual Habsburg armies and their overall numerical inferiority now placed them at serious risk of defeat.

GERMAN MOVEMENTS IN THE NORTH

In East Prussia a similar situation developed for much the same reasons. In difficult terrain – thick pine forests and a patchwork of small lakes – that favoured the defence, the Russian First Army failed to follow up its initial successes. This allowed the Germans to withdraw large numbers of troops from the front around Gumbinnen. Making use of East Prussia's efficient rail network, they were then able to redeploy the greater part of their available troops in order to deal with the Russian Second Army advancing from the south.

NEW COMMANDERS

German forces in the East were now under a new command. After the defeat at Gumbinnen on August 20, General von Prittwitz had telephoned the German high command. He appears to have lost his nerve, recommending that the German Eighth Army abandon East Prussia and withdraw to the Vistula. On hearing

Russian prisoners captured at Tannenberg
Pictures of the 125,000 Russians taken at Tannenberg gave an enormous boost to the Germans' faith in the efficiency and fighting qualities of their armies. The mighty Russian "steamroller" was not the threat that had been feared.

this, Moltke, the German commander-in-chief, decided Prittwitz should be dismissed and arranged for him to be replaced by Count Paul von Hindenburg with Erich Ludendorff as his chief of staff. The two men, who had never met before, formed such a successful partnership that they would take over the German high command in 1916. The aristocratic Hindenburg was the figurehead; Ludendorff, who came from humble origins, was the brains.

Hindenburg and Ludendorff reached East Prussia to take over command on August 23. Even before they arrived, a plan, prepared by Colonel Hoffmann, operations officer on Prittwitz's staff, to redeploy German troops to the south to counter the advancing Russian Second Army had already put into action.

THE BATTLE OF TANNENBERG

The Russian Second Army was increasingly disorganized and exhausted as it advanced in the direction of Osterode and Allenstein in its attempt to get behind an enemy that it believed to be still concentrated in the Gumbinnen area. By August 24 formations from I Corps had arrived in the Lautenburg area and on the following day the first clash took place between flanking formations around Soldau. Meanwhile, to the east, the leading elements of the Russian VI Corps had advanced as far as Bischofsburg.

By August 25–26, the situation on both sectors of the front, in East Prussia and southern Poland, curiously were mirror images of one another. In both sectors were armies – Russian in the north and Austrian in the south – advancing in the belief that they faced a defeated enemy and that they would be able to complete successful battles of encirclement, and both unaware of the enemy concentrations that would bring about their defeat.

THE TRAP IS SPRUNG

Dawn on August 26 found the Russian Second Army persisting with its advance in the direction of Allenstein. The army's commander, Alexander Samsonov, was confident that his flanks were in no immediate danger, despite his forces on the left having already run into the enemy around Soldau. On the same day German forces, having marched south from Gumbinnen, routed the Russian VI Corps in front of Bischofsburg, even as other German forces completed their preparations for counter-offensives against the Second Army's centre and left flank. These began on the 27th.

German advance in East Prussia
Throughout the Tannenberg campaign, the Germans had the advantage of fighting on home soil, exploiting their knowledge of the region's forests and lakes. In addition, the intact railway network allowed rapid redeployment of troops.

THE BATTLE OF TANNENBERG

AUGUST 17–31, 1914

Responding to the needs of their French allies, the Russians quickly mounted an invasion of German territory to distract the Germans from their invasion of France. Because the Russians were also engaged on the border with Austria-Hungary in the south, they sent only two armies into East Prussia. Their plan misfired completely as one of the invading armies was surrounded and crushed by the Germans.

KEY

➡ Russian advance	⌐ Russian position
⇨ Russian retreat	⌐ German position
➡ German advance	⊠ German fort/fortified town
⇨ German retreat	✵ Major battle
	▨ Major railway

The Russian advance
August 17–23

The two Russian armies advanced with a wide gap between them. When the Germans moved against the First Army, they were defeated at Gumbinnen, but then swiftly withdrew to meet the challenge of the Second Army.

August 20–23
Two German corps en route by rail to reinforce the German lines to the south

Night of August 20
German forces counterattack. Despite some success against the Russian XX Corps, the Germans are repulsed and withdraw

Night of August 17
Unauthorized attack by General François, commander of 1 Corps, drives the Russian force back to the frontier

August 17–20
Russian 1st Army crosses East Prussian border. Four corps of the German 8th Army have moved forward to defend

August 23
Advance of Russian 2nd Army under General Samsonov

The battle switches to the south
August 24–26

Unaware of the troop movements that had brought the bulk of the German Eighth Army south to meet his advance, Samsonov ordered his army forwards. The first encounters took place on August 26. The Russian First Army meanwhile made slow progress, uncertain of the forces that were ranged against it.

August 24
Russian XV Corps confronts entrenched German XX Corps. Fierce fighting rages all day. German forces withdraw to Tannenberg

August 24
Hindenburg commits almost all his troops to the southern flank

August 25
Rennenkampf pushes slowly westwards, unaware of weakness of German opposition

August 26
On Samsonov's northern flank, the Germans repulse an advance by Russian VI Corps

Night of August 25
François' 1 Corps reaches Seeben area by train

August 26
German forces take Seeben, and force Russian troops to withdraw from Frankenau area

The German victory, August 27–31

Outgunned and outmanoeuvred, Russian forces in the centre were defeated in every major engagement. As they attempted to retreat, they found their escape route barred by German I Corps.

August 27–28
German forces are moved south to complete encirclement

August 27–28
Remnants of Russian VI Corps withdraw across the border

August 30–31
Russian attempts to break through François' line are turned back. 125,000 Russians are captured

August 27
Under deadly bombardment from German I Corps, Russian I Corps suffers heavy casualties, and withdraws south

August 28
German I Corps, under François, advances eastwards, forming a line that will block Russian escape route

August 28–29
Samsonov orders continuation of Russian attack in the centre. Under heavy bombardment from German XX Corps, Russians start disorganized retreat

Hindenburg and his staff
Hindenburg (in the light coat) poses with his staff. His chief of staff, Ludendorff, stands on his right and Colonel Hoffmann on his left.

Trenches in Galicia
These well-camouflaged Austro-Hungarian trenches were carefully constructed with earth and brushwood cover and loopholes for the soldiers' rifles, but would prove vulnerable to heavy artillery fire.

The Russian I Corps was crushed around Usdau on the 27th, and on the 28th the Germans moved against the enemy centre around the village of Tannenberg, from which the battle would take its name. Though the Russian forces that had been committed to the advance on Allenstein were pulled back to counter this attack, the battle was already lost. The German advantages of artillery and supply, plus the depth of the previous Russian penetration in the centre, ensured that the Russians could not regain the

Russian columns
Russian troops advance through Galicia in pursuit of the retreating Austro-Hungarian armies. The Russians had a lot of ground to cover before battle could be rejoined, and lines of supply became seriously overstretched.

safety of Polish territory before the German I Corps secured Willenberg and closed their line of withdrawal. By August 30 three Russian corps had been destroyed and another two had been put to flight.

THE FIRST BATTLE OF THE MASURIAN LAKES
Following the disintegration of the Russian Second Army and the suicide of Samsonov, Hindenburg and Ludendorff switched their attention to

Rennenkampf's First Army. This had been advancing towards the fortified city of Königsberg in the north, while its left flank was making slow progress through the Masurian Lakes region. On hearing the news of Tannenberg, Rennenkampf withdrew to a line between the Masurian Lakes and the Baltic Sea. The regrouped German Eighth Army was ready to go over to the offensive on September 5 and, on the 9th/10th German I Corps struck a damaging blow against the Russian left flank. Aware that his army was in danger of being encircled, Rennenkampf ordered a withdrawal. Distracted by a brief but effective Russian counterattack, the Germans did not pursue fast enough to trap the Russians, but by September 13 had driven them out of East Prussia.

THE FALL OF LEMBERG
In the south, events unfolded very differently. Around Komarov, the Russian Fifth Army persisted until August 31 with an offensive that might have resulted in its being encircled and destroyed. Fortunately for the Russians, the depleted Austrian Third Army, advancing from the Lemberg area, had run into two full-strength Russian armies. Heavily defeated, the Third Army withdrew and the Russians occupied Lemberg on September 3.

The Austro-Hungarian commander-in-chief, Conrad von Hötzendorf, tried to switch the Fourth Army against the open right flank of the advancing Russian Third Army. In its turn, however, the Russian command sought to envelop the Austrian Fourth Army by directing the Third Army northwards. A series of battles were fought in the Lemberg–Rava Russka sector. The Russian Eighth Army, meanwhile, dealt with a reinforced Austrian Third Army and part of the Austrian Second Army in the area to the south of Lemberg.

THE AUSTRO-HUNGARIAN RETREAT
If the Russians had made more effective use of their Fifth Army, they might have routed either or both the Austrian Third and Fourth Armies. Even so, by

Russian victory in Galicia
The Austro-Hungarians had the better of the first battles, fought in southern Poland, but they did not realize that the greater Russian threat came from the east. Without sufficient forces to counter it, they were defeated in a series of battles around Lemberg and forced to retreat.

WARSAW
Bug
9TH ARMY
Brest-Litovsk
Pripet Marshes

POLAND
Lodz
Vistula
RUSSIAN EMPIRE

Opoczno
Radom
Ivangorod
4TH ARMY
5TH ARMY

Sept 18
German 9th Army arrives to reinforce Austrians
Lublin
Kholm

AUG 23–25
Krasnik
Austro-Hungarian victory
Sandomierz
AUG 26–SEPT 1
Komarov
Austro-Hungarian victory
Rovno
3RD ARMY

9TH ARMY
SILESIA
Katowice
Vistula
San
1ST ARMY
SEPT 3
Rava Russka
Russian victory

Cracow
Tarnow
Jaroslau
Przemysl
Lemberg
3RD ARMY
AUG 26–30
Gnila Lipa
Russian victory

AUSTRIA-HUNGARY
4TH ARMY
GALICIA
Dniester
Sept 11
General Austrian withdrawal ordered; troops eventually move 160 km (100 miles) to west

CARPATHIAN MOUNTAINS
Stanislaw
8TH ARMY
2ND ARMY
AUG 23–SEPT 1
Austrian 2nd Army is redeployed from Serbia

0 km 20 40 60 80 100
0 miles 20 40 60 80 100

THE GALICIAN FRONT	
Aug–Sept 1914	
⌒ Furthest line of Austrian advance	⊞ Fortified city/town
⋯ Austrian line after retreat, Sept 26	– – Major railway
➡ Austrian advance (Aug)	✹ Major battle
➡ Russian counterattack	▨ The Allies (and allied states)
➡ Austrian retreat (Sept)	▨ Central Powers (and allied states)
➡ German troop movement	

September 11 Russian superiority of numbers and position prevailed along the whole of the Galician front. The Austrians, whose Fourth Army narrowly escaped encirclement, broke off the battle. Thus, at the very time when the Germans, having broken the Russian First Army's left flank on September 10, were clearing East Prussia, the Austrians were beginning a disorderly withdrawal of over 160 km (100 miles) and appealing to their ally for help. In the opening battles on this front they had suffered 350,000 casualties. The Germans responded by reconstituting four of the Eighth Army's corps as the German Ninth Army, which was transported south into the Katowice-Cracow area by the end of the month.

RUMPLER TAUBE

~

THE FRAIL, BIRDLIKE Rumpler Taube ("Dove"), first produced in in 1910, was already something of an antique by 1914. Nevertheless, the Germans and Austrians used it as their main reconnaissance plane during the first few months of the war. One even flew over Paris dropping bombs and leaflets. On the Eastern Front, Taubes played an important role in the Tannenberg campaign, providing information on the movements of the Russian armies. In the Galician theatre, with greater distances to be covered, it was less effective, its maximum airborne endurance being only four hours. It was also vulnerable to fire from the ground. In 1915 Taubes were relegated to the role of pilot-training.

The engine gave a top speed of only 96 kph (60 mph)

With its pale linen-covered wings, the Taube was hard to spot at heights over 360 m (1,200 ft)

Control in flight was by warping – twisting the wings and tail as in early Wright brothers aircraft, rather than by means of ailerons

Russian trenches
Although campaigns on the Eastern Front in 1914 were extremely mobile, with cavalry advancing to reconnoitre enemy positions, once two armies came face to face, they quickly entrenched in similar fashion to the Western Front.

At the Battle of the Marne, the French halted their
retreat, counterattacked the pursuing Germans and
forced them back to the Aisne. The southern half of
the front then became fixed and the fighting moved
north through Picardy to Flanders in a series of
manoeuvres known as the "Race to the Sea". The last
major battle of the year in the West was fought at
Ypres, after which the Western Front became
stabilized from Switzerland to the Sea.

~

SEPTEMBER 1
Joffre orders armies to fall back
south of Paris as far the Seine

SEPTEMBER 2
French government secretly
evacuated to Bordeaux by train

SEPTEMBER 5
French 6th Army attacks right
flank of German 1st Army. Start
of Battle of the Ourcq

SEPTEMBER 6
French 5th Army and BEF halt, turn
round and advance towards the
Marne. Start of Battle of the Marne

SEPTEMBER 7–8
Foch's 9th Army in fierce fighting
in marshes of St Gond

SEPTEMBER 9
German 1st and 2nd Armies split as
French 5th Army and BEF advance;
decision taken for German retreat

SEPTEMBER 9–13
Belgian sortie from Antwerp
reaches Louvain

SEPTEMBER 12
German forces recross the Aisne
and take up strong defensive
positions

SEPTEMBER 14
Moltke dismissed and replaced
by Falkenhayn; Germans halt
Anglo-French offensive along
the Aisne. First use of aircraft
radio to direct artillery

SEPTEMBER 15
First use of aerial photography
for ground forces by
Royal Flying Corps

SEPTEMBER 22–26
Battle of Picardy

SEPTEMBER 26
Somme action; French driven out
of Péronne

SEPTEMBER 26
Arrival of Indian troops at
Marseille

SEPTEMBER 27
Start of Battle of Artois

SEPTEMBER 28
Germans start bombardment of
forts surrounding Antwerp

OCTOBER 1
Start of desperate fighting just east
of Arras; French 10th Army prevents
German breakthrough

OCTOBER 3
Belgians start withdrawal from
Antwerp towards Ghent

OCTOBER 4
German forces reach Belgian coast

OCTOBER 10
Surrender of Antwerp

OCTOBER 12
German occupation of Lille. Battle of
La Bassée

OCTOBER 16
Start of Battle of the Yser.
Start of Battle of Armentières

OCTOBER 18
Start of First Battle of Ypres

OCTOBER 30
Belgians succeed in flooding land to
east of Yser Canal, thus bringing
German advance to a halt

NOVEMBER 11
Last great German attack at Ypres

NOVEMBER 22
End of First Battle of Ypres

KEY	
▬ Siege of Antwerp Aug 20–Oct 10	▬ Battle of the Aisne Sept 12–28
▬ Anglo-French retreat to the Marne Aug 24–Sept 5 and Battle of the Marne Sept 6–11	▬ Race to the Sea Sept 17–Nov 22

From the Marne to First Ypres

IN THE COURSE of the German advance to and
beyond the Marne, both sides experienced
difficulties arising from the transfer of troops. The
various armies also had problems co-ordinating
movements and operations with their neighbours.
Gaps could not always be closed and, whether in
advance or retreat, armies struggled to maintain
contact with their flanking formations, while on the
western end of the line they had to look to their
exposed open flanks.

The French had redeployed large numbers of
men from their right flank to form the Sixth Army
and the Foch Detachment (soon to become the
Ninth Army). In spite of this they managed to

French soldiers at the Marne
The battle was fought in open country and the soldiers
used hedges, ditches and sunken roads for cover. If there
was none, they dug rudimentary trenches and foxholes.

maintain their positions on the right, opposite
Lorraine. Their second major problem was to
ensure proper co-ordination between the retreating
Fourth and Fifth Armies and between the Fifth
Army and the British Expeditionary Force.

One of the Germans' main problems was that its
three armies on the right had all had to sacrifice
men in the course of their advance. These had been
needed to mask Antwerp, hold down central
Belgium and besiege the the fortified towns of Givet

JOSEPH JOFFRE
~

KNOWN TO HIS TROOPS as "Papa Joffre", Joseph Joffre (1852–1931) led
the French army into the First World War. Even before the outbreak of
war, he had adopted a doctrine of "attack at all costs". As chief of the
general staff from 1911, he rid the French army of "defensively-minded"
commanders and lobbied for increased military spending. Following victory
at the Battle of the Marne in September 1914, Joffre was hailed as the
saviour of France. An autocratic leader, he had no qualms about
withholding information from the French government, which led the Briand
administration to attempt to bring him into line towards the end of 1915.

Joffre showed an equally unshakable nerve in victory and adversity. He
faced serious setbacks with the repeated failure of the French army to break
through in Champagne and Artois in 1915. It was, however, his failure to
prepare adequately against the German offensive at Verdun that finally led
to his ousting in December 1916. Still very popular, he was promoted to the
ceremonial role of Marshal of France.

THE FRENCH ARMY

THE FRENCH ARMY in 1914 had a peace-time establishment of some 700,000 officers and men. In July 1914 the French army mustered a total of 67 infantry, three colonial infantry and ten cavalry divisions. The standard establishment of a division – with 400 officers and 15,470 men – was two infantry brigades, each with three regiments, a cavalry squadron and a regiment of artillery, plus engineers and support troops. France possessed 173 metropolitan infantry regiments, most with three battalions, one of which was a reserve unit. In addition, in North Africa there were units of XIX Corps, which was commonly known as *l'Armée d'Afrique*, while elsewhere in France's empire there was *La Coloniale*, drawn from regular troops and men from pre-1789 colonies. At the outbreak of war, with first-line reservists, France was able to mobilize about 1,100,000 men. In the course of the war France mobilized a total of between 3.5 and 4 million men.

France, with a relatively small population and low birthrate, raised such numbers only by conscripting 84 per cent of its eligible manpower and, after 1912, extending the period of service to three years. The manpower problem confronting the French army was fundamental, as was the high command's unreasoning adherence to a doctrine of attack. These were not the only serious problems that it had to face. In the "75" it had the best field gun of any army, but few heavy and medium guns. The standard 1907 St Etienne machine-gun was mechanically unreliable, while the 1893 Lebel rifle was inaccurate. The army's relationship with the government was always difficult, while poor rates of pay meant that in 1914 it lacked its full establishment of officers, warrant officers and NCOs. It has been suggested that about one in ten of its soldiers did not speak French but a local dialect or *patois*.

IDENTITY DISC

LEBEL (1893 MODEL)

The magazine held eight

ST ETIENNE REVOLVER

8-mm ammunition

Firearms
The French Lebel was less accurate than the rifles of other armies. Troops at the start of the war were issued with a model dating from 1893. It continued in use throughout the war, but most soldiers preferred the 1915 Berthier.

Képi with cover

Uncovered képi

FORAGE CAP

CANTEEN

CLASP KNIFE

Légion d'honneur
France's highest decoration was instituted by Napoleon in 1802.

French artillery
A gun crew demonstrates the loading of a 75-mm field gun, the pride of the French Army and a significant factor in the victory on the Marne in September 1914.

Knapsack

Bayonet

French uniform of 1914
It seems astonishing today that the French went off to fight the First World War in bright red trousers and dark-blue overcoats. The only concession to camouflage in 1914 was a cover worn over the képi. A less conspicuous blue uniform was introduced in 1915, along with the Adrian steel helmet.

and Maubeuge. The Second and Third Armies had each given up a corps while the First Army had had to surrender the equivalent of three corps.

Unable to transfer formations from Alsace-Lorraine to the right flank because of the wrecked Belgian railway system, the Germans had neither the manpower nor the time to take or mask Paris. By now there was scarcely any effective control from OHL, the German high command. To make matters worse, the commanders of the three German armies of the right wing – Kluck, Bülow and Hausen – were not noted for their compatibility. This reduced communication between the three armies to a minimum.

A Change of Plan

To have attempted to move west of Paris at this point would have left all the advancing German armies west of Sedan over-committed along an extended front. For this reason Kluck's First Army moved south with the aim of passing to the east of Paris. As the direction of the French Fifth Army's retreat became clear, Kluck shifted the direction of his advance to the southeast. This promised to close the gap between the First and Second Armies. The Germans still held the initiative and the advantage of numerical superiority. The French attempt to stand on the Somme with the Sixth Army, the BEF and the Fifth Army in the last days of August came to nothing. The Anglo-French retreat continued.

Hit by shrapnel
The transport line of the British 1st Middlesex Regiment comes under fire as it nears the Marne on September 8. The man clutching his head has been badly wounded. The attack left the regiment's water cart riddled with holes.

BATTLE OF THE MARNE
5–12 SEPTEMBER, 1914
~

The French are justifiably proud of their victory on the Marne. Their initial offensives against Alsace and Lorraine had been costly failures and the French armies had been wrongly positioned to meet the German invasion. Nevertheless, they were able to redeploy their forces to launch a counterattack against the advancing German armies. The key event in the Battle of the Marne took place just to the east of Paris: the attack launched by the Sixth Army against the right wing of the German First Army led to the creation of a gap between the German First and Second Armies. In heavy fighting further to the east, the French halted the German Second, Third and Fourth Armies.

KEY

French advance	French position
British advance	British position
German advance	German position
German retreat/withdrawal	Road

The counter-offensive, September 5–6
Late on September 4, Joffre issued an order to the French armies to stop their retreat on the following day. He also agreed that the French 6th Army should attack the right wing of the German 1st Army just to the east of Paris.

Sept 5
French 6th Army encounters Gronau's Reserve Corps. Gronau attacks, defeating leading French divisions

Sept 6
Gronau withdraws to a strong defensive position west of the Ourcq

Sept 6
BEF advances northwards

Sept 5
Kluck sends some troops back across the Marne, where he has left only a Reserve Corps, commanded by General von Gronau

Sept 6
French 5th Army advances northwards, but is held back by part of German 1st Army

Sept 6
Left wing of German 2nd Army forces Foch's 9th Army back south across St Gond marshes

The battlefield
The Battle of the Marne involved a series of engagements stretching from the Ourcq to Verdun. After the general German retreat on September 9, dead men and horses lay scattered over a vast area of northeastern France.

GALLIENI AND THE PARIS GARRISON

About this time the commander of the Paris garrison, General Joseph Gallieni, in effect assumed a field command. The garrison had recently been strengthened by the arrival of North African troops by train and the despatch of reinforcements from the Alsace-Lorraine sector. The French also became aware of German intentions to pass to the east of Paris. Captured documents, taken from a German corpse, outlined the First Army's proposed line of advance from the Oise to the Ourcq. On September 3 the French government left Paris for Bordeaux and Joffre was still insistent on a general retreat as far as the Seine. Gallieni and his staff, however, had now had confirmation of the German change of direction from aerial reconnaissance and glimpsed the possibility of mounting a counter-offensive.

THE FRENCH 75-MM FIELD GUN

DEVELOPED IN THE 1890s, the French "75"mm marked a revolutionary change in the design of field artillery. Its hydraulic recoil mechanism enabled very rapid, accurate fire without the need to re-lay the gun after each shot. The *"soixante-quinze"* had a crew of nine and a six-horse team to pull the gun, along with its ammunition limber. The gun enjoyed great success at the Marne, both in support of attacking infantry and halting German advances with volleys of shrapnel. However, it lacked the power or high trajectory to be effective against well-made trench systems.

The gun normally fired 6 rounds per minute, but when the need arose, crews could manage up to 20 rounds per minute

Bullet-proof shield

Recoil mechanism

Impact fuse

Time fuse

Shoe brake

HIGH EXPLOSIVE SHELL

SHRAPNEL SHELL

THE BATTLE OF THE MARNE

The German First Army, after discounting the possibility of a major French counterattack from the direction of Paris, continued to pursue the BEF and reached the Marne on September 3. On the same day the French abandoned Reims. Joffre, meanwhile, provided himself with a scapegoat for past defeats by dismissing Lanrezac as commander of the Fifth Army and replacing him with Franchet d'Esperey. It was also at about this time that the German high command realized that the First Army was caught between two objectives: it could press forward to complete the encirclement of the French armies east of Paris, but it also had to guard against a counterattack by the Army of Paris.

Throughout September 4 Gallieni sought to secure Joffre's agreement to his proposed attack, to which the BEF and the French Fifth Army had to contribute. It was not until late on this day that Joffre authorized the halting the Anglo-French retreat and ordered general offensive operations for September 6, as Gallieni had requested.

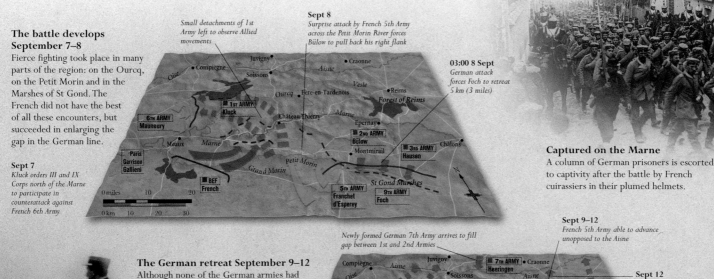

The battle develops September 7–8

Fierce fighting took place in many parts of the region: on the Ourcq, on the Petit Morin and in the Marshes of St Gond. The French did not have the best of all these encounters, but succeeded in enlarging the gap in the German line.

Sept 7
Kluck orders III and IX Corps north of the Marne to participate in counterattack against French 6th Army

Small detachments of 1st Army left to observe Allied movements

Sept 8
Surprise attack by French 5th Army across the Petit Morin River forces Bülow to pull back his right flank

03:00 8 Sept
German attack forces Foch to retreat 5 km (3 miles)

Captured on the Marne
A column of German prisoners is escorted to captivity after the battle by French cuirassiers in their plumed helmets.

The German retreat September 9–12

Although none of the German armies had suffered a serious defeat, the position of the First and Second Armies had allowed the BEF and the French 5th Army to march into the gap between them. Since the German First Army stood in danger of being completely cut off from the other armies, the order was given to retreat to the Aisne.

Sept 9
BEF crosses Marne, dividing German First and Second Armies

Newly formed German 7th Army arrives to fill gap between 1st and 2nd Armies

Sept 9–12
French 5th Army able to advance unopposed to the Aisne

Sept 12
German armies cross the Aisne pursued by British and French

Sept 9
Bülow orders Second Army to retreat

On September 5 the German First Army advanced on the Grand Morin River with four corps spread over 50 km (30 miles) and closed to within 8 km (5 miles) of the BEF and the French Fifth Army. The other German armies to the east, however, were encountering unanticipated resistance and the German First Army was made aware, by a liaison officer, Colonel Richard Hentsch, that the high command wanted it to retire north of the Marne. As it was, on September 5 and 6 the attack by Maunoury's Sixth Army against the right flank of the German First Army just to the east of Paris forced Kluck to change his plans. The German forces facing Maunoury amounted to one Reserve Corps commanded by General von Gronau. This put up considerable resistance, even launching a counterattack against the leading French formations before withdrawing to positions to the west of the Ourcq River. Gallieni had to rush reinforcements from the city to support Maunoury's army. All available forms of transport were pressed into service, including 600 Renault taxis. These made two trips each, carrying five men at a time, thus transporting 6,000 soldiers to the front. Their contribution to the battle brought them lasting fame as "the taxis of the Marne".

This new development forced Kluck to turn his army westwards. On September 7–8 he redeployed forces from its centre and left flank to support Gronau on the threatened right flank. In doing so, the First Army became separated from the Second Army to the east. It was into the gap thus presented that the BEF and the French Fifth Army

advanced on the morning of September 9, and it was among the congested columns in the rear of the First Army that the German decision to conduct a general withdrawal was taken that same day. With communications between the German First and Second Armies, and between the high command and these two formations, all but collapsed, the decision was taken by Hentsch. He ordered the First Army to withdraw to the Soissons area (see map page 55). With the information that a new army was being raised at St Quentin, he drew the approximate line to be reached during this withdrawal phase on a map provided by the First Army's chief of staff. By the 12th the German First Army had retired behind the Aisne, and only the Allies' lack of fresh troops with which to exploit German disarray had prevented the withdrawal from degenerating into a rout.

A NEW PHASE OF THE WAR

To the west was an open flank, stretching from Compiègne to the sea and from the Somme to Antwerp. This was an area in which both sides had formations but neither had the upper hand. In the aftermath of the German retreat from the Marne,

> *I spend my day and night in a trench. I have got a hole, partly burrowed out and partly roofed over with branches, just big enough to lie down, it is rather monotonous. I get out for meals but I have to be with my guns day and night as we are in the most forward trench waiting for the attack that never comes, as a matter of fact I think our position is too strong for the Germans' liking, they shell us constantly but we laugh at them from our burrows like rabbits. I couldn't tell you why we are fixed like this but we shall be very glad when we move forward again as this cave life is not to our liking.*

CAPTAIN ARTHUR MAITLAND, 2ND BATTALION ESSEX REGIMENT, IN A LETTER TO HIS PARENTS FROM THE AISNE, SEPTEMBER 30, 1914

and with manoeuvre impossible in the static conditions east of Reims, the attention of both sides focussed on the Aisne and the open flank.

THE BATTLE OF THE AISNE

Events on the Aisne and to the north unfolded more or less simultaneously, though it was to be the operations on the Aisne that were to become the better known. Here, on the high ground north of the river, the German retreat was halted and fresh troops moved up to close the 30-km (18-mile) gap between the First and Second Armies. At this point Moltke was dismissed as German chief of staff and replaced by the Prussian war minister, Erich von Falkenhayn. The positions the Germans established on the Aisne were easily defended, being sited on a ridge along the north side of the river. This sector of the Western Front came to be known as the Chemin des Dames after the road that had been built along the ridge in the 18th century for the daughters of Louis XV to go for drives in their carriages.

British and French forces, arriving on the Aisne one day behind the First Army, attacked across the river immediately but against an enemy that had established a rudimentary trench system and held major advantages bestowed by choice of ground. The main Allied efforts were made on September 13–14, but to little purpose, and late on the 14th the French and British began to entrench.

French troops awaiting an attack
This staged French photograph of 1914 shows troops entrenched in a commanding position with an aeroplane overhead ready to spot any movement by the enemy. The reality of trench warfare was not quite so neat and tidy.

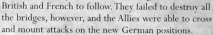

Blowing up a bridge over the Aisne
As the Germans retreated over the Aisne, they blew up bridges after they had crossed, making it difficult for the British and French to follow. They failed to destroy all the bridges, however, and the Allies were able to cross and mount attacks on the new German positions.

JOHN FRENCH

FRENCH HAD BEEN a successful cavalry commander during the South African War of 1899–1902. This led to his being chosen to command the BEF in August 1914. He was, however, to prove inadequate to the task.

French suffered a complete loss of confidence when forced to retreat after his first engagement in August at Mons, and Kitchener, the British Secretary of War, had to make a personal visit in September in order to strengthen his resolve. He was persuaded that the British forces should join the French counter-offensive on the Marne, where victory temporarily boosted his confidence. However, his uncertainty as a leader returned in 1915, manifesting itself in errors of judgement during the Artois-Loos offensive in September and October. His difficulties were compounded by his poor relationship with the French commanders and with his own field officers, and in December 1915 he was replaced by Douglas Haig.

For the remainder of the war, French served as commander of the British home forces, in which role he had responsibility for dealing with the 1916 Easter Rising in Ireland. He was later made Lord Lieutenant of Ireland.

British troops in Flanders
A column of British soldiers advances in single file across a field in Belgium in October 1914. At this stage of the war units were still operating in areas where neither side was aware of the enemy's strength.

THE RACE TO THE SEA

On September 14 the German high command instructed its forces on the Aisne to pin down the Allied troops, while an attempt was made to outflank them by moving troops to the west. Some three days later Joffre issued similar orders to the French. As a result the Battle of the Aisne continued until September 27, when it was allowed to die.

In the meantime, both the French and Germans made unsuccessful attempts to outflank the other, first in the region around Noyon on the 18th and then on the upper Somme on the 23rd/24th. As the battle moved northwards through the fields of Picardy and Artois towards the Belgian border, both sides continued to try to outflank the enemy, but neither could secure sufficient advantage of position and numbers. In the first days of October the French retained Arras and La Bassée in the face of determined German attacks, but were obliged to cede Lille and Lens before the two sides fought each other to a standstill in this sector (see map page 62).

This sequence of manoeuvres came to be known, rather confusingly, as the "Race to the Sea". Neither side was actually trying to reach the sea before the other, it was just that each failed attempt

The retreat from Antwerp
Cars line up in one of Antwerp's main squares in readiness for the evacuation in the final days of the siege. The decision to evacuate most of the Belgian field army was taken on October 6. Its commander, King Albert, left Antwerp around noon on the 7th.

to sidestep the enemy's forces happened to extend the entrenched front line further to the north and closer to the English Channel.

THE FALL OF ANTWERP

The end of the Battle of the Aisne coincided with the start of German siege operations at Antwerp. After the Germans' triumphal progress through central Belgium in the third week of August, some 70,000 Belgian troops took refuge in Antwerp, the "national redoubt". From there they mounted two sorties and sent saboteurs into German-occupied territories. The second sortie on September 9–13 penetrated as far as Louvain. For more than a month the German forces around Antwerp could do no more than mask the city and contain the garrison's sorties, but at the end of September the situation changed. Beginning on the 28th, with 160

ARMOURED CARS

~

IN THE MOBILE WARFARE that marked operations in Belgium and northern France in the last stages of the "Race to the Sea", primitive armoured cars could be seen driving along the flat roads of Flanders. The first to use them were the Belgians. The RNAS (Royal Naval Air Service) had a squadron of planes based at Dunkerque that flew reconnaissance sorties over the area. They also had a number of cars, used both for reconnaissance and for going to the rescue of pilots who had been shot down. As such journeys became more hazardous, the cars were provided with improvised armour of boiler plate. Finally it was decided to order customized cars from Rolls-Royce, fully enclosed in armour with a revolving turret. Unfortunately, by the time they arrived in December, the brief period of mobile war was already at an end.

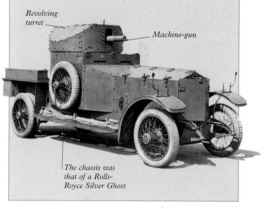

Revolving turret
Machine-gun
The chassis was that of a Rolls-Royce Silver Ghost

heavy and super-heavy siege guns in the line, the Germans set about the systematic destruction of the city's outlying fortifications.

TOO LITTLE, TOO LATE

Though a small British force of Royal Marines arrived overland in Antwerp on October 4, the morale of a garrison that believed itself to be otherwise abandoned was low. The Belgians' doubts about the strength of Antwerp's fortifications proved well-founded. They were no match for the Germans' super-heavy siege artillery: the formidable Krupp 420-mm "Big Berthas" that had done so much damage at Liège, backed up by highly effective Austrian 305-mm Skoda howitzers. While

Belgian carbineers
The carbineers with their distinctive top hats played a major role in the defence of Antwerp. The Belgians used small carts drawn by dogs to carry machine-guns, ammunition and even wounded men.

the big guns pounded the forts, the field artillery bombarded the trenches that ran between the forts with a mixture of high-explosive and shrapnel shells.

On October 6, when the Belgian defensive line behind the Nete River was forced, the decision was taken to abandon the city. King Albert and the Belgian government left the following day for Ostend. With German forces south of Antwerp trying to cut off the Allied line of retreat, some of the garrison were captured or crossed the border into the Netherlands, where they were interned. The city was finally occupied on October 10.

To the west of Antwerp, Belgian and French forces rejected the possibility of standing on the Terneuzen Canal, which linked Ghent to the sea. Instead they began to concentrate in front of Bruges. The British 7th Division was landed at Zeebrugge on October 6 and advanced as far as Ghent. It then retreated to join the other Allied forces around Ypres.

German forces in Belgium
Infantrymen enjoy the luxury of motorized transport during the fighting in Belgium in 1914. Most of them are wearing *Pickelhauben* (spiked helmets), but with cloth camouflage covers to stop them from glinting in the sun.

THE LAST DAYS OF MOBILE WAR

Meanwhile German cavalry was operating in the No Man's Land between Ypres and Lille and German and Allied forces were working their way northwards from the Somme in their indecisive attempts to outflank each other. They clashed around Arras and Lens on the October 7 and around Hazebrouck and Armentières on the 8th. This meant that there was virtually no room left in which to manoeuvre.

To the north, the Belgian army decided to stand on the Yser. The river was canalized along its last stretch flowing from Dixmude to the sea, and its high embankments commanded the low-lying land to the east, making it a good position to defend. The Belgians would have to face the re-formed German Fourth Army, reinforced by troops freed after the fall of Antwerp. This army, under the command of Duke Albrecht of Württemberg, prepared for a possibly decisive offensive along the coast and from Ypres against the ports of Boulogne and Calais.

THE BRITISH ARMY OF 1914

THE BRITISH ARMY of 1914 contained no conscripts – it was a small professional army of 250,000 men. With a history of reliance on the all-powerful navy for the security of the British Isles, there had been no need to maintain a vast standing army like that of Germany, France or Russia. In 1914 Britain sent an expeditionary force of six infantry divisions and one cavalry division, some 150,000 men, to the aid of France. In August four divisions moved up onto the French left flank to face the German armies advancing into France from Belgium. In October, when the British were engaged in fierce fighting at Ypres, they were joined by an Indian corps and some Territorial units. By the end of the year, the BEF had been reduced to half its original strength, with over 30,000 killed and more than 50,000 wounded. A new army was needed; it would be raised from the men who responded to the call for volunteers made in August 1914 by Lord Kitchener, the minister for war.

British Hussars advancing in open country
In 1914 cavalry was used mainly to screen the flanks of infantry formations and for reconnaissance. Here the Eleventh Hussars move north to Flanders in the final stage of the "Race to the Sea".

LEE ENFIELD .303
RIFLE AND
AMUNITION

WEBLEY
REVOVLER

Knapsack

WATER
BOTTLE

Bayonet

CLASP
KNIFE

WIRE
CUTTERS

ENTRENCHING
TOOL

British uniform and equipment
The British went to war in the khaki they had worn since the South African War (1899–1902). A major innovation in 1916 was the introduction of steel helmets.

Scottish troops marching to the front
In 1914 many Scottish regiments fought in their kilts and glengarry caps. The Germans were astonished at the sight and the German press carried some highly fanciful artistic impressions of the Scots in battle.

THE FINAL PHASE OF THE RACE TO THE SEA

The final phase of the "Race to the Sea" is usually reckoned to be synonymous with the First Battle of Ypres. In reality the last Allied and German offensives in Belgium and France before the front stabilized resulted in four battles fought on a 56-km (35-mile) sector from La Bassée to the sea between October 16 and November 11. At the outset there were many gaps in both fronts, but neither side was able to exploit them. The combination of a lack of room in which to manoeuvre, the speed with which reinforcements were moved into this sector, and the fact that neither side possessed any advantage of position and timing that enabled it to dictate events, ensured that these battles ended indecisively.

In part, the course of these final-phase operations was shaped by the occupation of Lille on October 12, which gave the Germans the key industrial centre of northern France even before their main effort opened on the Yser on the 16th. It was in an attempt to retake Lille that the British launched two offensives, also on the 16th. These resulted in battles around La Bassée and Armentières, in which some British formations found themselves opposed by the same German formations they had faced on the Aisne. With no advantage of numbers, artillery or timing on which to base their offensives, the British were held and, in some areas, ultimately thrown back beyond their original start lines.

THE FIRST BATTLE OF YPRES

Even before these British efforts faltered, however, the focus of attention had switched to the north. On October 16 French cavalry and the British V Corps began to move forward from Ypres, only to be confronted on the 18th by three corps of the German Fourth Army. On the same day French armies in the north were ordered to hold rather than attempt to advance. Meanwhile to the south of Ypres the German Sixth Army advanced to recapture recent losses around Armentières. By the 26th the Allied defences around Ypres had been reduced to a salient at no point more than 8 km (5 miles) from the city. French forces had, however, arrived to take over the northern part of the British line.

In the last days of October the crisis of the battle to the north along the Yser was reached. In order to

Indian troops
The Indian Corps landed at Marseille in September 1914 and saw action at Ypres in October and November. Here men of the 129th Baluchis have improvised a defensive position on the outskirts of the town of Wytschaete, to the south of Ypres.

This is a terrible war and I don't suspect there is an idle British soldier in France. I wonder where it will end; one hears so much. There has been more fighting and loss of life crowded into seven weeks than there was in the whole of South Africa. It is awful what the Brigade of Guards have lost and being like one big regiment one knows everyone and feels it all the more.

LIEUTENANT NEVILLE WOODROFFE, 1ST BATTALION IRISH GUARDS, IN A LETTER TO HIS MOTHER. WOODROFFE WAS KILLED IN ACTION AT YPRES ON 16 NOVEMBER

halt a much superior enemy that had fought its way across the Yser and was threatening to breach the Nieuport-Dixmude embankment, the Belgians, having ruled out a further withdrawal, decided on the drastic measure of flooding a large area of low-lying land. They did this by opening the sluice-gates to the sea at high tide. The operation had to be perfectly timed and the first attempts failed. Eventually a large area east of the Yser between Nieuport and Dixmude was successfully flooded, bringing large-scale operations in this area to a halt after October 30.

After more than a week of heavy but inconclusive fighting along the Ypres salient, on October 30 the Germans began a major attempt to secure the city, their main effort being made by a reinforced Sixth Army between Messines and the Menin Road. The kaiser had optimistically established himself with his field headquarters in Flanders in the expectation of a triumphal entry into Ypres along the Menin Road on October 31.

In the first two days of the offensive, the Germans made – by the standard of later battles for the salient – substantial gains. The British defence was almost reduced to breaking point. On the 31st the village of Gheluvelt on the Menin Road was defended by the remnants of five British battalions, reduced to about 1,000 men, the strength of a single battalion. This tiny force managed to hold off an attack by 13 German battalions for over an hour. Gheluvelt eventually fell, but in the heavily wooded country on either side of the Menin Road the German attacks lost their cohesion. The superior fieldcraft and marksmanship of the British defenders gave them a telling advantage over the young, inexperienced German formations.

LAST ATTEMPT AT A BREAKTHROUGH

With French forces stabilizing the line, German attacks around the salient continued for a week as the German high command hesitated between making a final effort at Ypres and switching forces to the East to support the Lodz offensive. A renewed effort, along the entire front between Dixmude and Messines, was ordered for November 10. What

Refugees fleeing Ypres
Scenes like this were common all over western Belgium, as families – their children and a few possessions loaded into carts – fled from the advancing German armies.

remained of Dixmude was taken, but no gains of any significance were registered elsewhere. On the 11th the Prussian Guard, despite breaking the British line, was cut to pieces in an action that effectively marked the end of the battle. After that the Germans undertook only local offensives in order to improve their tactical position in readiness for the coming winter. The battle is reckoned to have finally ended on the 22nd, two days after the BEF was relieved by the French.

THE STABILIZED FRONT

The battles of the final phase of "The Race to the Sea" are significant for three

The formation of the Western Front
From September to November 1914 the fighting in France moved steadily northwards. Once the Germans had dug in along the Aisne in mid-September, the action switched to the open flank to the northwest. A series of attempts by both sides to turn the enemy's flank brought the action north to Belgium, where the Allied line joined up with that of the Belgian army retreating from Antwerp.

reasons. First, they were the last battles of the opening phase of the war and represented the failure of both sides to turn the other's flank and maintain the momentum of mobile warfare. Second, political considerations now determined that the Allies, having held on to their positions, including a small part of Belgium, at very heavy cost, could not voluntarily withdraw from any part

> "… of the 1,100 officers and men that came out at the start we have Major Yeadon and about 80 men left. I believe you have plenty of soldiers at home. Well, we could do with a few here."
>
> CORPORAL GEORGE MATHESON, B COMPANY, 1ST BATTALION, THE QUEEN'S OWN CAMERON HIGHLANDERS, WRITING AFTER THE FIRST BATTLE OF YPRES

Map labels:

NETHERLANDS

BRITAIN

BELGIUM

GERMANY

LUX.

FRANCE

THE RACE TO THE SEA
Sept–Nov 1914

- Major German attack (with date)
- Major French attack (with date)
- Major battle (with date)
- Allied front line November 1914
- French sector
- British sector
- Belgian sector
- German front line November 1914
- Fortified town/city
- The Allies (and allied states)
- Central Powers (and allied states)
- Neutral states

Oct 21–29
Belgians open sluices along Yser Canal to let in seawater at high tides. Resulting flooding thwarts German attempts to cross the Yser

Oct 6–13
Belgian Army retreats from Antwerp via Ghent to line along the Yser

OCT 16–30
Yser

OCT 19–NOV 22
First Ypres

Oct 19–Nov 11

Oct 19–Nov11
Fiercest fighting of the "Race to the Sea". British and French hold on to salient around Ypres, which remains in Allied hands throughout the war

OCT 10–NOV 2
La Bassée

Sept 30

Sept 27–Oct 12
French 10th Army holds off attempted German breakthrough

SEPT 27–OCT 12
First Artois

Oct 1

Oct 4–8

Sept 27–28

Oct 5

Sept 22–26
French 2nd Army attempts to outflank German right wing

Sept 24

SEPT 22–26
First Picardy

Sept 22

Sept 18

Sept 17–18

SEPT 12–28
Aisne

Antwerp

Ostend
Nieuport
Oct 16–30
Dixmude
Ghent
BRUSSELS
Armentières
Lille
Charleroi
Maubeugie
Cambrai
Lens
Arras
Albert
Péronne
Royes
Noyon
Compiègne
Soissons
Reims
Verdun
Château Thierry
Chantilly
Abbeville
Hazebrouck
St Omer
PARIS
Nancy

Sambre
Oise
Aisne
Marne
Ource
Seine
Somme
Lys
Yser

0 km 20   40   60   80
0 miles 20   40   60   80

The Cloth Hall at Ypres 1914
The Cloth Hall, begun around 1200, was a proud symbol of the textile trade that flourished in medieval Flanders. Here it smoulders after being set on fire during a bombardment in the First Battle of Ypres. This was nothing to the shelling it would suffer in later battles: by the end of the war it had been reduced to rubble. Its reconstruction was finally completed in 1962.

of the front. This was despite the limited value of what they held and the fact that the Germans occupied superior positions along virtually the whole of this sector. Third, the final phase of operations witnessed an appalling blood-letting. The German initiative throughout most of this phase was the result of having to hand formations hastily raised from the class of 1914, many of them recruits with just two months' training. The loss of so many of them at Ypres led to the battle being known as the "Massacre of the Innocents".

THE COST OF FIRST YPRES

British, French and German casualties at the First Battle of Ypres totalled 250,000. British losses, which left the battalions sent to France in August with an average of one officer and 30 men of their original establishments (about 1,000 men), prompted the comment that "The high command and staff officers survived: the old army was beyond recall." So, too, were both sides' hopes of a short war and early victory. The kaiser reluctantly accepted that there was to be no breakthrough along the Belgian coast and a tiny corner of Belgium remained in Allied hands. The salient around Ypres would see many more battles, but would never fall to the Germans.

THE KINDERMORD
~

AT THE OUTBREAK OF WAR, over 35,000 German university and technical college students volunteered enthusiastically for the army. They received just eight weeks training – much of it from elderly officers of the reserve whose military ideas were rooted in the Franco-Prussian War of 1870–71 and who had little idea of the killing power of modern artillery and machine-guns. Instead of being divided up and sent to different units, almost all these volunteers went to make up the numbers in the hastily re-formed German Fourth Army. On October 20 Falkenhayn sent this army to the support the Sixth Army in a desperate attempt to break through in Flanders. The losses sustained as the students and other young men were launched against the Allied lines were more horrific than any experienced by the Germans to date. One of the worst episodes was at Langemarck to the northeast of Ypres on November 10. The slaughter came to be known as the *Kindermord* (the Massacre of the Innocents) and the verdict of those who witnessed it and survived was: "The men were too young and the officers too old."

Youthful enthusiasm
Students in Berlin cheer the declaration of war at the beginning of August. By November many of these young men, and thousands like them from all over Germany, lay dead on the battlefield of Ypres.

POLAND, GALICIA AND SERBIA
OCTOBER – DECEMBER 1914

~

In the closing months of 1914, war on the Eastern Front was exceptionally mobile. The Germans launched an offensive on Warsaw, but withdrew, allowing the Russians to advance towards Silesia. The Germans then struck again from the north, but were halted at Lodz. The Austro-Hungarians fell back almost to Cracow, but defeated the Russians in December, when they also made a third unsuccessful attempt to invade Serbia.

~

OCTOBER 1
Russian victory at Augustowo on East Prussian frontier

OCTOBER 4
Start of first German-Austrian offensive in Poland

OCTOBER 9
Germans reach the Vistula, lay siege to fortified town of Ivangorod

OCTOBER 9
Austrians relieve Przemysl

OCTOBER 15
Battle for Warsaw joined along entire length of Vistula front

OCTOBER 17
Russian reinforcements reach Warsaw front and save city from capture; Hindenburg orders withdrawal; Germans destroy rail lines and roads as they retreat

OCTOBER 23
Germans abandon attack on Ivangorod

NOVEMBER 1
Germans back at start line of advance

NOVEMBER 1
Start of third Austro-Hungarian invasion of Serbia

NOVEMBER 3
Mackensen's 9th Army switched by rail to new positions between Posen and Thorn

NOVEMBER 4
Austrians defeated at Jaroslau in Galicia; they withdraw almost to Cracow

NOVEMBER 11
Start of second German-Austrian advance into Poland, driving wedge between Russian 1st and 2nd Armies

NOVEMBER 10
Russians again besiege Przemysl

NOVEMBER 14
Russian armies set to advance to Silesia

NOVEMBER 16
Russians call off advance into Silesia; 5th Army sent north to help 2nd Army

NOVEMBER 18
Start of Battle of Lodz. Fierce fighting all round the city halts German advance

NOVEMBER 19
Russian 5th Army arrives to force back Mackensen's right, which is threatening to encircle Russian 2nd Army

NOVEMBER 24
German XXV Reserve Corps fights way out of perilous situation to the east of Lodz with 16,000 prisoners

DECEMBER 2
Austrians take Belgrade

DECEMBER 5
Start of Battle of Limanova; Austrian victory halts Russian advance on Cracow

DECEMBER 6
Russians withdraw from Lodz

DECEMBER 6
Serbs defeat Austrians at Kolubra River

DECEMBER 8
Austrians suffer heavy defeat south of Belgrade

DECEMBER 9
Battle for Warsaw; heavy fighting between Germans and Russians

DECEMBER 12
Start of Austrian counter-offensive from Hungary; recapture of key Carpathian passes

DECEMBER 15
Serbs reenter Belgrade; end of third Austrian invasion of Serbia as Austrians withdraw across border

DECEMBER 17
End of Battle of Limanova

KEY
- Campaigns in Poland
- Campaigns in Galicia
- Third Austro-Hungarian invasion of Serbia Nov 1–Dec 15

New Offensives in the East

Austro-Hungarian troops behind the line
An Austro-Hungarian infantry regiment enjoys a moment of respite from the war on the Galician front. In the autumn of 1914 the Russians came perilously close to crushing the Austro-Hungarian armies in this sector.

Because of the difficulties of the Austro-Hungarian armies in Galicia during early September, the Germans decided on an offensive against Warsaw. This opened on September 29. Ironically, with the defeated Austro-Hungarian armies reaching the safety of the Tarnow-Gorlice position in the first days of October, the immediate crisis facing the Central Powers had passed. Indeed, with the Austro-Hungarian high command having realized that the Russian forces that had advanced across Galicia were mostly unsupported cavalry, its forces went over to the offensive on October 4.

FIRST ADVANCE ON WARSAW

Przemysl, besieged by the Russians on September 24, was relieved by the Austro-Hungarian First Army on October 9, by which time elements of the Ninth German Army had reached the Vistula.

By October 12 they had almost reached Ivangorod and were about 20 km (12 miles) from Warsaw. Within another five days, however, the Central Powers' intentions had unravelled, the chief reason being that the Russian high command had correctly anticipated the German move. As the German Ninth Army came to the Vistula, two armies were committed to trying to hold German forces in the area above Warsaw, while elements from no fewer than four armies crossed the river below Warsaw in an attempt to strike at the Ninth Army's open left flank. As this threat materialized, the Germans had to abandon their offensive and began to withdraw.

To the south the Austrian First Army was obliged to abandon most of its gains and to leave the garrison of Przemysl to withstand a second siege. By November 1 the German Ninth Army was back on its original start line, having conducted a thorough destruction of communications in order to forestall a general Russian advance. The Germans then swiftly redeployed their forces by train, transporting the Ninth Army to the Posen-Thorn area in order to renew its attempt to clear the west bank of the Vistula. Failure had not invalidated the original German intention, merely ensured a renewed attempt in the near future.

RUSSIA POISED TO ADVANCE

The German offensive of September–October 1914 was successful in the sense that it provided immediate relief to the hard-pressed Austro-Hungarian armies in Galicia. But this relief was short-lived and the failure of the German offensive worsened the strategic position of the Central Powers by bringing no fewer than four Russian armies into western Poland. This, in its turn, presented the Russian high command with a dilemma. For the first time Russian armies were gathered in a position and strength that would allow them to move against Silesia. However, the immediate problem faced by the *Stavka*, the Russian high command, was whether to move against the German sector of the front or the positions held by the inferior Austro-Hungarian armies.

The Russian Southwest Front command insisted that the main effort be made in western Galicia, against the weaker enemy, but in the event the *Stavka* sought to compromise by authorizing offensives against both enemies. By dividing its available forces, however, the *Stavka* in effect condemned both offensives to failure. Even more seriously, the Germans, having broken the Russian signals ciphers, by late October were aware of Russian intentions and order of battle. The slowness of the Russian advance across a devastated western Poland provided the Germans with the chance to frustrate Russian plans. As a result of the superior strategic mobility provided by their railways, they were able to move the Ninth Army north into the Posen-Thorn sector in readiness for an offensive against the rear of the Russian armies to the south. At the same time, the Austro-Hungarian armies, reassured by the promise of German reinforcements, began to thin their forces in Galicia in order to support the German Ninth Army's right flank. Thus evolved the Central Powers' plan to clear western Poland and crush Russian forces against the upper Vistula.

The siege of Przemysl
A slow-moving column of ox- and mule-wagons brings supplies to the Russians besieging Przemysl in Galicia. The town was under siege from September 24 to October 9, then again from November 10 to March 22, 1915.

Russian infantry receiving a fresh issue of ammunition

A short while ago when we marched through Galicia and constantly expected to meet the enemy, every soldier was supposed to have not just the regular amount of 120 cartridges, but much more. Sometimes, every one of us had up to 300 cartridges. They weigh almost one pud (16 kg/35 lb). On those long marches, these heavy loads bothered the men. To remedy the situation they threw the cartridges into the ditches where no one picked them up.

J. OSKINE IN *LE CARNET D'UN SOLDAT*

Russian troops advancing through barbed wire
Trenches and defensive systems did not present enormous obstacles on the Eastern Front at this stage of the war as the front line shifted almost on a daily basis.

Russian Maxim gun
The Russian machine-gun was similar to the German Maxim, but heavier and more difficult to transport. Here a Maxim is mounted on a motorcycle sidecar for use against aircraft.

Hungarian forces, with their left flank held and right flank crumbling as Russian pressure mounted, faced exactly the same danger as they had nearly three months previously at Lemberg. By November 25, the Russian Fifth Army, having played its part in stopping the German offensive at Lodz, turned south to face the Austrian Second Army, which was forced to withdraw. The situation now facing the Austro-Hungarian forces had become desperate. However, the decision was taken to withdraw most forces to the Cracow area and to move the Fourth Army south of the Vistula in order to take the Russian Third Army in the flank as it approached the ancient Polish capital. Despite the morale-sapping defeats that Habsburg armies had sustained over the

THE BATTLE OF LODZ

The German offensive opened on November 11 from positions between the Warta and Vistula and immediately broke through a poorly deployed and even more poorly commanded Russian First Army. Within five days, the Germans, with a potentially decisive superiority of numbers, had fought and won a battle at Kutno, split the Second and First Armies and were closing on Lodz.

On November 16, however, the *Stavka* halted the Russian offensive in western Poland and ordered the Fifth Army north to support the Second Army in the defence of Lodz. As a result, on November 18–19 the Germans pressed forward in the belief that all the Russian armies were in retreat and that Lodz would fall. In the event, the Russian Second Army managed to hold the German right flank. The Fifth Army, after a march of some 110 km (70 miles) on appalling roads in just two days, losing half its men in the process, moved to counter the German XXV Corps as it tried to encircle Lodz.

A CONFUSED OUTCOME

Had the Russian First Army moved in support, the German left flank would have been overwhelmed, but a combination of courage and luck, and ineptitude on the part of the Russian First Army's commander, allowed XXV Corps to extricate itself. The Germans fought their way out of a seemingly hopeless position, bringing with them 16,000

prisoners and 64 captured guns. After facing the prospect of disastrous defeat, the Russians had briefly enjoyed the expectation of victory, but in the end the battle could not be counted a victory for either side. In the aftermath, the *Stavka* decided to concentrate on operations against Austria-Hungary in Galicia and the Carpathians.

THE BATTLE OF LIMANOWA

To the south, the battle developed along lines that neither side had anticipated. The Austro-Hungarian high command had assumed that German success would weaken Russian forces in the north and that the Galician front would remain quiet. Both these assumptions proved incorrect. Though the Habsburg Second Army's offensive opened on November 16 and met with early local success, the Russians proved stronger than expected and their Fourth Army yielded little ground. On the right flank, the consequences of having stripped the front had to be paid as the unsupported Russian Third Army, advancing across the San, moved into the Tarnow area by November 20. With the Germans held before Lodz, and unable to provide the support that had been promised, the Austro-

German supply column
The campaigns of late 1914 saw German and Russian troops covering enormous distances as they crossed and recrossed Poland. Road and rail links rapidly deteriorated, causing problems of supply for both sides.

LODZ AND LIMANOWA
NOVEMBER – DECEMBER 1914

It was in the heavy fighting at the end of 1914 that the Eastern Front became fixed. By the end of the year an almost continuous front stretched from East Prussia to the Carpathians in the south. The key battles in this process were Lodz, where the Russians halted a determined German attempt to break through towards Warsaw, and Limanowa, where the Austro-Hungarians drove back the Russians who were threatening to take Cracow.

KEY

⬅ Russian advance	⌒ Russian position
◫ Russian retreat	⌒ German position
➡ German advance	⌒ Austro-Hungarian position
◫ German withdrawal	⊠ Fortified city/town
➡ Austro-Hungarian advance	⚜ Major battle
◫ Austro-Hungarian retreat	▦ Major railway

Russian prisoners captured in Poland
This group of prisoners being escorted by German reserves during the Polish campaigns of late 1914 reflects the wide range of peoples serving in Russia's armies.

previous three months, the Fourth Army, supported by the German 47th Reserve Division, moved onto the offensive in the last days of November. In fierce battles around around the towns of Lapanow and Limanowa, the Russian Third Army was beaten and forced to retreat to the east, and the threat to Cracow was eliminated. Perhaps even more significantly, the activities of the Russian Eighth Army were halted. This army had advanced to the Carpathians, where it had secured various passes and was preparing for what would have been a barely opposed advance into the plains of Hungary. Its operations were halted in order to concentrate

The German attack on Lodz November 1914
In the north, the German Ninth Army executed a bold manoeuvre, redeploying by train in order to launch an attack between the Russian First and Second Armies. To the south the Russian armies advanced slowly on a wide front, their objectives an invasion of Silesia, an offensive against Cracow and to take the passes through the Carpathians.

November
Advancing Russian 8th Army wins control of the approaches to Carpathian passes

November
Austrian 2nd Army transferred from Carpathians to strengthen German line

Nov 4–10
German 9th Army withdraws by rail to Posen, where it prepares to attack the Russian 1st and 2nd Armies

Nov 11
Renewed offensive by German 9th Army is successful, driving a gap between Russian 1st and 2nd Armies

Nov 15
Russian II Corps defeated at Kutno and retreats to the east

Nov 1
Front line at start of Russian offensive

November
Russian 3rd Army advances towards Cracow, reaching Tarnow by Nov 20

Nov 16
Advance towards Silesia called off by Russian high command

Nov 19
Russian 5th Army, having moved swiftly northwards, halts the German advance

Nov 23
After a bitter battle east of Lodz German troops escape northwestwards

Dec 5–17
Despite determined Russian resistance, Austrians win battle around Limanowa

Dec 3
Austrian forces advance towards the towns of Lapanow and Limanova

Dec 6
Russians make voluntary withdrawal from Lodz

Austro-Hungarian recovery December 1914
At the start of December the Russians were confident of taking Cracow and advancing into the Carpathians, but attacks by the Austrian 4th Army on the flank of the Russian 3rd Army south of Cracow proved the turning point in the campaign.

Dec 8–15
Boroevic's 3rd Army seizes the opportunity to attack Russia's exposed southern flanks

Dec 12
The Russian 8th Army ordered to withdraw. Russian invasion of Hungary has been prevented

December
Russians continue to besiege Przemysl. The city eventually surrenders on March 22, 1915

Dec 1
Front line at beginning of December

Dec 31
Russian front line at end of the year

Franz Conrad von Hötzendorf
~

Austro-Hungarian chief of staff from 1906, Conrad von Hötzendorf (1852–1925) had been a close associate of the assassinated Archduke Franz Ferdinand. At the outbreak of war, he attempted to handle his twin objectives – the defence of Galicia and the invasion of Serbia – by first concentrating on the Balkans. When the Russians mobilized more quickly than expected, he was forced into a chaotic transfer of troops from Serbia. The Gorlice-Tarnow Offensive of May 1915 succeeded in regaining territory previously lost to Russia, but an offensive in August that year led to massive Austro-Hungarian casualties. By this time, Germany had little or no respect for Conrad's leadership and took control of the successful Serbian campaign. In contrast, Conrad's Trentino Offensive against Italy in 1916 did not receive German support and ended in failure. By September 1916, Austria-Hungary had been forced to accept German command on all fronts. In March 1917 Conrad was demoted to field command of the Trentino front and remained in that position until his dismissal, following a further unsuccessful offensive, in July 1918.

Russian forces on the upper Vistula. The opportunity that the Russians lost here in November 1914 never presented itself again.

Russian Weaknesses
Thus ended a month in which the Russian and Austro-Hungarian armies had demonstrated remarkable resilience, but from which they, and particularly the Russians, nevertheless emerged as losers. While success on the Eastern Front had eluded the armies of all three empires, the Russian failure was the most acute. Having failed to secure any telling victory when at the peak of their powers in the first weeks of the war, the Russians had subsequently gained no decisive success either in western Galicia or in the Carpathians, and their threat to Silesia had been eliminated. Moreover, their position west of the Vistula was now difficult to defend. This the Russians acknowledged on

Dugout in Galicia
Russian soldiers prepare for a long winter. Campaigning in the Galician sector of the Eastern Front did not stop during the winter of 1914–15. The Russians continued to launch attacks on the passes through the Carpathians.

December 6, when they abandoned Lodz and withdrew to a line closer to Warsaw. The Germans, despite having failed in two major offensives, held a clear strategic advantage at the end of the year.

The Third Invasion of Serbia
While the Austro-Hungarians had at least managed to regain some of the ground lost to the Russians in Galicia, they still had embarrassing unfinished business in Serbia. A third offensive got under way in November. The Serbian armies, ably led by the veteran Putnik, fell back across the Kolubra River until they reached good defensive positions. The Austrian armies followed, securing Valjevo, though they made slow progress in increasingly wet and wintry weather. The Serbian army also gave ground in the north, abandoning Belgrade, which was occupied on December 2. On the following day, however, with the front now east of a flooded Kolubra, the Serbian army, having received shipments of French ammunition, mounted its counterattack. Over the next six days they forced the Austro-Hungarian armies to relinquish all their conquests to date and abandon the offensive.

The Cost of the Campaign
With the capital re-occupied by Serbian forces on December 15, the third Austro-Hungarian invasion of Serbia in 1914 was comprehensively defeated. The cost of three offensives had been 227,000 killed, wounded and missing from a total of 450,000 troops committed to the campaigns. Serbian casualties numbered about 170,000 from a total of 400,000. These losses were devastating enough to a small country such as Serbia, but an even greater cost was exacted by the typhus epidemic that ravaged Serbia in the ensuing winter months.

Serbian troops advancing
After a series of well organized retreats, the Serbian army switched to the offensive on December 3. The old king, Peter, appeared in the trenches to urge on the troops.

THE AUSTRO-HUNGARIAN ARMY

IDENTITY TAG

IN MILITARY TERMS, Austria-Hungary was the least of the great powers. Its army had the cumbersome title of the *Kaiserliche und königliche Armee* (Imperial and Royal Army) because the Emperor of Austria was also king of autonomous Hungary. In theory the Joint Army, as it was also known, was able to muster 32 infantry and nine cavalry divisions and to put into the field some 1,300,000 officers and men. The real peace-time establishment, however, was about 450,000, and the balance was made up with recalled reservists. In addition, Austria and Hungary each possessed a separate national army, the *Landwehr* and the *Honved* respectively. The reserve (or *Landsturm*) numbered a further million men. With Austria-Hungary calling up only 29 per cent of its eligible manpower for service, the reserve divisions were manned by older conscripts and second-grade conscripts, the latter's period of service being 20 weeks spread over a two-year period.

Austria-Hungary, like Russia, lacked the industrial base needed to wage a protracted war and was not well served in terms of railways and rolling stock for moving formations swiftly between fronts. About one-quarter of all conscripted soldiers were illiterate, and most of the conscripts from the subject nationalities did not understand German or Hungarian. In addition, most of the subject nationalities – Czechs, Slovaks, Poles, Romanians and southern Slavs – had linguistic and cultural links with the empire's various enemies.

Austrian artillery
Despite its lack of a large industrial base, Austria-Hungary did manufacture some good artillery pieces, such as the 305-mm howitzer produced at the Skoda works in Prague.

INFANTRY CAP

INFANTRY TUNIC

COMBAT KNIFE

Uniform
The blue-grey uniform worn by the Austro-Hungarians at the start of the war dates from 1909. The red stripes on the collar indicate an infantry regiment (in this case a German-speaking one). In 1916 Austria-Hungary adopted a new *feldgrau* uniform similar to that worn by their German allies.

BOOTS

STEYR-MANNLICHER CARBINE (1895 MODEL) AND BAYONET

Firearms
The brand new Steyr factory, completed in 1914, produced the army's 8-mm Mannlicher rifles and carbines, as well as pistols and machine-guns.

STEYR 9-MM AUTOMATIC PISTOL (1912 MODEL)

Cocking lever

Water-filled barrel-jacket to prevent barrel overheating

Muzzle flash hider

Collapsible tripod

Trigger and two-handed grip

Schwarzlose machine-gun
Designed by a German engineer, the Schwarzlose was adopted by the Austro-Hungarian army in 1907. The fact that it had just ten main working parts made it a very reliable gun. Captured Schwarzloses were often used by Russian and Italian troops.

Ammunition box

Belt holds 250 rounds of 8-mm ammunition

THE WIDENING WAR

1914–1916

~

ALTHOUGH THE FIRST WORLD WAR AFFECTED EVERY
PART OF THE WORLD TO SOME EXTENT, IT WAS
ESSENTIALLY A EUROPEAN WAR, CAUSED BY
A BREAKDOWN IN RELATIONS AMONG THE GREAT
EUROPEAN POWERS, THAT SPILT OVER TO OTHER
CONTINENTS. AT THE SAME TIME, AS THE ALLIED
POWERS STRUGGLED TO MATCH THE MANPOWER OF
THEIR ENEMIES, TROOPS RAISED IN DISTANT PARTS
OF THE BRITISH AND FRENCH EMPIRES WERE SENT
TO FIGHT ON THE BATTLEFIELDS OF EUROPE.

~

A long way from home
Algerian troops of the Armée d'Afrique prepare
couscous in a village in northern France in 1914.
At least 150,000 Algerians saw service in France
in the course of the war, along with 39,000
Tunisians and 14,000 Moroccans.

NEW THEATRES OF WAR

WARS HAD BEEN FOUGHT BETWEEN EUROPEANS ON OTHER CONTINENTS BEFORE,

ESPECIALLY IN THE 18TH CENTURY WHEN FRANCE, SPAIN AND BRITAIN COMPETED

FOR COLONIES AND TRADE. BY THE LATE 19TH CENTURY THE SITUATION HAD

BECOME VERY DIFFERENT. COLONIAL CONFLICTS WERE INVARIABLY RESOLVED BY

CONFERENCES AND COMPROMISES. HOWEVER, WHEN FULL-SCALE WAR ERUPTED

IN EUROPE IN 1914, IT IMMEDIATELY SPREAD OUTWARDS TO THE COLONIES.

I T GRADUALLY BECAME CLEAR that the First World War would involve an unprecedented consumption of manpower. Hundreds of thousands of troops were recruited outside Europe, especially from the British and French empires, and they fought in all theatres of the war, including the Western Front – some 80,000 Africans died fighting on the battlefields of Europe.

Staffs may plan strategies, but wars are unpredictable. The expectations of 1914 – that the war would be short and decided in Europe – were totally confounded in a matter of months. The stalemate in the trenches promised a war without foreseeable end, and the entry of other powers – particularly the Ottoman Empire and Italy – extended it to the Middle East and southern Europe. After the Turkish entry into the war in November 1914 the British found themselves involved in three separate, non-European theatres.

GERMANY'S COLONIES

As Germany was late in entering the imperial scramble for "a place in the sun", its colonies tended to be areas of little interest to older competitors. In spite of nervousness about German expansion, the British did not discourage a German takeover of uncolonized territories of Africa – Togoland, Cameroon, East Africa and Southwest Africa. Although their total area was huge, they were, for the most part, thinly populated with hardly any resources, industrial development or infrastructure.

The war in Africa was fought predominantly by African, and some Asian, troops, except in Southwest Africa, where the Allies were represented by white South Africans and Rhodesians. Among white colonists, opinion was opposed to war, which they feared would encourage resistance to White rule. The Africans themselves had no say in the matter, and although some African troops were allegedly volunteers, most were, in fact if not officially, conscripts. All the European powers, especially the French, also recruited Africans to fight on the battlefields of Europe.

Germany's African colonies were surrounded by British, French or Belgian possessions and cut off from reinforcement by Allied command of the sea. Inevitably, they were short of supplies, including guns and ammunition (Lettow-Vorbeck's men in East Africa sometimes made their own). Their position appeared hopeless and all had surrendered by the end of 1915 except East Africa, where the last shot of the war was fired

Alpine warfare
Fighting on the Italian front was trench warfare with a difference. Here Austro-Hungarian troops in the Dolomites are dug in at a height of over 3,000 m (10,000 ft).

"The country was undisciplined and so was the army: we have taken care of the problem by the usual and proper means, the shooting of insubordinates to prevent the sparks from turning into a fire."

COUNT LUIGI CADORNA, CHIEF OF THE ITALIAN GENERAL STAFF

two weeks after the armistice in Europe. Although campaigns were on a very small scale compared with those in Europe, casualty rates were high, especially among the porters. Many more died from disease and starvation than were killed in battles.

Almost the whole African continent was affected by the war. Oppressive recruitment policies and the general social and economic dislocation caused by war provoked local disturbances in many parts of the continent. However, notwithstanding high rates of desertion, African soldiers in general demonstrated remarkable loyalty and stoicism. Educated Africans generally supported the Allies, hoping – vainly as it turned out – for post-war rewards in the form of civil rights and equal opportunities.

Germany also had a number of tiny bases in the Pacific, important only for their wireless and cable stations, plus the enclave of Tsingtao, seized from China in 1897, which was the only significant German overseas naval base. None lasted long, the islands mostly falling after minimal resistance to Australian and New Zealand forces. Tsingtao required more effort before it fell to the Japanese who, on the basis of their 1911 treaty with Britain, entered the war to further their own long-term strategic aims.

ITALY ENTERS THE WAR

Since unification, Italy had been eager to establish its "great-power" status. Despite rapid industrial development in the north, the economy remained primarily agrarian. The division between north and south (where 90 per cent were illiterate) grew wider than ever. Meanwhile Italy's imperialist dreams led to a disastrous invasion of Abyssinia (Ethiopia) in 1896. Slight consolation for that defeat was gained when Libya was taken from the Turks in 1912.

In 1882 Italy had joined the Central Powers in the Triple Alliance, but the precise terms of the treaty enabled it to declare neutrality in 1914. Italy's chief territorial ambitions were to acquire the Italian-speaking regions within Austria-Hungary – the Trentino, part of the southern Tyrol, Trieste and Istria. These, and more, were promised by Britain and France in the secret Treaty of London, signed on April 26, 1915.

Strategically, Italy was of little significance. It offered few advantages to its new allies apart from forcing the Central Powers to fight on another front. The decision to declare war was taken by a group of ministers backed by the King. Neither the military nor parliament was consulted. Most civilians showed no enthusiasm for the war and the Italian army was seriously under-prepared. Deficiencies in equipment since the Libyan war had not been made good. There were only a hundred or so heavy guns available. General Cadorna, the ruthless chief of staff who enjoyed virtually unlimited authority, had only seven of 25 divisions fully operational.

THE OTTOMAN TURKS

After their defeat in the Balkan Wars (1912–13), the Turks needed a substantial ally. They turned to Germany, which reaped the benefit of its long diplomatic courtship and substantial investments (including the as yet unfinished Berlin–Baghdad Railway). Germany also provided a military mission that undertook to bring the Turkish army up to date and educate a new class of officers.

The Ottoman Empire, historically a land power, had little in the way of a navy. The British had undertaken to rectify this situation, and two dreadnoughts destined for Turkey were being built in British shipyards. On the outbreak of war the British, to Turkish fury, requisitioned them. At that time two German ships, the battlecruiser *Goeben* and the light cruiser *Breslau*, were stationed in the Mediterranean. On August 3 they shelled two French ports in North Africa, then sailed for the Dardanelles, escaping the bemused British fleet, which had expected them to break out west not east. After a short delay, they were admitted to sanctuary off Constantinople. It was Britain's turn to protest, but the Turks claimed the ships were replacements for their lost dreadnoughts. Although the Turkish cabinet was still divided on whether to join in the war, the die was effectively cast. On October 29, the *Goeben* and *Breslau* attacked Russian ports in the Black Sea. Declarations of war duly followed.

TURKISH WAR AIMS

The Turks hoped to restore their authority where it had been lost or superseded, chiefly in the Balkans and North Africa. Their strategy was based on political rather than military considerations and committed them to an impossible number of major enterprises, fighting simultaneously against Britain and Russia with little aid from their allies. Their first and heaviest campaign was fought against their traditional enemy, Russia. In the winter of 1914–15 Enver Pasha, the Turkish minister of war, chose to launch an offensive across their common border in the Caucasus, in spite of the hostility of the terrain.

In North Africa the Italians had taken advantage of Turkish weakness to acquire Tripolitania and Cyrenaica in 1912. Farther east, Egypt was still nominally within the Sultan's dominions but it had been administered by the British, ostensibly "advising" the Khedive, ever since their troops crushed a nationalist revolt in 1882. In November 1914 the Khedive proclaimed his loyalty to the Sultan, principally because he wished for German favour (and perhaps because he happened to be in Constantinople at the time). To the Germans the

Ill-fated British advance into Mesopotamia
British cavalry pass the ruined 6th-century palace of the Persian king Khosrow I at Ctesiphon. In 1915–16 a British force made rapid progress up the Tigris, but after a clash with the Turks at Ctesiphon, turned back to Kut, where it was besieged for almost five months before surrendering.

"Through the Narrows of the Dardanelles and across the ridges of the Gallipoli Peninsula lie some of the shortest paths to a triumphant peace."

WINSTON CHURCHILL, URGING THE CASE FOR
A RENEWED OFFENSIVE AT GALLIPOLI, SUMMER 1915

Suez Canal, closed to them by the British, was an attractive strategic target. Egypt therefore became the objective of the second Turkish offensive of the war early in 1915.

PERSIA AND MESOPOTAMIA

In the Middle East the situation was more complicated. Persia was dominated by European powers, but in 1907, after a century of rivalry in the region, Russia and Britain, worried by German expansion, reached an agreement to respect Persian independence. The two powers carefully defined their own spheres of interest, Russian in the north and British in the south. In practice this was little short of annexation: the Anglo-Persian Oil Company's refinery at Abadan became virtually an outpost of the British Empire.

On the outbreak of war the Persian government declared its neutrality, but Britain, wary of the Turks and anxious to protect its oil interests, moved troops to Bahrein (Bahrain) in the Gulf. When Turkey entered the war nearly two months later, they advanced to Shatt al'Arab, the great channel formed by the confluence of the Tigris and Euphrates, which the Turks claimed as their territorial waters. Turkish forces in Mesopotamia were thin and scattered, a factor that encouraged the British in an over-ambitious advance.

THE DARDANELLES CAMPAIGN

Similarly thinly defended was Gallipoli, the Turkish peninsula on the European side of the Dardanelles, the strait that divides Europe from Asia. Allied possession of the strait could lead to the capture of Constantinople and the reopening of the route to the Black Sea and Russia's southern ports.

The motive for an attack on the Dardanelles was a request from Russia (January 2, 1915), hard-pressed by the Turks in the Caucasus, for relieving action by their allies. Such an initiative also appealed to the British and French as an alternative to the impasse on the Western Front. One keen supporter was Winston Churchill, at the British admiralty, who had sent ships to bombard the forts at the mouth of the Dardanelles soon after Turkey entered the war. Attempts to force the straits by naval power alone failed and it was decided that an amphibious operation was necessary. Thus was born the disastrous Allied expedition to Gallipoli.

The *Goeben* and *Breslau* at Constantinople
The German battlecruiser Goeben (right) and her escort the Breslau (left) escaped their British pursuers in August 1914 to reach the safety of the Dardanelles. The ships were then renamed and nominally purchased by the Turkish navy.

The Dardanelles Expedition

In the trenches at Anzac Cove
An Australian sniper aims his home-made periscopic rifle. In Gallipoli's cramped, shallow trenches with the Turkish lines so close, periscopes became essential equipment.

W HEN IT WAS FIRST MOOTED, the idea of a Dardanelles venture seemed an appropriate way to make use of British sea power. British ships had bombarded the entrance to the straits on November 4, 1914 even before hostilities had officially begun, and on December 13 the submarine *B11* sank the Turkish guardship *Messudieh* at Chanak Kale. These two attacks sacrificed the element of surprise by alerting the Turks to British intentions. The Turks set about strengthening their defences, sowing 344 mines in the straits by March 1915 and siting torpedo tubes at the Narrows. Between February 25 and March 14 the British carried out bombardments and put ashore landing parties to destroy Turkish positions. In spite of this, British and French attempts to sweep the straits failed ignominiously in the face of Turkish artillery.

After these setbacks London decided that an amphibious assault might be necessary, the navies being given one last chance to force the straits unaided. The attempt was made, with 16 battleships, on March 18. Three were sunk, one beached, and two severely damaged, while the minefields guarding the Narrows were untouched. These failures reflected the essence of the Dardanelles problem: a naval assault could not prevail because Turkish guns could not be silenced until the minefields were cleared, and the minefields could not be cleared until the guns were silenced.

CHANGE OF PLAN

The belated decision was taken to conduct a full-scale amphibious operation to clear the Turkish guns from the landward side. In the absence of proper liaison arrangements between army and navy and with a lack of specialist landing craft, preparations were far from perfect. Nevertheless, by April 21 the newly arrived commander, Sir Ian Hamilton, had assembled 77 ships at the island of Lemnos and 75,000 men – the ANZAC Corps, the Royal Naval Division, the British 29th Division and one French Colonial division. The time spent in this effort, however, allowed the Turks to reinforce and reorganize their troops under German command. Beaches that could be assaulted were lightly held while strong reserves were deployed locally.

THE OTTOMAN EMPIRE

~

THE OTTOMAN EMPIRE suffered a succesion of military defeats in the early years of the 20th century. It also underwent serious internal upheaval. The Young Turk revolution of 1908, which led to the abdication of Sultan Abdul Hamid the following year, was a largely bloodless affair. The Young Turks who filled the important positions in the cabinet at the outbreak of war – men such as Talaat Bey and Enver Pasha – were energetic reformers with ambitions to modernize the empire. In 1914 the military was in the midst of long-needed reforms. Older, high-ranking officers were being replaced by better-trained – but inexperienced – younger men. Some good weapons were available (Mauser rifles and Krupp guns), but they were in short supply. Transportation was undeveloped, the treasury was empty, and the country depended on imports of German coal and steel, as well as armaments and machinery.

Turkish infantry uniform
Apart from the traditional kalabash hat, the design of the Turks' uniforms showed the influence of their German advisers.

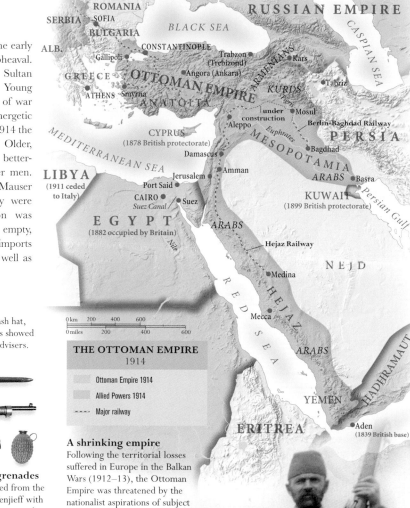

BAYONET

9.5-MM MAUSER CARBINE (1887)

Turkish infantry weapons
The Turks were issued with Mauser rifles, including the 1898 model used by the German Army as well as various older weapons.

Turkish grenades
These ranged from the antique Tufenjieff with its rope fuse to modern fragmentation grenades.

THE OTTOMAN EMPIRE 1914

- Ottoman Empire 1914
- Allied Powers 1914
- ---- Major railway

A shrinking empire
Following the territorial losses suffered in Europe in the Balkan Wars (1912–13), the Ottoman Empire was threatened by the nationalist aspirations of subject peoples, such as the Arabs, Kurds and Armenians.

Turkish army
 Attempts were made after the failures of the Balkan Wars to modernize the army. Conscription was a lottery, and the main effort fell upon the Anatolian peasant. He was a courageous, dogged soldier, but equipment was all too often out-of-date or absent.

Military leaders
The Turkish war minister Enver Pasha (*left*) was apt to ignore the advice given him by the German general Liman von Sanders (*above*).

Turkish prisoners
Despite the horrors of the fighting on
Gallipoli, the Allied troops respected
"Johnny Turk" as a fair and honourable opponent.

THE LANDINGS

With the defence dispersed in order to meet the
threat of landings in the Gulf of Xeros, on Gallipoli
itself or in Asia, the initiative lay in Allied hands (see
maps, pages 80–81). The landings of April 25,
however, miscarried by narrow but critical margins.
The Anzacs were put ashore 1.5 km (1 mile) north
of the intended beaches. The resulting confusion
delayed an advance on the Sari Bair ridge, giving
the leading elements of the Turkish 19th Infantry
Division time to occupy it. Checked and then
confined to a very shallow beachhead, the Anzac
forces were denied permission to evacuate their
precarious, cliff-ledge positions.

The British 29th Division, which consisted of
regular soldiers, veterans of garrison duty
throughout the British Empire, landed around
Cape Helles, the tip of the Gallipoli peninsula, at
five beaches, Y, X, W, V and S. They were
transported in rowing boats towed by steam
launches, two of them commanded by naval cadets
aged just 13. On V Beach, as troops tried to
disembark from the steamer *River Clyde* and the
smaller boats accompanying her, they were mown
down by Turkish machine-gun and rifle fire,
suffering over 1,200 casualties. Forces scheduled for

that beach were diverted to W Beach and, by
nightfall on the 25th, footholds had been secured on
all five beaches, and forces from Y Beach had
advanced almost to Krithia. There, however, they
encountered advancing Turkish forces and, having
withdrawn to their beachhead, they evacuated Y
Beach on the 26th as a result of confusion of orders.
To the south, a continuous front was established on
that day but a general offensive along the line on the
28th failed as fresh Turkish forces were fed into the
battle. By May 8 the deadlock at Cape Helles was as
complete as that on the Western Front.

THE BRITISH DILEMMA

During the summer the Turks tried to drive the
Allies back to the shore with a series of very costly
attacks. On May 19 suicidal charges were launched
along the whole length of the Anzac front. By noon
that day the Turks had suffered 10,000 casualties
and over 3,000 dead, dying and wounded lay in No
Man's Land. As the bodies decayed in the heat,
the situation became unbearable. A truce
was arranged for May 24 and for nine
hours men from both sides dug
graves, many exchanging
gifts and fragments of
conversation. Equally
costly attacks and
counterattacks
continued at
Cape Helles

Turkish camp
Turkish troops held in
reserve could enjoy the
relative comfort of a
military camp. Allies not
in the line were shipped
back to base on the
island of Lemnos.

throughout the summer with little change in the
front line. The Allied forces, living on unsuitable
food such as bully beef and biscuit, sharing their
crowded trenches with makeshift latrines and
millions of flies, were ravaged by dysentery.

THE SECOND PHASE

All the while London grappled with the
consequences of failure. The British choice was
either to evacuate or to reinforce, but an evacuation,
during the short summer nights, was technically
impossible. The decision was taken to renew the
offensive. A further landing would be made at Suvla
Bay, timed to coincide with an offensive from Anzac
Cove against the heights of Sari Bair.

The failure of the renewed British offensive in
August 1915 has generated much controversy.
Apologists for the Gallipoli venture claim that it
could have succeeded had the divisions of IX Corps
put ashore at Suvla Bay on August 6 pushed
forward to secure the Anafarta Ridge – they were
barely opposed and should have been able to turn
the Turkish defences on Sari Bair. This line of
argument has seized on obvious targets: a hopelessly
inadequate command system and certain equally
inadequate generals. Troops moved to and fro

A precarious toehold
After the landing on April 25
the troops at Anzac Cove
dug in wherever they
could. Their makeshift
scrapes and burrows
on the cliffs offered
little protection
from enemy
shelling.

THE ANZACS
~

THE AUSTRALIAN AND NEW ZEALAND ARMY CORPS was raised at the beginning of the war. Australia (total population 5 million) provided 322,000 volunteers, New Zealand (1 million) a remarkable 124,000. Anzacs served on the Western Front, in the Middle East and – most notably – in Gallipoli, where their heroic fight in a hopeless cause made a permanent impact, commemorated annually on Anzac Day, April 25.

Australians, with their team spirit and egalitarian scorn for the English class system, received military training at school. The New Zealanders of 1914 mostly sprang from pioneer conditions, reared with guns and spades; moreover, they were culturally committed to the idea of the Empire. The Anzacs came to be regarded as the finest soldiers of the war, and their high casualties reflected their courage and aggression. Australia lost 60,000 men killed, New Zealand 17,000. Yet the survivors of Gallipoli, returning to their Egyptian base, took a more deprecatory view of themselves, and wearily sang:

> *We are the ragtime army, The A.N.Z.A.C.,*
> *We cannot shoot, we won't salute, What bloody use are we?*

No worries mate
This photograph of an Australian carrying a wounded friend to the dressing station became an emblem of the spirit of the Anzacs amidst the horrors of Gallipoli.

Before the landings
Troops of the Australian and New Zealand Army Corps (ANZAC) on their way from the Greek island of Lemnos to the landing at Anzac Cove.

---

across the Suvla Plain, lacking clear orders and maps, or returned to the landing places because they had no water. Hardly any artillery had been landed, so the commanders on shore chose to wait until more arrived. Meanwhile the advance on Sari Bair was being executed with considerable daring and determination. The Anzacs, reinforced by one and a half divisions of British and Gurkha troops, had a clear idea of their objectives, but advancing by night over unfamiliar ground, one of the columns got hopelessly lost. Only small units reached the crest of the ridge at Chunuk Bair and Hill Q, but Turkish reserves, ably directed by Mustafa Kemal, regained the ridge and the moment of opportunity had passed.

ACCEPTING FAILURE

The failure of the August offensive was due to a combination of factors. It was in part the result of IX Corps' not having understood its part in a plan that anticipated success elsewhere, in part because the Anzac offensive failed to carry its objectives and in part because of the speed and effectiveness of the

reaction of Turkish forces. This last factor is one of particular importance and is often overlooked. Much has been made in British histories of the narrowness of the margin between success and failure, and indeed there were occasions, both in April and August 1915, when victory only narrowly eluded the British. By the same token, the British also came perilously close to comprehensive defeat,

Evacuation of Cape Helles, January 8, 1916
Debris, including unwanted stores and equipment, litters the shoreline at W Beach on Capes Helles. This photograph was taken on the day of the evacuation of British and French troops from the tip of the Gallipoli Peninsula.

Recruitment
Young Australians volunteered for the armed services in such numbers that there was no need to introduce conscription.

A CALL FROM THE DARDANELLES
"Coo-ee-
Won't YOU
come?"
ENLIST NOW

most certainly in April. The failure to clear the Sari Bair ridge and the Turkish containment of the beachhead at Suvla spelt the end of British hopes of success at the Dardanelles. Even so, the decision to abandon the expedition was put off for some time. Hamilton was removed from command on October 16 but his successor was in turn removed after having recommended evacuation on the 31st. November, however, saw the onset of winter and, on December 7, the British cabinet authorized an evacuation that was completed, without loss and without any soldiers being left behind, from Anzac Cove and Suvla Bay on December 19–20 and from Cape Helles on January 8–9, 1916.

THE GALLIPOLI CAMPAIGN

APRIL 1915 – JANUARY 1916

When the Ottoman Empire entered the war in November 1914, the Allies' maritime links with Russia's southern ports on the Black Sea were severed. The British and French determined to to seize the Dardanelles, with the aim of then sailing on to attack the Ottoman capital, Constantinople. It was hoped this might force the Turks out of the war and reopen the sea-route to the Black Sea. After various failed attempts to force the Dardanelles by Anglo-French naval forces, it was decided to land troops on the Gallipoli Peninsula on the European side of the Dardanelles in order to silence the Turkish guns guarding the straits. The two landings of April 25, 1915 both fell far short of their objectives. The troops at Cape Helles and at Anzac Cove were halted by a determined Turkish defence. A renewed offensive came in August with the landing of two fresh divisions at Suvla Bay. Again the offensive was contained by the Turks and, with no prospect of a breakthrough, the Allied troops were evacuated at the end of the year.

KEY

➡	British or Anzac landing/advance	⌒	French position
◼➤	British or Anzac retreat	⌒	Turkish position
➡	French landing/advance	⊠	Turkish fortified town
➡	Turkish advance	⋀	Turkish encampment
·····	Allied objective	⚓ ⚓	Turkish minefield
⌒	British or Anzac position	✹	Major battle
		▬▬	Road

Going through their paces
Australian and British troops exercising at Cape Helles in December 1915, keeping up the illusion for the watching Turks that there was to be no withdrawal from Gallipoli.

Diversionary attack by Royal Naval Division

THE LANDINGS OF APRIL 25 AT ANZAC AND HELLES

Mustafa Kemal quickly deployed 19th Turkish Division along crest of Sari Bair to contain the ANZAC landing

Ground held by ANZAC troops at end of first day after overcoming Turks defending the beach

Actual landing was a little to the north of intended landing site. This caused confusion and delay in establishing beachhead

Anzac Cove, April 25
15,000 Australian and New Zealand troops failed to gain the heights of Sari Bair before they were occupied by Turkish reinforcements.

Despite successful unopposed landing, troops here evacuated on April 26 after Turks launch counterattack

Ground gained by Allies by dusk on first day

Allied warships shell Turkish positions before and during the landings, but their fire is largely ineffective

French landing at Kum Kale

Disastrous landing of River Clyde; hundreds of disembarking troops mown down by Turkish machine-guns

The landings at Cape Helles, April 25
Only at V and W beaches did the landings meet serious opposition, the Turks inflicting heavy casualties as the British disembarked.

April 28
A bloody encounter, known as the First Battle of Krithia, results in Allied advance of just a few hundred metres

May 8
Turkish front line

French troops, despite success at Kum Kale, are withdrawn and transferred to the right of British line at Helles

British and French progress at Helles to May 8
Fierce fighting as the British and French struggled towards Krithia resulted in 10,000 Allied casualties in the first three days.

May 6–8
Second Battle of Krithia ends in stalemate, with both the Allies and the Turks securely entrenched

May 8
British and French front line

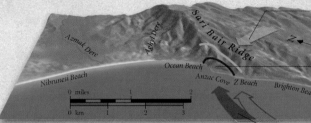

Anzac Cove
Troops enjoy a period of respite between bouts of Turkish shelling as they walk along the narrow beach at Anzac.

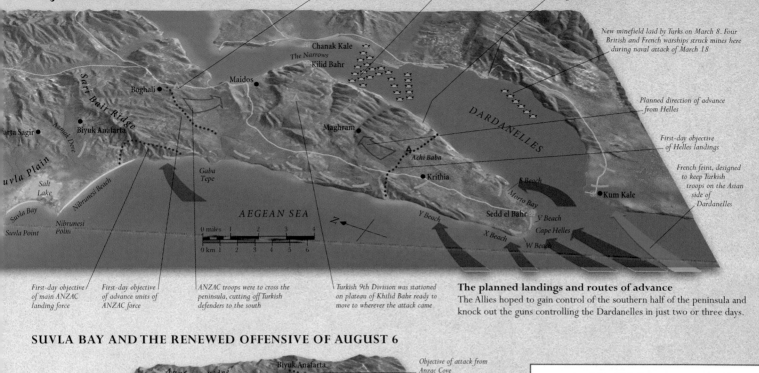

THE STRATEGIC AIMS AND FIRST-DAY OBJECTIVES OF THE LANDINGS

Most of Turkish 19th Division was concentrated just south of Boghali

Turkish minefields guarding narrowest parts of the Dardanelles

Mobile Turkish howitzer batteries active on both sides of the straits

New minefield laid by Turks on March 8. Four British and French warships struck mines here during naval attack of March 18

Chanak Kale

The Narrows
Kilid Bahr

Maidos

Boghali

Sari Bair Ridge

Biyuk Anafarta

arta Sagir

Chunuk Dere

uvla Plain

Salt Lake

Suvla Bay

Suvla Point

Nibrunesi beach

Nibrunesi Point

Gaba Tepe

DARDANELLES

Maghram

Achi Baba

Krithia

Kum Kale

S Beach

Morto Bay

Sedd el Bahr

V Beach

Y Beach

X Beach

Cape Helles

W Beach

Planned direction of advance from Helles

First-day objective of Helles landings

French feint, designed to keep Turkish troops on the Asian side of Dardanelles

AEGEAN SEA

N

0 miles | 1 | 2 | 3 | 4

0 km | 1 | 2 | 3 | 4 | 5 | 6

First-day objective of main ANZAC landing force

First-day objective of advance of ANZAC force

ANZAC troops were to cross the peninsula, cutting off Turkish defenders to the south

Turkish 9th Division was stationed on plateau of Khilid Bahr ready to move to wherever the attack came

The planned landings and routes of advance
The Allies hoped to gain control of the southern half of the peninsula and knock out the guns controlling the Dardanelles in just two or three days.

SUVLA BAY AND THE RENEWED OFFENSIVE OF AUGUST 6

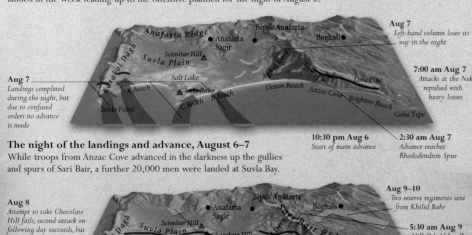

Objective of attack from Anzac Cove

Anafarta Ridge

Karakol Dagh

Anafarta Sagir

Biyuk Anafarta

Boghali

Scimitar Hill

Suvla Plain

Salt Lake

Suvla Bay

Lala Baba

Suvla Point

Nibrunesi Point

Aghyl Dere

Lone Pine

Anzac Cove

Brighton Beach

Gaba Tepe

Suvla was defended by a force of about 1,500 – they had no machine-guns, only a few howitzers concentrated on Anafarta Ridge

5:30 pm Aug 6
Attack at Lone Pine gains Turkish first trench, but Turkish line holds

0 miles | 1 | 2 | 3

0 km | 1 | 2 | 3 | 4

20,000 reinforcements landed at Anzac Cove

Before the landings at Suvla, August 6
The situation at Anzac had changed little since May, but 20,000 fresh troops were landed in the week leading up to the offensive planned for the night of August 6.

Anafarta Ridge

Karakol Dagh

Anafarta Sagir

Biyuk Anafarta

Boghali

Scimitar Hill

Suvla Plain

Salt Lake

A Beach

Lala Baba

C Beach

B Beach

Suvla Point

Ocean Beach

Aghyl Dere

Lone Pine

Anzac Cove

Brighton Beach

Gaba Tepe

Aug 7
Left-hand column loses its way in the night

7:00 am Aug 7
Attacks at the Nek repulsed with heavy losses

Aug 7
Landings completed during the night, but due to confused orders no advance is made

10:30 pm Aug 6
Start of main advance

2:30 am Aug 7
Advance reaches Rhododendron Spur

The night of the landings and advance, August 6–7
While troops from Anzac Cove advanced in the darkness up the gullies and spurs of Sari Bair, a further 20,000 men were landed at Suvla Bay.

Biyuk Anafarta

Anafarta Sagir

Boghali

Scimitar Hill

Chocolate Hill

Karakol Dagh

Suvla Plain

Salt Lake

A Beach

Lala Baba

C Beach

B Beach

Suvla Point

Suvla Bay

Nibrunesi Point

Ocean Beach

Sari Bair Ridge

Aghyl Dere

Lone Pine

Anzac Cove

Brighton Beach

Gaba Tepe

Aug 9–10
Two reserve regiments sent from Khilid Bahr

5:30 am Aug 9
Hill Q held briefly by small group of Gurkhas and soldiers of the 6th South Lancashire Regiment

Aug 8
Attempt to take Chocolate Hill fails; second attack on following day succeeds, but with heavy casualties

Aug 9
Two Turkish divisions from Bulair reach Suvla by forced march

Aug 8
Chunuk Bair held briefly by New Zealand and British troops

The Turkish counterattacks, August 9–10
Turkish reinforcements swiftly contained the threat at Suvla and drove the Anzacs back from their positions on Sari Bair.

THE EVACUATION
~

That the evacuation of Gallipoli was effected without the loss of a single man was a triumph of careful planning. At Suvla and Anzac there were some 83,000 men and 5,000 animals. Troops were taken off night after night, leaving a rearguard of 20,000 to convince the Turks that all was normal. This final group was taken off on the night of December 19/20. Ingenious devices were rigged up to fire rifles automatically as the trenches were gradually stripped of men. In the end the Turks suspected nothing, nor did they at Helles three weeks later when the procedure was repeated. The Turks attacked on January 7, but were met by such fierce defensive fire that they assumed the Allies planned to maintain the front. That night and the next the remaining troops were evacuated.

Early departures from Suvla Bay
Soldiers being towed away from Suvla on a raft during the days leading up to the final evacuation. This was completed under cover of darkness.

French field kitchen at Gallipoli
The presence of a division of French troops, chiefly North African Zouaves and Senegalese Riflemen, in the Allied landings on Gallipoli is often forgotten. This was increased to two divisions for the renewd offensives in August.

CAUCASUS, MESOPOTAMIA AND EGYPT

NOVEMBER 1914 – APRIL 1916

Turkish troops were spread thinly over the Ottoman Empire and Turkish war aims were many and various. The Turks hoped to regain territory lost in recent wars from Russia and Italy and to consolidate their hold over non-Turkish, non-Muslim peoples in their empire. At the same time they needed to oblige their German allies by threatening British interests in the Middle East such as the Suez Canal and Persian oilfields.

1914 NOVEMBER 11
Russian offensive against Koprukoy repulsed by Turks

1914 NOVEMBER 22
Force from India occupies Basra to protect oil pipeline from Persia

DECEMBER 22
Turks launch offensive towards Sarikamish

DECEMBER 29
Turks stage short occupation of Tabriz in northwest Persia

1915 JANUARY 17
Battle of Sarikamish ends; Turkish forces, weakened by advancing across mountains in winter, suffer humiliating defeat

1915 JANUARY
Turks assemble troops at Beersheba to cross Sinai and attack Suez Canal

FEBRUARY
Turks initiate policy of deporting Armenians, which is thinly disguised genocide

JANUARY 30
Russians recapture Tabriz

FEBRUARY 3–4
Unsuccessful Turkish attacks on Suez Canal

APRIL 11
British forces led by Sir John Nixon repel Turkish attack on Basra

MAY 19
Russians briefly occupy Van, following Armenian uprising

JUNE 3
British General Townshend takes Amara on Tigris

JULY 25
British occupy Nasiriya on Euphrates

SEPTEMBER 26–28
Battle of Kut al-Amara; British forces defeat Turks

NOVEMBER 24
Battle of Ctesiphon ends; British retreat to Kut al-Amara

NOVEMBER 22
Start of Battle of Ctesiphon, southeast of Baghdad

DECEMBER 7
Turks begin siege of Kut al-Amara

1916 JANUARY 17
Russians force evacuation of Koprukoy, four days after mounting attack

1916 JANUARY 18
British make first of three failed attempts to relieve garrison at Kut al-Amara

FEBRUARY 7
Mus taken by Russian forces

FEBRUARY 11
Russian offensive on Erzerum begins

FEBRUARY 15
Turkish 3rd Army starts to abandon Erzerum, mostly withdrawing towards Erzincan

FEBRUARY 26
Russians take Kermanshah as they advance into western Persia

APRIL 18
Trebizond, abandoned by Turks, is occupied by Russians

APRIL 26
Agreement between British, French and Russians on future partition of Ottoman Empire; British commitments conflict with promises to Arab leaders

APRIL 29
End of siege of Kut al-Amara as British forces surrender to Turks

KEY

- Caucasus and Armenia Nov 1914–April 1916
- Mesopotamia and Persia Nov 1914–April 1916
- Egypt Jan–Feb 1915

Turkey's War on Many Fronts

TURKEY'S ENTRY INTO THE WAR dramatically extended the area of fighting. This alarmed the hard-pressed Russians in particular. In the Caucasus, a region conquered by Russia a century earlier, the Russians were worried about the loyalty of their Muslim subject peoples. The Turks were even more concerned by the many Christian Armenian communities on their side of the border.

Turkish prisoners in Ardahan
In the winter of 1914–15 the Turkish Third Army was virtually destroyed and almost all its guns captured. These prisoners were fortunate not to have frozen to death.

THE CAUCASUS CAMPAIGN

The idea of an offensive in the Caucasus appealed to war minister Enver Pasha, not only because he hoped for support among the various peoples of the Caucasus, but also because the main theatre for the Russians was so far away. Germany approved his plan, which suited its own strategic interests.

As the Allies did not declare war on the Turks until November 5, no serious campaigning was anticipated in the Caucasus in the winter of 1914–15. But a Russian advance into eastern Anatolia, checked at Koprukoy, stung Enver Pasha, who took command of the Third Army in person on December 19, into an unwise counter-offensive.

The difficulties of campaigning in mid-winter in a region that contained hardly any roads or rail lines (the main means of transport was baggage animals), were seriously underestimated. Enver's plan involved large-scale deployment at an altitude sometimes over 3,000 m (9,800 ft), in temperatures

Armenian refugees

The majority of the Armenians killed in 1915 were driven from their homelands into the Syrian Desert. There they either died of starvation or thirst or were killed by Turkish troops or bands of outlaws.

that would freeze an ungloved hand to a rifle barrel on contact. The main objective was the town of Sarikamish, about 45 km (30 miles) southwest of Kars, but by the time the Turks reached it, their X Corps, which spearheaded the attack, had already lost about one-third of its men. Although one Turkish division briefly entered the town, Sarikamish had still not been taken when Russian reinforcements started to arrive by railway from Kars. Enver was reluctant to withdraw and his

Fighting in the Caucasus

The advantage on this front lay with the Russians, but because of commitments on the Eastern Front, they were often unable to exploit their victories. Following the collapse of Russia in 1917 the Turks were able to recover all their lost territory.

troops suffered a disastrous defeat at the hands of the Russian commander, General Mishlaevski. By the time the fighting ended on January 17, the Turkish Third Army had lost up to 90,000 men out of a total of 130,000. According to some estimates, 30,000 Turkish soldiers simply froze to death.

Russia's commitments in other regions prevented the exploitation of this victory until the following winter, when the Russian Army of the Caucasus captured the

Victims of the massacres

Estimates of the Armenians killed range widely: figures as high as 3 million are quoted, but impartial sources suggest a death toll of between one million and 1,500,000.

fortress of Erzerum on February 16. Following a series of amphibious operations along the Black Sea coast, Russian forces took the port of Trabzon (Trebizond), disrupting supplies to the re-formed Third Army. Determined resistance by the Turks could not prevent further losses, Bayburt and Erzincan falling in July.

ARMENIAN MASSACRES

As well as fighting the Russians in the Caucasus, the Turks were waging a parallel campaign against their own Armenian subjects. With the rise of Armenian nationalism in the 19th century, relations between the two peoples had deteriorated rapidly. Alleging Armenian support for and collaboration with Russian forces, the Turkish authorities began a programme of forced deportation and massacres. The killings continued from April 1915 until 1917. Some groups were murdered in cold blood, others were driven into the desert to die of thirst or starvation. When challenged by the US and other countries, the Turks claimed these horrors were necessary measures of national security; Armenians condemned the policy as nothing short of genocide.

Grand Duke Nicholas in the Caucasus

When he was dismissed as commander-in-chief of the Russian armies in 1915, Nicholas, cousin of Tsar Alexander III, was despatched to take over command of the Army of the Caucasus.

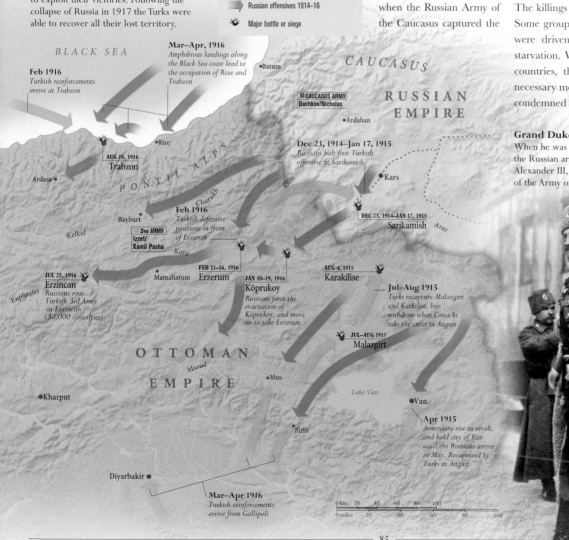

THE CAUCASUS FRONT
1914–1916

Turkish advances and retreats 1914–16

Russian offensives 1914–16

Major battle or siege

BLACK SEA

CAUCASUS

RUSSIAN EMPIRE

Mar–Apr, 1916
Amphibious landings along the Black Sea coast lead to the occupation of Rize and Trabzon

•Batum

Feb 1916
Turkish reinforcements arrive at Trabzon

CAUCASUS ARMY
Dashkov/Nicholas

•Ardahan

•Rize

AUG 18, 1916
Trabzon

Ardasa •

PONTIAL ALPS

Dec 23, 1914–Jan 17, 1915
Russians halt first Turkish offensive at Sarikamish

•Kars

Oltu

Charukh

Bayburt •

Feb 1916
Turkish defensive positions in front of Erzerum

Kelkid

3RD ARMY
Izzet/
Kamil Pasha

Kara

DEC 23, 1914–JAN 17, 1915
Sarikamish

Aras

JUL 25, 1916
Erzincan
Russians rout Turkish 3rd Army at Erzincan (30,000 casualties)

Euphrates

Mamahatum

FEB 11–16, 1916
Erzerum

JAN 10–19, 1916
Köprukoy
Russians force the evacuation of Köprukoy, and move on to take Erzerum

AUG 4, 1915
Karakilise

Jul–Aug 1915
Turks recapture Malazgirt and Karkilise, but withdraw when Cossacks take the cities in August

JUL–AUG 1915
Malazgirt

OTTOMAN
EMPIRE

Murad

•Mus

•Kharput

Lake Van

•Van

Apr 1915
Armenians rise in revolt, and hold city of Van until the Russians arrive in May. Recaptured by Turks in August

•Bitlis

Diyarbakir •

Mar–Apr 1916
Turkish reinforcements arrive from Gallipoli

0 km 20   40   60   80   100
0 miles   20   40   60   80   100

EGYPT AND MESOPOTAMIA

Turkish defeats can be partly explained by the number of campaigns they fought simultaneously. Enver Pasha's ambitious attack in the Caucasus, though the largest, was but one of three offensives they undertook in 1914–15, in addition to fighting elsewhere, notably at Gallipoli, where the Turks won a major victory.

As it became likely that the Turks would side with the Central Powers, Britain took steps to safeguard its interests in the Gulf and in particular the newly important resources of southern Persia that fuelled the new, oil-burning battleships. The Sixth Indian Division was installed in Bahrein (Bahrain) in October and when war was declared, an expeditionary force was sent to the Shatt al-Arab. Within a month it took Basra, the main city of southern Mesopotamia, and advanced to Qurna at the junction of the Tigris and Euphrates.

Persia itself was neutral, but on the outbreak of war the Russians occupied the north and the British parts of the south. The Turks invaded the north and by January 1915 reached Tabriz, before a Russian counterattack drove them back to the border. Minor fighting continued, with Russian cavalry combating Turkish formations and Persian irregulars.

Another Turkish offensive, encouraged by Germany, was aimed at the Suez Canal. The canal was vital to the Allies' communications and its seizure would be a serious setback and an embarrassing blow to the prestige of the British

Scouting over Egypt
A German Rumpler C1 flies over the Pyramids of Giza. The Germans flew bombing raids from Palestine in 1915 in support of the Turkish attack on the Suez Canal.

Empire. The Turks were also keen to regain those parts of North Africa that Italy had wrested from them less than three years earlier.

Egypt was nominally still part of the Ottoman Empire, but the British had exercised political control since the 1880s and the economy was mostly in the hands of Europeans. When the Khedive declared loyalty to his overlord, the Ottoman sultan in Constantinople, the British threw him out and established a "protectorate". They also closed the Suez Canal to their enemies and used Egypt as a staging post for the thousands of imperial troops – Australians, New Zealanders and Indians – making their way to Europe via the canal.

As in the Caucasus, the Turks faced a formidable geographical obstacle. They had to cross the Sinai desert, a hostile landscape without water bar a few wells, depending largely on camels for transport. Moreover, to avoid

detection, the Turks chose the most difficult route.

The task was given to the Fourth Army, based in Damascus and commanded by Ahmad Cemal (Djemal). He was not a soldier by profession, and although he had a gifted German chief of staff, Kress von Kressenstein, the two men did not cooperate well. The Turks had German-made pontoons to cross the Canal, and confidently anticipated an Arab revolt in their favour in Egypt. About 50,000 Arab volunteers, including Sinai Bedouin, did join the Fourth Army, but the Egyptian city-dwellers, though they had little love for the British, were not prepared to act on their inclinations, and without their support the Turkish attack had little hope of success.

PROBLEMS OF SUPPLY

The Fourth Army comprised only 19,000 men, which German logistics experts thought was already too many to be supplied across the Sinai (in a study of 1907 the British had calculated that a trans-Sinai dash was only possible for a strike force of two or three thousand). The British had nearly four times as many men in Egypt, though they were widely scattered and of mixed fighting quality.

The objective was well-chosen and the planning was excellent – not a man was lost in the desert – but the Turks still needed the advantage of surprise, an improbable condition. Allied intelligence had suggested a likely invasion from the east and, inevitably, the army was spotted from the air as it advanced across the barren desert. By the time the Turks reached the canal on February 3, the British were ready for them, dug in on the western bank. As the attack was about to start, a sandstorm caused delay and confusion. In a week's fighting, only in

Campaigns in the Middle East
The major offensives in this region – the Turkish attack on the Suez Canal and the British advance into Mesopotamia – were ill conceived. Both broke down as a result of stretched lines of supply and communication.

EGYPT AND MESOPOTAMIA
1915–1916

➡ British offensive	- - - Major railway
▮➡ British retreat	╲ Oil pipeline
➤ Turkish offensive	Ottoman Empire
╲➤ Turkish retreat	The Allies (and allied states)
✿ Battle or siege	Neutral states

Transport in Sinai
Camels played an important role in supplying the troops defending Suez and in the later advance into Palestine.

Aleppo
Mosul
OTTOMAN EMPIRE
PERSIA
CYPRUS
Homs
Tigris
Tripoli
Tikrit
Beirut
April 29, 1916
The British surrender Kut
1916
British build railway across Sinai ready for attack on Palestine
1915
Turkish troops, attempting to seize the Suez canal, are turned back by British defenders
DAMASCUS
SYRIAN DESERT
Haifa
Nov 22–26, 1915
The British advance to Baghdad is turned back at Ctesiphon. The British withdraw to the garrison at Kut al-Amara
BAGHDAD
SEPT 26–28, 1915
DEC 5, 1915–APR 29, 1916
Kut al-Amara
Jaffa
NOV 21, 1915
Ctesiphon
JUN 3, 1915
Amara
JERUSALEM
MESOPOTAMIA
FEB 4, 1915
May 1915
After the Turks attempt to retake Basra, British troops are reinforced, and move up the Karun valley, forcing a withdrawal to Amara
JUL 24, 1915
Nasiriya
Ahwaz
Gaza
El Arish
Beersheba
Euphrates
Port Said
FEB 3, 1915
Ismailia
MAY 30, 1915
Qurna
Abadan
CAIRO
Suez Canal
Suez
Petra
ARABIA
Nov 6, 1914
British launch Mesopotamian offensive, taking Basra on Nov 21
NOV 21, 1914
Basra
Fao
Persian Gulf
Nile
Aqaba
EGYPT
SINAI
0 km 100 200 300
0 miles 100 200 300
KUWAIT
(British protectorate)

Guarding the Suez Canal
ANZAC troops dig gun
emplacements in
preparation for any
renewed Turkish attack
on the Suez Canal.

two or three places did the
Turks manage to erect pontoons across the
canal. Their bridging equipment was quickly
disabled by Indian troops. Cemal Pasha, who had
banked on establishing a bridgehead across the
canal immediately and had supplies for only a brief
period, broke off the attack in disgust and withdrew
under cover of night. The British commander, Sir
John Maxwell, who had planned a defensive battle
from the start, was not prepared to pursue.

The Turks did not give up the idea of an attack on
Egypt and gained a potentially useful ally through
the cooperation of the Senussi (Zanussi), an Islamic
sect based in Libya but with supporters over a huge
region. The Senussi were at first favourable to the
British, but their position changed when Italy, which
had seized most of the Libyan
coastline in 1911–12, entered the
war on the Allied side.

The Turkish Fourth Army,
however, was in no condition to
repeat its march across the Sinai,
and although some ambitious
schemes were contemplated by the
Turks, they achieved little beyond
forcing the British to maintain a
large garrison in Egypt.

ADVANCE UP THE TIGRIS
In Mesopotamia, General Sir John
Nixon, commanding the British
and Indian expeditionary force,

concluded that
its position was vulnerable.
In an attempt to ensure his forces around Basra
from Turkish attacks he sent a force of little over a
division, under General Townshend, up the Tigris
valley to capture the town of Kut al-Amara.
Townshend's success in taking Kut at the end of
September 1915 inspired a misplaced euphoria that
prompted London to authorize him to move
directly against Baghdad. Although there were few
Turkish forces in the region, it was a foolhardy plan.

Townshend's men advanced partly on land and
partly by boat up the river. In November, they met

a Turkish force at Ctesiphon, 32 km (20 miles) from
Baghdad. The battle was indecisive but Townshend,
conscious of the fragility of his communications,
decided to withdraw to Kut, where his troops dug
themselves in within a bend of the Tigris. They
were soon encircled by the Turks, who constructed
earthworks sufficient to withstand, on the one side,
sorties from Kut and, on the other, attacks by a
small British relief force. Four attempts were made
to relieve Kut. In the last a thousand men died.
Shortly afterwards, the annual floods covered the
plain, and Kut was cut off beyond hope of relief.
Townshend's men were exhausted, under siege
for five months with supplies for two, and some
Indian soldiers were starving to
death rather than eat horsemeat.
After the surrender of April 29,
1916, Townshend and his officers
were well treated, but the
remaining 12,000 British and
Indian troops, who were already
in poor health, were marched
1,900 km (1,200 miles) to prison
labour camps in Anatolia, where
more than a third of them died.

Stripped for action
A party of British signallers manhandles
a cablewagon across a Mesopotamian
river. Good communications were
vital in the desert environment.

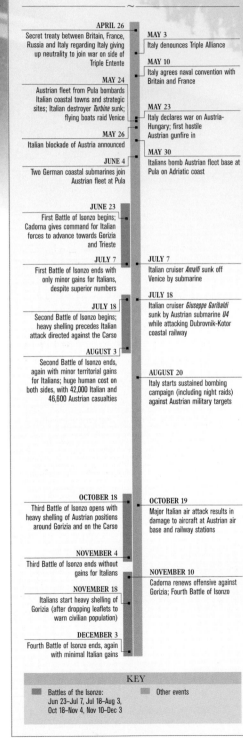

The Isonzo Front

ITALY ENTERS THE WAR
APRIL – DECEMBER 1915

~

Italy's reason for declaring war was to gain territory, so its armies went on the offensive from the start. The year 1915 was dominated by Italian attempts to break through on the Isonzo River, but there were also naval encounters and bombing raids across the Adriatic. The Austro-Hungarians defended grimly throughout 1915, but whenever they lost territory, even a single hilltop, were under orders to recapture it at all costs.

~

APRIL 26
Secret treaty between Britain, France, Russia and Italy regarding Italy giving up neutrality to join war on side of Triple Entente

MAY 3
Italy denounces Triple Alliance

MAY 10
Italy agrees naval convention with Britain and France

MAY 24
Austrian fleet from Pula bombards Italian coastal towns and strategic sites; Italian destroyer *Turbine* sunk; flying boats raid Venice

MAY 23
Italy declares war on Austria-Hungary; first hostile Austrian gunfire in

MAY 26
Italian blockade of Austria announced

MAY 30
Italians bomb Austrian fleet base at Pula on Adriatic coast

JUNE 4
Two German coastal submarines join Austrian fleet at Pula

JUNE 23
First Battle of Isonzo begins; Cadorna gives command for Italian forces to advance towards Gorizia and Trieste

JULY 7
First Battle of Isonzo ends with only minor gains for Italians, despite superior numbers

JULY 7
Italian cruiser *Amalfi* sunk off Venice by submarine

JULY 18
Second Battle of Isonzo begins; heavy shelling precedes Italian attack directed against the Carso

JULY 18
Italian cruiser *Giuseppe Garibaldi* sunk by Austrian submarine *U4* while attacking Dubrovnik-Kotor coastal railway

AUGUST 3
Second Battle of Isonzo ends, again with minor territorial gains for Italians; huge human cost on both sides, with 42,000 Italian and 46,600 Austrian casualties

AUGUST 20
Italy starts sustained bombing campaign (including night raids) against Austrian military targets

OCTOBER 18
Third Battle of Isonzo opens with heavy shelling of Austrian positions around Gorizia and on the Carso

OCTOBER 19
Major Italian air attack results in damage to aircraft at Austrian air base and railway stations

NOVEMBER 4
Third Battle of Isonzo ends without gains for Italians

NOVEMBER 10
Cadorna renews offensive against Gorizia; Fourth Battle of Isonzo

NOVEMBER 18
Italians start heavy shelling of Gorizia (after dropping leaflets to warn civilian population)

DECEMBER 3
Fourth Battle of Isonzo ends, again with minimal Italian gains

KEY
█ Battles of the Isonzo:
Jun 23–Jul 7, Jul 18–Aug 3,
Oct 18–Nov 4, Nov 10–Dec 3

█ Other events

Trench clubs
Savage hand-to-hand fighting over disputed trenches was a feature of the battles of the Isonzo. Pictured here are two Italian trench clubs and a well-made, flexible Austrian truncheon (centre).

ITALY ENTERED the war on May 23, 1915, declaring war only on Austria-Hungary, from which it hoped to gain the territory promised by the Treaty of London, negotiated with the Allies in April. For topographical reasons this was a singularly ambitious task. The border between Austria and Italy, nearly 650 km (400 miles) long, passed through high mountains, which naturally favoured the defence. There were only two areas where the Austro-Hungarian defences might be breached, through the passes to the Trentino to the north, and via the valley of the Isonzo River in the Julian Alps to the east. The Trentino route was ruled out because the passes were in Austrian hands and heavily fortified. The main Italian effort throughout the war was therefore launched across the Isonzo towards Slovenia, Trieste and Istria. This presented huge problems for troop concentration

Italian gun emplacement 1915
The Italians were very short of artillery, especially heavy artillery, at the beginning of the war. Here a 305-mm howitzer has been installed in the Val Dogna on the Carnic front in order to bombard an Austrian fort.

and mobility. The Italian supply lines were always vulnerable to attack from the Trentino, so some forces always had to be diverted in that direction. It also required clearing the vast, windswept Bainsizza plateau to the east, a series of desolate, rocky ridges.

The Central Powers were aware of Italy's negotiations with their enemies, and by the time war was declared the Austrians were ready. With only seven divisions in all, they were heavily outnumbered, but were superior in artillery and machine-guns. In initial skirmishes in June, Italian Alpine troops climbed the 2,300-m (7,500-ft) Monte Nero overnight and swept the few defenders from the summit. This early success created unrealistic expectations. The main advance began on June 23 with an artillery barrage that destroyed the monastery of Sveta Gora, a Slovene national treasure, but not many defence posts. Commander-in-chief Cadorna aimed to take Gorizia (whence half the inhabitants had fled) and the bleak Carso plateau, gateway to Trieste. Casualties in the First Battle of the Isonzo (there would be ten more) were heavy – over 30,000 Italians, 20,000 Austrians. A shortage of front-line doctors meant that many Italian wounded were left unattended, and transport problems caused severe shortages of food and water. Some Italian officers forced their men forward at gunpoint, and both sides threw rocks when ammunition ran out (the Italians had as yet no grenades).

THE ITALIAN FRONT
1915

➤ Italian advance Jun 1915
▢ Territory occupied by Italy Jun 1915
↖ Austrian front line Dec 1915
☙ Main areas of fighting on the Isonzo River
---- Major railway
▢ The Allies (and allied states)
▢ Central Powers (and allied states)

On July 7, with Italian advances minimal, Cadorna called a halt to the offensive. Dismissing 27 generals, he blamed the failure on everyone but himself.

The Second Battle of the Isonzo began on July 18, the main objective being Monte San Michele on the edge of the Carso. This time the artillery barrage was heavier and more effective. Every shell bursting in the limestone terrain discharged a hail of rock fragments more deadly than bullets to soldiers without steel helmets. The Italians gained the summit, but were driven off next day in a counter-attack spearheaded by knife-wielding Bosnians. The Italians retook it on July 25, and were again pushed off. The tactics of the Austrian commander Boroevic were simple: if a position was lost, recapture it immediately.

Fighting on the Carso gradually died away with Trieste still over 30 km (20 miles) distant. A fruitless

The first four battles of the Isonzo
Shots were exchanged all along the front in 1915, but the only serious fighting was on the Isonzo. Estimated Italian casualties were at least 230,000, Austrian about 165,000.

assault on the upper Isonzo continued, but heroism was unavailing against well-entrenched machine-guns. Cadorna was still convinced he could break through, but he needed two months for recovery and reinforcements – one was the young socialist firebrand Mussolini.

The Third Battle of the Isonzo began on October 18 with a three-day artillery barrage. Gorizia was now Cadorna's objective. The Italians reached its suburbs but could not take the town, and the offensive ended at the beginning of November. The Fourth Battle began a week later (November 10) and lasted into December. Italian gains remained insignificant and one regiment mutinied.

High-altitude training
Italian Alpini troops march up a glacier. The Alpini led many of the most daring attacks on the Austro-Hungarian lines as well as arranging the supply of positions high in the mountains.

Italian troops crossing the Isonzo by ferry
The Isonzo front did not simply follow the river. In their initial advance the Italians gained a number of bridgeheads on the east bank, while the Austrians managed to hold on to key defensive positions on the west bank.

~

The war in this theatre was soon concluded with the swift takeover of all the German possessions in the Pacific. The only lengthy operation was the siege of Tsingtao, conducted for the Allies by the Japanese. One potential danger to British interests was the German Far East Squadron, but its commander, Admiral von Spee, chose to sail for the South Atlantic, where his ships were hunted down off the Falkland Islands.

~

SEPTEMBER 2
Japanese land on the Shantung peninsula for attack on Tsingtao

SEPTEMBER 11
Australian force lands at Herbertshöhe in Neu Pommern (New Britain) in the Bismarck Archipelago

SEPTEMBER 22
Arrival of British force at Laoshan Bay to support Japanese attack on Tsingtao

OCTOBER 7
Yap, in the Caroline Islands, occupied by Japanese, who quickly take over the Caroline, Mariana and Marshall Islands

OCTOBER 16
Japanese launch general attack on Tsingtao

NOVEMBER 2
Austrian cruiser *Kaiserin Elizabeth* sunk at Tsingtao

NOVEMBER 7
Surrender of Tsingtao

NOVEMBER 14
Nauru occupied by Australian forces

DECEMBER 1
German squadron succeeds in rounding Cape Horn en route for the Falklands

DECEMBER 14
German armed merchant cruiser *Cormoran* interned at Guam

AUGUST 30
German Samoa occupied by New Zealand forces

SEPTEMBER 7
German squadron under Admiral von Spee cuts British Pacific cable off Fanning Island

SEPTEMBER 17
German New Guinea and surrounding colonies surrender to Australian forces

SEPTEMBER 22
Von Spee attacks Papeete in Tahiti

OCTOBER 16
First New Zealand forces leave for Europe

OCTOBER 17
First Australian forces leave for Europe

NOVEMBER 1
Battle of Coronel in Pacific: von Spee's squadron sinks British ships *Monmouth* and *Good Hope*, with no survivors

NOVEMBER 26–29
Von Spee's ships meet fierce storms off coast of Chile

DECEMBER 8
Battle of Falkland Islands: von Spee's ships caught and destroyed by British squadron; 1,800 men, including von Spee and his two sons, killed

KEY

▨ China and the northern Pacific Aug 30–Dec 14

■ New Guinea and the South Pacific Sept 11–Oct 17

▨ Voyage of Spee's squadron Aug 22–Dec 8

German Possessions in the East

FROM A BRITISH POINT OF VIEW, the German threat in the Far East was essentially a naval one, specifically the possible depredations the East Asiatic Squadron, commanded by Admiral Graf von Spee and based at Tsingtao, might make on maritime trade and troopships. Although Britain and Japan were allied by treaty, Japan was only obliged to assist Britain in the event of an unprovoked attack on its Far Eastern possessions (chiefly Hong Kong). Other countries with interests in the region – including the US, Australia, New

Japanese battery at the siege of Tsingtao
The Japanese success at Tsingtao was a foregone conclusion. They were able to call on 100 siege guns with 1200 shells each and also used aircraft to drop bombs.

Zealand and the Netherlands – also feared Japanese expansionism. However, Britain's naval strength in the Pacific was hardly superior to Germany's, and the German ships were more modern. Australia had just five cruisers (one a battlecruiser) and three destroyers, and New Zealand had only begun to train a navy less than a year earlier. In these

A token presence
Japanese soldiers cast curious glances at the South Wales Borderers arriving to join the force besieging Tsingtao.

circumstances, Britain asked Japan for assistance in taking Germany's main overseas naval base, the port of Tsingtao (Quingdao) on the Shantung peninsula. The Japanese operation was supposed to be strictly limited and Chinese neutrality was not to be infringed. On August 23 Japan declared war on Germany.

The Japanese landed forces in Chinese territory – 130 km (80 miles) north of Tsingtao at Lungkow Bay, where they established a supply base, while simultaneously blockading the coast. The main force landed nearer the objective at Laoshan Bay, but still in Chinese territory. The build-up was slow, aggravated by heavy rain, and the main advance only began on September 23. The Japanese had 60,000 men (including one British and one Indian battalion sent from Tientsin). Meyer-Waldeck, the German commander, having called in every man from out-stations, had fewer than 5,000 men. The heavy guns of the port's fortifications could be trained back to cover the landward approach, but within a month the Germans were running low on ammunition. On November 7 Meyer-Waldeck asked for terms.

MOPPING UP THE ISLANDS

In October the Japanese 1st South Seas Squadron moved into Micronesia, where Germany had several small bases on islands purchased from Spain

The taking of Tsingtao
This lithograph shows the novel tactics employed by the Japanese at Tsingtao. They maintained a shrapnel bombardment at night and moved up their trenches in the dark despite the German searchlights.

in the 1880s. These islands were valuable to Japan not only for strategic reasons, but also for natural resources such as phosphates.

The German naval squadron had left the area in mid-September, when von Spee sailed for the South Atlantic (see page 176), and within the next month the Japanese mopped up all the German bases in the Caroline and Marshall Islands.

The Australians and New Zealanders were dismayed by this unanticipated Japanese expansion, but they had similar goals of their own. The British invited them to help take over Germany's possessions in the South Pacific but, far from committing them to London's authority as requested, they meant to hold on to them. They agreed that longitude 170° E should

constitute the dividing line between Australia's possessions (to the west) and New Zealand's (to the east).

Escorted by Australian ships, 1,400 New Zealanders landed in Samoa, where they met no resistance. The squadron then covered an Australian invasion of German New Guinea, where the German commanders were a captain in the reserves and a police officer, with few men and no guns. On September 17 they surrendered German New Guinea, the Bismarck Archipelago and the Solomon Islands. Some resistance continued in Papua, from German missionaries and a surveying expedition led by a man named Detzner. He was still at large when the war ended. By the time the Australians and New Zealanders had completed their conquest of the southern islands, the Japanese had taken over the islands of Micronesia to the north.

Regime change
The British flag is hoisted in German Samoa on August 30, 1914 after the bloodless takeover of the colony by New Zealand troops.

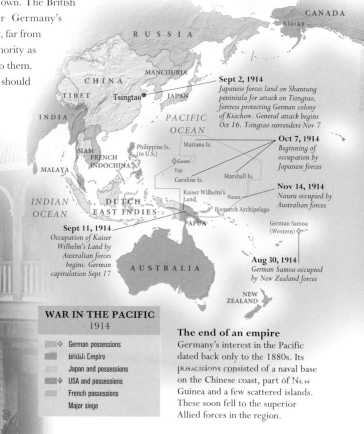

Sept 2, 1914
Japanese forces land on Shantung peninsula for attack on Tsingtao, fortress protecting German colony of Kiachow. General attack begins Oct 16. Tsingtao surrenders Nov 7

Oct 7, 1914
Beginning of occupation by Japanese forces

Nov 14, 1914
Nauru occupied by Australian forces

Sept 11, 1914
Occupation of Kaiser Wilhelm's Land by Australian forces begins. German capitulation Sept 17

Aug 30, 1914
German Samoa occupied by New Zealand forces

WAR IN THE PACIFIC
1914

- German possessions
- British Empire
- Japan and possessions
- USA and possessions
- French possessions
- Major siege

The end of an empire
Germany's interest in the Pacific dated back only to the 1880s. Its possessions consisted of a naval base on the Chinese coast, part of New Guinea and a few scattered islands. These soon fell to the superior Allied forces in the region.

CAMPAIGNS IN AFRICA
AUGUST 1914 – SEPTEMBER 1916

~

Germany had four overseas possessions in Africa: two in East Africa (Togoland and Cameroon), German East Africa and German Southwest Africa. None could be resupplied by sea and all were bordered by colonial territories of their enemies. In spite of this, all the German forces in Africa put up strong resistance to invading Allied forces. In East Africa, the campaign led by Lettow-Vorbeck lasted until the end of the war.

~

1914 AUGUST 6–8
French contingent from Dahomey (Benin) occupies coasts of Togo

1914 AUGUST 15
Raid by 300 Germans on British East Africa threatens Uganda Railway

AUGUST 26
German governor of Togo surrenders as French and British advance on Kamina

SEPTEMBER 25
French take Kousséri in north of Kamerun

SEPTEMBER 27
Kamerun capital Douala surrenders to French and British force

OCTOBER 10
Rebel Boer troops, who have crossed into German Southwest Africa, declare war on Britain; disaffected elements in South Africa rise against government

NOVEMBER 2–5
British landing at Tanga in German East Africa ends in humiliating defeat

DECEMBER 25
South African units land at Walvis Bay

1915 JANUARY 13
South African forces take Swakopmund

1915 JANUARY
Last resistance by rebel Boers crushed by government troops

MARCH 1
Start of British blockade of German East Africa

MAY 20
Windhoek, capital of Southwest Africa, surrenders to South African troops

JUNE 26
Advance from French Equatorial Africa reaches Lomié in Kamerun

JULY 9
Surrender of German forces in Southwest Africa at Tsumeb

SEPTEMBER
End of rainy season. Start of four-pronged advance on Yaounde, summer capital of Kamerun

DECEMBER 26
Two British gunboats, transported overland from Cape Town, start operations on Lake Tanganyika

1916 JANUARY 1
French and British columns reach Yaounde in Kamerun

1916 FEBRUARY 9
British boats secure control of Lake Tanganyika

FEBRUARY 18
Last German garrison in Kamerun, at Mora, surrenders

MARCH 5
British offensive in region of Mt Kilimanjaro. German forces thereafter fight skilful rearguard action under Lettow-Vorbeck

SEPTEMBER 4
Dar es Salaam surrenders to British forces, who go on to capture other coastal ports of German East Africa

SEPTEMBER 19
Belgian forces, having advanced through Rwanda and Burundi, take Tabora on Tanganyika railway

KEY

- West Africa Aug 1914–Feb 1916
- East Africa Aug 1914–Sep 1916
- Southwest Africa Aug 1914–Jul 1915

War in Africa

THE NUMBERS ENGAGED IN COMBAT in Africa were small: Lettow-Vorbeck remarked that a company in Africa corresponded to a division in Europe. There was virtually no artillery, the machine-gun being the heaviest and most potent weapon. More men died of disease than in combat, and supply was a bigger problem than fighting. There were very few roads or railways, and in tsetse-ridden areas especially, where pack animals could not be used, all depended on human porters. More Africans were enlisted as porters than soldiers.

Togoland, a narrow strip between the British Gold Coast and French Dahomey, contained Germany's most important overseas wireless station at the capital, Kamina. French and British troops fought a brisk campaign and a junior officer, Captain Bryant, left in command of the Gold Coast Regiment, took the capital on August 25, and the Germans destroyed the wireless station before surrendering.

The War in Africa
After Germany's defeat, its former African possessions were taken over by Britain, France, Belgium and South Africa under League of Nations mandates.

South African cavalry
The heroes of Southwest Africa, it was said, were the horses; human losses in the campaign were relatively light.

Cameroon (Kamerun) was a different matter, a little-known terrain of great mountains and plateaus, dense jungles and swamps. Most of the development was in the small coastal strip. As elsewhere, the German colony was surrounded by enemies. Its forces in 1915 peaked at about 5,000, including 1,500 Europeans. Allied forces, drawn mainly from West Africa, eventually amounted to nearly 25,000, but poor planning and lack of

WAR IN AFRICA
1914–1916

- British Empire
- French possessions
- German possessions
- Belgian possessions
- Italy and possessions
- Portugal and possessions
- Ottoman Empire
- Area of conflict

PORTUGAL SPAIN ITALY GREECE
MOROCCO TUNISIA OTTOMAN EMPIRE PERSIA
RIO DE ORO ALGERIA LIBYA EGYPT ARABIAN PENINSULA
FRENCH WEST AFRICA FRENCH EQUATORIAL AFRICA ANGLO-EGYPTIAN SUDAN ERITREA FR. SOMALILAND BR. SOMALILAND
PORT. GUINEA SIERRA LEONE LIBERIA GOLD COAST TOGO Kamina NIGERIA Douala CAMEROON RIO MUNI (to Spain) FRENCH CONGO BELGIAN CONGO ABYSSINIA IT SOMALILAND BRITISH EAST AFRICA GERMAN EAST AFRICA Dar es Salaam INDIAN OCEAN
ANGOLA N. RHODESIA PORTUGUESE EAST AFRICA
GERMAN SOUTHWEST AFRICA Windhoek S. RHODESIA BECHUANALAND MADAGASCAR
ATLANTIC OCEAN UNION OF SOUTH AFRICA

Aug 6–8, 1914
French and British forces invade. Germans surrender on Aug 26

Sept 1914
Allies secure capital Douala. A protracted campaign follows. Allies' converging offensives lead to eventual German capitulation, Feb 18, 1916

Aug 1914
German forces withdraw to capital, Windhoek. South African forces capture Windhoek May 20, 1915, and Germans surrender July 9

1914–18
A protracted campaign. German forces extend campaign to Portuguese East Africa

intelligence hindered their progress. In late August, British troops from Nigeria crossed the border in several places, but were thrown back. The only successful offensive was against the colony's capital and main port, Douala, which fell to French Senegalese troops on September 27.

Tropical rains and skilful defence combined to hold up any significant Allied advance until late in 1915, when they finally pushed into the central region, forcing many Germans to seek refuge in Spanish territory. Even so, the last German stronghold, at Mora in the north, did not surrender until February 1916.

The conquest of Southwest Africa (Namibia), a vast but sparsely inhabited country, was undertaken largely by white South African (and Rhodesian) troops. They numbered about 70,000, but included many Afrikaners, not regular soldiers, who were anti-British, having fought in the Boer (South African) War (1899–1902). About 11,000 rebelled, but a much greater number remained loyal and the "Boer Rebellion" disintegrated by January 1915.

The South Africans invaded from the sea and overland, the main objective being the capital, Windhoek. In one rapid advance 3,000 men traversed 400 km (250 miles) of the Kalahari Desert in two weeks. Following the German abandonment of the south, forces under the command of General Botha, South Africa's prime minister, took

Indian troops lying dead at Tanga
The disastrous British landing at Tanga in German East Africa in November 1914 resulted in over 800 casualties.

Windhoek on May 20, 1915. Facing insuperable odds, the Germans continued to resist in the north until July 9, when they surrendered to Botha.

GERMAN EAST AFRICA

The greatest of the colonial "side-shows" was East Africa. It lasted as long as the war in Europe. The British had many more troops in the region, eventually topping 100,000 men, mainly from Africa and India. They also commanded the sea. The Germans had 15,000 at most, predominantly local African askaris, but they did have a master of bush warfare in General Lettow-Vorbeck.

The British gained control of Lake Victoria and Lake Tanganyika, but an ill-organized expeditionary force landing at the coastal port of Tanga was repulsed. Thereafter, commitments elsewhere meant that no

PAUL VON LETTOW-VORBECK

~

GENERAL LETTOW-VORBECK (1870–1964) was one of the most remarkable soldiers of the First World War. Appointed military commander of German East Africa in January 1914, he remained undefeated throughout the war by a British army that was ten times the size of his force of Germans and askaris. Lettow-Vorbeck was a master of bush warfare. He knew he could not take on the enemy in a major engagement, and made expert use of mountains, bush and forest to elude his pursuers. His tactics were often very cunning: he positioned his men to lure mounted enemy troops into tsetse-ridden areas, where their horses died. After his victory at Tanga in November 1914 he withdrew inland and launched frequent lightning attacks on the forces sent after him. In late 1917 he led his troops into Portuguese East Africa, from where they continued to make raids against the enemy Hearing belatedly of the armistice while in Rhodesia, he surrendered on November 25. Fêted as a national hero in Germany, he also won the admiration of his adversaries. After the war, he led the Freikorps that put down the Spartacists in Hamburg.

serious effort was made to dislodge the Germans until early 1916, when, the war in Southwest Africa having ended, the South African General Smuts took command. Somewhat out of his depth in the different conditions of East Africa, Smuts was anxious to avoid unnecessary slaughter, especially of his South Africans. In major fighting in the region of Kilimanjaro in 1916, Smuts was unable to entrap the highly mobile German troops. The Germans retreated south, again avoiding encirclement, but lost more men in a fierce battle fought in heavy rain in December. The number of fit men who remained under Lettow-Vorbeck's command was down to 8,400, and food was a major problem.

The key battles of 1917 were fought around Kilwa and Lindi near the coast. German casualties, though much smaller, were relatively more serious. Having moved into Portuguese East Africa, Lettow-Vorbeck's capture of Namakura in July brought vital booty – food, rifles, ammunition and ten machine-guns. He moved north and west, entering Northern Rhodesia in November 1918. On November 12, the last battle of the war was fought between Lettow-Vorbeck's askaris and 750 men of the King's African Rifles. Hearing of the armistice the following day, Lettow-Vorbeck finally surrendered formally on November 25.

Sabotage
The Central Railway, which ran from Dar es Salaam to Lake Tanganyika, was destroyed by the Germans as they retreated south in 1916 pursued by British forces.

THE BRITISH AND FRENCH EMPIRES AT WAR

LARGE NUMBERS OF NON-EUROPEANS from the British and French empires fought on the battlefields of Europe in 1914–18. The two empires had been created and maintained by British and French troops; now the relationship was reversed with imperial forces helping to sustain the mother countries.

The French army in 1914 consisted administratively of three separate organizations: the Metropolitan Army, l'Armée d'Afrique and La Coloniale (restricted to French overseas citizens and subjects from post-1789 colonies not in North Africa). The colonial armies raised both complete divisions and smaller units for incorporation within the Metropolitan Army. Over 200,000 Algerians, Moroccans and Tunisians served in Europe. From the start of the war Germans found themselves faced by Zouave infantry and spahi cavalrymen from North Africa and Tirailleurs Sénégalais (Senegalese Riflemen) from West Africa. There were also significant contributions from Madagascar and Indo-China.

Britain's declaration of war was binding on all parts of the Empire. The dominions of Australia, Canada and New Zealand associated themselves willingly with Britain's cause, and saw themselves, as overseas British, bound to come to the defence of the mother country. However, on the Western Front both the Canadians and Australians insisted their formations were held in national corps rather than as parts of the British Army. They came to be regarded as imperial shock troops and their contribution to the war was crucial in creating a new independent sense of nationhood. The case of South Africa was somewhat different. With a European male population of military age of 244,000, it raised perhaps three divisions, but the costs of its operations, other than in German Southwest Africa, were borne by Britain. It sent troops to East Africa and maintained an infantry brigade on the Western Front.

India began the war with a long-service professional army of some 241,000 men. The Indian Army fought on the Western Front (in 1914–15) and in the Middle East and East Africa. It was to take until 1917 before the army was re-organized in a way that permitted major expansion. Such was its growth that in November 1918, when 548,311 men served in the Indian Army, India had become the imperial strategic reserve. Had the war continued into 1919, India was to have assumed responsibility for the entire Middle East and Salonika.

The contribution the colonies made to the war was immense, not least in terms of labour, whether for the military or in industry. The war brought ideas of national self-determination to subject peoples. French colonial troops and labour in France enjoyed the privilege of citizenship. However, peace saw a return to pre-war colonial attitudes.

Zouave club
This hand-carved trench club is decorated with the head of a Zouave, a soldier of the crack North African infantry force founded in 1834.

West African troops
Six battalions of Tirailleurs Sénégalais were shipped to France to fight in the opening weeks of the war. In all 163,000 served on the Western Front. Some 30,000 of them died.

Spahi uniform
The main items were a short red jacket, Turkish-style trousers, a large cape and a turban wound round a *chechia* (a small fez).

SPAHI LEATHER BAG

BOOTS
soft inner boot

normal shoe

Algerian spahis
In the first months of the war detachments of spahi cavalry were a common sight on the roads of northern France. Later, like other cavalrymen, they would fight as infantry in the trenches.

Gurkhas in France
In the course of the war 100,000 Gurkhas enlisted in the Indian Army. Gurkha regiments fought on the Western Front and in Egypt, Gallipoli, Mesopotamia, Palestine and Salonika.

Join the A·I·F
This is Serious!
ENLIST NOW

Join the AIF
Recruiting posters for the AIF (Australian Imperial Force) gave the impression that volunteers would be joining their mates in an exciting adventure on the other side of the world.

Send-off from Melbourne
The first troopship for Europe sailed on October 17, 1914. Australia, with a population of 2,300,000 males of military age, recruited 416,809 men.

Annamites in French shell factory
Some 50,000 Annamites (Vietnamese) and 13,000 Chinese from French Indo-China worked in France's munitions factories and in the army's labour corps.

Laying railway track
Indian labourers worked with the Indian Army in Mesopotamia and other parts of the Middle East. They also worked on the Western Front, as did labourers from China, South Africa, Egypt, the West Indies, Malta, Mauritius, the Seychelles and Fiji.

WAR AND THE RISE OF THE STATE

1915

~

AS IT BECAME APPARENT THAT THE WAR WAS GOING TO
LAST FAR LONGER THAN ORIGINALLY ANTICIPATED, THE
GOVERNMENTS OF ALL THE BELLIGERENT STATES
INCREASED THEIR CONTROL OVER MUNITIONS AND
OTHER KEY INDUSTRIES. THEY ALSO, TO VARYING
DEGREES, ADOPTED POLICIES AIMED AT LOOKING AFTER
THE WELFARE OF THE PEOPLE REQUIRED TO WORK
IN THESE INDUSTRIES AND SUPPORT THE WAR EFFORT IN
GENERAL. WITH THE INTRODUCTION OF MANY NEW
REGULATIONS, THE STATE BEGAN TO INTERVENE IN
PEOPLE'S LIVES AS IT HAD NEVER DONE BEFORE.

~

Shell factory
As the need for munitions became more urgent,
the British government took direct control of their
production, employing thousands of women in
dangerous jobs such as filling shells with explosive.

FACING NEW REALITIES

AT THE END OF 1914 ALL THE COMBATANT NATIONS STILL EXPECTED VICTORY IN
THE NOT TOO DISTANT FUTURE. THE WINTER WOULD OBVIOUSLY LIMIT IMMEDIATE
OPERATIONS, BUT IT WAS GENERALLY BELIEVED THAT THE MOMENTUM OF WAR
WOULD BE REGAINED IN THE SPRING IF THE PRODUCTION OF SUFFICIENT SUPPLIES
OF WEAPONS AND AMMUNITION COULD BE ORGANIZED.

THE DEMAND FOR MUNITIONS had outstripped supply very early in the war: the Prussian War Ministry's stock of artillery shells, for example, had virtually run out after six weeks. It was apparent to many that if the vast material requirements of the war were to be met, governments – which still exercised few bureaucratic controls outside their finance and military departments – would have to undergo fundamental change. They would not only have to assume direct control of industry but would also have to actively promote the welfare of their citizens – a task that was, eventually, to prove impossible for Russia and the Central Powers. Industry could not function, and the armies could not be supplied with manpower and material,

unless the civilian population was kept supplied with adequate food, heating and light. To this end, the British and French governments in particular adopted an interventionist approach as it became apparent that the war was not going to end quickly.

In France, which – like Germany – faced a massive shortage of shells almost immediately, the government took steps to ensure that as many private companies as possible were involved in the manufacture of munitions. Almost 2.5 million men were conscripted during the first weeks of the war but, by the end of 1915, 500,000 had been sent back to work in the factories that were under military jurisdiction. In Britain, where the Defence of the Realm Act (DORA) was introduced in 1914 to give the government powers to direct the

economy and various aspects of public life, little was done initially to ensure an adequate supply of munitions. It was only when the scale of the British army's munitions shortages became apparent, in the spring of 1915, that steps were taken by the government to boost the production of munitions, including the establishment of national factories.

Conscription was not introduced in Britain until May 1916. The success, however, of efforts in 1915 to recruit a mass volunteer army – 2.6 million men by the end of the year – meant that here, as in France, the government had to take an active role in ensuring that industrial and agricultural production continued. Women were encouraged in both countries, and in all the other belligerent states, to undertake the work formerly done by men.

"People out here seem to think that the war is going to be quite short. Why, I don't know; personally, I see nothing to prevent it going on forever."

BRITISH CAPTAIN, COLWYN PHILLIPS,
WRITING TO HIS MOTHER ON MARCH 12, 1915 FROM THE YPRES SALIENT

CHOICES FACING GERMANY

Over the winter of 1914–15 the combatants in the war not only had to consider how best to increase their production of munitions; they also had to reconsider their military strategy. Arguably Germany faced greater dilemmas than any other power. In attempting to implement the Schlieffen Plan, it had stood on the defensive in the east while it pursued victory against the French in the west. It had not, however, been able to stay on the defensive in the east once Russia had completed its initial mobilization and prepared to launch offensives into the Carpathians and East Prussia. Germany was now faced with the question of whether it should strengthen its forces in the east, so reducing the likelihood of victory in the west.

Despite the failure of the Schlieffen Plan, Falkenhayn, the German chief of staff, still believed at the beginning of 1915 that victory had to be won in the west. He was unconvinced by the argument being voiced by Hindenburg and Ludendorff – heroes of the German victory over the Russians at Tannenberg in East Prussia in August the previous year – that Germany's interests were now best served by standing on the defensive in the west and taking offensive action in the east. In his view, Russia would always trade space for time and the security of its troops. By ordering the withdrawal of its armies, it could induce the Germans to advance across a country whose sheer size and primitive communications systems, plus the lack of any major objective in front of which the

German cavalry
On the relatively fluid Eastern Front the cavalry was able to play a more significant role than on the Western Front where the trench system signified deadlock.

Russians might be trapped and annihilated, would make victory difficult to achieve. Falkenhayn, however, could not ignore the fact that Hindenburg and Ludendorff had the ear of the kaiser.

Falkenhayn could also not ignore the weakness of Austria-Hungary – a weakness that caused the Germans to view their ally with increasing contempt. The losses of 1914 among the Austrian and Hungarian troops and long service elements of the Imperial Army had been particularly serious. The halting of the Russian offensive against Silesia and the partial German success at Lodz forestalled any immediate move by Russia against Austria-Hungary. At a time, however, when Austria-Hungary could not confront Russia with any real confidence, it also faced the need to continue the war against Serbia, which in 1914 had driven out, and so humiliated, the Austro-Hungarian armies that had invaded it. Austria-Hungary's problems were to be further increased by the Italian declaration of war in May 1915.

THE PROBLEMS FACING RUSSIA

Russia also faced problems in 1915, problems that were partly caused by an increase in the number of fronts on which it had to fight. Turkey's entry into the war on October 29, 1914 presented Russia with a further front in the Caucasus. This, combined with the losses incurred in the opening months of the war, meant that throughout 1915 Russia could not face Austria-Hungary and Germany with more than an equal number of troops along the 960-km (600-mile) Eastern Front.

The sheer length of this front, stretching from Memel on the Baltic coast to Czernowitz just east of the Carpathians, coupled with insufficient manpower, meant that neither the Austro-Germans nor the Russians were able to concentrate along it in great numbers. Lacking the labour necessary to build complicated trench systems, both sides focused on launching offensives rather than strengthening defensive positions.

From December 1914, the war in the East became comparatively fluid. Initially the Russians pushed back the Austro-Hungarians in the Carpathians, in preparation for an attack on Hungary. Austro-Hungarian and German forces, however, then launched an offensive in May that succeeded in driving the Russians from Galicia by the end of June and from Poland by September.

The Russians were finally able to bring the onslaught to a halt only after they had suffered some two million casualties. The Central Powers had not driven Russia out of the war, but they had exposed many of its army's weaknesses. In addition to huge shortages of basic equipment, weapons and shells – shortages that were to be eased by considerable increases in war production in the summer of 1915 – the Russian army continued to be dogged by the perennial problems of political appointments and appalling administration. There was also a chronic shortage of good-quality junior officers and a lack of proper training at all levels, problems whose seriousness many senior officers failed to appreciate throughout 1915.

Marching to position
Hungarian soldiers march to their positions on the Dniester River, near Lemberg, during the successful Austro-German offensive of May–September 1915, in which the Russians were driven out of Galicia and Poland.

THE WEST ENTRENCHED

It was a very different story on the Western Front, which was viewed by both France and Britain as the most important theatre of operations, where the outcome of the war would in all probability be decided. With most of Belgium and a large area of northern France in German possession, the French – from whom the British took their lead in 1914–15 – were intent on clearing national territory. This meant attempting to undertake offensive action against an enemy which, after November 1914, had the pick of the ground and was able to develop a strong defensive system of trenches.

Trench systems of a rudimentary nature had been constructed in the first months of the war. Then, as it became apparent that there would be no immediate victory for either side, both set about constructing more elaborate systems – generally between 90 and 360 m (100 and 400 yds) apart – the position of which was barely to change for three years. Indeed, the Germans were to add "a tier a year", thus ensuring that their front line could not be broken in a single offensive. What were intended by the Allied strategists to be decisive battles turned into operations in which tens of thousands – sometimes hundreds of thousands – of men were killed for very little gain. In 1915 the Allies launched several campaigns in Champagne and Artois, none of which achieved their objectives.

One of the main reasons for the stalemate that developed on the Western Front was the superiority of defensive firepower – in the form of long-range artillery, accurate rifles and machine-guns. Another was the superiority of strategic mobility over tactical movement: any breach in the front could always be sealed by a defence that was able to move formations by rail to the threatened sector more quickly than an attacker under fire could move on foot or horseback across the battlefield. Adding to the difficulties of the attacking army was the inadequacy of communication systems: effective command and control of operations on the front

"...a thousand complexities of thought and sentiment prevented men, on both sides, from breaking the net of fate in which they were entangled, and revolting against that mutual, unceasing massacre..."

BRITISH FRONT-LINE CORRESPONDENT, PHILLIP GIBBS,
IN HIS BOOK, *REALITIES OF WAR*

French troops in Artois
Throughout 1915 the French struggled to break through the German lines in Artois. They launched and the British launched major offensives in both the spring and autumn of 1915, but the advances they made were negligible.

line would only become possible with the miniaturization of the radio. In the First World War most communication was through field telephones whose connecting wires were constantly being destroyed by artillery bombardments.

These military explanations, however, do not in themselves make the three-year deadlock totally understandable. The nations warring on the Western Front were only able to fight on,

increasingly determined to fight to the finish to justify the losses already incurred, because the vast majority of troops were prepared to take part in the continuing slaughter.

In his book, *Realities of War*, the British front-line correspondent Phillip Gibbs describes the situation confronting the men in the trenches. They were in "a devil's trap from which there was no escape". This trap encompassed "old tradition, obedience to

the laws of war, or to the caste which ruled them, all the moral and spiritual propaganda handed out by pastors, newspapers, generals, staff officers, old men at home, exalted women, female furies, a deep and simple love for England, and Germany...".

On both sides, the societies involved had a social cohesion that meant they simply refused to collapse under the strain of a war that should by rights have destroyed them.

Deadlock in the West

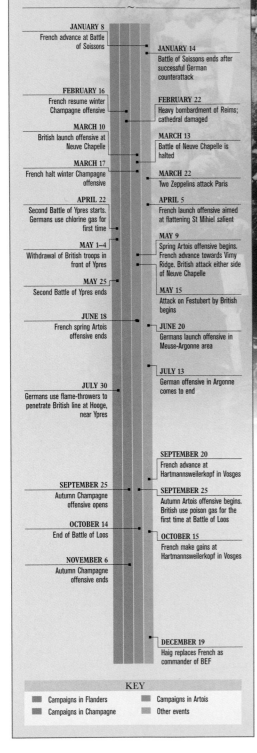

German trench, winter 1914–15
German trenches at this time were very basic compared with those developed later in the war, but the French generally found it impossible to break through them.

O N DECEMBER 10, 1914 the French Tenth Army conducted the first of a series of attacks in Artois, primarily directed against Vimy Ridge. Ten days later, at the opposite end of the bulge in the front line between Flanders and Verdun (see map page 140–41), the Fourth Army attacked along a 32-km (20-mile) front to the east of Reims, in Champagne. Neither operation was a success.

WINTER CAMPAIGNS

In Artois, in atrocious weather and thick mud, a few villages changed hands at the cost of some 8,000 French casualties. In Champagne, exhaustion and the same bad weather led to the offensive being broken off in the first week of January. It was resumed again on February 16, but by the time it came to a halt on March 17, the French had secured the forward German defence lines in just one sector, around "Hill 180". They had done so at the enormous cost of 240,000 casualties.

There was no disguising the extent of the French strategic failure in Artois and Champagne, which largely stemmed from the lack of heavy artillery necessary to destroy the forward German defensive positions. Even in the midst of failure, however, the French and British had to prepare for the next phase of operations. It was agreed that the British would take over the French sector in front of Ypres, so freeing the French for offensive action elsewhere. A combined spring offensive would then be mounted in Artois – the British against the German positions on Aubers Ridge and the French against those on Vimy Ridge. There would also be a full-scale French offensive in Champagne.

The plan soon had to be revised as it became clear that the British would not be able to relieve the French at Ypres because of a shortage of troops. This, coupled with the defeats suffered by the French in December and January, meant that the French could not undertake a spring

Artois offensive. The British then proposed an attack at the ruined village of Neuve Chapelle in Artois as a demonstration of resolve and to complement the French effort in Champagne.

BATTLE OF NEUVE CHAPELLE

The British launched their attack at 7:00 am on March 10 with the immediate objective of taking the village of Aubers less than 1.5 km (1 mile) away. Given artillery and ammunition shortages, plus the certainty of major operations later in the year, the logic behind an unsupported attack at Neuve Chapelle was questionable. It was, however, these same shortages that mainly accounted for whatever success was achieved. Unable to mount a prolonged preliminary bombardment, the artillery opted for a 35-minute hurricane barrage against a very narrow sector, some 3,600 m (4,000 yds) long, in which the British and Indian troops together outnumbered the opposing German forces by 5 to 1.

As a result of careful rehearsals and detailed planning, the British attack achieved total surprise. Neuve Chapelle was secured in the first hour and a breach was created in the German line. What happened next, however, was an illustration of

some of the problems presented by trench warfare. Losses incurred in the assault phase prevented the proper consolidation of gains, and the break-through sector, some 1,800 m (2,000 yds) wide and up to 1,080 m (1,200 yds) deep, was too narrow to provide any real chance of opening and maintaining a breach. The British also failed to feed reserves into the battle quickly enough to prevent the defence from reconstituting the front. This failure was due to inadequate communications and a lack of proper co-ordination at corps level, and provided the German defence with some five hours respite at a time of maximum vulnerability.

Though the British were able to hold off a German counterattack, the attempt to resume the offensive and drive on to Aubers Ridge was abandoned after three days, on March 13. A total of 7,000 British and 4,200 Indian soldiers had been killed or wounded. The Germans had suffered an equal number of casualties.

PLANS FOR A MAY OFFENSIVE

On March 29, at Chantilly, British and French commanders agreed to revive the plan that had been abandoned during the winter – and launch an

attack on the Aubers and Vimy ridges in May. What the Allies did not foresee at this stage was the launch in April of the only major German offensive on the Western Front in 1915 – at Ypres.

SECOND BATTLE OF YPRES

On the evening of April 22, the German Fourth Army launched an offensive on the French sector of the Allied positions around the Ypres salient with the aid of a new weapon: poisonous gas. After a short but intense bombardment in which heavy siege artillery was used, two German corps attacked behind clouds of chlorine gas released from 5,730 cylinders. With no protection against the gas, the two French divisions in the line retreated rapidly, leaving an 8-km (5-mile) gap to the left of the Canadian First Division's position. By nightfall the Germans had taken the villages of Langemarck and Pilckem. They did not, however, have sufficient reserves. Consequently, with their infantry wary of following behind their gas too closely, the Germans were unable to exploit what was to prove to be their best chance of breaking open the Allied front in the West in 1915.

CHRISTMAS TRUCE OF 1914

~

FREEZING RAIN DURING November and December 1914 left both sides struggling with flooded trenches and appalling conditions. This led to something of a "live-and-let-live" arrangement along much of the northern sector of the Western Front, especially between the British and German troops. December 24 brought a frost. The ground hardened and the smell of decomposing flesh abated. The Germans placed lighted Christmas trees along their trenches and soldiers on both sides sung Christmas carols to each other in comradely greeting. Next morning a fog lifted to reveal frost-covered trees in brilliant sunlight. All firing stopped and there was shouting between trenches, followed by soldiers moving into No Man's Land. Gifts were exchanged, and both sides took the opportunity to bury their dead.

Allied commanders insisted that such an event should never recur. In subsequent years there were orders to shoot anyone attempting to fraternize with the enemy.

Royal gift
For Christmas 1914, some 427,000 British forces received a brass box containing tobacco, or writing materials and sweets. The scheme, funded by public donation, was the idea of Princess Mary, whose photograph was also enclosed.

Winners' cup
Several football matches took place between German and British troops during the truce. This beer mug is believed to have been awarded by German troops to a winning English side.

Friends for a day
German and British troops met in No Man's Land, shook hands and exchanged gifts of chocolate, tobacco and cigarettes, their hostility temporarily forgotten.

Collecting the dead
The French did not only suffer huge losses in Artois and Champagne. They also incurred some 65,000 casualties in their unsuccessful attempt in April to eliminate the St Mihiel salient, and between June 20 and July 13 they suffered a further 32,000 casualties in the Argonne sector.

SPRING OFFENSIVES IN ARTOIS

The German effort at Ypres, despite its considerable initial success, failed largely because Falkenhayn's main aim at this time was to cloak the redeployment of forces to the east. To that end, he denied the German Fourth Army the necessary reserves. The Allied Artois offensives in the spring were also to fail, with the French effort falling between an attempt to break open the front and the more modest aim of achieving tactical gains across a restricted sector.

FRENCH ADVANCE TO VIMY RIDGE

The French Tenth Army opened its offensive with a six-day artillery bombardment involving over 1,200 guns. Then, on May 9, troops began to advance towards Vimy Ridge. Those who survived the German machine-gun fire succeeded in advancing over 5 km (3 miles) in just 90 minutes, breaking open the German front and reaching the villages of Vimy and Givenchy. As at Neuve Chapelle, this initial success was due to very detailed planning. But again, as at Neuve Chapelle, French gains, across a 7-km (4-mile) stretch of the front, were too narrowly concentrated, and losses too heavy, for effective exploitation to be possible. On the following day the French positions on Vimy Ridge were eliminated by counterattacks.

BRITISH OFFENSIVES

As part of their attempt to take Aubers Ridge, the British launched an attack either side of Neuve Chapelle on May 9. They had only enough shells to maintain a preliminary bombardment for 40 minutes – and few of the shells were high-explosive. Consequently, little damage was inflicted on the German defences, and the British and Indian forces became easy targets for the German machine-guns. They had suffered 11,000 casualties by the time their attack was abandoned the next day.

Between May 15 and 27 the British undertook a second, and very different, offensive at Festubert. This time there was a 60-hour preliminary bombardment to wear down German manpower.

By April 24 the British and Canadians had reconstituted the defence and had improvised protection against gas, but they were unable to prevent the Germans from gaining St Julien and Gravenstafel. In a series of counterattacks that followed, the Allied forces failed to recover any lost ground. They had wholly inadequate artillery support and were completely overwhelmed by concentrated German machine-gun and artillery fire.

ALLIED WITHDRAWAL

From this point the Allies faced an impossible choice at Ypres. If Allied artillery was kept around and to the west of Ypres, it could not properly support the infantry, but if it was moved forward it would be completely dominated by a much superior enemy. Withdrawal was inevitable, though political considerations meant that Ypres and Belgian territory could not be totally abandoned.

The withdrawal began on May 1. The next day, a German gas-supported attack was halted for the first time and, by the 4th, the British Second Army's withdrawal to a new main line of resistance was completed. On this line the Germans attacked the Frezenberg Ridge on May 8–9, and the Bellewarde Ridge on the 24th and 25th. Mutual exhaustion then ensured that the battle was allowed to die. The Allies had suffered 58,000 casualties, the Germans 38,000.

Only on the first day of the attack had the Germans had any real chance of strategic success. Subsequently, they had discovered that, though gas could be an effective weapon, there was always the danger of it being blown back by the wind over their own, often unprotected, infantry. However, while the Germans had failed to take Ypres, they had succeeded in taking all the high ground and all but surrounding the town. The British were left holding Ypres but in a position of very considerable military disadvantage.

> "The horrible part of it is the slow lingering death of those who are gassed. I saw some hundred poor fellows laid out in the open … slowly drowning with water in their lungs …"

GENERAL CHARTERIS, WRITING IN HIS DIARY ON APRIL 28, SIX DAYS AFTER THE FIRST GAS ATTACK AT YPRES

GAS ATTACKS

THE FIRST USE OF POISON GAS was at Ypres on April 22, 1915. The Germans released chlorine from canisters and relied on the wind to blow gas clouds to the enemy position. After this, both sides began to use different types of gas, including phosgene, an insidious weapon that had little immediate effect but struck soldiers down 24 hours later. Both gases caused a painful death over a number of days by asphyxiation. The gas that caused the greatest number of casualties was mustard gas. It had the effect of rotting the body both inside and out, so that the skin blistered and the mucous membrane was stripped off the bronchial tubes. The pain was almost unendurable and could last for up to five weeks. It was hard to counteract and victims who survived were left scarred for life.

The first improvised protection used by the Allies at Ypres consisted simply of water- or urine-soaked handkerchiefs and towels. Within three days, cotton pads dipped in bicarbonate of soda had been rushed to the front. Later in 1915 block gauze pads soaked in hyposulphite solution, with an extra flap to cover the eyes and tapes to tie round the head, were used. The British and French went on to develop more elaborate forms of protection. From late 1917 the box respirator, which used charcoal or antidote chemicals to neutralize the gas agents, became standard British issue. The antidotes were only effective for 30 minutes, however, at which point the respirator had to be changed – a potentially fatal procedure.

GAS ALARM RATTLE

Gas masks
Early gas protection for British and French troops consisted simply of goggles and a gauze pad. Next came flannel hoods impregnated with phenol, and incorporating mica eye-pieces. Later masks included a rubber-tipped metal tube that was held between the teeth for exhalation. The Germans quickly developed a mask that had a cylindrical screw-fitted filter, still in use in 1917.

Goggles

EARLY FRENCH GAS MASK AND GOGGLES, 1915

Cotton wadding mask

EARLY BRITISH "HYPO" GAS HELMET, 1915

GERMAN M1915 GAS MASK, 1917

FRENCH M2 GAS MASK, 1916

Gas alert
At the first sign of gas, whistles or rattles would be sounded. Soldiers, such as these French troops, would have to find and fit their gas masks as quickly as possible.

German gas shells
Gas shells, first used by both sides in 1916, contained liquid gas, which evaporated on impact. They were a more effective way of delivering gas to enemy lines than relying on the wind.

Primitive protection
Cameronians (Scottish Rifles) in 1915 stand ready for action, wearing early gas masks. These consisted simply of goggles and gauze and provided little protection against chlorine and phosgene.

TRENCH WEAPONRY

~

TRENCHES CREATED A NEW, largely unanticipated, demand from all armies for weapons with which to fight at very short range. The result was the revival of weapons such as fire and grenades. Fire – created by igniting petrol spray with an incendiary bomb – was first used in October 1914, in the Argonne-Meuse sector. A flamethrower was used for the first time on February 26, 1915 against French positions outside Verdun. The first concerted use of flamethrowers was on July 30, 1915. A total of six were employed against the British at Hooge in the Ypres salient, at a point where the trenches were less than 4.5 m (5 yds) apart. Even at such close range, most losses were incurred when the infantry emerged from cover to be attacked by the waiting Germans, rather than by the flames themselves.

In August 1914 only the Germans possessed mortars: a total of 160. During 1915, however, the production and use of many different types of mortar expanded rapidly on both sides. In the first quarter, British factories produced 75 mortars and 8,000 shells; in the last quarter, 524 mortars and 180,000 shells. By July 1916 British infantry divisions had three batteries of light mortars and three of medium mortars, each consisting of four weapons. Single batteries of heavy mortars came later. By 1918 the British had 3,022 mortars on the Western Front.

By spring 1916 the British standard weapon was the light 3-in (7.5-cm) Stokes mortar, which could fire 30 rounds a minute, but initially was employed only to fire smoke rounds. In May 1916 the British introduced a medium mortar, which fired a 132-kg (60-lb) projectile from

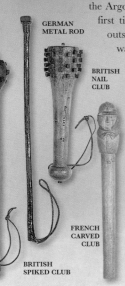

GERMAN
METAL ROD

BRITISH
NAIL
CLUB

FRENCH
CARVED
CLUB

BRITISH
SPIKED CLUB

Trench clubs

Some of the weapons used in hand-to-hand fighting in the trenches were almost medieval in appearance. Clubs, many of which were home-made, proved especially useful for night trench raids and patrols.

German 76-mm minenwerfer

The standard German trench mortars were known as *minenwerfers* (bomb-throwers). They came in three sizes, this 76-mm gun being the smallest. By 1917 every German infantry battalion had four of these light mortars. *Minenwerfer* required large teams to move them: six men for the 76-mm, 21 men for the huge 26-cm version.

Shell loaded into barrel end. Barrel rifled to increase range and velocity

Recoil chambers

Elevation gauge

Fired by pull lanyard

Elevation wheel

Detachable wheels for transport. These were removed before firing

Base plate for stable firing platform

HIGH EXPLOSIVE 76-MM
MINENWERFER SHELL

prepared positions within 140 m (150 yds) of the enemy line. The British heavy mortar, introduced in late 1916, fired a 68-kg (150-lb) projectile to a maximum range of 915 m (1,000 yds). It had to be fired from 7.5 m (25 ft) below the surface, and could gouge out a trench to about the same depth. The German equivalent was a 90-kg (200-lb) version with a range of 550 m (600 yds).

Though used extensively by the Allies during the Russo-Japanese War of 1904–05, the grenade – a hand-thrown bomb detonated by impact or a timed fuse – was only widely issued to German forces in 1914. The British had almost none until spring 1915, and their first Mills Mark II grenades often exploded in the hand of the thrower. It was not until 1916, with the Mark III, that such accidents were reduced to one in 20,000. A total of 75,000,000 grenades were manufactured in Britain, and a discharger cup was devised so they could be fired from a rifle, thus increasing their range. Grenades became so important that orders for their supply were given priority over those for rifle ammunition.

Germans practising the use of flamethrowers

In 1915 flamethrowers came with inflammable liquid sufficient for two minutes' action over a maximum distance of 18 m (20 yards). Most front-line positions, however, were further apart than this, so making it impossible to use the flamethrowers effectively.

FRENCH "HAIRBRUSH"
GRENADE, 1915

BRITISH MK III
PERCUSSION
GRENADE, 1915

Early percussion and improvised grenades

Many early percussion grenades were fitted with streamers, a parachute or a propeller to ensure that they would fall head-first and detonate on hitting the ground. Hand-made grenades, like the French example shown here, had to be ignited before throwing.

FRENCH P2
GRENADE, 1914

Mortar shells

Mortars were used to deliver high explosive, shrapnel, smoke and gas. The larger shells were easy to spot as they were lobbed over on a high trajectory. They could be dodged, but their huge explosive power still sapped morale.

GERMAN 21-CM TRENCH MORTAR SHELL

BRITISH 3-IN STOKES MORTAR SHELL

Shrapnel grenade

Hollow-tailed grenade is fitted onto firing peg

Tail fins

Elevation scale

Firing peg

Traverse scale

Base plate for stable firing platform

High explosive grenade

Smoke grenade

Loading a 17-cm *minenwerfer*
High explosive shells weighed 49.5 kg (109 lb) and a gun crew could fire 30–35 of these per hour. With the lighter gas shells they could manage a rate of 40–45 per hour.

German grenade-thrower

The *granatenwerfer* was a simple trench weapon issued in large numbers to the infantry. The grenade had a small propellant charge in its hollow tail. This was ignited by a pin in the firing peg.

GERMAN ROUND GRENADE WITH CARRY CLIP, 1915

FRANCO-ITALIAN BESOZZI, 1915

BRITISH HALES RIFLE GRENADE, 1915

Fragmentation grenades

The Allies favoured pineapple-shaped grenades intended to explode into the maximum amount of shrapnel. The chief problem with all designs was the fuse. The Besozzi, for example, had a crude phosphorus-tipped fuse that was struck like a match. The British settled on the Mills with its lever that had to be held firmly against the grenade until on release it ignited the 5-second fuse.

FRENCH F1 OFFENSIVE GRENADE, 1916

GERMAN "DISCUS" GRENADE, 1915

FRENCH CITRON FOUG, 1915

FRENCH P1, 1915

Grenades diversify

Grenades took on many interesting shapes: lemons, lamp bulbs, toffee apples and even discuses. Grenades where the thrower struck the grenade to start a time fuse included the Citron Foug. Percussion grenades, which detonated on impact, included the French P1 and the German "discus" or "tortoise" grenade designed to detonate whichever side struck the ground.

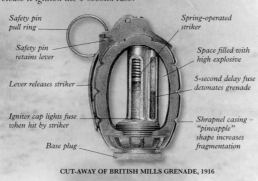

Safety pin pull ring

Safety pin retains lever

Lever releases striker

Igniter cap lights fuse when hit by striker

Base plug

Spring-operated striker

Space filled with high explosive

5-second delay fuse detonates grenade

Shrapnel casing – "pineapple" shape increases fragmentation

CUT-AWAY OF BRITISH MILLS GRENADE, 1916

The ostensible objective was to secure positions just 900 m (1,000 yards) in front of the British defensive line – an objective that was achieved, but at the cost of 16,000 British and Indian casualties.

SECOND ADVANCE ON VIMY RIDGE

After May 10 the French Tenth Army's effort degenerated into a series of local actions until June 16, when it staged its second major offensive in Artois. The French had learned from their experiences on May 9, and now concentrated more artillery and infantry for the attack. They had also brought up reserves close to the front in order to try to exploit success effectively. But on this occasion the defence was also stronger than it had been on May 9, and the German Sixth Army concentrated artillery fire on No Man's Land once the assault began. Just one of six French corps managed to break the German front. As in May, however, the corps' success in seizing positions on Vimy Ridge was costly and short-lived as, unsupported, its gains were quickly eliminated by German counterattacks. On the 18th, the futility of continuing the battle was recognized by the French high command, and a halt was called. The French had incurred around 100,000 casualties in the five weeks of this offensive; the Germans 60,000.

One of the lessons drawn by the French and British planners from the spring offensives was that additional infantry was required. For the British this meant a lengthening of their front as more divisions arrived in northern France. It was also concluded that the assault sector should be widened in order to break the defence over too great a distance for it to be easily sealed, and heavier and longer bombardment should be employed to neutralize the enemy's defensive positions. Applying these lessons meant that, appalling as the losses in Artois were, far greater losses were to be incurred in the battles that followed over the next 30 months.

AUTUMN OFFENSIVES IN ARTOIS AND CHAMPAGNE

Following the failure at the Dardanelles and Russian defeats in Poland (see pages 76–79 and 116–19), it became essential that a major Anglo-French effort should be launched on the Western Front. The French had originally planned to launch two simultaneous major offensives in July, in Artois and Champagne. In June and July, however, their intentions changed, and it was agreed that the British First Army should make the main effort in Artois, with limited French support, while three French armies undertook the main effort in Champagne.

With some 35 French divisions assembled in Champagne and six British divisions committed to an attack on Loos in Artois, the Allies possessed a marked advantage over a German defence that had only six divisions in reserve on the whole of the Western Front. In both Artois and Champagne, however, the Germans had the pick of the ground and since the spring offensive they had strengthened their defences. A second, heavily wired, main line of resistance was sited some 2,275 m (2,500 yds) behind the first and, wherever possible, on reverse slopes. The Germans' heavy artillery and ammunition supply was also far superior to that of the British and French combined, and they possessed more and better mortars, grenades and trench-fighting equipment than the Allies.

The reality of the situation in late summer 1915 was that, for all their efforts, the British and French were no better placed to unlock the enemy defence than they had been in the spring. As a result, the offensives that opened on September 25, after a four-day artillery bombardment, conformed to the pattern of those that had gone before: in the opening hours of the assaults both the British and French made considerable but uneven gains. As the defence re-formed itself, however, the attacks degenerated into a series of grim, unco-ordinated local struggles for insignificant features until both sides were exhausted.

BATTLE OF LOOS

In the attack that began on Loos on September 25, among the mines, slag heaps and fortified villages of Artois, the British used poison gas for the first time. They released 150 tons of chlorine from over 5,240 cylinders and a light wind carried it slowly towards the German lines. Over 600 Germans fell victim to the gas, which also drifted back to the British trenches where it caused huge confusion and many casualties, but few deaths.

The British advanced rapidy, at one point covering a distance of more than 3,600 m (4,000 yds). Loos itself was captured in the first hours of the attack, and the German first-line defences over a 6-km (4-mile) front, between Auchy and Lens, collapsed. The German Sixth Army made preparations to evacuate its positions in both the British and French sectors. The British, however, failed to move reserves into the line in sufficient time and strength to exploit the advantage that had been won, enabling the Germans to reconstitute their defence along their second line.

The British attack between Hulluch and Lens on the second day, mounted without artillery support,

collapsed, and some of the previous day's gains, including the Hohenzollern Redoubt in the north, were lost. At Hulluch, each advancing British column of up to 1,000 men presented an easy target to the German machine-gunners. In the words of a German regimental diary, "Never had the machine-gunners such straightforward work to do nor done it so effectively. They traversed to and fro along the enemy's ranks unceasingly." Similar scenes occurred further south as the British advanced on the Hugo Wood. Such was the slaughter that the Germans called the battle the "Field of Corpses of Loos". In just two days an estimated 6,000 British troops were killed. The battle continued until October 14, but the British failed to make any gains and suffered some 50,000 casualties.

Collecting from the dead
Gathering up weapons from the fallen after battle was common practice. In 1915 rifles and ammunition were in too short supply to be wasted.

Action in the Argonne
Fighting continued in the Argonne sector throughout 1915. Here German soldiers dig a trench in the autumn, when they launched a number of attacks.

Loos after the battle
Men of the 15th Scottish Territorial Division were among the troops who captured Loos from the Germans on September 25, the opening day of the attack.

To the south the French incurred some 48,000 casualties in securing Souchez on September 26 and establishing themselves on Vimy Ridge, thus forcing the Germans to move reserves from Loos to this sector. The French retained their positions on Vimy Ridge until the following year, although most of their attention now switched to Champagne. The Germans had suffered some 56,000 casualties in checking the Allied attacks.

CHAMPAGNE OFFENSIVE
In Champagne the French Second Army made significant gains on September 25. It broke open the German front over a distance of some 4 km (6 miles), and advanced up to 3 km (2 miles) in less than an hour. In certain sectors the French advance secured positions behind the German Third Army's second main line of resistance, and gains were consolidated to a depth of about 5 km (3 miles). The Second Army's success was partly the result of the main weight of the assault falling upon the

weakest part of the German line. But with the arrival of reserves and fresh artillery after the 26th, the Germans were able to reconstitute their defence, causing the Second Army, despite explicit orders to the contrary, to break off the battle.

There were to be a number of attacks, both in the Champagne region and in Artois, until early November, after which the failure of the Anglo-French autumn campaign was admitted at a cost of some 144,000 casualties (compared to 85,000 German casualties). There was a further, seemingly

unimportant, consequence. In order to increase their heavy artillery for the Champagne offensive, the French had stripped their fortresses at Verdun of their artillery, and it was to Verdun that the thoughts of Falkenhayn now turned.

Major offensives on the Western Front
During 1915 the Allies made repeated attempts to break through the German lines in Artois and Champagne. Neither their campaigns, nor that of the Germans at Ypres, were successful, and by the end of the year the Western Front was much as it had been at the beginning.

> When (the officer's) platoon had run about 20 yards he signalled them to lie down and open covering fire. The din was tremendous. He saw the platoon on the left flopping down too, so he whistled the advance again. Nobody seemed to hear. He jumped up from his shell-hole and waved and signalled 'Forward'. Nobody stirred. He shouted: 'You bloody cowards, are you leaving me to go alone?' His platoon-sergeant, groaning with a broken shoulder, gasped out: 'Not cowards, sir. Willing enough. But they're all f.....g dead.' The Pope's Nose machine-gun traversing had caught them as they rose to the whistle.

EXTRACT FROM *GOODBYE TO ALL THAT* BY ROBERT GRAVES, WHO TOOK PART IN THE BATTLE AT THE AGE OF 20

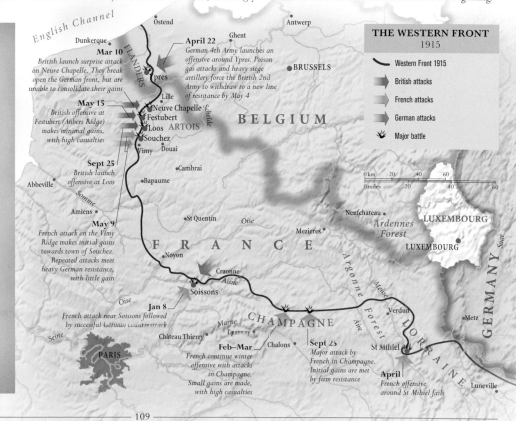

THE WESTERN FRONT
1915

Western Front 1915
British attacks
French attacks
German attacks
Major battle

April 22
German 4th Army launches an offensive around Ypres. Poison gas attacks and heavy siege artillery force the British 2nd Army to withdraw to a new line of resistance by May 4

Mar 10
British launch surprise attack on Neuve Chapelle. They break open the German front, but are unable to consolidate their gains

May 15
British offensive at Festubert (Aubers Ridge) makes minimal gains, with high casualties

Sept 25
British launch offensive at Loos

May 9
French attack on the Vimy Ridge makes initial gains towards town of Souchez. Repeated attacks meet heavy German resistance, with little gain

Jan 8
French attack near Soissons followed by successful German counterattack

Feb–Mar
French continue winter offensive with attacks in Champagne. Small gains are made, with high casualties

Sept 25
Major attack by French in Champagne. Initial gains are met by firm resistance

April
French offensive around St Mihiel fails

English Channel
Ostend
Antwerp
Ghent
Dunkerque
BRUSSELS
Ypres
Lille
Neuve Chapelle
Festubert
Loos   ARTOIS
Souchez
Vimy
Douai
BELGIUM
Schelde
FLANDERS
Abbeville
Somme
Amiens
Cambrai
Bapaume
Oise
St Quentin
Neufchateau
Ardennes Forest
LUXEMBOURG
LUXEMBOURG
F R A N C E
Mezieres
Noyon
Craonne
Aisne
Argonne Forest
Meuse
Verdun
Metz
LORRAINE
GERMANY
Saar
Soissons
Oise
Seine
Marne
Château Thierry
Epernay
Chalons
CHAMPAGNE
St Mihiel
April
Luneville
PARIS

0 km 20 40 60
0 miles 20 40 60

TRENCH SYSTEMS ON THE WESTERN FRONT

THE TRENCHES THAT STRETCHED down the Western Front, from the English Channel to the Swiss border, varied considerably between different armies and over time. The German trenches in 1917–18 were superior to those of the British and French and were vastly more sophisticated than those of 1914–15.

Dug with miniature picks, shovels and spades, the first trenches were improvised. They were really little more than rifle pits that had been linked together. The assumption that they were only temporary, and that mobile warfare would be resumed in spring 1915, meant that the first trenches were not developed substantially. In fact, throughout the war the French – committed as they were to offensive operations – had a trench system that was the least developed defensively, with only two main lines. This, however, did not prevent them from protecting their trenches with sandbags and lining them with timber.

In British sectors there were three lines of trenches: the front, support and reserve. The front comprised connected fire and command trenches. The fire trenches were continuous but not straight. They consisted of sections known as "firebays", up to 9m (10yds) long, separated from each other by "traverses", which made a crenellated pattern when seen from above. The traverses protected the soldiers in one firebay from the blast of a shell landing in an adjacent bay, and provided shelter from enfilading fire – an attack down the length of the trench. The command trenches consisted of officer command posts, dug-outs for rest, and latrines. Leading to the front were communication trenches, along which telephone cables to battalion and battery headquarters were laid, and fresh reserves and supplies were moved. These were also constructed to minimize blast effect, and had slit trenches for emergency cover.

This forward system, which was protected in No Man's Land by substantial barbed wire entanglements, was some 90m (100yds) in front of what was known as the support line. This held reinforcing troops but had no command line or positions. The reserve line, in which were housed further reinforcements, was generally some 360–540m (400–600yds) behind the support line. Behind the reserve line, and beyond the range of small-arms fire, were the artillery positions. Either within the trench system or independent of it, concrete fortifications might be used to create strongpoints.

The Germans, who were generally more committed to a defensive strategy on the Western Front between spring 1915 and February 1918, gradually developed a three-line system similar to that of the British, but considerably deeper – as much as 5km (3 miles) deep by 1917. With the pick of the ground, the Germans were able to burrow deep into uplands, or use caves such as the Caverne du Dragon below the Chemin des Dames, to house up to 1,000 men.

The distance between the front-line systems of the two sides was generally around 90–360m (100–400yds), though in some sectors it could be measured in single figures, and in other sectors it was as much as 900m (1,000yds). In certain sectors, such as the Vosges mountains, individual strongpoints took the place of trenches.

Communication trench
British soldiers wait in a communication trench on their way to the front. All movement had to be below ground level, out of sight of enemy fire and observation posts. Nevertheless, signallers on both sides were often exposed as they relayed messages using semaphore, or when acting as runners between trenches.

Trench network
The map shows German trenches (in blue) as detected by French intelligence operations. The French trenches to the south, were omitted in case the map fell into German hands.

Keeping watch

A periscope was a useful device for observing the enemy without running the risk of getting shot. It consisted of a tube with two mirrors, one at either end, placed at a 45-degree angle to the sides of the tube so that the image from the upper mirror was reflected in the lower one. More elaborate models provided stereoscopic vision.

A RANGE OF PERISCOPES

Fields of barbed wire

Trenches were usually protected by belts of barbed wire. On the German side the belt was 45–90 m (50–100 ft) deep, and often survived artillery bombardments.

GERMAN BARBED WIRE

BRITISH BARBED WIRE

BRITISH RIFLE WITH CUTTERS

Trench lining

Trench walls were lined with different materials, depending on what was available. Wattle was common in the Argonne and Vosges, but planking and sandbags were widely used elsewhere.

Wire cutters

With No Man's Land a sea of barbed wire, cutters were vital equipment. Although parties were often sent out under cover of darkness to cut the wire in advance of an attack, soldiers frequently became entangled in wire and turned into easy targets for enemy fire. Wire cutters – maybe on the end of a rifle – could save a man's life.

BRITISH FOLDING WIRE CUTTERS

FRENCH WIRE CUTTERS

GERMAN WIRE CUTTERS

German dead in the Meuse sector, April 1915
The French renewed an offensive in the Meuse sector on
April 9, storming the Crête des Eparges. In the action
that followed, some Germans were overwhelmed while
still in their trenches and killed in hand-to-hand fighting.

The Eastern and Balkan Fronts

POLAND, GALICIA AND SERBIA
JANUARY – DECEMBER 1915

~

On May 2 the Central Powers launched a major offensive in Galicia, between Gorlice and Tarnow, which drove the Russians back out of Galicia within seven weeks. In mid-July they began to advance through northern Poland. The Russians retreated rapidly and by mid-September they had lost their Polish provinces. The following month German, Austro-Hungarian and Bulgarian forces successfully invaded Serbia.

~

JANUARY 31
German attack at Bolimov on the Vistula front involves first recognized use of gas

JANUARY–MARCH
Attacks by Austrians, supported by Germans, and counterattacks by Russians, in atrocious conditions for control of the passes in the Carpathians

FEBRUARY 7–22
German victory at winter battle of the Masurian Lakes

MARCH 22
Przemysl, with garrison of 120,000, surrenders to Russians

MARCH 26
Successful Russian counterattack in Carpathians takes Lupkow Pass

APRIL 21–30
Preparation for combined German and Austrian offensive in Galicia

MAY 2
Gorlice-Tarnow Offensive begins; German 11th Army spearheads breakthrough on a wide front

MAY 15–23
Germans and Austrians cross the San River

JUNE 3
Przemysl retaken

JUNE 22
Lemberg retaken

JUNE 23–27
Germans and Austrians cross the Dniester

JULY 21–AUGUST 8
Siege of Ivangorod

AUGUST 5
Germans enter Warsaw

AUGUST 7
Russians repulse Germans near Riga

AUGUST 16
Russian army withdrawn to Brest-Osovyets-Kovno line

AUGUST 18
Fall of Kovno

AUGUST 26
Brest-Litovsk falls to Germans

SEPTEMBER 5
Tsar assumes command of Russian army with Alexeyev as his chief-of-staff

SEPTEMBER 3
Grand Duke Nicholas effectively dismissed, appointed Viceroy of Caucasus

SEPTEMBER 18
Germans take Vilna (Vilnius)

SEPTEMBER 25
German advance against Russians comes to a virtual standstill

OCTOBER 7
German and Austrian forces begin to cross Sava and Danube rivers

OCTOBER 9
Germans and Austrians take Belgrade

OCTOBER 11
Bulgarian troops enter Serbia from the east, sealing fate of Serbia

OCTOBER 22
Bulgarians occupy Kumanovo

NOVEMBER 5
Nis falls, giving Germans and their allies rail link with Turkey

NOVEMBER 16
Bulgarians take Prilep and Serbs evacuate Monastir

NOVEMBER 25
Order given for Serbian army to retreat through Albania

DECEMBER 4
German pursuit of retreating Serbians is halted

KEY

■ German offensive in the north Jan 31–Feb 22
■ Combined German-Austrian offensive in Poland May 2–Sept 25
■ Campaigns in Carpathians Jan–Mar
■ Campaign in Serbia Oct 7–Dec 4

WHILE ON THE WESTERN FRONT the opposing armies struggled to make any significant advance in 1915, on the Eastern Front the situation was to prove more fluid. The year began, however, with a series of Austro-Hungarian and German offensives that did not achieve a great deal.

THE WINTER CAMPAIGNS

As 1915 opened, the Austro-Hungarians launched an offensive in the Carpathians with the aims of ensuring the relief of the Austrian garrison in the fortress town of Przemysl and forestalling a Russian attack on Hungary. To the north the Germans planned a major offensive that would forestall any renewed Russian attempt to advance further into East Prussia from the Masurian Lakes region by pushing the Russians back beyond the Vistula.

THE CAMPAIGN IN THE CARPATHIANS

In the south, though German forces supported the Austro-Hungarian armies in the Carpathians, the two sides were evenly matched. This, combined with the fact that most of the fighting had to take place in narrow mountain passes where neither side was able to secure any telling tactical advantage, meant that the main battles – on the Dukla, Lupkow and Uzhok passes opposite Przemysl and the Verecke and Wyszkow passes to the east – achieved almost nothing. The cold and snow sometimes claimed whole sub-units overnight, adding to the sense of futility experienced by the troops. In the words of General von Kralowitz, chief of staff of the Austrian X Corps:

> "Every day hundreds froze to death; the wounded who could not drag themselves off were bound to die … there was no combating the apathy and indifference that gripped the men."

Only in March, and in the most southern sector of the front, were the Austro-German forces able to make any gains, driving the Russians to positions behind the Dniester. This success, however, failed to prevent the Russians from securing the surrender of Przemysl, and its garrison of 120,000 officers and men, on March 22. As winter gave way to spring, the Russians, having recovered the Dukla and Lupkow passes and driven their defenders 48km (30 miles) to the south, made preparations for an invasion of Hungary.

BATTLE OF THE MASURIAN LAKES

Within the German high command there had been many weeks of argument between the "Westerners" and "Easterners" about whether Germany should adopt an offensive strategy in the East. This argument – both the product and cause of a deepening antipathy between Falkenhayn on the one hand and Hindenburg and Ludendorff on the other – was settled in January 1915 with the decision to mount an offensive from East Prussia's Masurian Lakes region into eastern Poland. The somewhat grandiose intention was to force the Russian evacuation of the Vistula salient northwest of Warsaw, and ultimately to cut the Warsaw–Vilna (Vilnius) line of communications. Holding attacks were to be mounted on the Narew River while the German Eighth and Tenth Armies made the main effort on the Gumbinnen-Johannisburg sector, encircling and annihilating the Russian Tenth Army before it could withdraw into the safety offered by Kovno and Grodno. The

Hungarian artillery
Hungarians manning the guns in the northern Carpathians struggled with snow and freezing temperatures during the early months of 1915.

German armies would then develop their offensive to the south. Following a diversionary attack by the German Ninth Army at Bolimov (to the west of Warsaw) on January 31, the Eighth and Tenth Armies opened their offensive on February 7 in blizzard conditions, with the temperature 40° below zero. With no superiority of numbers but perhaps a 9 to 1 advantage in artillery, the Tenth Army immediately broke open the weak right flank of its opposite number. However, though the two German armies trapped and destroyed the bulk of the Russian Tenth Army, it took them so long to do so that they were unable to exploit their success. In the third week of February, the Russian Tenth Army fought itself to destruction in the Augustow Forest (suffering 50,000 casualties), thus buying time for the *Stavka* to reconstitute the front. In March the Germans voluntarily ceded – and Russian attacks recovered – some of the ground that had changed hands in February. Meanwhile, across the

Russian prisoners in Augustow
Up to 30,000 Russian troops were taken prisoner by the Germans during the battle in Augustow Forest that destroyed the Russian Tenth Army in February 1915.

Niemen River a surprise Russian offensive resulted in the capture of Memel on the 17th and an assault on Tilsit on the 20th. On the 21st a hastily-improvised German counterattack, supported by warships, resulted in the recapture of Memel, two days before the Austrians in Przemysl capitulated to the Russians. By the end of March the German forces in the Niemen sector had recovered all the ground lost earlier that month: they subsequently captured the Latvian port of Libau (Liepaja) on May 8.

These offensives produced no lasting strategic advantage for either side but were significant in a number of ways, including the first use of gas on the Eastern Front.

Advance of the German cavalry
As Russian troops retreated in haste, they sometimes omitted to destroy the bridges over rivers and so failed to delay the onward sweep of the Austro-German forces.

I pushed the clothes back (on one man) and saw a pulp, a mere mass of smashed body from the ribs downwards ... The soldier's dull eyes were still looking at me and his lips moved, but no words came. What it cost me to turn away without aiding him, I cannot describe, but we could not waste time and material on hopeless cases, and there were so many others waiting.

FLORENCE FARMBOROUGH, BRITISH NURSE IN A MEDICAL
UNIT ATTACHED TO THE RETREATING RUSSIAN FORCES

Among ruins near the Nida River
During their advance across Poland, Austro-Hungarian troops take up positions among the shattered remains of buildings.

Shells filled with xylyl bromide, a tear-producing chemical agent, were fired by the Germans into Russian positions at Bolimov on January 31, but the intense cold made the chemical freeze, and so it did no harm. More importantly, the winter campaign represented a significant weakening of both Austria-Hungary and Russia, and a strengthening of the position of Hindenburg and Ludendorff in their dealings with their superiors as a result of growing German commitments on the northern and southern sectors of the Eastern Front.

ADVANCE ACROSS POLAND

In the spring of 1915 there was a deepening awareness in Germany of the need to support Austria-Hungary. It was also aware of the need to take some form of offensive action that would cow Italy and Romania, thereby ensuring their increasingly dubious neutrality. In the view of the Austro-Hungarians, an offensive against Serbia was more likely to goad Italy into war than ensure its passivity. Consequently, Falkenhayn planned a major offensive commitment in Galicia, which was to be led by the German commander, Mackensen.

GORLICE-TARNOW OFFENSIVE

The Austro-German offensive opened on May 2 between Gorlice and Tarnow. The aim was to break open the Russian Third Army's front and advance eastwards, so trapping major enemy formations against the Carpathians. The Russian army had no more troops at its disposal than the Germans and Austro-Hungarians, and it also suffered from a severe lack of rifles and shells. At a time when 200,000 rifles were needed each month for new recruits, only 70,000 were being manufactured, often making it necessary for soldiers to wait for others to be killed so that they could take possession of their weapons. Furthermore, the Germans had over one million shells available to them in the Gorlice-Tarnow sector – far more than the Russians. Over 700,000 German shells were fired in a preliminary four-hour bombardment on the evening of May 1, and within 24 hours the Russians had been driven out of Gorlice.

The Russian Third Army was unable to resist the advance of the Austro-German forces, which now proceeded rapidly. On May 6, the Austrian Fourth Army captured Tarnow, taking over 30,000 Russian prisoners. On the 8th the German Eleventh Army began to close in on the San River, 130km (80 miles) from its start line. Two days later the Russian Eighth Army began to evacuate its positions along the Carpathians, to avoid being trapped, and by the 11th the whole of the Russian front south of the Vistula was in retreat. Counterattacks between May 15 and 22 checked the Austro-German forces around Opatow, but in the second half of May they were able to establish themselves east of the San.

After a brief period of reorganization, the Austro-German forces resumed the offensive on June 12, and by the 17th had broken through the fronts of the Russian Third and Eighth Armies.

Collecting weapons
Austro-Hungarian infantry collect weapons from a captured Russian trench. The Russians were very short of rifles and they could ill afford to lose them to the enemy.

Offensives in Galicia and Poland
The Russians could do little to resist the advance by the Austro-Hungarians and Germans that began on May 2 between Gorlice and Tarnow, and by the end of June they had lost Galicia. The relentless onslaught of the Central Powers was resumed on July 13 when they turned their attentions to northern Poland. By mid-September the Russians had also been driven out of Poland.

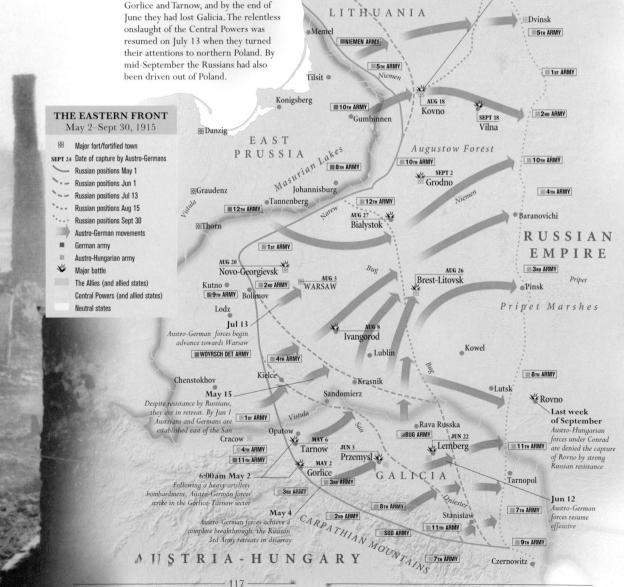

THE EASTERN FRONT
May 2–Sept 30, 1915

⊠ Major fort/fortified town
SEPT 24 Date of capture by Austro-Germans
⌒ Russian positions May 1
- - Russian positions Jun 1
-·- Russian positions Jul 13
-··- Russian positions Aug 15
···· Russian positions Sept 30
➤ Austro-German movements
■ German army
■ Austro-Hungarian army
💥 Major battle
▨ The Allies (and allied states)
▨ Central Powers (and allied states)
▨ Neutral states

Aug 18
German Tenth Army takes Kovno. Subsequent assaults on Vilna are met with firm Russian resistance until Sept 18

Jul 13
Austro-German forces begin advance towards Warsaw

May 15
Despite resistance by Russians, they are in retreat. By Jun 1 Austrians and Germans are established east of the San

6:00am May 2
Following a heavy artillery bombardment, Austro-German forces strike in the Gorlice–Tarnow sector

May 4
Austro-German forces achieve a complete breakthrough; the Russian 3rd Army retreats in disarray

Last week of September
Austro-Hungarian forces under Conrad are denied the capture of Rovno by strong Russian resistance

Jun 12
Austro-German forces resume offensive

LATVIA
Riga
LITHUANIA
Libau MAY 8
Dvinsk 5TH ARMY
Memel
NIEMEN ARMY
5TH ARMY
Niemen
Tilsit
Konigsberg
10TH ARMY
Kovno AUG 18
SEPT 18 Vilna
1ST ARMY
Danzig
Gumbinnen
2ND ARMY
EAST PRUSSIA
8TH ARMY
10TH ARMY
Augustow Forest
SEPT 2 Grodno
10TH ARMY
Masurian Lakes
Graudenz
Johannisburg
12TH ARMY
Niemen
4TH ARMY
Tannenberg
Narew
AUG 27 Bialystok
Baranovichi
Vistula
12TH ARMY
Thorn
1ST ARMY
Bug
RUSSIAN EMPIRE
Novo-Georgievsk AUG 20
AUG 5 WARSAW
AUG 26 Brest-Litovsk
3RD ARMY
Pinsk Pripet
Kutno
2ND ARMY
9TH ARMY Bolimov
Lodz
Pripet Marshes
AUG 8 Ivangorod
Kowel
WOYRSCH DET ARMY
Lublin
Bug
4TH ARMY
Chenstokhov
Kielce
Krasnik
8TH ARMY
Sandomierz
Lutsk
1ST ARMY
Vistula
Rovno
San
Rava Russka
Cracow Opatow
MAY 6 Tarnow
JUN 3 Przemysl
BUG ARMY JUN 22
Lemberg 11TH ARMY
4TH ARMY
11TH ARMY
MAY 2 Gorlice
3RD ARMY Tarnopol
3RD ARMY
GALICIA
Dniester
2ND ARMY
8TH ARMY
Stanislaw
7TH ARMY
SUD ARMY 11TH ARMY
CARPATHIAN MOUNTAINS
7TH ARMY
9TH ARMY
Czernowitz
AUSTRIA-HUNGARY

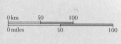
0 km 50 100
0 miles 50 100

AUGUST VON MACKENSEN

~

AUGUST VON MACKENSEN (1849–1944) was one of the most impressive German field commanders of the First World War, renowned for operations requiring speed and surprise. After contributing as a corps commander to the German victory at Tannenberg in August 1914, he joined the Ninth Army in Poland and as its commander led it in the capture of Lodz in December.

In May 1915 Mackensen, as commander of the Eleventh Army, spearheaded the successful Gorlice-Tarnow offensive in Galicia. Promoted to field marshal, he further displayed his mastery of breakthrough tactics in the German summer advance through Poland. In September he commanded the Central Powers' invasion of Serbia, and in the autumn of 1916 he led the multi-national Danube Army during the successful Romanian Campaign. He spent the remainder of the war overseeing the occupying forces in Romania.

Refugees during the Russian retreat
Forced to leave their homes, refugees not only suffered considerably themselves but added to the difficulties of the retreating Russian troops by blocking the roads.

The Russians were in no state to put up a strong resistance, having incurred 412,000 casualties in May alone and lacking 500,000 rifles by mid-June. On the 17th they accepted the loss of Galicia, and on the 20th, with Austrian forces closing in on Lemberg – the most important of the east Galician cities – they gave orders for its evacuation. The city was captured on the 22nd. In just seven weeks the Austro-German offensive had pushed the Russian armies back to the start lines from which they had begun the war in Galicia.

ADVANCE ON WARSAW AND BREST-LITOVSK

Having transformed the position in the south, Falkenhayn and Conrad now agreed to continue the offensive with an advance on Brest-Litovsk. With the Russian forces now facing Galicia, the renewed offensive would necessarily involve frontal attacks and was unlikely to secure Brest ahead of a Russian withdrawal from central Poland. This, however, did not present a problem to Falkenhayn, whose basic aim was to conquer Poland and eliminate any immediate or direct threat to the Central Powers. Concerned to release formations for operations elsewhere, he was not prepared to accept Hindenburg and Ludendorff's plan to attempt to cripple Russia through an offensive that began on the Baltic coast and made its main effort in the Kovno-Vilna sector. The

advance into northern Poland began on July 13. The Russians proved unable to resist it, and on August 5, Warsaw – which had been under Russian control since 1815 – fell to the Germans. The Germans drove on, leaving a force to surround and besiege the fortress of Novo-Georgievsk with its garrison of 90,000 men. The garrison surrendered on the 20th. Further south Ivangorod was besieged from July 21 and captured on August 8, and Brest-Litovsk was secured on the 26th and Bialystok on the 27th. An understrength German Tenth Army took Kovno on August 18.

At this point Falkenhayn inconsistently sanctioned an assault on Vilna. The German armies pushed back the Russian flank to the north of the city but failed to inflict more than a local defeat on a well-conducted defence. The city was voluntarily ceded by the Russians on September 18 as part of a deliberate Russian retreat. Russian forces then successfully defended Molodechno, retook Smorgon and inflicted a local defeat on the Germans around Logishin. Knowing that any further Austro-German success would be hard won, Falkenhayn closed down offensive operations in the east on September 25.

As a result of the fighting for possession of Poland, 750,000 Russian soldiers had been sent to prisoner-of-war camps, where conditions were generally appalling. Civilians had also suffered

Frozen in time
Two Russian soldiers, caught in barbed wire and turned into easy targets for the Austro-German forces. The Russians suffered around 1,000,000 casualties during the the Austro-German advance through Poland.

considerably. The Russian government had ordered the complete evacuation of the country, and to this end whole communities were driven from their villages. Deprived of any regular means of livelihood, many were to die from starvation or succumb to epidemics.

RUSSIAN LOSSES IN POLAND

Russia had lost some of its richest and most heavily industrialized provinces and its threat to the Central Powers was broken. Despite, however, losses on a scale that would have finished any other army, the Russians withdrew from Poland in surprisingly good order and remained aggressive even in defeat. The capture of Vilna alone cost the German Tenth Army 50,000 casualties. Furthermore, in the last week of September, as Austro-Hungarian forces sought to secure a victory in the south, the Russians inflicted a very sharp and severe defeat on them in front of Rovno. The Habsburg armies may have incurred as many as 300,000 casualties before German forces stabilized the situation by recapturing Lutsk.

Destroyed bridge over the San at Przemysl
On June 3, after heavy fighting, Austro-German forces retook the fortress town of Przemysl, which the Austrians had lost to the Russians in March.

> "Men who had fought in several wars and many bloody battles told me that no horrors of a field of battle can be compared to the awful spectacle of the ceaseless exodus of a population…"

RUSSIAN GENERAL GOURKO DESCRIBING THE REFUGEES
WHO FLED DURING THE RUSSIAN RETREAT IN POLAND

THE CONQUEST OF SERBIA

In the first months of 1915, the Austro-Hungarians had been concerned that their involvement in a another offensive against Serbia would encourage Italy to declare war. It was only after the Italian declaration of war in May, followed by the defeat of the Russians in Galicia and Poland, that the Austro-Hungarians and Germans felt ready to consider the elimination of Serbia from the war. They did so, but from very different perspectives. For Austria-Hungary, a Balkans campaign represented no more than the opportunity to deal with Serbia, but for Germany it was also a means of re-establishing overland communications with Turkey and securing the support of Bulgaria.

A SECONDARY ROLE FOR AUSTRIA-HUNGARY

Austria-Hungary was painfully aware of its need for German support: the three offensives it had launched against Serbia in 1914 had all failed, with the loss of 227,000 men. Germany, however, was not prepared to play a supporting role, recognizing that it would have to take the lead in so important a task as the conquest of Serbia. In the event, Austria-Hungary's defeat at Rovno during the campaign in

Advancing Bulgarians

Two Bulgarian armies invaded Serbia from the east on October 11. Here Bulgarian infantry can be seen advancing towards Serbian lines on the opposite hillside.

Poland in September 1915 rendered it unable to play anything but a secondary role.

In fact, by the time the German Eleventh Army took up its positions below Belgrade in order to lead Austro-German forces across the Save and Danube rivers, the success of the campaign was assured. In the autumn of 1915 Serbia was considerably weaker than in the previous year, partly because of the heaviness of its 1914 losses and partly because of the typhus epidemic that was still affecting the country. Added to this was the fact that during the summer of 1915 the Germans had drawn Bulgaria to their side, its bitter rivalry with Serbia being critical in making it decide to conclude an alliance on September 6. Aware of Bulgaria's intentions to invade their country, the Serbs had no alternative but to disperse their depleted formations along extended front lines. In doing so they found themselves facing an enemy that possessed overwhelming advantages of position, timing and numbers. The Serbs had only around 200,000 troops to face over 300,000 under the overall command of Mackensen. They were also desperately short of artillery and ammunition.

Compounding Serbia's difficulties was the failure of Allied attempts to provide effective aid. After a long delay, an Anglo-French force finally began to arrive in Salonika on October 5. It was planned that this force would advance through Macedonia and provide direct support for the Serbian army. As events were to prove, however, it represented little more than strategy by gesture.

THE ADVANCE ON BELGRADE

The Austro-German forces launched their attack on October 6. They captured Belgrade on the 9th, but made only very limited gains during the first ten days because of the strength of Serbian resistance and the problems experienced in moving heavy equipment over the rivers. The state of the Serbian army, however, meant that whatever success it commanded in these opening days was transitory. It was subjected to an ongoing attack that would have ensured defeat even without the Bulgarian invasion of the 11th. The Bulgarians advanced to Kumanovo, through which the vital north-south railway ran, and captured it on the 22nd. This ensured that no relief force would arrive from Salonika, while the Serbian army could not attempt to withdraw through Macedonia.

RETREAT THROUGH THE MOUNTAINS

With the German Eleventh Army outflanking or reducing successive Serb positions in the Morava valley, the Serbian army was forced into the mountains. The Germans were unwilling to contemplate either an attempt to encircle the Serbs to the west or a move southward that might lead to a commitment against Greece. Consequently, reasoning that the remnants of the Serbian army were unlikely to survive a winter retreat through the mountains of Albania, they withdrew five divisions.

The German calculation proved to be more or less correct. By mid-November the Serbian army, with King Peter and the government, had withdrawn to Kosovo. Defeated at Gnjilane on November 22, the army was forced on the 25th to order its formations to withdraw to Albania. So began a terrible 160-km (100-mile) march by some 200,000 Serbian troops and civilians through the mountains. In the course of three weeks, thousands died from cold, hunger and disease, or at the hands of Bulgarian troops and Albanian tribesmen.

As, during December, Austro-Hungarian forces moved to occupy Montenegro, some 150,000 Serbian troops survived the mountains to reach the Albanian coast. In January 1916 they were evacuated by Allied ships from Durazzo and Valona to Corfu, where many more were to die from hunger.

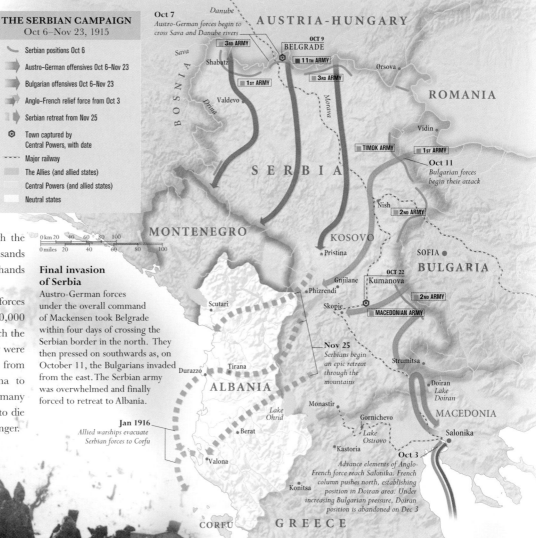

THE SERBIAN CAMPAIGN
Oct 6–Nov 23, 1915

- Serbian positions Oct 6
- Austro-German offensives Oct 6–Nov 23
- Bulgarian offensives Oct 6–Nov 23
- Anglo-French relief force from Oct 3
- Serbian retreat from Nov 25
- ⊙ Town captured by Central Powers, with date
- ---- Major railway
- The Allies (and allied states)
- Central Powers (and allied states)
- Neutral states

Oct 7
Austro-German forces begin to cross Sava and Danube rivers

Oct 11
Bulgarian forces begin their attack

Oct 22

Nov 25
Serbians begin an epic retreat through the mountains

Oct 3
Advance elements of Anglo-French force reach Salonika. French column pushes north, establishing position in Doiran area. Under increasing Bulgarian pressure, Doiran position is abandoned on Dec 3

Final invasion of Serbia
Austro-German forces under the overall command of Mackensen took Belgrade within four days of crossing the Serbian border in the north. They then pressed on southwards as, on October 11, the Bulgarians invaded from the east. The Serbian army was overwhelmed and finally forced to retreat to Albania.

Jan 1916
Allied warships evacuate Serbian forces to Corfu

Serbian retreat over the Drina
In the winter of 1915 the Serbian headquarters staff were among those who retreated through the Albanian mountains. With them was Radomir Putnik, celebrated military leader of the Serbs, who had to be carried in a sedan chair because of ill health.

Map labels: AUSTRIA-HUNGARY, Danube, Sava, Drina, Morava, BOSNIA, Shabatz, BELGRADE, OCT 9, 3RD ARMY, 11TH ARMY, 1ST ARMY, 3RD ARMY, Valdevo, ROMANIA, Orsova, Vidin, SERBIA, TIMOK ARMY, 1ST ARMY, Nish, 2ND ARMY, KOSOVO, Pristina, SOFIA, BULGARIA, MONTENEGRO, Scutari, Gnjilane, Phizrendi, Kumanova, 2ND ARMY, Skopje, MACEDONIAN ARMY, Durazzo, Tirana, ALBANIA, Lake Ohrid, Berat, Monastir, Strumitsa, Doiran, Lake Doiran, MACEDONIA, Gornichevo, Lake Ostrovo, Salonika, Valona, Kastoria, Konitsa, CORFU, GREECE

THE HOME FRONT
AUGUST 1914 – NOVEMBER 1918

From the beginning of the war, governments in all the belligerent states introduced measures to increase their control over industrial production and the welfare of the population. How far-reaching and effective these measures were varied from country to country. France and Britain adopted a more interventionist approach than the others, with the result that their populations suffered privation rather than starvation.

1914 AUGUST 8
Defence of the Realm Act (DORA) passed in Britain

SEPTEMBER 8
"State of War" regulations applied to whole of France

1915 JANUARY
British women are employed as munitions workers

MAY
"Shell scandal" in Britain results in new Ministry of Munitions; in France, further action taken to boost military production

JULY-AUGUST
"Great Retreat" from Poland triggers economic and political turmoil in Russia

1916 MAY 1
British summer time introduced as "daylight saving" measure

MAY 25
Universal conscription introduced in Britain

DECEMBER 7
New War Cabinet organizes Britain for total war

MARCH 8
"February Revolution" leads to tsar's abdication and creation of liberal Provisional Government

1917 MARCH 28
Formation of Women's Auxiliary Army Corps in Britain

MAY-JUNE
Strikes and unrest among French civilians at same time as mutinies in army

NOVEMBER 6-7
"October Revolution": Bolsheviks take over Provisional Government

1918 JANUARY 1
Food rationing for individuals introduced in Britain

JUNE
"Spanish flu" reaches Britain after spreading from Middle East

JULY
French government takes control of key war production industries

1914 JULY 30
Austro-Hungarian War Production Law is put into effect

AUGUST 8
Germany's Department of War Raw Materials (KRA) is set up

1915 APRIL
Ration cards introduced for "war bread" in Vienna and other Austro-Hungarian towns

JULY 1
Formation of Central War Industries Committee to coordinate war production

JULY 12
German coal industry placed under state control

1916 JANUARY 1
Riots in Austria-Hungary force down government-fixed price of bread and flour

AUGUST 29
Under the Hindenburg Programme, Germany is organized as a war economy

OCTOBER
Famine, distress and political unrest in Russian cities; wave of strikes in Petrograd

1917 JANUARY
"Turnip winter" in Germany after failure of potato harvest

MAY 24
Strikes in Vienna's war production factories

AUGUST
Food riots in German towns

NOVEMBER
Vienna is close to starvation as war production doubles

1918 JANUARY
1,500,000 German workers strike; widespread food riots in Austria-Hungary

10 JUNE
Representation of the People Act gives vote to some British women

NOVEMBER
Revolutionary strikes erupt all over Germany

KEY
- Events in France and Britain
- Events in Russia
- Events in Germany and Austria-Hungary

The Home Front

French women making rifle barrels
Once the shortage of armaments became clear in the early months of the war, existing factories were adapted for the production of munitions, and women were drawn into working in them.

AT THE OUTSET OF THE WAR, the talk was of weeks, or possibly months, of combat. None of the countries involved was prepared for a conflict that would last for years and devour an unprecedented mass not just of human beings, weapons and ammunition, but also of food, coal, clothes, boots, medicine, soap, tents, spades, wire, transport vehicles and horses. To wage such a war, governments had to direct, and in some cases assume direct control of, particular key industries. It also had to sustain the workforce in these industries.

INTERVENTIONIST APPROACH IN FRANCE

At the outbreak of war, all classes in France combined in patriotic unity. The government of "Sacred Union" – President Poincaré's description of the coalition formed on August 26 – embraced a uniquely wide political spectrum and was granted exceptional powers over economic affairs and national security. Arrest without trial and very strict censorship were introduced and, in December,

politicians were forbidden to visit the front (though this was later permitted under certain conditions).

Like the other combatants, France had not foreseen the importance of shell-guzzling heavy guns, and within a matter of weeks it was facing a shell shortage. Its ammunitions industry was producing about 100,000 shells per week, but the actual requirement was more like 700,000. In addition to this shell shortfall, the French war

Cutting back on alcohol consumption
All the powers involved in the war introduced measures to reduce alcohol consumption. In France, bar opening hours were restricted and resources were diverted from the production of wine and pastis to that of foodstuffs.

economy was challenged by the effect of German occupation, which included about two-thirds of France's iron and steel capacity, and 40 per cent of its coal mines. The government recalled thousands of conscripts to return to the industrial war effort and the number of workers in the French armaments industries rose from just 50,000 in 1914 to 1.7 million by 1918. One-third were women, who were increasingly taking over men's jobs in a wide range of occupations in heavy and light industry and transport, and doing clerical work.

THE FRENCH WAR ECONOMY

In the first months of the war, France's economy was totally disorganized – with a resulting sharp rise in unemployment. The industrial crisis was largely overcome during 1915, but at the cost of increasing national debt. The revival of the working-class movement from 1916 brought further disruption, and in May–June 1917, coinciding with the mutinies among the troops, over 70 industries were hit by strikes in Paris and St Etienne, the chief armaments centre.

Nevertheless, the majority of workers adhered to the patriotic ideal, and most French people backed Clemenceau, who in November 1917 became, at the age of 76, both prime minister and war minister. With a war cabinet of only five members, he was a virtual dictator, suppressing all criticism and prosecuting any public figure who expressed defeatist attitudes.

The middle classes were generally hardest hit economically, at least in relative terms. Salaries were frozen while the cost of living more than doubled. It was matched by wage rises among munitions workers, though not by the smaller rises in other industries. Soldiers' families received subsistence payments of 1.25 francs per day plus 50 sous for each child. Together with the rise in food prices (though there was no serious food shortage in France), the payments made many peasant households better off. Peasant families, however, suffered relatively higher casualties than those of urban workers.

GOVERNMENT CONTROL IN BRITAIN

Within days of the outbreak of war, the British government was empowered by the Defence of the Realm Act (DORA) to direct the economy and public life. It lost no time in taking control of the railways, buying up all the raw sugar, regulating prices, guaranteeing banks, printing more paper money, doubling income tax and raising customs duties. The long arm of DORA even reached out to

Ploughing up London's Richmond Park
War-time shortages encouraged resourcefulness on the home front. In the country, pasture was converted to arable land. In towns and cities, recreational parks served as vegetable gardens.

THE ESCALATING COST OF WAR

DURING THE WAR public expenditure increased on an enormous scale. The first war-time budgets were considerably higher that any peace-time budget, and continued to rise throughout the war. In Britain expenditure increased by almost 500 per cent between 1914 and 1917, followed by a dip in 1918. In Germany it increased by just over 500 per cent up to 1917, in France by 560 per cent up to 1918, and in Russia by 315 per cent up to 1916. It is hard to determine exactly how much of this rise represented an increase in military expenditure together with other expenditure related directly to the war effort, such as spending on transport and the bureaucracy required to implement various controls. Among the reasons for the huge increase in spending was a rapid rise in inflation and the requirement to pay interest on an ever-increasing national debt. No country was able to finance the war from taxation. All had to rely on borrowing from other countries and from their own population, who were encouraged to support the war effort by buying government war bonds.

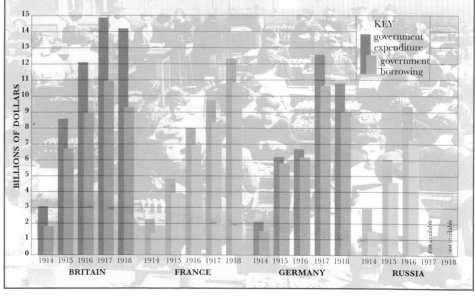

KEY
government expenditure
government borrowing

BILLIONS OF DOLLARS

| 1914 1915 1916 1917 1918 | 1914 1915 1916 1917 1918 | 1914 1915 1916 1917 1918 | 1914 1915 1916 1917 1918 |
| BRITAIN | FRANCE | GERMANY | RUSSIA |

SHORTAGES AND RATIONING

THE AGE-OLD CONNECTION between food and military success was expressed by Napoleon's dictum: "An army marches on its stomach". The First World War, however, saw a new situation, in which civilian populations far from any battlefield became vulnerable to war-induced famine and disease.

Food was a matter of life and death in war-time Russia's northern cities, where by 1917 there were endless queues for minimal, unregulated supplies of the most basic provisions. The bread queues of Petrograd, where people gathered for hours every day – and sometimes every night – acted as unofficial information centres and became hotbeds of revolution. Queuing also became part of life in war-time France, where government rationing of coal, oil and some foods began in 1918.

In Britain, the war meant privation rather than starvation. By the end of 1916, government controls meant that food retailers were only allowed half of their usual stocks, which they rationed on a household basis. Gradually, state controls over the distribution of food were tightened. Early in 1918, by which stage intensified submarine warfare was seriously affecting food imports, rationing for individuals was introduced, principally of sugar, tea, margarine, bacon, cheese and butter and then, from April, of meat.

On the outbreak of war, German civilians trusted the state's promise of a short war. They were not prepared for the effects of the Allied blockade, which began to bite within months, particularly in Hamburg and Berlin. In 1915 Berliners were the first Germans to be issued with bread ration cards. Before long, meat, dairy products, potatoes, sugar, cereals and soap were only

obtainable through ration cards. As meat grew scarce, people resorted to such dubious delicacies as pickled walrus and boiled crow. The black market flourished, and everywhere there were queues. The winter of 1916–17 was known as the "turnip winter" because, after a disastrous potato harvest, turnips and beets became staples.

A similar situation of acute shortages, poorly administered, ever-shrinking rations, "ersatz" substitution foods and rampant profiteering was enacted in the towns and cities of Austria-Hungary. Riots and, eventually, revolts were triggered by the food crisis, which began when supplies of grain and oil were drastically affected by the Russian advance through Galicia in 1914. To add to the tension between war workers and war bosses, the political gap between Austria and Hungary widened as, by 1917, Hungarian grain was feeding the army while civilians in the western, Austrian half of the empire were starving.

French ration cards
In France there was rationing of foodstuffs such as bread and sugar, but in fact fuel shortages were the main problem. Severe restrictions were placed on the use of public and private lighting, and oil and coal for domestic heating were strictly rationed. War-time winters saw affluent Parisians congregating in well-heated hotel lobbies.

Waiting in line
Armed with baskets, French women put in their waiting hours. Long queues for government-controlled rations of essential foods and commodities became an everyday sight in the towns and cities of the home fronts.

Fishing for victory
On every home front, civilians were urged to contribute to the war effort by being economical, especially with food. The French were encouraged to catch and eat more fish so as to conserve national livestock resources.

MANGEZ MOINS DE VIANDE
POUR MÉNAGER NOTRE Cheptel

DO YOUR BIT
H.M.S.
SAVE·FOOD

KOMMANDANTUR
de Marcq-en-Barœul

Faisant suite à mon ordre du 1er Juin, les prix des légumes à partir du 1er Juillet prochain seront les suivants :

Belles salades de toute nature.	**0.10**	l'une
Oseille.	**0.10**	le kilog
Petits pois.	**0.75**	»
Fèves.	**0.50**	»
Haricots verts.	**0.75**	»
Beaux choux.	**0.15**	l'un
Navets.	**0.15**	la botte de 10 beaux navets
Carottes.	**0.35**	la botte de 10 belles carottes
Beaux bouquets	**0.05**	l'un

Toutes les quantités, petits pois, fèves, haricots verts, carottes, oignons, poireaux, pommes de terre, etc., ne pourront être exportés en dehors de la Commune, sans autorisation de la Commandantur.
Marcq-en-Barœul, le 1er Juillet 1917.

Der Ortskommandant.

Price controls
This poster lists the prices of vegetables as determined by a local military commander in German-occupied France. In practice, peasant farmers often found ways of getting round government regulations and official price controls.

Combating shortages
While soldiers and sailors were "doing their bit" by fighting on land and at sea, non-combatants on the home front were asked by their governments to save food and cut down on waste in the interests of the war effort.

German rations
In Germany, most basic foods were rationed by separate local authorities. Ration cards took account of the holder's age, health and employment, but the quantities obtainable varied from locality to locality, arousing much resentment.

encompass Britain's horses, 165,000 of which were requisitioned for army service within the first months of the war. However, little was done in the early months to increase the supply of shells.

In the spring of 1915 Britain experienced a "shell scandal". Newspapers took the line of General French, who blamed the failure to break through on the Western Front on a shortage of shrapnel and high-explosive shells. The government was stung into action, and created a new Ministry of Munitions under the future prime minister Lloyd George, who set about co-ordinating, controlling, and boosting production in all of the country's armaments industries. In addition to the established armament firms, there were now national factories, specializing in the mass production of rifles, shells, small arms ammunition, powder and explosives. This was dangerous work, often done by women who became known as the "munitionettes".

Trusting in the overwhelming superiority of its navy, Britain was the only major European power without conscription. Indeed, at the outset, there was so much patriotic enthusiasm in Britain that the army could barely cope with the number of volunteers. Despite the huge losses on the Western Front, there were enough volunteers until May 1916, when conscription was introduced.

In the previous year it had become apparent that relying on volunteers was having an adverse effect on the production of munitions. The National Registration Act had been introduced with the aim of establishing what proportion of men of military age were still eligible for service and what proportion were employed in work vital to the war effort. These men, who were employed on the railways and in mining and agriculture, as well as in munitions, were not to be enlisted in the army.

To improve workers' efficiency, there was a campaign against the consumption of alcohol that included such measures as watering down beer and reducing pub opening times. Working hours were extended, with "summer time" – by which all the clocks in Britain were put forward by an hour – being introduced in May 1916. At the same time, the new Ministry of Food supervised agriculture and, eventually, introduced rationing.

Many war-time initiatives were to develop into permanent institutions. Britain's Medical Research Council, for example, began as a war-time medical committee. During the war the citizens of both Britain and France not only learnt to live with a plethora of new regulations – curfews, rations, passports and the like. They also came to expect greater government involvement with their welfare.

Patriotism and profit
This 1916 poster invites Russians to help the motherland in her hour of need, and make themselves a good profit, by buying government war bonds at 5.5 per cent interest. The extra finance was needed to boost production in the war industries.

DEPRIVATION IN RUSSIA

Counting, like all the other belligerent states, on a short campaign, the Russian War Ministry had made no long-term plans. It also failed to appreciate the importance of industry to the war effort. Existing stocks of weapons and ammunition only lasted for the first few weeks of the war, and instead of responding to calls of alarm from generals at the front, the tsarist government dismissed them. By the spring of 1915 the shortages were so bad that whole battalions of the Russian army were being trained without rifles, while in battle some Russian troops depended for weapons on those taken from the dead and wounded.

The munitions crisis eased after the summer of 1915, when a new, tsar-approved War Industries Committee began to co-ordinate the supply of materials and orders to the big armaments factories. Between January and April 1915 the whole army had received only 2,000,000 shells, although the stated requirement of the *Stavka* (Supreme Command) was 3,500,000 per month. By the autumn of 1916 production had risen to 4,500,000 shells per month. The production of rifles had also increased, from around 70,000 per month in 1915 to 111,000 per month, but this was still well short of the estimated monthly requirement for 200,000.

While the supply of munitions improved, the soldiers continued to be deprived of the most basic requirements. On the occasion of one inspection by the tsar, a single company was kitted out by dint of raiding several regiments' resources, leaving the unseen men in the trenches without boots, knapsacks, trousers and hats. In the absence of any competent government action, Russia's war effort was supported by volunteers. In towns and cities patriotic clubs and committees organized the collection and distribution of the food, linen and medicine donated by the public, and women volunteered themselves as nurses to the ever-increasing number of casualties. From June 1915, under the leadership of liberal aristocrat Prince Lvov, a movement based on the Russian empire's network of local councils, the Zemstvo Union, took on the job of supplying and supporting the army. Its volunteers led the way in setting up field canteens and medical units at the front, evacuating the wounded, helping refugees and providing relief to soldiers' families. Meanwhile, civilians starved. This was partly because of problems with the production of food, particularly after the loss of Poland in 1915. More significant, however, was the inability of the Russian railway system to ensure the proper distribution of food or, indeed, anything else.

SHORTAGES IN GERMANY

In common with all the other governments of the belligerent states, Germany was so beguiled by the short-war fallacy that it had no plans for a continuing war. It was certainly not prepared for

Working as painters
Once the men had been called up, the young, the old and the female were called upon to fill the labour gap. Here, watched by their foreman, French women paint and label railway carriages.

Conscientious Objectors

~

ONCE THE WAR BEGAN, a great tide of patriotism rolled over any pacifist inclinations of Christians, feminists, anarchists and socialists all over Europe. As the only major combatant state without a conscripted army, Britain was also the only country where open opposition to the war on religious or political grounds continued to be an option, but it was a distinctly uncomfortable option. As the death toll on the Western Front mounted, and the national war effort intensified, pacifist dissidents were increasingly vulnerable to popular rage.

The various strands of the pacifist movement united in opposition to conscription, which came for unmarried men early in 1916, and then, in May, for all men. Conscription represented a sharp break with Britain's tradition of voluntary military service and, in framing the new Military Service Acts, the government was mindful of this tradition. The Conscription Acts allowed for the exemption of non-religious "conscientious objectors" as well as members of Britain's historic peace churches, notably the Society of Friends (Quakers).

In theory, the Military Service Acts were generous – and far ahead of the times – but in practice many "conchies" were treated as criminals. For many of the elderly worthies who made up the local tribunals, which were set up to hear claims for exemption, conscientious objectors were unprincipled "shirkers" who only wanted to save their own skins. Across Britain, there was wide variation in the fairness and efficiency of the tribunals, and great confusion over the difference between "absolutists" and "alternativists". One in ten of the 16,500 men who applied for exemption were "absolutist" pacifists like Stephen Hobhouse, a Quaker who, rather than agree to serve with the Friends' Ambulance Unit as a condition of exemption, was sent to prison, where his brutal treatment caused an outcry. The majority of the conscientious objectors were "alternativists", who agreed to non-combatant military service and spent the rest of the war working in hospitals, farms and kitchens.

Behind bars
A "conchie's" picture of prison life: hard work, harsh words and the consolation of a weekly visit.

White feather campaign
In Britain, female vigilantes handed out white feathers to able-bodied, young men not in uniform as tokens of their supposed cowardice.

the Allied blockade, which cut off Germany from its overseas sources of food and essential raw materials. Within a few days, however, the Minister of War had set up a War Materials Department (KRA) which set about collecting supplies and distributing them among businesses producing for the war effort. Without this, and the skill of German scientists in devising substitutes for unobtainable materials, it is doubtful whether Germany would have been able to stay in the war.

The KRA system was reasonably effective until 1916, when the massive requirements of the battles at Verdun and on the Somme revealed the need to increase production. In place of the partnership between the government on the one hand, and industry and the army on the other, a

Using new skills in aeroplane production
A young woman, using woodworking and joinery skills, puts the finishing touches to an aeroplane propeller blade at a factory in Ipswich, eastern England. Before the war, few women had acquired such skills.

WOMEN IN INDUSTRY AND ON THE LAND

WARS HAVE ALWAYS INVOLVED women as carers and casualties and victims, but the first "total" war called for the participation of more women than ever before in many more ways. In Britain, where there was already a strong movement for female democratic rights, suffragette leader Emmeline Pankhurst demanded women's "right to serve", and do more than "nurse soldiers or knit socks". Women's willingness – and war-time requirements – facilitated the entry of thousands of "munitionettes" into the war industries.

Unlike the suffragettes, so many of whom were "ladies" and highly educated, most of "Tommy's sisters" in the war production factories were ordinary, unskilled working women. Before turning their hands to the operation of machine lathes, and the manufacture of everything military – from guns and gas masks, to shells and aeroplane propellers – many of them had worked as domestic servants.

The war was also a stimulus to the opening up of new employment opportunities in France. Women were drawn into the revamped French factories first by private employers and later by the state. By 1918 more than a million French women were working in national defence, armaments and aeronautics. In Austria-Hungary, too, where by 1916 42.5 per cent of workers in heavy industry were female – as compared with 17.5 per cent in 1913 – the war had the effect of diverting women from traditional female jobs into "skilled men's work".

By 1915 women in Germany were working at everything from chemicals, electrical equipment, and metalwork to precision instruments and leather goods, and by 1918 they formed 55 per cent of the industrial workforce. Although the pressure on them to volunteer for industrial war work was higher than in Britain and France, their health and safety conditions were much worse. In France, for example, young mothers were not permitted to do munitions work, but this was not the case in Germany where 60-hour weeks were not uncommon for women of all ages.

The war drained millions of men from the land. On small family farms, women and grandfathers and children coped as they have always coped in times of crisis, and shouldered the extra burden themselves. In France the drop in food production was compounded by German occupation, and was so serious that by 1917 the government had released 300,000 soldiers from the army to work on the land. Forced labour was the German government's solution to the land crisis, and by 1918 100,000 Belgians and 600,000 Poles were at work on German farms and factories.

In Britain, women were asked to take the place of the men who had been diverted from agriculture. The first official, government-sponsored organization was the Women's Forage Corps, founded in 1915, and this was followed by the Women's Forestry Corps and the Women's Land Army.

NATIONAL SERVICE WOMEN'S LAND ARMY

GOD SPEED THE PLOUGH AND THE WOMAN WHO DRIVES IT

Women in agriculture
Over 113,000 women took up agricultural work in Britain during the war. Initially, many were part-time volunteers. The Women's Land Army was formed in 1917 in response to the need for a full-time, paid workforce. Thousands of women joined up, but ex-soldiers and German prisoners of war continued to be of vital importance to agricultural production.

Munitions workers
Munitions meant more than guns and shells, the term being applied to everything required by the war machine, from gas masks to propellers. These women are making aircraft components.

Fodder-makers
Summer 1918, a team of British women, members of the Forage Corps, operate a monster hay-baling machine driven by a steam engine. It was the job of the Women's Forage Corps to provide food for the thousands of horses on which the army depended.

Dangerous work
As precautions against the risks of explosion and TNT poisoning, British munitions workers were equipped with overalls, caps and gloves. Even so, female shell-fillers were nicknamed "canaries" because the powder turned their skin bright yellow.

A woman's touch
In French war production, women were concentrated in the chemical, wood and transport sectors, where they generally performed handling tasks and specialized in operating all sorts of machine tools, from lathes to welders.

virtual military dictatorship over the entire economy – the Hindenburg Programme – was established. A War Office was set up with responsibility for labour, weapons, munitions, raw materials, and food supplies for the armed services, but it failed to meet up to expectations. Because of the continuing Allied blockade, Germany's war production could not match that of its enemies, even though the munitions workers worked longer hours while surviving on much less food.

The food-related crimes of speculation, hoarding and adulteration were rife on the German home front, and the worst affected civilians were the urban poor. German city-dwellers got used to spending much of their waking lives in queues. Women would get up in the middle of the night, and take their knitting and sewing to the shops, hoping to be among the first at the scene of a morning food delivery. People who waited in line, only to find that supplies had run out, and who were then forced to join yet another queue, were said to be dancing a "polonaise".

Bread became so scarce in the German capital that an escaping British prisoner-of-war was recaptured when his sandwich, made of white bread and obtained in a parcel from home, gave him away. Although Berlin was far from any front line, life there was utterly changed by the war. Theatres, museums and street markets were closed, and there were cuts in public transport, electricity and street lighting. As early as 1915 Berlin had lost its copper roofs and wrought iron railings, and coal carts were pulled by old horses, donkeys and even circus elephants.

MILITARIZATION IN AUSTRIA-HUNGARY

The 51.3 million people in the Austro-Hungarian Empire were the subjects of Franz Josef I, who was titled the emperor of Austria and the king of Hungary. While the Austrian half of the empire was largely industrialized, with factories capable of producing armaments and heavy machinery, the Hungarian half had a predominantly agrarian economy. They shared an imperial currency and a customs union, but each half had considerable control over its own national armies and resources.

In 1914 Austria-Hungary had the theoretical advantage of a war production law, which allowed for the "militarization" of life on the home front. Thus, the railways were strictly for army or army-related use, and men under 50 who were not deemed fit enough for combat duty were still liable for work in the war production factories. A pre-war law banning night work by women was lifted,

Waiting for the soup
The huge city of Berlin was particularly vulnerable to the effects of the Allied blockade. By 1916 thousands of Berliners depended on the soup doled out from kitchens set up by the German Women's National Service.

as was the traditional ban on Sunday working, and the wages of war workers were kept to a government-controlled minimum.

A poor harvest in 1914, combined with the destruction of so much farmland on the Eastern Front and the impact of the Allied blockade, meant that Austria's industrial war workers were soon beginning to experience the effects of food shortages. Increasing tension between workers and their military bosses was matched by the tension between Austria and Hungary. The war disrupted the symbiotic relationship between Austria's factories and Hungary's farms, and the imperial government lacked the authority and power to impose or enforce a centralized food policy. As a result, urban Austria slowly starved while rural Hungary had a surplus. An embittered Viennese writer described the war as an operetta for which Berlin supplied the libretto and Budapest the music, which was an elegant way of expressing Austria's increasing deference to German militarism and dependence on Hungarian grain.

Composed of 15 nations, the Habsburg empire did not command the undivided loyalty of its subjects. In fact, the multi-national character of Austria-Hungary was a factor in the young Adolf Hitler's decision to enlist as a German rather than an Austrian soldier. The loyalty of the starving populations of the cities of central Europe was further strained by the unchecked behaviour of "profiteers", ruthless entrepreneurs who took conspicuous advantage of hard times on the home front. Theatregoers in Budapest, for example, were disturbed by the sounds of the war-enriched devouring black market salami and gherkins.

THE IMPACT OF THE WAR ON WOMEN

WOMEN'S ROLES EXPANDED during the First World War, moving beyond the traditionally sanctioned realm of Kinder, Kirche, Küche ("children, church and kitchen") in all of the combatant states. Although the war-time press made much of the obvious novelty of females driving omnibuses and ambulances, and wearing overalls and trousers for their jobs in heavy industry, there were no less significant changes in spheres such as medicine, where women were already established.

Florence Nightingale was never as close to the action as the front-line nurses of the First World War. Mairi Chisholm and her colleague Elsie Knocker (later the Baroness de T'Serclaes) joined a "flying column" and ran a wound-dressing post from a cellar on the Western Front: "We started the day by being heavily shelled – shrapnel just bursting their heads off". The Scottish Women's Hospitals (SWH) was founded by Scottish surgeon Elsie Inglis, who died in Russia in 1917 and whose very first enquiries at the War Office were met with: "Go home and sit still".

Scottish Women's Hospitals ran 14 fully equipped hospitals on every Allied front except those controlled by the British army, which was supported by the VADs (below). Led by Mabel Stobart, the SWH unit in Serbia stayed with the Serbian army throughout the "Great Retreat", a march of epic heroism and hardship over the mountains of Albania and Montenegro. One of the British women, Flora Sandes, joined the Serbian infantry and having survived combat, and a serious wound, ended the war as a commissioned officer.

Flora Sandes' career as a soldier was unusual, but there were other unusual women. The Russian army's all-female Battalion of Death was organized by Maria Bochkareva, who had worked as a factory foreman before the war. After making a direct appeal to the Tsar, she was allowed to become a soldier and spent two years in the trenches. In 1917, when she had achieved the rank of sergeant, she formed her Women's Battalion of Death in the hope of raising the morale of her fellow soldiers, and shaming them into a victorious drive against the enemy. The commander-in-chief on the southern sector of the front, General Brusilov, supported Bochkareva's initiative because he believed that Russia's war effort would gain from greater participation by patriotic volunteers of both sexes. Bochkareva's women shaved their heads and wore regular army uniforms and before they left for the front, they assembled in Moscow to be blessed by the Russian Church.

The effect of the war on "white collar" women was less spectacular, but more enduring. In France alone, the state bureaucracy mushroomed as a result of the war effort, increasing by 25 per cent in just four years. An army of women typed the letters and lists, and answered the telephones of war-time government agencies and offices. The rise of office jobs was just one of the changes that were well underway in industrialized countries before 1914, but which the war accelerated and made more obvious. After 1918, prosperous British households suffered from "servant problems", and fewer young women were prepared to work as maids.

Voluntary Aid Detachments
Britain's Voluntary Aid Detachments pre-dated the war and included men and women. But as the army claimed more and more men, most of the volunteer support workers were female.

V.A.D.
NURSING MEMBERS . COOKS . KITCHEN-MAIDS .
CLERKS . HOUSE-MAIDS . WARD-MAIDS .
LAUNDRESSES . MOTOR-DRIVERS . ETC.
ARE URGENTLY NEEDED

QUEEN MARY'S ARMY AUXILIARY CORPS.
The GIRL behind the man behind the gun.
ENROL TO-DAY FULL PARTICULARS AND FORMS OF APPLICATION FROM THE NEAREST EMPLOYMENT EXCHANGE. ASK AT POST OFFICE FOR ADDRESS.

A moving hospital
A British nurse tends to her patients while they are being transported by ambulance train from the front to hospital. Of all the war-time women's organizations, the British women's medical services were undoubtedly among the most professional.

EDITH CAVELL

~

EDITH CAVELL (1865–1915), the daughter of a Norfolk clergyman, was the matron of a nursing school in Brussels, which became a Red Cross hospital for the care of wounded men from both sides of the Western Front. She became involved in an underground movement that helped more than 200 English, French and Belgian soldier-prisoners to escape from German-occupied Belgium into neutral Holland. Along with the Belgian resistance organizer, Philippe Baucq, Nurse Cavell was arrested by the local German authorities and condemned to death. Her execution by firing squad on October 12, 1915 caused a wave of revulsion and fierce anti-German propaganda in Britain and the USA. Her own last reported words were: "I realize that patriotism is not enough. I must have no hatred or bitterness towards anyone".

Brevet de Marraine
A French government certificate acknowledges the holder as a "marraine". The marraines (literally, godmothers) were women who sponsored individual soldiers in the French Army by writing letters to them. The idea behind the scheme was that these concerned yet cheerful penpals would keep up morale at the front and assure the soldiers in the trenches that their efforts and sufferings were appreciated by those at home.

Transport workers
As the men of Berlin left for the front, women donned uniforms and began to run the city. As well as driving horse-drawn buses and mail-wagons, they operated the city's trams. This war-time substitution crew, which includes a boy, was photographed in 1917. After 1918, few of these women would continue in their war jobs. Nevertheless, important precedents had been set for women's work.

Coping alone
By removing millions of men from their families, the war had a huge impact on the role of women. For thousands of mothers, the war years were a testing balancing act between duties of home-making in a time of exceptional privation and the demands of war work.

BATTLES
OF
ATTRITION
1916

~

FOLLOWING THEIR FAILURE TO BREAK THE STALEMATE
ON THE WESTERN FRONT IN 1915, BRITAIN AND FRANCE
PLANNED A MAJOR OFFENSIVE ON THE SOMME IN THE
SUMMER OF 1916. BEFORE THIS COULD TAKE PLACE,
HOWEVER, THE GERMANS LAUNCHED THEIR OWN MAJOR
OFFENSIVE IN FEBRUARY AT VERDUN. BOTH OFFENSIVES
WERE TO BECOME GREAT BATTLES OF ATTRITION,
COSTING THE LIVES OF HUNDREDS OF THOUSANDS OF
MEN FOR LITTLE GAIN. THE ALLIES ONLY MET WITH
SUCCESS ON THE EASTERN FRONT, DURING THE BRUSILOV
OFFENSIVE, AND EVEN THIS WAS SHORT-LIVED.

~

French and British troops in a trench
On the Western Front, from Flanders to the
Somme, British and French soldiers met as
they took over sections of the front line from
each other. The position of this line was to
change very little during 1916.

STALEMATE AND SLAUGHTER

THE ALLIES ENTERED 1916 WITH A CERTAIN OPTIMISM. BRITAIN NOW HAD

38 DIVISIONS ON THE WESTERN FRONT, AND RUSSIA COULD AT LAST MATCH THE

NUMBER OF GERMAN AND AUSTRO-HUNGARIAN DIVISIONS ON THE EASTERN FRONT.

BRITAIN AND FRANCE WERE ALSO CONVINCED THAT THE FAILURES OF 1915 COULD BE

ATTRIBUTED TO SPECIAL FACTORS THAT WOULD NOT BE REPEATED IN THE FUTURE.

IN REALITY, THE ALLIES had many reasons to be concerned. They had widening commitments at Salonika and in the Middle East, plus the continuing campaigns in Cameroon and East Africa to pursue. Much more serious, however, was the weakening of Russia as a result of its territorial and manpower losses during 1915. Russia had never been able to conscript more than a relatively small part of its available manpower, and by the end of 1915 it was clear that it would exhaust its supply of trained soldiers within a year. For Russia, victory in 1916 was essential.

MISREADING THE LESSONS OF 1915

Beneath Allied confidence in late 1915 was a failure to realize the exact nature of the problems associated with offensive action. In the course of the year German wire defences on the Western Front had been considerably thickened, and it had become apparent that high explosive was the only means of cutting through the fields of barbed wire. Prolonged bombardment, however, not only resulted in the loss of surprise, but also overlooked the fact that the defence was continually evolving and increasing in strength.

By the end of 1915 the German defence on the Western Front was still far removed from the system that was to be in place by 1917, but the defensive positions being prepared for front-line troops were elaborate and formidable. Moreover, by the end of 1915 the British remained badly under-equipped in terms of heavy artillery, and they had only remedied their shortage of shells by sacrificing quality. The Russians had overcome the worst of their equipment shortages so that virtually every soldier at the front now had a rifle. However, even more than the British, they had insufficient supplies of all types of artillery. On top of these deficiencies was the fact that British and Russian planning for a breakthrough was rudimentary.

Both Britain and France were aware of Russia's increasing weakness and their own in-effectiveness in diverting German attention away from the Eastern Front. Consequently, at and after the Chantilly conference (December 5–8, 1915), they drew up a plan of campaign based on unity of action. The British high command favoured an attack in Flanders supported by an amphibious landing behind the German flank, but the French insisted on an attack on the Somme. Ostensibly this was because the terrain there was better than in Flanders. The real reason, however, was simply that it was on the Somme that the British and French armies met. Without any major railway close to the

Somme landscape
From the last week of June 1916 a series of relentless bombardments, in which millions of shells were fired, produced a landscape of total desolation.

> *"A shell-hole strewn with bully-tins, broken weapons, fragments of uniform, and dud shells, with one or two dead bodies on its edge… this was the never-changing scene that surrounded each one of all these hundreds of thousands of men."*

GERMAN WRITER ERNST JÜNGER DESCRIBING THE
SOMME BATTLEFIELD IN HIS NOVEL, *STORM OF STEEL*

Somme in which the British would play their full part. It was agreed that the Russians would mount an offensive in mid-June 1916 while the Italians would attack in August at the same time as the British and French began their offensive on the Somme. There was, however, disagreement between the British and French over who should be responsible for the preliminary attacks that would divert German attention from the scene of the main effort. The French high command insisted that the British stage these attacks while the British high command, aware of the limitations of the new divisions coming into the line, resisted the demand. German attention was diverted from the Somme nonetheless, though in a way that neither the British nor the French anticipated.

FALKENHAYN'S PLAN

By the end of 1915 there appeared to be no immediate demands upon Germany's resources and attention from secondary theatres of war. Aware that in 1916 the French would renew their offensive efforts and the new armies of Britain would enter the field in strength, Falkenhayn reasoned that it was time once again to take the initiative in the West. He believed that Britain was the cornerstone of the alliance opposing Germany. Recognizing, however, that it was not possible to strike directly and fatally at Britain, he concluded that Germany should strike indirectly in 1916 by attacking France. He argued that if the French people could be made to understand clearly that "in a military sense they have nothing more to hope for, (the) breaking point would be reached, and England's best sword knocked from her hand". The means to be employed was not to break the French front *en masse*, but to bleed France to death by attacking an objective "for the retention of which the French would be compelled to throw in every man they have". The objective he selected was Verdun.

front, an attack on the Somme lacked any real strategic purpose, while the openness of the terrain and the naturally strong defensive position of the Germans in the sector meant there was no tactical rationale. In fact, the French high command, recognizing that the breaking of the German front in a single battle was very unlikely, sought a battle of attrition on the

THE BATTLE OF VERDUN

Falkenhayn's plan for the Verdun offensive has been criticized for its ghoulishness, although his intentions were really not very different from those of British and French commanders on the Western Front at this time. The plan was, however, flawed by one fundamental ambiguity. To draw the French into a killing zone where the artillery could do its work, German forces had to mount their effort against an objective worth defending. If, however, it was worth defending, for the Germans it was worth taking. Falkenhayn could not reveal what his real intention was to the formations committed to the offensive, and he hesitated between prosecuting the battle as planned and setting out to take Verdun, which would have defeated his own purpose. In fact, the losses suffered by the Germans were to be almost as high as those of the French: between February 21, when the first attack was launched, and the end of March, the Germans suffered over 81,600 casualties while the French suffered 89,000. By the end of the year a German advance of just a few kilometres had resulted in almost a million casualties.

Caring for the wounded
Gordon Highlanders transport a wounded comrade along the Albert-Bapaume road in July 1916 – just one of the 630,000 Allied casualties incurred during the Battle of the Somme.

THE ITALIAN AND EASTERN FRONTS

Early in the year Conrad von Hötzendorf, chief of staff of the Austro-Hungarian army, sought German agreement to an expedition against Italy, reasoning that eliminating Italy from the war, or inflicting a major defeat on it, would free Habsburg forces for the Eastern Front. Conrad requested that the Germans provide four divisions for the assault and take over part of the Austro-Hungarian line in

Galicia in order to release divisions for the attack. However, such was the poor state of relations between Conrad and Falkenhayn that the request was not even acknowledged. Conrad went ahead and withdrew six divisions from Galicia without informing Berlin in an attempt to carry out the offensive against the Italians in April. At the same time Falkenhayn, in preparing for the Verdun offensive, stripped the southern sector of 90 per cent of its German forces. In fact, bad weather in the Trentino was to delay Conrad's attack until May with what proved to be disastrous implications for the Austro-Hungarians on the Eastern Front.

During the summer of 1915 the Russians had been defeated in Galicia and pushed out of Poland, suffering two million casualties in the process. They had also seen the removal of their commander-in-chief, Grand Duke Nicholas. They had, however, made what was in many ways an impressive recovery in September. The fact that on September 1 Tsar Nicholas II assumed personal command of the army, despite his lack of military knowledge, was coincidental.

In agreeing to tie its summer 1916 effort to that of the British and French, the Russians had insisted that all the Allies should undertake relieving offensive action if one was subjected to German attack. They wished to ensure that there would be no repetition of the events of 1915 when the British and French had been singularly ineffective in diverting German attention during the Central Powers' summer offensive. The German attack at Verdun and the subsequent French request for assistance was not something they had anticipated.

"A short time ago death was the cruel stranger, the visitor with the flannel footsteps ... today it is the mad dog in the house ... One eats, one drinks beside the dead, one sleeps in the midst of the dying, one laughs and one sings in the company of corpses ..."

GEORGES DUHAMEL, FRENCH DOCTOR SERVING AT VERDUN

Lying as he fell
The remains of a German soldier, killed in a British assault on Beaumont-Hamel, in November 1916. Trench rats grew fat on a diet of human flesh.

THE BRUSILOV OFFENSIVE

The Russian attempt to come to the aid of France initially resulted in failure north of the Pripet River, where they launched an attack on Vilna (Vilnius) in March. Only around Lake Naroch did they achieve any success, but even their few gains were elminated by German counterattacks in April. However, Brusilov, commander of the Southwest Front, then proposed an offensive that was to inflict a devastating defeat on the Austro-Hungarian army. Launched on June 4, the offensive succeeded partly by achieving total surprise. Within eight days the Austro-Hungarian front south of the Pripet had given way and the Russians had taken 250,000 prisoners. The result was a collapse in morale and ultimately the integration of German and Austro-Hungarian forces under German command.

THE SOMME

Meanwhile, the offensive on Verdun was having a major impact on British and French plans for the Somme campaign. As the French commitment at Verdun deepened, so their planned role on the Somme diminished. In June, when the Germans renewed their Verdun offensive, the British brought forward the date of the Somme offensive. On July 1 over 100,000 Allied troops began a battle that was to last until November 18. By that date the Allies had failed to take a single town of any size and had incurred 630,000 casualties. The Germans, too, had suffered terrible losses. Falkenhayn, before being removed from command in August 1916, had insisted that "not a foot's breadth of ground must be voluntarily abandoned". In fighting to defend every foot of ground at the Somme, the Germans incurred over 660,000 casualties.

French involvement at the Somme
Although they did not play as great a role as originally planned in the Battle of the Somme, the French met with more success than the British during the initial advance.

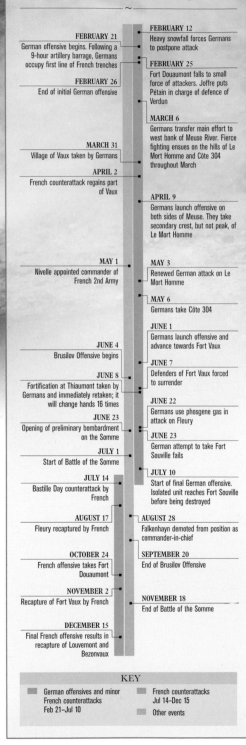

Battle of Verdun

The moment of death
This image – thought to be a still from a German film about the Battle of Verdun – captures a French soldier being thrown backwards by the force of a bullet. He was just one of over 500,000 French casualties of the battle.

Verdun was a fortified city surrounded by a ring of forts that were held by skeleton garrisons and had almost no heavy artillery. These had been dispatched to the Champagne battlefields in 1915 by a French high command that saw no need to maintain strong defensive positions around Verdun. It did not believe the Germans would attack Verdun, even as Falkenhayn made his very thorough preparations at the beginning of 1916 to launch an offensive in the sector in front of the city that would "bleed France white".

In a huge feat of organization, the Germans moved some 1,400 guns up to a 5-km (3-mile) front east of the Meuse River, ready for an assault by their Fifth Army on February 12, 1916. In the event, a ferocious blizzard forced a postponement and gave the French the opportunity to make some much-needed improvements to their defences.

The German Fifth Army possessed a clear advantage over the opposing French Second Army. On the 5-km (3-mile) front, between the Meuse and Orne, where its main effort was to be made, it had mustered nine divisions compared to the two available to the French. As well as this advantage in manpower, the Germans had a 4 to 1 advantage in artillery and had secured clear superiority in the air.

The Germans also had a telling logistical advantage. The Fifth Army was served by no fewer than a dozen rail lines, of which ten were broad gauge, and had secured bridges over the Meuse. Three rail lines met at Verdun, but the southern route had been severed by the German capture of St Mihiel in 1914, while the main route to Paris could be closed by German artillery fire. This left the French with the totally inadequate combination of one narrow gauge rail line and one road, both from Bar-le-Duc, along which to transport men and supplies. They also had no ready means of transferring forces from one bank of the Meuse to the other except through Verdun itself.

ADVANCE TO FORT DOUAUMONT

The German offensive finally began on February 21 with a shot from a Krupp 380-mm (15-in) naval gun that hit the cathedral in Verdun almost 32km (20 miles) away. After a massive nine-hour artillery bombardment, which buried many French soldiers alive in their trenches, at 4:00pm three German corps – a total of 140,000 men – began to move forward. By the end of the day one of the corps had occupied the Bois d'Haumont, but the other two had run into greater resistance than anticipated. The French troops fought tenaciously, making local counterattacks in the face of a continuing artillery attack. They could not, however, hold back the German advance for more than an hour or two, and on the 25th the Germans reached Douaumont, the greatest of the forts surrounding Verdun.

Many of Douaumont's guns had been removed the previous year and 500 infantrymen had been withdrawn. As a German regiment advanced towards it, the majority of the six regular and 57 Territorial gunners now manning the fort were inside, listening to a lecture. Just one gun was in action as the Germans overcame the few defenders in the surrounding trenches, and a lone sergeant climbed into the fort. The sergeant managed to fid and lock up both the gunners and the men who had been listening to the lecture, and he was shortly joined by two German officers, one of whom now took command of the fort. Douaumont had been lost without a shot being fired in its defence.

FRENCH RESISTANCE

The loss of Douaumont was a disaster for the French and could well have led to their deciding to withdraw from Verdun to a more defensible line. Instead Pétain, the much-respected general who was appointed on the night of the 25th to organize Verdun's defence, set about keeping the city out of German hands. The French army poured men, artillery and aircraft into the area as a spring thaw set in, turning the area into a quagmire and adding to the misery of the soldiers on both sides. The German Expressionist painter Franz Marc was to write on March 3: "For days I have seen nothing but the most terrrible things that can be painted from a human mind". The next day he was dead, one of over 400,000 casualties to be suffered by the Germans in the Verdun sector.

By the end of February the French had secured at least a rough equality in the air and in the number of heavy guns in the area. Pétain – a steadying and inspiring influence – ordered the re-arming of the forts around Verdun, and the extension of trenches and field positions so that infantry and forts might better support one another. Nonetheless, for the next two months the French situation on the heights of the Meuse remained desperate.

In Germany the fall of Douaumont was regarded as a victory that foreshadowed the fall of Verdun itself. In reality Germany's best chances of victory had gone by the 25th. Had the attack not been delayed for nine days, the Fifth Army would have fallen upon a wholly unprepared defence. In any event, a full-scale infantry assault on the first day might well have carried the French position. It had been a mistake to restrict the attack to the east bank of the Meuse, which meant that the German forces, even on the 22nd and 23rd, were subject to heavy enfilading fire from French artillery that was concentrated on the hills across the river.

LA VOIE SACRÉE

~

THE ROAD BETWEEN Bar-le-Duc and Verdun played such a vital role in the battle that it was subsequently christened the Voie Sacrée or Sacred Way. Along its 72km (45 miles), day and night, there were normally 3,500 trucks on the move, ferrying men, ammunition and supplies to the beleaguered city. During the initial crisis of February 21 to March 6 it delivered 23,000 tons of ammunition, 2,500 tons of other material and 190,000 men. One truck passed every 14 seconds, submitting the road surface to considerable wear and tear. Over the course of ten months, 8,500 men from 16 labour battalions worked to keep the road in a good state of repair and open.

The special unit responsible for controlling traffic and servicing the vehicles numbered 300 officers and 8,500 men; there were 30 breakdown trucks always on the road and repair crews stationed beside it. A broken-down vehicle was immediately moved to the roadside so as not to interrupt the flow of precious supplies. Automobile repair shops at Bar-le-Duc and Troyes worked ceaselessly, as did the hydraulic presses turning out solid rubber tyres.

Alongside the road ran a narrow-gauge single-track railway, *Le Meusien*. This was able to move about 1,800 tons of supplies per day. It carried the bulk of the food for the army in Verdun – some 16,600 officers and 420,000 men, not to mention 136,000 horses and mules – and brought back many of the wounded from the front.

Mending the road
Members of 16 labour battalions worked on resurfacing the road, breaking and shaping the stone which they first had to quarry.

Joining the queue
French infantry line up for transport to the front along the Voie Sacrée. The road was narrow in February, but it would soon be doubled in width under Pétain's orders.

ACTION ON THE WEST BANK

On March 6 the Germans began an attempt to clear the west bank and secure Le Mort Homme and Côte 304. Fighting for possession of these two hills continued through March. It also continued on the east bank around the ruins of the village of Vaux, which in one month changed hands 13 times.

On April 9 the Germans launched an offensive on both sides of the river, across a 32-km (20-mile) front. They took the secondary crest of Le Mort Homme on the first day, but they subsequently failed in their attempt to take the summit. Four days later all operations on the west bank ground to a halt in the relentless rain. Fighting, however, continued on the east bank around Forts Douaumont and Vaux, throughout April.

The German Fifth Army had lost some 120,000 men by the end of April. However, on May 3 it renewed its effort on the west bank of the Meuse no weaker in manpower and artillery than it had been at the start of the campaign ten weeks previously. Pétain had maintained forward defensive positions on the west bank of the Meuse to hold on to the main crest of Le Mort Homme and the neighbouring Côte 304. The French, however, could not withstand the renewed German advance. By May 6 the Germans had gained control of Côte 304 and by the end of the month they had cleared Le Mort Homme of all French troops.

The French, now under Nivelle, launched a series of attacks on the east bank, one of which reached, but failed to retake, Fort Douaumont on May 22–23. It was not until June 1 that the Germans could undertake a renewed offensive on the east bank and advance towards Fort Vaux, where they met with particularly strong resistance.

BATTLE OF VERDUN

FEBRUARY 21 – DECEMBER 18, 1916

~

The battle in front of Verdun was the longest single battle of the First World War. It was the only major German offensive undertaken on the Western Front between November 1914 and March 1918, and brought France perilously close to disastrous defeat at various times between February and July 1916. The German attacks on the east bank of the Meuse in February resulted in the capture of Fort Douaumont and forced the French to abandon the Wöevre Plain, but they failed to secure any major tactical advantage for the Germans. In March and April they captured the main French positions on the west bank before becoming embroiled in further attacks and counterattacks on the east bank in which, after July, neither side was able to secure the advantage. This situation changed in October when the French began a series of attacks that resulted in the recapture of Fort Douaumont and the end of the battle.

KEY

⌐	French front line	⊠	Fort/fortified site
⌐	German front line	▧	Road
➔	German advance	▧	Railway
➔	French advance		

The initial German attacks February 18–April 30
Initially the Germans concentrated on attacking French positions on the east bank of the Meuse. This was a mistake, and in March they began to attack on the west bank.

Mar 6
Germans shift their attack to west bank of Meuse

Apr 9
A renewed assault takes secondary, but not main, crest of Le Mort Homme

Montfaucon

Bois d'Avocourt

Avocourt

Parois

Domba...

French front-line trench
Many French trenches at Verdun were very basic. Soldiers would sometimes shelter from the rain in holes they had dug in the side of the trench, though they then ran the risk of being buried alive by the mud thrown up by the explosion of a shell nearby.

Raynal, leader of the defence of Fort Vaux
When Major Raynal – shown here flanked by his second-in-command and a German officer – was finally forced to surrender Fort Vaux, the Germans treated him as a hero.

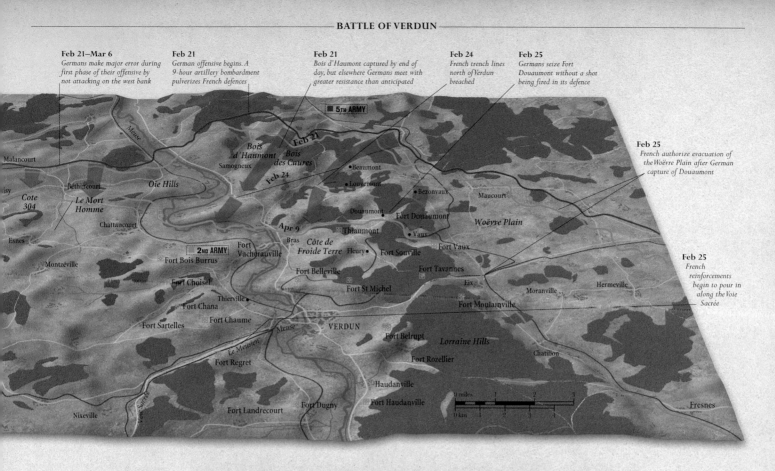

Feb 21–Mar 6
Germans make major error during first phase of their offensive by not attacking on the west bank

Feb 21
German offensive begins. A 9-hour artillery bombardment pulverizes French defences

Feb 21
Bois d'Haumont captured by end of day, but elsewhere Germans meet with greater resistance than anticipated

Feb 24
French trench lines north of Verdun breached

Feb 25
Germans seize Fort Douaumont without a shot being fired in its defence

Feb 25
French authorize evacuation of the Woëvre Plain after German capture of Douaumont

Feb 25
French reinforcements begin to pour in along the Voie Sacrée

Attrition on the east bank
May 1–August 8
With the German capture of the main French positions on the west bank, the Germans made one final attempt to defeat the French on the east bank before the Somme offensive began.

May 3
Germans renew offensive on west bank of Meuse, taking Côte 304 on May 6

Jun 1
Germans renew attack. Fort Vaux and Thiaumont are taken by Jun 9

Jul 10
Germans succeed in reaching Fort Souville, but are turned back by French counterattacks

Jun 23
Germans reach ridge line that commands Verdun and Meuse bridges, and Côte de Froide Terre

French attacks
October 24–December 18
The commander of the French forces, Nivelle, launched a series of attacks on October 24 that drove back the Germans on the east bank and ended the threat that they posed to Verdun.

Dec 15
Final offensive by the French results in recapture of Louvemont and Bezonvaux

Nov 2
French retake Fort Vaux

General Pétain
As commander of the defence of Verdun (February 25–April 30), Pétain saved it from being captured.

Oct 19
French mount their heaviest preliminary bombardment of the war so far against German-occupied Fort Douaumont

Oct 24
Following bombardment, French launch counterattack and retake Fort Douaumont

DEFENCE OF FORT VAUX

The German bombardment of Fort Vaux began on June 1, at one point firing shells at the rate of 1,500 to 2,000 an hour. Inside were 600 troops, many of them injured, under the command of Major Raynal. Just before dawn on the 2nd, the barrage suddenly stopped and two German battalions moved forward. By mid-afternoon they had overwhelmed the defenders and occupied a large part of the superstructure. Raynal was determined to resist, and he and his men withdrew to the underground corridors where a grim battle was fought in the darkness with grenades and machine-guns. On June 4 the Germans used flamethrowers in an attempt to drive out the French with asphyxiating black smoke. With all radio contact severed, at midday Raynal sent out his last message by carrier pigeon: "We are still holding our position, but are being attacked by gases and smoke of very deadly character. We are in need of immediate relief. Put us into communication with Souville again at once for visual signalling. We get no answer from there to our calls. This is our last pigeon!"

The following day the first French relief force arrived. Like the four that followed, it suffered terrible casualties in the course of trying, but failing, to relieve the garrison. The men in the fort were now suffering from lack of water and in their desperation they were licking the moisture on the walls or drinking their own urine. On June 7 Raynal decided that there was no alternative but to surrender. Remarkably, in their brave defence of the fort, the French garrison had suffered a hundred casualties; the Germans had suffered over 2,740.

On June 8 the German Fifth Army reached the fortification at Thiaumont, within 5km (3 miles) of Verdun. In almost getting to Pétain's designated last line of resistance in front of the city, the Germans had inflicted appalling losses on the French, stretching their defence to breaking point. The French were now confronted by the very real prospect of losing Verdun and, with it, many of their guns. They were, however, determined to hold on to the city no matter what the cost. In the words of Pétain, writing to Joffre on June 11: "Verdun is menaced and Verdun must not fall. The capture of the city would constitute for the Germans an inestimable success which would greatly raise their morale and correspondingly lower our own."

In the second week of June, when the defences around Thiaumont consisted mostly of gaps, there was a pause in the fighting. On June 4 the Russian Brusilov Offensive had been launched (see pages 148–50) and had quickly overwhelmed the opposing Austro-Hungarian forces along a 450-km (300-mile) front. Falkenhayn was now forced to suspend operations at Verdun in order to attend to the needs of the Eastern Front.

Trench near Douaumont
The heroic French counterattacks at Verdun gave rise to the slogan "on les aura" ("we'll get 'em"), used here on a war-bond poster. But while the French succeeded in recapturing the Verdun forts and occupying German trenches, they did so at terrible cost. Almost 650,000 men lost their lives in the ten-month long battle.

"What a bloodbath, what horrid images, what a slaughter. I just cannot find the words to express my feelings. Hell cannot be this dreadful."

ALBERT JOUBAIRE, FRENCH SOLDIER AT VERDUN

GERMAN OFFENSIVE ON FORT SOUVILLE

The Germans renewed their offensive at Fleury on June 22, their objective to take Fort Souville, which overlooked Verdun itself and all the bridges over the Meuse. Like the advance of February 21–25, this latest advance raised the question for the French high command of whether it should evacuate the east bank. While, however, this may have been conceivable in February, it was totally out of the question in June. Too much had been invested in holding Verdun, and too much artillery was in place on the east bank, for the French to accept defeat and reorganize their defences on the west bank.

Surprised by the German use of phosgene gas near Fort Souville on the evening of June 22, the French lost Fleury the following day. However, an immediate counterattack brought the German advance in this critical sector to a halt. A further German offensive planned for early July was then delayed for two days by torrential rain that turned the battlefield into a morass of mud. The attack was finally launched at midnight on the 10th, with the French artillery being engulfed by gas until well after the German infantry had begun to advance. The Germans succeeded in reaching Souville and made further gains in the next two days, but these were eliminated by a French counterattack on the 14th.

The fact that the tide of battle had been brought to Souville a second time was a reflection of German failure to make the decisive breakthrough. A German victory at Verdun no longer appeared to be a real possibility. This did not mean, however, that the battle was allowed to die. The summer passed with a series of local attacks and counterattacks, the Anglo-French Somme offensive launched on July 1 denying the German Fifth Army the reserves needed for a resumption of large-scale operations. Indeed, repeatedly subjected to French artillery fire, the Germans would have relinquished many of their gains if shattered villages such as Fleury had not now acquired an exaggerated significance. After Falkenhayn's dismissal on August 28, the German leadership sought to limit commitments at Verdun as pressure from the French intensified.

The success of French offensives in the last three months of the battle stemmed largely from the employment of the creeping barrage, a tactical innovation developed by Nivelle, in which artillery fire moved forward in stages, just ahead of the advancing infantry. In a rapid attack on October 24 the French recaptured Fort Douaumont in the process of recovering ground that the German Fifth Army had taken four months to capture. On November 2 Fort Vaux was retaken. The final French attack on December 15 resulted in the recapture of Louvemont and Bezonvaux, lost in the first days of the original German attack. Both sides then allowed the battle to die.

The resilience of the French at Verdun was as remarkable as it had been unanticipated by Falkenhayn when planning his offensive on the city. It strengthened French morale, but it also came at the cost of an estimated 542,000 French casualties, of whom about half were killed. Also unanticipated by Falkenhayn was the number of German casualties. The Germans lost almost as many men as the French – 434,000 – in the course of achieving an advance of just 8 km (5 miles) or less along a 32-km (20-mile) front during ten months of fighting.

Railway gun

Both sides used railway guns at Verdun. The French brought up two massive 40-cm (16-in) Modele 15 howitzers to pound the defences of Fort Douaumont before finally recapturing it on October 24.

NIEUPORT 17

~

INTRODUCED IN MARCH 1916, the Nieuport 17 played a major role in France winning back control of the skies over Verdun from the Germans. An improved version of the Nieuport 11, the "*bébé*", the first fighter to compete successfully against the formidable German Fokker Eindecker, the larger Nieuport 17 was soon nicknamed the "*superbébé*". With a ceiling of 5,300 m (17,388 ft), it could easily outclimb its chief rival, the Fokker E.III. Armed with a single Vickers machine-gun, it was flown by many French aces, including Charles Nungesser, ten of whose 43 victories were scored over Verdun. The Nieuport was the first plane ever to be equipped with air-to-air rockets. On May 22 five out of six German balloons in the Verdun sector were shot down in flames by French airmen.

The synchronized Vickers .303 machine-gun fired through the propeller. Early versions had a Lewis gun fitted on the top wing

The 9-cylinder, 110-hp rotary engine gave a top speed of 177 kph (110 mph)

The struts were often fitted with Le Prieur rockets, used for shooting down observation balloons

OBSERVATION AND COMMUNICATION

Before 1914 the belief in the primacy of offensive action largely negated the need for strategic reconnaissance, while cavalry was expected to provide adequate tactical reconnaissance. In the war's opening weeks, however, aircraft successfully conducted strategic reconnaissance at Tannenberg and the Marne, and cavalry failed to provide adequate tactical reconnaissance.

Trench systems – with an area behind the enemy system to which access was impossible except from the air – changed requirements. At the strategic level proper reconnaissance could only be conducted by aircraft and cameras. The wireless was needed for the rapid transmission of reports. The British had designed and tested an airborne wireless before August 1914, but they only put it into general service in 1915. During the Artois offensive in May, they employed aircraft that spotted targets and reported to the artillery by morse transmissions. Morse keys were, however, difficult to use while flying, and in February 1916 airborne wireless telephony – the transmission of voice messages – was tested for the first time. Instead of aerials, the first sets had a trailing wire that had to be reeled

in as necessity dictated. A reliable transmitter became available in sufficient numbers to equip formations in early 1917, but the British kept the majority of aircraft with wireless telephony around London for home defence. Just two squadrons on the Western Front were similarly equipped, and these were not given an offensive role in case a set was captured and copied. The range of these sets was about 160 km (100 miles), rising to 290 km (180 miles) in 1918.

At the tactical level, observation had a crucial role to play in directing artillery fire, and could be conducted from balloons linked by telephone cable to command posts on the ground. The first balloons for tactical reconnaissance were produced by the Germans and the French, and the latter supplied one to the British army in May 1915. At this stage responsibility for airships and balloons was vested solely in the Royal Navy. By 1916 the Royal Flying Corps had assumed responsibility for balloons on the Western Front, though their two-man crews were drawn exclusively from the artillery. Ultimately the British were to have a balloon company for each of their five armies on the Western Front.

Message shells
Case
Shells were used to send written messages up the line.

Message holder

Cap

Telephone communication
The field telephone enabled artillery forward observation officers to relay the results of shelling back to the gunners, so that they could adjust their aim accordingly.

Bird's-eye view
A soldier on a ladder inside this fake tree, peered through a peep-hole and passed down information on enemy positions to a colleague, who transmitted it to the artillery battery.

Wireless communication
Wireless sets that received and transmitted morse messages were used by troops once they had moved beyond the reach of field telephone cables.

Portable field telephone
A portable telephone was carried in a leather shoulder bag. In addition to a telephone handset for verbal communication, it had a key for transmitting morse when the line became too noisy for speech to be heard clearly.

Observation from a great height
Balloons anchored to the ground were an ideal way of observing enemy activities, but the operator had little chance of survival if a gas-filled balloon was set alight by enemy fire.

Parachute flare cartridge

Star shells

GERMAN FLARE PISTOL

BRITISH PARACHUTE FLARE PISTOL

Star shells
Magnesium flares, known as star shells, were fired into the air to send pre-arranged signals, often using different colours. Some shells had parachutes that slowed their descent. Star shells were also used to illuminate No Man's Land and reveal enemy activity.

Dog messengers
Dogs were used by both sides to carry messages between trenches, in tubes attached to their collars. They were trained to leap barbed wire, and their speed and agility made them difficult targets for snipers.

Pigeon post
Often the only means of communication, pigeons were widely used to carry messages from the front to headquarters. During the German siege of Fort Vaux near Verdun, the French defenders relied on pigeons to carry their requests for help.

Nonetheless, French avoidance of defeat at Verdun was very dearly bought. Many French divisions moving up to Verdun saw themselves as lambs being driven to the slaughter. As they approached they heard the constant roar of the great guns, reminding them, in the words of one soldier, of "a gigantic forge that ceased neither day nor night". All around was a sea of mud in which stood a few solitary tree stumps – all that remained of the once extensive forests. The so-called communications trenches that began up to 3 km (2 miles) from the front line were often little more than ditches surrounded by water-filled shell craters into which heavily-burdened soldiers might fall and drown. Invariably hanging above this desolate scene was a pall of smoke and the stench of rotting corpses. Few could go through such an experience without being psychologically scarred for life.

Unlike the Germans, who fed reinforcements to the divisions that were in place, the French rotated divisions in the line. As a result, four-fifths of the French army saw service in the war's longest, and one of its most horrific, battles.

ACTION ON VIMY RIDGE
While the French were pouring virtually all their forces into the Verdun sector, the British were active on Vimy Ridge in Artois. In the autumn of 1915 the French had given up their struggle to recapture the ridge from the Germans. Instead they had spent the winter months tunnelling deep underground, creating a system of galleries and saps. However, as the British were to discover on their arrival in March, the Germans had dug deeper and more extensively. A battle began for control of the mine shafts, in which the tunnellers of both sides attempted to blow up sections of the line above. By mid-May eight British and five French tunnelling companies had begun to get the upper hand, but on May 21 the Germans launched a surprise offensive which began with an intensive bombardment of the British front line. Those who survived were half buried in earth and unable to prevent the Germans moving forward to construct a new line.

On the 23rd the Germans began to bombard the British lines again. Although this time the British were ready to launch their own offensive, they lost many men to accurate German shelling. By late May the British had suffered almost 2,500 casualties while the Germans had suffered over 1,340. With the British high command refusing to divert any artillery from the Somme to Vimy Ridge, there was no likelihood of the Germans being driven off the ridge in the immediate future.

With the aim of reducing German pressure on the French at Verdun, the Russians launched an offensive in March north of the Pripet River. This achieved litttle. Far more successful was the Brusilov Offensive south of the Pripet in June, though by September it had petered out. The Romanians invaded Austria-Hungary in August, thus provoking a campaign of conquest by the Central Powers that ended with the defeat of Romania.

1916 MARCH 18
Russian offensive from positions east of Vilna begins; limited gains at cost of heavy casualties

1916 APRIL 4
Brusilov takes up position as commander of Russia's Southwest Army Group

APRIL 14
Naroch battle ends after Russians beaten back by Germans

APRIL 14
Brusilov proposes offensive over extended front

JUNE 6
Russians capture Lutsk; German reinforcements dispatched from Verdun; Austrian from Trentino

JUNE 4
Start of Brusilov Offensive; Austrian line soon broken in two places

JUNE 16
Germans launch counterattack; few gains made

JUNE 18
Czernowitz falls to Russians

JULY 28–AUGUST 17
Battle of Kowel; Russians fail to take the town

MID-AUGUST
Release of German troops from Western Front means Central Powers now have more divisions south of the Pripet than Russia

AUGUST 27
Romania declares war on Austria-Hungary

AUGUST 27
Romania invades Transylvania

SEPTEMBER 18
Falkenhayn arrives to assume command of Romanian campaign. German-Austrian 9th Army launches attack at Vulcan Pass

SEPTEMBER 1
Mackensen's Danube Army, made up of Bulgars, Turks and Germans, invades Dobruja from the south

SEPTEMBER 20
Brusilov offensive comes to halt

SEPTEMBER 20
Romanians, aided by Russian and Serbian forces, halt advance by Danube Army

OCTOBER 16
Russians launch attack towards Vladimir-Volynskiy in unsuccessful attempt to resume Brusilov Offensive

OCTOBER 10
Bulk of Romanian troops now driven out of Transylvania

NOVEMBER 21
Craiova falls to Falkenhayn's forces

NOVEMBER 23
Part of Mackensen's army crosses Danube to link up with Falkenhayn in attack on Bucharest

DECEMBER 5
Oilfields of Ploesti blown up by British

DECEMBER 6
Fall of Bucharest

DECEMBER 7
Beginning of Romanian retreat on all fronts

1917 JANUARY 7
Romanian campaign ends

KEY

■ Lake Naroch offensive Mar 18–Apr 14	■ Romanian campaign Aug 27, 1916–Jan 7, 1917
■ Brusilov Offensive Jun 4–Sept 20	

Russia Fights Back

Putting on a brave face
This picture of Russian front-line troops gives no hint of the equipment shortages that had bedevilled the army since the outbreak of war, nor of the spirit of defeatism that was spreading among the troops in early 1916.

IN THE SPRING OF 1916 the Russian armies had twice as many men as the Germans and Austro-Hungarians in both the northern and central sectors of the Eastern Front but only about the same number in the south. It was therefore predictable that the Russians, when asked by the French to mount an attack that would divert German attention from Verdun, should choose to do so north of the Pripet River and advance towards Vilna (Vilnius). The Lithuanian town contained an important railhead and was at the centre of a major road network, which meant it was well worth recapturing from the Germans.

VILNA AND LAKE NAROCH

The Russian offensive opened on March 18. However, there was a notable lack of co-ordination between army groups and between artillery and infantry. There was also little knowledge of enemy positions because of a lack of reconnaissance, forcing much of the artillery to fire blind: one of the artillery bombardments became known, after the corps commander, as "Pleshknov's *son et lumière*". Despite the length of front, the attacks were very narrowly directed, with the result that the attacking forces were mown down by flanking fire. The

Russian troops who managed to reach the German trenches found themselves shelled by German artillery who had received two week's warning of what was to come as a result of the only too common lack of Russian security. Only in one sector, around Lake Naroch, where the Russians attacked on the 21st across the ice and through thick fog, did they achieve any success. However, the few small gains made were eliminated by German counterattacks in April.

Perhaps the only surprising aspect of this action was that the Germans were obliged to move three divisions to the threatened sectors and sustained 20,000 casualties. The Russian armies lost some 110,000 men, including 12,000 fatalities from frostbite. According to the Russians' own figures, 300,000 Russian troops, with artillery support on a scale greater than that available even to the Central Powers in 1914 and 1915, had been routed by 50,000 Germans. The debacle left the Russian armies in this sector badly demoralized.

THE RUSSIAN ARMY

~

IN 1914 THE RUSSIAN army had around 1.3 million men, with a reserve of about 4 million. In theory there were an additional 22 million men of combat age, but almost half were exempt from conscription. There was a belief in Europe that the Russian army would have a steamroller effect, but this failed to materialize. In 1914 alone, Russia lost the equivalent of its first-line strength, and in its disastrous retreat from Poland in 1915 it lost a further 3 million. As a result, successive call-ups merely covered losses rather than increasing numbers. There was also a shortage of trained officers, the majority of whom were killed in 1914–15. In 1916 an infantry regiment of 3,000 troops had only 12 officers.

The Russians had not anticipated a protracted war and suffered from material shortages throughout 1915. The production of 70,000 rifles a month fell fell far short of requirements – under-estimated at 200,000 a month – and unarmed reinforcements were a common sight in 1915. The need to import 2,300,000 rifles also gave rise to logistical problems caused by having ten different rifles in service.

By the summer of 1916 the army was better equipped and organized, but by the autumn Russia's mounting economic problems were impinging on troops, who were consequently becoming increasingly poorly fed and clothed. Even more ominous was the fact that Russia stood at the end of its manpower resources. After March 1917 the available reserves would not cover normal losses.

КТО
ПОДПИШЕТСЯ НА

Russian cavalry
The main weapons of the cavalry were the lance and the sabre. They also carried a rifle over the shoulder.

Bebout
A knife such as this, with a carved handle and sheath, was carried by a gunner, to be used in close fighting instead of a bayonet.

PAPAKHA

EPAULETTES

Hand grenade
A pre-war design, this stick grenade had an effective time fuse that was activated as the handle was released.

Russian uniform
Khaki was adopted by the Russians as the colour for their uniforms as early as 1907. The winter hat, the papakha, carries the oval cockade in the Romanov colours.

COAT

Moisin-Nagant rifle
Like all Russian rifles, this 7.62-mm (0.3-in) rifle was used with its bayonet fixed. Rifle production reached 111,000 a month in 1916, but demand still outstripped supply.

Revolver
This Moisin-Nagant revolver would have been carried by machine-gunners and artillery men.

THE BRUSILOV OFFENSIVE

Following the Naroch debacle, the new commander of the Russian Southwest Front, Brusilov, made a radical proposal. It was clear that lengthy preparations and prolonged bombardments sacrificed the element of surprise and enabled the defender to ensure adequate reserves were in position to counter any break-through. Furthermore, relative shortages of guns and shells enforced concentration on frontages that were very narrow, adding to the ease with which breaches could be sealed. Brusilov recommended that the armies under his command should launch a general offensive, with each army attacking along 48-km (30-mile) frontages after a brief bombard-ment, thus tying down enemy reserves and preventing effective counterattack. By paying very careful attention to artillery fire plans, ensuring

Austro-Hungarian prisoners
The Austro-Hungarian forces in Galicia were completely unprepared for the offensive launched by Brusilov on June 4, and by June 10 over 193,000 of them had been taken prisoner by the Russians.

AUSTRO-HUNGARIAN DEBACLE

Brusilov's proposals were not well received within the Russian high command. However, the defeats of the Italians in the Trentino in May (see pages 232–33) led to appeals for a Russian diversionary offensive, and with only the four armies of the Southwest Front able to take action immediately, Brusilov was authorized to begin operations on June 4.

The Brusilov Offensive spelt disaster for the four Austro-Hungarian armies along the 450-km (300 mile) front that stretched from the Pripet to Czernowitz. Thinly spread over an extended front, they had invested far too much confidence in the strong defensive positions they had prepared, and, critically, they had not expected attack. In many sectors they had dug trenches up to 8m (20ft) deep – sometimes five lines of them – and with sufficient supplies of food and water, the troops had made themselves comparatively comfortable.

close co-ordination between artillery and infantry, sapping to within 100m (110yds) of enemy positions and constructing defensive shelters for reserves, Brusilov sought to minimize weaknesses. His formula represented a radical departure from anything seen previously on the Eastern Front.

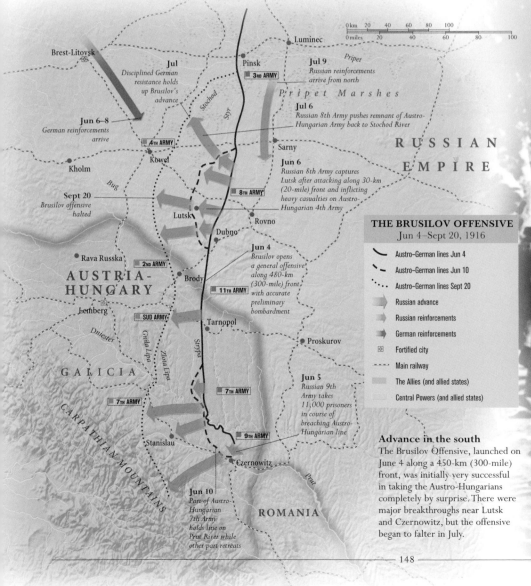

Advance in the south
The Brusilov Offensive, launched on June 4 along a 450-km (300-mile) front, was initially very successful in taking the Austro-Hungarians completely by surprise. There were major breakthroughs near Lutsk and Czernowitz, but the offensive began to falter in July.

The Russian bombardment on June 4 took the Austro-Hungarians completely by surprise. The Russian forces advancing behind it found that many enemy forces had become trapped in their deep shelters and had no alternative but to surrender.

Immediately south of the Pripet Marshes, the Russian Eighth Army under Kaledin advanced along a 30-km (20-mile) front towards the town of Lutsk, which it took on June 6 after overwhelming the Austro-Hungarian Fourth Army. By June 10 the Fourth Army had lost 60,000 men, and despite being helped by marshy terrain that channelled Russian attacks, it only just managed to hold Russian drives intended to eliminate German positions. Relief was to come only on June 16, when four German divisions withdrawn from Verdun and four Austro-Hungarian divisions withdrawn from the Trentino went into action. Initially these divisions made only slight gains while suffering heavy losses.

Further south, breakthroughs on a smaller scale were made by the Russian Eleventh and Seventh armies. In the far south the Austro-Hungarian Seventh Army initially stood its ground behind the Dniester River, using all its reserves to withstand an attack by the Russian Ninth Army under Letchitsky. It was, however, forced to retreat when the Russians broke through defences north of the river on June 7.

ALEXEI BRUSILOV

~

THE MOST SUCCESSFUL RUSSIAN GENERAL of the First World War, Brusilov (1853–1926) was charged at the war's outbreak with leading the Eighth Army in Galicia. Here he quickly demonstrated the innovative planning techniques and tactical flexibility that were his trademarks. Despite combining early successes with defeat by the Austro-Hungarians in Galicia in the summer of 1915, Brusilov was appointed as commander of the Southwest Front (the Russian term for an army group) in March 1916. In June he was responsible for an offensive of unprecedented effectiveness that took Russian armies back to the foothills of the Carpathians. One of only two offensives in the war to be named after their commanding general, it is often considered to have fatally impaired the effectiveness of the Austro-Hungarian army.

Following the Russian "February Revolution" in 1917, Brusilov became commander-in-chief of the Russian army. However, after directing the Kerensky Offensive in July, he was replaced by Kornilov. He was not involved in the initial stages of the Russian Civil War, but in 1920 he led the Red Army into Poland.

By mid-June the Seventh Army had been almost completely destroyed, losing over 100,000 men, after being split in two by the Russians. As one part retreated westwards, the other attempted to hold positions along the Prut River west of Czernowitz, before withdrawing southwestwards to the Bukovina region.

By the end of the month the Russians had advanced over 96 km (60 miles) in sections of the front south of the Pripet, and had taken 350,000 prisoners and more than 700 guns. They were ready to press on towards the Carpathian foothills.

Russian field hospital
Although the Russians met with great success in the initial stages of the Brusilov Offensive, they continued to suffer enormous casualties. By the end of July they had incurred 450,000 and their reserves had fallen from 400,000 to 100,000 men.

By the end of July the Southwest Front's offensive was faltering. The advantage of surprise was inevitably dissipating itself and the Russians were beginning to become exhausted. Lacking reinforcements, Brusilov now concentrated on taking action to protect his northern flank, which was exposed to German forces that separated his armies from the Russian army group in the central sector. On July 28 he launched an assault north of the Pripet Marshes in an unsuccessful attempt to capture the important railway junction of Kowel.

INCREASED GERMAN INVOLVEMENT

The German offensive at Verdun had come to a halt by the end of June, and with the attack on the Somme in July revealing the Allied hand, the Germans were free to move good-quality formations to Galicia. By mid-August, the release of 18 divisions from the Western Front brought the number of German divisions south of the Pripet to 24, which meant that the Central Powers had 72 divisions in comparison with Brusilov's 61. Perhaps more importantly, the German high command had insisted on a number of

changes to give itself virtually total control of the Austro-Hungarian armies at both the operational and administrative levels. By insisting on German appointments to command and staff positions, and by integrating German and Austro-Hungarian formations ultimately to company level, Berlin ensured that Vienna lost its freedom of action everywhere except on the Italian Front. Austria-Hungary might have resented the German connection and after 1916 hope to conclude a peace that would leave the Empire intact, but after the Brusilov Offensive its separate existence was little more than a fiction. With the entry of Romania into the war on August 27, the Germans extended the command arrangements they had imposed upon Austria-Hungary to both Bulgaria and Turkey.

Romania's entry into the war extended Russia's commitments over another 400km (250 miles) of

Russians standing over Austro-Hungarian dead
Although the Brusilov Offensive came to an end in September, sporadic fighting continued in the Carpathians through October, adding to the estimated total of 1.5 million casualties suffered by the two sides.

front and were later deemed by the Russian military to have cost them the chance of securing Kowel. In reality, had such a chance existed then it was in June rather than in August and September. Although the last actions of the main Brusilov Offensive south of the Pripet did not take place until September, Brusilov's real effort was over after July.

EFFECTS OF THE OFFENSIVE

The Brusilov Offensive is seen as evidence of what Russian armies could achieve when well commanded and led. However, it ultimately involved very heavy Russian losses – almost a million men, half of them prisoners – for what were strictly limited gains. Both at the time and after the offensive ended, its costs caused domestic anguish. The various towns that were captured and military successes that were registered generated no popular enthusiasm, merely the knowledge that what had been gained would be lost.

> "In the mountains, bad, quite inadequate shelter, icy cold, rain and mist. An excruciating life."
>
> FROM THE DIARY OF AUSTRIAN GUNNER
> (AND PHILOSOPHER) LUDWIG WITTGENSTEIN, JULY 15, 1916

RUSSIA IN TURMOIL

~

DURING THE SUMMER OF 1915, as the Russian army was driven back eastwards across Poland, hundreds of thousands of refugees, their homes and farms destroyed, headed for the cities and towns. Along with disease, misery and panic, there were widespread rumours of treachery, which focused on the Tsarina Alexandra, a German princess by birth.

The catastrophe exposed the incompetence of Russia's autocratic government, but Tsar Nicholas II had neither the will nor the wit to change. Instead of liberalizing his regime by appointing efficient, experienced ministers, and securing the support of the duma (Russia's parliament), the zemstvos (municipal councils) and the industrialists' War Industries Committee, Nicholas decided to rule like a true autocrat and take personal command of the Russian army. In his absence, power passed to the tsarina, who was herself under the demonic influence of the faith-healer Rasputin.

While Nicholas was away at the front, Alexandra and Rasputin began to exercise a disastrous influence over government appointments. From September 1915 to February 1917 Russia had four prime ministers, five ministers of the interior, three foreign ministers, three war ministers, three ministers of transport and four ministers of agriculture. "I am here, don't laugh at silly old wifey," wrote Alexandra to her husband, "but she has trousers on unseen."

The Russian bourgeoisie was in despair. The Zemstvo Union – based on a network

Rasputin surrounded by court admirers
Rasputin's hypnotic powers, which apparently relieved the suffering of the haemophiliac Crown Prince Alexis, gave him a powerful emotional hold over the tsarina.

of local councils – had become virtually a state within a state, but could do little to alleviate the ever-worsening situation. The scarcity of food and fuel, rampant inflation, the collapse of the transport system and the rapidly rising crime rate were combining to create an explosive, revolutionary situation.

At the outset of the war many liberal-minded Russians had hoped that a successful military campaign would unite the Russian people and forestall the need for radical reform of the state. However, they now came to the conclusion that radical reform was a pre-condition for military success. In December 1916 Rasputin was murdered by a group of young nobles hoping to save the honour of Russia and the imperial family. But they were too late. Russia was already on the brink of a revolution that would consign the Romanov dynasty to history.

НА
ПОМОЩЬ
ЖЕРТВАМЪ
ВОЙНЫ

"War victims need your help"
Russian citizens were exhorted to rally round and support those wounded in the war, who could expect little help from the autocratic, inefficient government.

Recruiting troops at Bogorodsk, near Moscow
Heavy Russian losses throughout 1914–16 meant that there was a constant need to call up more men just to maintain numbers. A shortage of weapons in the first two years meant that many soldiers were not even equipped with rifles. The supply of munitions, however, began to improve as the political situation deteriorated.

Promoting war bonds
In common with other governments, the Russians raised extra funds by encouraging citizens to invest in war bonds. This poster promises a return of 5.5 per cent, but investors never saw this money.

Помогайте армии
въ ея великомъ дѣлѣ
и подписывайтесь на

Наши города, села и храмы
ждутъ освобожденія
отъ вражескаго нашествія.

ВОЕННЫЙ 5½% ЗАЕМЪ.

THE ROMANIAN CAMPAIGN

At the beginning of 1916 Romania was still neutral and was seeking to exploit the opportunity provided by the war to advance its territorial ambitions – directed particularly against Austria-Hungary over Transylvania, but also against Russia over Bessarabia. It was, however, aware of the risks involved in pursuing such a policy if it failed to intervene on the winning side before the war's end. By 1916, following the conquest of Serbia, and the entry of Bulgaria into the war, the Central Powers had secured for themselves a potentially overwhelming advantage in the Balkans. But in the course of the year, Allied inducements, initial Russian success in the Brusilov Offensive, and the growing signs of Austria-Hungary's disintegration, prompted Romania to declare war on the Central Powers on August 27.

Allied support – in the form of an offensive from Salonika in Macedonia and a Russian move against Bukovina – provided the basis of a Romanian plan of campaign to stand on the defence against Bulgaria while striking through the Carpathian mountains against Austria-Hungary. However, by the time Romania had shown its hand, the Brusilov Offensive was faltering and Austria-Hungary and Germany had forces available with which to meet a new commitment in the Balkans. On top of this was the fact that, with the Salonika front quiescent, the Bulgarian army was able to spend the

Burning oil near Constanza
As the Romanian armies retreated, British agents played a major role in destroying oil dumps and wells in order to keep them out of the hands of the Central Powers.

summer of 1916 preparing for the expected Romanian intervention in the autumn. This meant that the imbalance of forces, in terms of both numbers and quality, was very clearly against Romania when it entered the war. The nature of the terrain added to the disadvantages it faced, as did the inadequacy of the Romanian rail system, which made it impossible to move rapidly between the two fronts facing Transylvania.

Austrian troops enter Bucharest, December 6
A Romanian attack on the Danube Army as it advanced towards Bucharest was defeated following the intervention of the Austro-German Ninth Army.

THE INITIAL OFFENSIVE

The initial Romanian offensive into Austria-Hungary, launched on August 27, met with little opposition and succeeded in advancing some 80km (50 miles) into Transylvania before being halted. On September 1, however, a combined army of Bulgarians, Turks and Germans invaded the region of Dobruja and advanced almost to Constanza before being repulsed by the Romanians with the support of Russian and Serbian formations. Then, as the Romanians began to send more troops to meet this threat, the Austro-German Ninth Army opened its counter-offensive on September 18 at the Vulcan Pass. The main effort unfolded in the centre over the next 16 days, and by October 10 the Romanians had been

High-level discussions
Mackensen (*left*), commander of the Danube Army, confers with Archduke Friedrich (*centre*), commander of the Austro-Hungarian First Army, during the Romanian campaign. Mackensen remained in command of the army of occupation in Romania until the end of the war.

forced to evacuate Hungarian territory. Within another two weeks the Austro-German Ninth Army had secured the critically important Predeal Pass. But shortly after, as the Russians extended their front southwards in support of the Romanians, the onset of winter brought the closing down of major operations in Moldavia.

THE ADVANCE OF THE CENTRAL POWERS

The Germans redirected their attention to Wallachia and the Dobruja and made advances in both areas. Craiova fell on November 21, and two days later the Danube Army, formed from units of each of the Central Powers, crossed the lower Danube around Sistova (Svishtov) and began to advance on Bucharest. Its consequent separation from the German Ninth Army provided a desperate Romanian army, which faced certain defeat if it remained on the defensive, with a final opportunity to counterattack and perhaps buy the time needed to allow more Russian reinforcements to arrive. The initial Romanian drive pinned down the left flank of the Danube Army. But as the Ninth Army moved to the

latter's support, the Romanian offensive collapsed and Bucharest fell on December 6.

The subsequent Central Powers' pursuit of the retreating Romanian armies was slowed by the poor state of the roads, but by the new year southern Moldavia and the whole of Wallachia and the Dobruja had been cleared of Allied forces. The Central Powers had gained control of Romania's oil- and grain-producing regions and Russia had been left with a widening commitment in its vulnerable southern regions. The situation in this

sector was to remain more or less unchanged until December 7, 1917 when Romania, left to its own resources after the Bolshevik Revolution in Russia, concluded an armistice with the Central Powers.

The Central Powers' invasion of Romania
The Romanian invasion of Transylvania, launched on August 27, was halted after an 80-km (50-mile) advance. An Austro-German offensive then drove the Romanians out of Hungary by October 10, while the Danube Army advanced northwards through the Dobruja. By December the Romanians had been defeated by stronger forces.

THE ROMANIAN CAMPAIGN
Aug 27, 1916–Jan 7, 1917

→ Romanian offensive into Transylvania
Aug 27–Sept 18, 1916

➘ Central Powers Front in Transylvania
Sept 18, 1916

⇒ Austro-German advance through Wallachia and Moldavia Sept 18, 1916–Jan 7, 1917

⇒ Danube Army advance through Dobruja
Sept 1, 1916–Jan 7, 1917

⌒ Central Powers front in Dobruja Sept 23, 1916

⌒ Romanian positions Nov 26, 1916

⌒ Central Powers front Jan 7, 1917

◉ Town captured by Central Powers, with date

--- Major railway

The Allies (and allied states)

Central Powers (and allied states)

0 km 20 40 60 80 100
0 miles 20 40 60 80 100

AUSTRIA-HUNGARY

RUSSIAN EMPIRE

Jassy

Prut

Maros

Klausenburg

TRANSYLVANIA

4TH ARMY

MOLDAVIA

Sept 18
Falkenhayn launches counterattack, forcing Romanians back through Vulcan Pass on Oct 10

1ST ARMY

Schossburg

Berlad

9TH ARMY

Hermannstadt

Sereth

Hatseg

Focsani

Galatz

Isman

T R A N S Y L V A N I A N   A L P S

Predeal Pass

OCT 14

2ND ARMY

Dec 1
Falkenhayn's forces advance after defeat of Romanian attack in front of Bucharest

Mehadia
Vulcan Pass
1ST ARMY
Campolung
Ploesti

OCT 25
Cernavoda

OCT 25
Constanza

Orsova

Aug 27
Romanians begin advance into Transylvania

W A L L A C H I A

DEC 6
◉ **BUCHAREST**

Oct 20
Mackensen's forces begin advance to Constanza and Cernavoda

R O M A N I A

Arges

NOV 21
Craiova

Aluta

SEPT 6
Turtukai

3RD ARMY
Danube

Sept 23
Front stabilized

D O B R U J A

Danube

Sistova

SEPT 9
Silistria

Nov 23
Danube Army begins advance on Bucharest

DANUBE
Mackensen

Rustuchuk

Sept 1
Combined army of Bulgarians and Germans crosses border

Varna

S E R B I A

B U L G A R I A

BLACK SEA

LIFE AT THE FRONT

THE AMOUNT OF TIME A MAN spent in the front-line trenches varied over the course of the war, but the most usual period of duty was between four and six days. At any one time, only a minority of soldiers were in "active" sections of the line – firing or being fired at. The rest were battling against hunger, sleeplessness and the miseries arising from the weather and their cramped, damp and unsanitary living conditions.

The quality of dugouts varied. While German reserves were relatively comfortable in deep bunkers, the French hunkered down in notoriously wretched trenches. Sleep in the trenches was a snatched luxury and clean water was in short supply. Most dugouts had a brazier for heat and for warming food; for toilets there were buckets, or the nearest shell-hole.

After heavy rain, trenches became mucky, stinking cesspits: breeding grounds for disease and the agonizing condition known as "trench foot". Another common complaint was "trench fever", spread by lice – another great scourge of the trenches. Soldiers could visit delousing stations behind the lines for baths and clean clothes, but within a few hours they would be "lousy" again. Rats, grown huge on the corpses of the dead, also played a part in the trench nightmare. Killing them was one way of relieving the boredom of life in the line.

Food was a major cause of complaint. Officially, each soldier was supplied with daily rations of about 4,000 calories, but in practice the rations carried up the lines at night were, at best, irregular and monotonous, at worst irregular and barely edible. British troops despised the tins of corned beef, or "bully", their usual fare, though German soldiers developed quite a taste for it. Maconochie's, a mixture of meat and root vegetables, was highly prized by the British.

Trench life became a world apart, with its own code of behaviour. "Mucking in" was the British term for looking out and looking after one another. Soldiers didn't always appreciate their official "rest" periods, which too often meant clearing roads, digging defences or shifting ammunition, as well as the tedium of drills and parades.

Alcohol ration

Chocolate ration, not to be eaten until the order is given

Mess kit
Every French soldier was issued with a mess kit (in a design unchanged since 1855), consisting of a cup, spoon and fork (but no knife), and containers for his vital alcohol and chocolate rations.

TIN OPENER

BISCUIT TIN

SWEETS

Front line rations
Rations generally came in tins so tin openers were vital equipment. The French issued their men with hard mint sweets and biscuits. Raisins, tobacco and chocolate were usually shared by the soldiers.

Field kitchen
If they were lucky, soldiers would receive hot food from a field kitchen, though meals usually had to be carried on foot up to the front and were, at best, lukewarm on arrival. A shortage of cooking vats meant flavours becoming intermingled, with tea tasting of vegetables.

Home comforts

German propaganda photographs showed soldiers at the front enjoying a comfortable life in their dug-outs. Packs of cards were issued that used images of the Kaiser, the Crown Prince and Graf Zeppelin, among other prominent Germans.

Anything for a laugh . . .

Humour was used to cheer up French troops (*top left*). The Germans used it to show an over-jolly image of the war. It even appeared on postcards (*right*) sent by soldiers loath to describe the true horror of their experiences.

Trench art

Life on quiet sectors of the front could be rather dull. To help pass the time some soldiers fashioned objects from spent cartridge and shell cases.

MODEL PLANE

LIGHTER

LETTER OPENER

ROLLING PAPERS

Getting comfortable

Soldiers of the Border Regiment, notoriously self-sufficient, rest in hollowed-out shelters in the side of a captured German trench in Thiepval Wood, August 1916.

Wash time

There was little chance to wash properly at the front, with water in short supply. Despite attempts to repel them, lice infested the clothes of almost every soldier and proved impossible to exterminate.

INSECT REPELLENT

Destruction on the Somme, 1916
German soldiers search through the wreckage of a Red Cross vehicle hit by a shell. Members of the medical services were frequently victims of shell fire.

Battle of the Somme

THE SOMME
JUNE 24 – NOVEMBER 18, 1916

~

On the first day of the Battle of the Somme, July 1, the British suffered 57,000 casualties for few gains. This set the pattern for the following five months. Both sides suffered hundreds of thousands of casualties as Allied troops battled for control of individual villages, ridges and woods. When the battle was finally allowed to die on November 18, the Allies had advanced little more than 13km (8 miles) on a 30-km (20-mile) front.

JUNE 24
Allies open barrage along 40-km (25-mile) front

JUNE 29
Planned Allied attack postponed

JULY 1
British advance first and suffer 57,000 casualties; French make gains south of Hardecourt

JULY 2
British capture Fricourt; French advance further, taking Herbecourt

JULY 7
British make unsuccessful attack on Mametz Wood

JULY 10
British capture Contalmaison and make another attack on Mametz Wood

JULY 13/14
Night attack on German line from Longueval to Bazentin-le-Petit

JULY 15
South African brigade takes Delville Wood but forced to abandon it on 20th. British reach High Wood but forced to withdraw on 16th

JULY 20
British attack for possession of High Wood; not finally captured until September 15

JULY 23
Australians involved in fighting for Pozières; finally captured on August 5

JULY 28
British recapture Delville Wood; further fighting for possession of wood until September 3

AUGUST 12
French gain the German third line of trenches from the Somme to Hardecourt

AUGUST 18
British advance to Guillemont, scene of fierce German resistance

AUGUST 24
French take whole of Maurepas

AUGUST 28
Falkenhayn replaced by Hindenburg. Falkenhyan's policy of holding ground whatever the cost abandoned

SEPTEMBER 3
Guillemont, with many prisoners, captured by British. Ginchy also taken, but British then driven out

SEPTEMBER 9
Ginchy retaken

SEPTEMBER 13
French mount successful attack southeast of Combles

SEPTEMBER 15
British offensive in which tanks used for first time in advance towards Flers

SEPTEMBER 25
British begin attack in Morval area; French attack against Bouchavesnes

SEPTEMBER 26
British launch attack on Thiepval Ridge, capturing Thiepval

SEPTEMBER 28
Attack in Morval area ends after capture of Combles and Morval

SEPTEMBER 30
Thiepval Ridge occupied except for part of Schwaben Redoubt

OCTOBER
Heavy rain makes battlefield a quagmire. Allied attacks continue, but there is no great new offensive

OCTOBER 7
British secure Le Sars, but further progress in this sector halted on slopes of Butte de Warlencourt. Butte finally taken November 5

OCTOBER 10
French make small advance on 5-km (3-mile) front south of the Somme

NOVEMBER 13
British attack at Beaumont Hamel and along north bank of the Ancre. Beaumont Hamel and Beaucourt captured

NOVEMBER 17/18
Overnight snow brings battle to an end

KEY
- ■ Initial major Allied offensive Jun 24–Jul 14
- ■ Period of attrition Jul 15–Sept 14
- ■ Second major Allied offensive Sept 15–Sept 30
- ■ Second period of attrition Oct 1–Nov 18

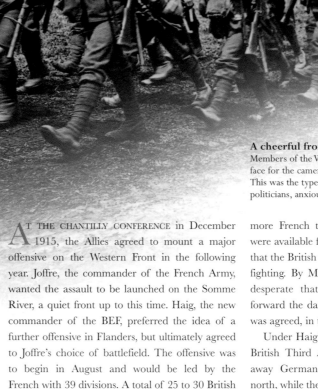

A cheerful front
Members of the Worcestershire Regiment put on a brave face for the camera on their way to the front on June 28. This was the type of image that was welcomed by British politicians, anxious to show the war in a good light.

At THE CHANTILLY CONFERENCE in December 1915, the Allies agreed to mount a major offensive on the Western Front in the following year. Joffre, the commander of the French Army, wanted the assault to be launched on the Somme River, a quiet front up to this time. Haig, the new commander of the BEF, preferred the idea of a further offensive in Flanders, but ultimately agreed to Joffre's choice of battlefield. The offensive was to begin in August and would be led by the French with 39 divisions. A total of 25 to 30 British divisions would be committed to the battle.

This planned division of responsibility for the Somme campaign was to change after the launch of the German offensive on Verdun in February. As more and

Shell blast
Artillery bombardments were used to try and break the Germans' resistance and destroy their barbed wire. But even the million shells with which the Allies pounded the Germans in the week prior to the attack of July 1 did not have the desired effect.

more French troops were sent to Verdun, fewer were available for the Somme, and it became clear that the British would have to bear the brunt of the fighting. By May, the situation at Verdun was so desperate that Joffre called on Haig to bring forward the date of the attack. A date of June 29 was agreed, in the event postponed until July 1.

Under Haig's original plan, two divisions of the British Third Amy under Allenby were to draw away German reserves at Gommecourt to the north, while the Fourth Army under Rawlinson plus the French divisions under Foch broke through the German trenches on a 30-km (20-mile) front. These attacking forces would then turn northwards, driving back the German flank and creating a gap for the British cavalry. Initially, Haig considered that if no breakthrough took place swiftly, the attack should be stopped. He had, however, changed his mind on this particular point by the time the attack began.

THE ROLE OF ARTILLERY

Rawlinson did not agree with aspects of Haig's plan. He doubted that a single major effort would be decisive and argued for a series of smaller, related attacks to secure positions of tactical advantage from which a battle of attrition could be launched. Although Rawlinson's formula was rejected, he shared with Haig and the French General Nivelle, an artillery expert, the belief that a massive artillery barrage over several days had the ability to inflict enormous damage on defenders.

Haig certainly had a massive supply of shells, which he assumed would be sufficient for his heavy guns and howitzers, posted less than 60 m (197 ft) apart over about 24 km (15 miles), to destroy the German defence, and for the field artillery to destroy the barbed wire. This would compensate for the inexperience of a large proportion of the British forces. The battle would, essentially, be won at the outset by the artillery, giving infantry the role of marching in and mopping up afterwards.

German casualties
A direct hit from a shell could kill a dozen men in an instant. Often, bodies would lie unburied or, if buried, would be disinterred by subsequent action. Soldiers sometimes had to live alongside such corpses for weeks on end.

These assumptions were, in fact, incorrect in 1916. Haig did not have the weight of guns and shells required to overwhelm the defence over a front that was extended to protect the advancing troops, in the centre, from enemy flanking fire. Besides a large number of dud shells, there were also technical deficiencies. The shells of 1916 burst on impact with the ground. Used against barbed-wire entanglements, they tended merely to throw the wire about, rather than create large gaps through which the infantry could advance unchecked.

British planning discounted past evidence that no bombardment, however massive, could create the opening for a breakthrough. It also ignored the hard-learned lesson that the attacking infantry should advance as fast as possible and employ fire-and-movement tactics, with each group periodically dropping to the ground, making use of any available shelter, to provide covering fire for others. Instead, the British troops were to advance in lines, almost shoulder to shoulder, at a steady pace.

Haig's strategic purpose was increasingly unclear. The small town of Bapaume, 16 km (10 miles) behind the German front, was his immediate objective, but first the Pozières ridge, between the Ancre and Serre rivers, had to be taken. Since the Germans held the advantage of high ground along the entire front and had considerably strengthened their defences as Allied intentions became evident, even this modest objective was optimistic. The French objective was the town of Péronne.

PRELIMINARY BOMBARDMENT

A small number of the British troops had served in Flanders or Gallipoli, but the vast majority were inexperienced volunteers who knew little of trench warfare. They were confident of making a dramatic breakthrough – and their optimism was increased by the massive artillery bombardment that began on June 24 and continued for over a week.

Field guns in batteries 900 m (1,000 yds) behind the front, together with heavy siege guns a further 1.5 km (1 mile) or so behind, bombarded a 24-km (15-mile) front, firing over 1,500,000 shells in seven days. Although most of the German troops on the Somme were battle-hardened units who had been in position for many months, a bombardment of such relentless ferocity was beyond their experience. In the words of Lieutenant Stefan Westmann, a German medical officer:

"Day and night, the shells came upon us. Our dugouts crumbled. They would fall on top of us and we'd have to dig ourselves and our comrades out. Sometimes we'd find them suffocated or smashed to pulp. Soldiers in the bunkers became hysterical – they wanted to run out, and fights developed to keep them in the comparative safety of our deep bunkers. Even the rats became hysterical and came into our flimsy shelters to seek refuge from this terrific artillery fire."

The Allied attack was supposed to begin on June 29, but was postponed for two days owing to heavy rain and the discovery by raiding parties that the bombardment had been less effective than hoped. Assurances then came from above that the wire was cut, but there was more than one soldier equipped with binoculars who could see for himself that, despite the pounding it had received, long stretches of the wire were still intact.

OVER THE TOP

It was a perfect summer's morning when on July 1, at 6:25, the final Allied bombardment began. Continuing for over an hour at a firing rate of 3,500 shells a minute, the noise was so intense that it could be heard as far away as England. When the guns stopped, the air was split by massive eruptions as the British exploded mines they had laid under the German defences. The awesome demonstration of destructive power heartened the attacking troops.

After the bombardment came a brief interval of silence before whistles blew to send the men up the scaling ladders. Once over the top, they formed lines holding their rifles in front of them, and began to walk towards No Man's Land. All advantage of surprise had been sacrificed, it was broad daylight, visibility was perfect, and there was little cover – conditions, in short, that heavily favoured the defenders. The advancing infantry could have been protected by a "creeping barrage", laid down by the field guns and moving just ahead of them. This tactic, however, was a new one that required exact

timing between the artillery and infantry, and was still in the process of being developed. It was to be used effectively at Verdun in October, but in July all that could be achieved was the bombardment of each enemy line at a pre-arranged time. In fact, afraid of hitting their own men, the gunners advanced the barrage beyond each line of German trenches long before the infantry reached it.

Ahead of the troops lay the German barbed wire, which in many places had gaps that were so few or so small that they created bottlenecks. They reduced the slow advance to a virtual standstill, as the Germans began to appear from their 9-m (30-ft) dugouts, hauling their machine-guns into place in a drill they had rehearsed many times.

KILLING FIELDS

From a distance the ragged lines of slowly advancing soldiers looked like clockwork dolls, and equally vulnerable, as individuals began to stagger and fall under the withering machine-gun fire before they had fired a shot themselves. As the first line of men disintegrated, the next line came under fire. The German artillery was in action too, and shrapnel vied with machine-gun bullets in clearing

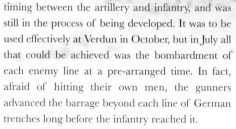

Helping the wounded
Although soldiers in offensive action were ordered not to break the line to give assistance to those who had fallen, many later risked their own lives to try and get the wounded back to safety. The Allies suffered 630,000 casualties on the Somme; the Germans even more.

...for the first short distance there seemed to be no casualties, but soon it became apparent that men were going down rather thicker that one realized... My officer called across to me and said, 'You stick to me, and I'll stick to you'. I said 'Right!' but immediately lost sight of him. I don't know what happened to him. At that point, to my great surprise, a hare ran along in front of me, its eyes bulging with fear, but I don't think it was half as frightened as I was.

TROOPER R. J. MASON OF THE 10TH HUSSARS DESCRIBING THE ADVANCE ACROSS NO MAN'S LAND

the ground of marching men. Whole battalions were reduced to a hundred or so men. Following orders, the lines continued to advance, further impeded by the bodies of the dead and wounded. More bodies, grotesquely posed, were tangled in the uncut wire. Elsewhere those firing the machine-guns concentrated on the gaps. The Germans were outnumbered and fighting for their lives, but eventually many of them tired of the easy slaughter and refrained from firing on wounded men attempting to drag themselves back to their own line. In a few places the British did manage to capture a German trench, but as no reinforcements reached them they were soon forced out again.

Behind the British lines the field dressing stations were overwhelmed. The wounded who seemed unlikely to survive were placed on one side and treated last, if at all. As the day ended, many of the bodies strewn about the battlefield appeared to come to life, as wounded men emerged from shell holes and depressions and struggled to to get back to their lines under cover of darkness.

A total of 13 British divisions went into action on July 1. By the end of the day, they had suffered over 57,000 casualties, a third of them killed – the highest total of any day in the history of the British army. The only progress they had made was in the southern sector, where the German-held villages of

Douglas Haig

~

As COMMANDER-IN-CHIEF of the BEF from 1915 to 1918, Douglas Haig (1861–1928) became a controversial figure. His name will always be associated with the sacrifice of hundreds of thousands of men – about which he showed little remorse – in the battles of attrition in 1916–17, such as the Somme and Third Ypres. He was widely regarded in Britain as the architect of victory in 1918, but this is disputable.

At heart a cavalry man, in the First Battle of Ypres he demonstrated some tactical skill against a numerically superior force. He subsequently became commander of the First Army and by December 1915 he had succeeded Sir John French as commander-in-chief of the BEF.

Despite Prime Minister Lloyd George temporarily putting the BEF under French command in 1917, Haig maintained the support of his field commanders. Whether he was sufficiently prepared for the German offensives in March and April 1918 is questionable. He has, however, been given much credit for the successful British advances that subsequently began in August at Amiens and his insistence that Germany would surrender before the end of the year.

Mametz and Montauban were captured. Haig's objective, Bapaume, was not reached on July 1 – nor in the five months of attacks that followed.

The five French divisions – all that could be spared – were mostly south of the Somme. They had heavier guns in support and gained some element of surprise by delaying their attack to the last moment. They encountered less opposition and

were more successful, taking 3,000 prisoners and forcing the evacuation of the Germans' second line during the night. But their objective, the town of Péronne, remained safely in German hands.

Transporting the wounded
Wheelbarrows, carts and planks – whatever was to hand – were used to carry the wounded back to the field dressing stations on the first day of the Somme offensive.

BATTLE OF THE SOMME
JULY 1–NOVEMBER 18, 1916

~

As a result of the German offensive on Verdun, the Battle of the Somme was fought largely by British troops with French support. The British planned to break through the German lines between Serre and Maricourt, and advance to Bapaume. The French objective was Péronne. In fact, neither Bapaume nor Péronne were to be captured in the five-month long battle. On the first day – when the British army suffered higher casualties than on any other day in its history – six German divisions withstood an attack by 13 British and five French divisions. Very limited progress was made in the southern sector; none was made in the north. Over the next two weeks the Allied troops inched forward to capture the German second line around Bazentin-le-Petit. The battle then went through a period of local encounters until a second attempt at a major advance was launched on September 15 with the aid of a new weapon – the tank. However, after some initial success at Flers, the battle again turned into one of attrition before dying out on November 18.

KEY		
British front line		French advance
French front line		Road
British advance		Railway

FOLLOW-UP ATTACKS

As a result of the failure on the part of the Allies to achieve the planned breakthrough on July 1, the Battle of the Somme became in effect one of attrition, with numerous limited offensives directed at specific villages, ridges or woods. Combat was ferocious, and a Somme battlefield in the wake of the fighting was, in the words of Christopher Nevinson, the British war artist, a hellish environment of "…shrieks, pus, gangrene and the disembowelled". The smell was indescribable.

The British, having repelled a German attempt to retake Montauban on July 2, renewed the offensive next day, but failed to take Ovillers, less than 1.5 km (1 mile) from the front. The French in the south again made better progress, breaking through the German second line of defences and taking many prisoners. Casualties were heavy; units of the Foreign Legion lost one-third of their men.

German troops with captured weapons
German machine-gunners valued the British Lewis machine-guns that were somewhat lighter than the models, such as the Maxim, with which they were issued.

On July 6-7 the British captured La Boiselle and Contalmaison, which the Germans regained hours later. A British attack on Mametz Wood was repulsed; it was taken a week later. After ten days of fighting, the Germans had been pushed back on average only one or two kilometres. At Verdun meanwhile, the failure of the last German attacks in June and July, combined with the demands of the Somme and the Eastern Front, had compelled Falkenhayn to go over to the defensive.

Wrecked German trench
When Allied troops managed to capture a German trench, they were amazed at how deep and strong it was. The Germans had spent many months improving their defences.

Flash hider

Water jacket

Backsight

Butt

Crank handle

Pistol grip

Spiked bipod

German Maxim MG 08/15
This lighter version of the 1908 Maxim – 19 kg (43 lb) when filled with water – was designed to be carried quickly into battle. It normally had a crew of three, but could be operated by a single gunner.

The initial offensive July 1–15

On the first day the British and French made minor gains in the south; in the north the British attacks in the area between Gommecourt and Thiepval made no headway at all. In a night attack on July 13, the British broke through the German lines along the Longueval ridge. On the 15th, High Wood was reached but not taken.

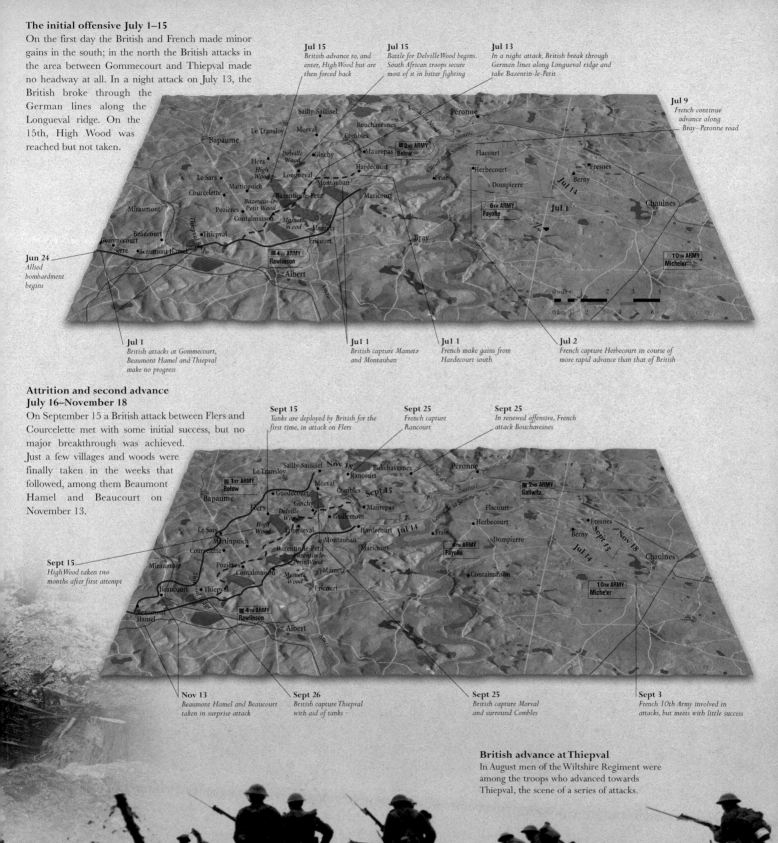

Jul 15
British advance to, and enter, High Wood but are then forced back

Jul 15
Battle for Delville Wood begins. South African troops secure most of it in bitter fighting

Jul 13
In a night attack, British break through German lines along Longueval ridge and take Bazentin-le-Petit

Jul 9
French continue advance along Bray–Peronne road

Jun 24
Allied bombardment begins

Jul 1
British attacks at Gommecourt, Beaumont Hamel and Thiepval make no progress

Jul 1
British capture Mametz and Montauban

Jul 1
French make gains from Hardecourt south

Jul 2
French capture Herbecourt in course of more rapid advance than that of British

Attrition and second advance July 16–November 18

On September 15 a British attack between Flers and Courcelette met with some initial success, but no major breakthrough was achieved. Just a few villages and woods were finally taken in the weeks that followed, among them Beaumont Hamel and Beaucourt on November 13.

Sept 15
Tanks are deployed by British for the first time, in attack on Flers

Sept 25
French capture Rancourt

Sept 25
In renewed offensive, French attack Bouchavesnes

Sept 15
High Wood taken two months after first attempt

Nov 13
Beaumont Hamel and Beaucourt taken in surprise attack

Sept 26
British capture Thiepval with aid of tanks

Sept 25
British capture Morval and surround Combles

Sept 3
French 10th Army involved in attacks, but meets with little success

British advance at Thiepval

In August men of the Wiltshire Regiment were among the troops who advanced towards Thiepval, the scene of a series of attacks.

BRITISH NIGHT ATTACK

In a surprise night attack on July 13, the British broke through the German lines across a 5.5-km (3.5-mile) sector along the Longueval ridge, taking Bazentin-le-Petit, west of Delville Wood. For a moment, penetration to a depth of around 900 m (1,000 yds) renewed hope of breaking through the entire German front, and brought Haig's beloved cavalry briefly into action. But poor communications, among other difficulties, allowed the Germans to restore their defences.

On July 15 British forces reached High Wood, but could not capture it. On the same day, to the east, the battle for Delville Wood began – the moment of truth for the South African Brigade that had been ordered to capture it. The fighting was marked by ruthless hand-to-hand combat as well as pulverizing bombardments that reduced the wood to shreds within two days. The South Africans had been told to hold the wood at all costs. A week later the 4th Regiment of the South African Infantry Brigade consisted of just 42 men.

Meanwhile, on July 19, Australians and New Zealanders from the Gallipoli campaign carried out a diversionary attack on Fromelles, far to the north, to prevent German reinforcements reaching the battlefield. The German defences appeared formidable, and since no reinforcements were moving southward, the main reason for the attack no longer existed. The Australian General Elliott, advised by a British staff officer that "a holocaust" was in prospect, questioned the need for the operation, but was told that it would be bad for morale to cancel it. The first Australian casualties were victims of their own supporting fire. The guns did not, however, disable the German machine-gun emplacements, and the result was as predicted. Total casualties were about 1,700 dead (plus 400 British), 4,000 wounded, and 500 captured.

The intense local battles of attrition that were typical of the Somme campaign were everywhere, resulting in tens of thousands of casualties on both sides. In an attempt (not the first) to capture Guillemont on August 8, one battalion lost half of its officers and one-sixth of its men.

In late July Haig learned that the British government was becoming restive at the casualties, but he thought another six weeks of "steady offensive pressure" would break the Germans. The weather continued fine: "not the weather for killing people" noted Harold Macmillan, a future British prime minister. But as autumn came it brought heavy rain and, with it, murderous mud.

THE DEVELOPMENT OF THE TANK

ODDLY IT WAS THE BRITISH NAVY that first realized the need for some kind of cross-country armoured vehicle. In the early months of the war armoured cars (see page 59) had been used by the Royal Naval Air Service based in Dunkerque. Once the front became fixed in November 1914, they were of little further use since they could not cross trenches or barbed wire. A number of men turned their minds to possible solutions to this problem. The War Office was sceptical, but Winston Churchill, First Lord of the Admiralty, took a keen interest and, in February 1915, established a Landships Committee. Many designs were considered, one specifically for bridging trenches, one for cutting wire, another to carry troops across No Man's Land. One school of thought favoured vehicles on huge wheels, another the caterpillar track used on tractors. In the end it was the caterpillar track that prevailed.

The design that was given the go-ahead was the creation of Walter Wilson and William Tritton, working at Fosters engineering works at Lincoln. When tested on February 2, 1916, government officials and army top brass were (with the exception of Kitchener) impressed and an order was placed for 100 machines. In essence this was the design that the British army would use for the rest of the war and thus the prototype came to be known as "Mother". It gave birth to the Mark I, which saw action at the Somme later in the year. This came in two versions: the "male", armed with two naval 6-pounders in sponsons (half-turrets projecting from the sides of the tank) and four machine-guns, and the "female", with seven machine-guns. The reason for the "female" version was a fear that male tanks might be swamped by masses of enemy infantry. Production of the Mark 1 began at Fosters and at the larger plant of the Metropolitan Carriage Co, Birmingham. To preserve the weapon's secrecy the name "tank" was coined because, without its guns, it looked like a vehicle for carrying water.

An unimpressive trial
On June 30, 1915 the Navy gave a demonstration of this American Killen-Strait tractor fitted with wire-cutters at the front. It was clearly not the answer to the deadlock in the trenches.

Little Willie
This prototype, produced by Tritton and Wilson in September, 1915, looked quite like the tanks of the future. Its trench-crossing abilities, however, were very limited and nobody gave it any serious consideration. It survives as a museum exhibit.

Disinformation
The army was determined that the first appearance of tanks on the Western Front should take the Germans by complete surprise. Accordingly the tanks' bodies (without sponsons or guns), when they were loaded on trains for transport from the factory, were labelled "to Petrograd" in case they were spotted by spies.

THE ENGINEERS

WILLIAM TRITTON

WALTER WILSON

THE TWO MEN given credit for designing and building the first tank are William Tritton, managing director of the Fosters factory in Lincoln, and Lieutenant Walter Wilson of the Royal Naval Reserve. In peacetime Wilson, a genius in matters of gearing, had been an engineer working on cars and lorries. The two men had both worked on a number of experimental designs before coming up with one that would be used in battle. Tritton, for example, had produced a giant trench-crossing vehicle with huge wheels, shown in the picture above behind its inventor. He and Wilson worked together on the Lincoln No. 1 machine (later known as "Little Willie"). It ran on American-made Bullock "Creeping Grip" tracks. In a trial these proved completely inadequate, so Tritton devised stronger, more reliable ones. However, "Little Willie" was superseded by a tank conceived principally by Wilson – a "quasi-rhomboidal" vehicle, on which the tracks ran all the way round the hull – the Mark I.

Mechanized warfare
Nobody knew quite what to expect of the new tanks when 50 of them were despatched to battlefield of the Somme in 1916. The general hope was that they would knock out machine-guns, crush barbed wire and serve as a shield for infantry advancing across No Man's Land.

Big Willie or "Mother"
Big Willie, the prototype of the first British tank, Mark 1, succeeded at its trials in January and February 1916 in crossing a 3-m (10-ft) trench and riding over a vertical obstacle 1.4 m (4 ft 6 in) high. This performance so outstripped that of any previous prototype that it was given the job. Its wheeled tail, for steering and balance, was dispensed with in later models.

Mark I tank
The tank used at the Somme was manned by a crew of eight: an officer and the driver sitting up front, a gunner and his mate in each sponson and two gearsmen who worked the gears on the drive shafts to the the sprocketed wheels that turned the caterpillar tracks. The tank was powered by a 105 hp Daimler engine originally designed to drive tractors.

The first tanks to go into battle were fitted with a roof of wood and wire to protect them from the full blast of grenades and shells.

The guns fitted in the sponsons were naval 6-pounders with their barrels cut down. When a tank went into battle it carried 324 rounds for each gun.

DAIMLER MARK IV TANK ENGINE

Loopholes for tank commander and driver

The Allied front line inched forward. At the beginning of September, it had advanced between 1.5 and 5km (1 and 3.5 miles) since July 1. The French had gone a little farther, but they were tied to the pace of the British advance. Ginchy (where the Irish secured a victory), Delville Wood and Guillemont were all finally taken before September 15, when the main British offensive was renewed.

A NEW WEAPON

Tactics had improved since July. The "creeping barrage" was now more effective at subduing enemy trenches, if not artillery. More important, on September 15 a new weapon appeared: the tank. This would eventually prove to be the antidote to the machine-gun and provide one of the solutions to the stalemate of trench warfare. In 1916 only 50 were available – not enough to be effective – and they were used in the wrong way, operating individually in support of infantry. But, like Hannibal's elephants, they had a dramatic psychological effect. The Germans initially felt quite powerless against what they saw as "monsters" that crawled along the top of trenches, enfilading them with continuous machine-gun fire.

In fact, about one-third of the tanks broke down, and many others were destroyed by artillery fire. Nevertheless, those that kept going long enough succeeded in driving the Germans out of the village of Flers, and they were largely responsible for the British advance on September 15 of about 1,800m (2,000 yds) on an 8-km (5-mile) front between Flers and Courcelette. This included High Wood, finally taken two months after the first attempt.

Conservative officers remained sceptical of the tank, and the German high command was not sufficiently convinced by what it has seen to press forward with developing their own tank. Haig, however, demanded 1,000 of them.

The British registered another advance ten days later, taking Combles on the 25th. On the following day, Thiepval – besieged since July 1 – was captured with the aid of 13 tanks. At Gueudecourt, with tanks and the support of spotter aircraft, they took 500 prisoners for only five men lost.

At the end of the month came heavy rain. The downpour rapidly demonstrated, once again, a

> "The mud makes it all but impassable, and now sunk in it up to the knees, I have the momentary terror of never being able to pull myself out."
>
> BRITISH SOLDIER MARK PLOWMAN DESCRIBING THE TRENCHES ON THE SOMME IN NOVEMBER

major disadvantage of bombardments by heavy artillery: they cut up the ground over which the infantry hoped to advance, and, once soaked by rain, it turned into mud. The consequence was described by the offical historian of the South African Brigade, John Buchan:

"There were now two No Man's Lands – one between the front lines, and one between the old enemy front and the front we had won. The second was the bigger problem, for across it must be brought the supplies of a great army. Every road became a watercourse, and in the hollows the mud was as deep as a man's thighs…Off the roads the ground was one vast bog, dugouts crumbled in, communication trenches ceased to be."

Behind the British front lay 9km (6 miles) of "sponge, varied by mud torrents". Artillery could not be shifted, and men died as a result of the sheer effort of carrying a message across the glutinous mud. A wounded man hesitated before seeking shelter in a shell hole, fearing that do so might mean being sucked down to his death.

Despite the conditions, October saw a series of British attacks of the kind that deservedly gave generalship in the First World War a bad name. Rawlinson, complaining that the bad weather "has given the Boche a breather", hoped to "be aggressive" all winter. But, after the capture of Beaumont-Hamel and Beaucourt, snow on November 17/18 brought the Somme campaign to an end. Bapaume was still in German hands.

POLICY OF FORWARD DEFENCE

The relative ease of the final British advances indicated German exhaustion. Falkenhayn's strategy of "forward defence", insisting that all lost ground be immediately recovered, regardless of inferior numbers and limited reserves, largely explained the bitterness of the August fighting.

MARK 1 TANK ADVANCES

Just before Zero Hour we heard this dammed racket, and I remember saying, 'What the hell is this?' Then these tanks appeared, one on our front and one a bit away from us. We were all absolutely flabbergasted. We didn't know what to think. We didn't know what they were because we hadn't been told anything about them. It was an amazing sight … They came up right in front of us and swung round and went straight for the German line. The barbed-wire entanglements had been pretty well smashed by our artillery but the tanks just rolled over what remained of them and smashed them all to pieces. They scared the guts out of the Germans. They bolted like rabbits.

BRITISH CORPORAL EDWARD GALE ON THE ARRIVAL OF TANKS AT THE SOMME

Stuck in the mud
Torrential rain in November 1916 turned the battlefield into a quagmire. Supplies of ammunition were badly delayed as roads became virtually impassable to man or beast.

German casualties were even higher than those of the Allies: about 660,000 compared with 630,000. By the end of August, when Hindenburg and Ludendorff took over, a rethink was clearly needed. In future the front line would be held lightly, and non-vital defences would be surrendered, thus restoring tactical flexibility to the defence.

Meanwhile, the Allies agreed to resume the attack on the Somme in the spring. Joffre, who resigned on December 12, added a rider: France had sufficient manpower for only one more major effort. It was clear, therefore, that in the following year the main burden of responsibility on the Western Front would pass from France to Britain.

THE ARTILLERY OF TRENCH WARFARE

THE FIRST WORLD WAR BEGAN as a war of movement and very quickly became a siege war, a fact that did much to determine how artillery developed. Initially, great faith was placed in field artillery, generally in the 75 to 85-mm (3 to 3.3-in) range, but the development of trench systems spelt the need for bigger guns and howitzers (which had short barrels and fired heavier shells on a high trajectory). Their volume of fire over protracted periods was deemed critical to infantry success, with saturation of the enemy defence system being considered far more important than the achievement of surprise.

In many ways the French offensives of spring and autumn 1915 reflect the transition from one system of warfare to the other. In the Artois offensive in May the French employed some 300 heavy guns. Just a few months later, in the Champagne offensive – for which three railway lines were built in order to get artillery and ammunition into position – they employed 2,000 guns in support of 11 corps against two German corps with 600 guns. The intensity of the French bombardment ensured the destruction of three German infantry regiments before rain transformed the battlefield into a sea of mud.

The battle in Champagne lasted 15 days and at heavy cost to the attacking French forces, but the lesson derived from it was that an even greater concentration of firepower was needed. In 1915 the British at Loos had only 12 guns per km (19 guns per mile) of front, and heavy guns were limited to 96 rounds a day – that is, one shell every 15 minutes. At Messines in 1917 they had 756 heavy guns and 1,510 field guns on a 13.5-km (8.5-mile) front.

As well as an increase in the number of heavy weapons, there were three major developments in artillery over the course of the war. First, various medium guns and howitzers were developed. Initially the maximum size was determined by what a horse team could draw, but in the final stages of the war, horses were replaced by tractors. Second, mobile artillery was developed in the form of the tank. This was a response to the fact that the shattering of defensive positions by artillery firepower made it virtually impossible for the artillery to move across the battlefield in order to repeat the process against the next enemy line. Third, a new kind of artillery – the rail gun – was developed when it became apparent just how expensive medium and heavy guns were in terms of manpower, their crews of up to 28 men invariably being subjected to intense counter-battery fire. Some rail guns, such as the British 9.2-in (234-mm) gun, the German 170-mm (6.7-in) Instant Gun and the American 14-in (356-mm) gun were standard weapons mounted on flatcars. However, the most famous model – the Paris Gun with which the Germans bombarded Paris in 1918 – was purpose-built.

GERMAN 77-MM FIELD-GUN

77-mm (3-in) shrapnel shell, known as a "whizzbang" by British troops

High-explosive 77-mm (3-in) shell

German whicker shell carrier

BRITISH 18-POUNDER FIELD-GUN

60-pounders at the Somme
The 60-pounder was Britain's largest field-gun, pulled by a team of heavy horses. Noted for its accuracy, it had a range of 9,400 m (10,300 yds).

Shrapnel shell

High-explosive shell

Gas shell

Smoke shell

Time fuse, lightly fitted so forced off by bursting charge

Field guns
The light, mobile field guns such as the French 75-mm (see page 55), the German 77-mm and the British 18-pounder did not have the weight of shell or the angle of fire to be effective against well-dug trenches and barbed wire. With their rapid rate of fire they still played their part in barrages, firing from batteries about 3 km (2 miles) behind the front line. When enemy troops were in view, they were loaded with shrapnel.

Bullets (steel balls) set in resin

Flash from fuse passes down central tube to ignite charge at base of shell

Cordite propellant charge

Brass shell-case

Bursting charge of loose fine-grain gunpowder

SHELL-CASE   PROJECTILE

18-pounder shrapnel shell
When the bursting charge exploded, it blasted away the fuse and projected the bullets through the nose of the shell.

German 305-mm howitzer

A gun crew prepares a well-concealed howitzer for firing. The gun had to be fired from a solid platform and its massive shells weighed 390-kg (858 lb). The Austro-Hungarians also had a 305-mm howitzer, made by Skoda.

Decorated dud

Many shells, especially in the first year of the war, did not explode. This British shell was fired in Flanders. The Germans in the opposing trenches painted it with a patriotic design and "Greetings from Flanders".

FRENCH ARTILLERY THEODOLITE

RANGE CALCULATOR

FRENCH ARTILLERY OFFICER'S BINOCULARS

Range-finding

Officers were well trained in the science of artillery and had many aids to calculate the required trajectory of fire. In the heat of a battle, however, communication with observation posts might be cut and batteries would often accidentally shell their own men.

DIAL SIGHT OF BRITISH 18-POUNDER FIELD-GUN

BRITISH 4.5-in HOWITZER

4.5-in (114-mm) high-explosive shell

British howitzers

At the start of the war, heavy howitzers were thought of as siege weapons, while lighter more mobile guns were intended for use on targets such as railway stations or bridges. Trench warfare brought them to the battlefield, sited in hollows and woods behind the lines. Once in place they were very difficult to move. The 9.2-in howitzer weighed 15 tons and it took 36 hours to dismantle it ready for transportation.

BRITISH 9.2-in HOWITZER

BRITISH 6.5-in HOWITZER

ramrod

EVENTS BEYOND THE BATTLEFIELD
1914–1918

~

IN THE ABSENCE OF CLEAR VICTORY ON LAND, THE

FIRST WORLD WAR WAS DECIDED BY SEA POWER.

IT WAS A SIEGE WAR, BUT ONE UNLIKE ANY OTHER

IN HISTORY – A SIEGE NOT OF CITIES BUT OF

CENTRAL EUROPE. SEA POWER WAS THE MEANS BY

WHICH BRITAIN, FRANCE AND THE USA, ABLE

TO DRAW ON RESERVES OF MANPOWER AND

INDUSTRIAL AND FINANCIAL RESOURCES FROM

THE OUTSIDE WORLD, WERE ABLE TO WAGE

AND ULTIMATELY WIN THE WAR OF EXHAUSTION

AGAINST THE CENTRAL POWERS.

~

Hunting for U-boats
One of the chief tasks of the British Navy was to seek
out and destroy the U-boats that threatened to drive
Britain from the war. The means of detecting U-boats
underwater was the hydrophone. One is seen here being
lowered from the deck of the Scottish trawler *Thrive*.

THE WIDER PERSPECTIVE

AS THE LAND WAR WAS FOUGHT OUT ON THE BATTLEFIELDS OF EUROPE, DECISIVE

EVENTS THAT ALLOWED THE COMBATANTS TO KEEP THEIR ARMIES IN THE FIELD WERE

TAKING PLACE IN THE WAR AT SEA. THESE AFFECTED RELATIONS WITH NEUTRAL STATES,

ESPECIALLY THE USA. IT WAS THE GERMAN DECISION TO RESUME UNRESTRICTED

SUBMARINE WAR IN 1917 THAT LED TO THE ENTRY OF THE USA INTO THE WAR.

I N THE COURSE of four centuries since 1500 Europe had established primacy over every continent in the world, but by the end of the 19th century it had passed the peak of its power. Two significant non-European powers – the USA and Japan – had emerged. It was the dealings of Europe in 1916–17 with one of these powers that would change forever the relationship of Europe with the outside world.

THE POWER OF THE USA

As early as 1890 the United States had emerged as the greatest manufacturing state in the world; by 1900 it produced more than Britain and Germany combined. Anglo-French attempts to involve the United States in the war on the side of the Allies was evidence of European awareness of the reality of American power. But America's declared policy was one of neutrality and President Wilson's government offered more than once to broker a peace settlement. In 1915, and again in 1916, American missions to various European capitals were politely received, but on December 12, 1916 the German chancellor, Bethmann-Hollweg, stated Germany's willingness to seek a negotiated end to the war and invited the United States to act as mediator between the belligerent powers. Such an unprecedented action – an initiative that would have established a non-European state as arbiter of Europe's disputes – was indicative of the seriousness of the situation in which Germany found itself at this stage of the war. What had prompted this invitation to the United States to act as mediator was the situation in the war at sea.

THE NAVAL WAR

The course of the war at sea in 1914–18 was largely determined by Germany's decision, taken around 1900, to build a fleet to rival the British navy. The policy was pursued with no regard to Germany's geographical position and its strategic inferiority to its potential enemy. Britain's ports commanded the North Sea and the English Channel, the only routes available to German ships if they wished to reach the open ocean. Britain responded to this challenge to its supremacy by joining in the naval arms race, and the German navy, the *Hochseeflotte* (High Sea Fleet), was never able to catch up and threaten British numerical superiority.

In 1906 Britain launched the *Dreadnought* – faster, more heavily armoured, and with more powerful guns than any battleship that had gone before. This was followed by the battlecruiser, faster still but less heavily armoured. The naval arms race intensified as all the powers, including France, Russia and even Austria-Hungary, decided that they needed dreadnoughts too. In the years 1906–14 Britain built a total of 32 modern dreadnoughts and battlecruisers;

The might of the British Navy
The *Queen Elizabeth*, launched in 1915, was the first of a new class of dreadnought armed with eight 15-in guns. These fired 870-kg (1,920-lb) shell a distance of 25 km (16 miles).

> *"All of us, from the commander-in-chief down to the latest recruit, shared the same opinion about the attitude of the English fleet. We were convinced that it would seek out and attack our fleet the minute it showed itself and wherever it was. This could be accepted as certain from all the lessons of English naval history."*

GERMAN ADMIRAL REINHARD SCHEER, WRITING IN HIS WAR MEMOIRS, 1920

Germany built 23. Many of the German ships were superior to their British counterparts, but the High Sea Fleet's numerical inferiority condemned it to spend the war acting as a coastal defence force.

THE PHASES OF THE NAVAL WAR

The war at sea can be conveniently divided into three main parts. The opening phase lasted until December 1914, by which time the Central Powers' shipping had been driven from the high seas and the threat presented by German warships outside European waters had been largely eliminated. After April 1915 there were no warships at all at large to challenge Allied naval supremacy.

The second period, between January 1915 and February 1917, was one in which, as the noose of economic blockade tightened on the Central Powers, Germany hesitated between waging a campaign against Allied merchant shipping and conducting fleet operations. The German navy wanted to fight, but the high command dared not risk the fleet in a classical sea battle. It aimed to weaken the British navy by means of mines and torpedoes until battle could be joined in circumstances where Germany held a significant advantage. Britain's naval strategy was similarly cautious. The decision, taken before the war, to impose a distant blockade on Germany, basing the Grand Fleet at Scapa Flow, ensured that the war at sea would remain a stand-off.

THE BATTLE OF JUTLAND

Both sides provoked skirmishes in the North Sea, designed to try to lure parts of the opposing fleet into battle with larger formations. One such encounter led to the inconclusive Battle of Jutland in 1916. This, the first and only time in the war the two fleets clashed, brought home to Germany the lesson that tactical victories in the North Sea were never going to improve its strategic situation. After the failure to inflict any lasting damage on the British fleet, the German high command was won round to the idea of an unrestricted submarine campaign against shipping. The third period of the naval war, after February 1917, witnessed a German offensive against shipping that initially proved very successful before being contained during and after the second half of 1917.

UNRESTRICTED SUBMARINE WARFARE

The great majority of the sinkings by German U-boats in the course of the war were conducted according to Prize Regulations. The submarine would stop the merchantman (its prize), allow the crew to take to the lifeboats, then finally sink the ship, normally by gunfire. In an "unrestricted" campaign, submarine commanders ignored these rules and would torpedo targets without warning.

In 1915 a number of ships had been torpedoed in this way, including the liner *Lusitania*, in which 128 American passengers had been drowned.

For Germany, 1916 had brought failure at Verdun, an increasingly serious defensive obligation on the Somme and the disastrous weakening of Austria-Hungary by the Brusilov Offensive. When the German approach to the United States to negotiate a peace came to nothing, there seemed no possibility of Germany defeating its enemies other than by means of a campaign against shipping. This, it was hoped, would drive Britain from the ranks of its enemies. Otherwise Germany faced defeat in a war of attrition and exhaustion.

"It is much more important to destroy a railroad station, a bakery, a war plant, or to machine-gun a supply column, moving trains, or any other behind-the-lines objective, than to strafe or bomb a trench. The results are immeasurably greater in breaking morale…in spreading terror and panic."

GIULIO DROUHET, ITALIAN GENERAL AND
ENTHUSIASTIC ADVOCATE OF STRATEGIC BOMBING

The problem with such a course of action was the certainty of American hostility. The United States had grown increasingly assertive in claiming its rights as a neutral state: the freedom to trade and the freedom of its citizens to travel. These rights had been challenged by previous German submarine actions. American indignation at the sinking of the *Lusitania* and other ships had reinforced the political, economic and historical links between the United States and Britain and France. Meanwhile American trade with Germany had dwindled almost to nothing as a result of the British blockade.

The Germans gambled that they could sink enough British, Allied and neutral shipping to starve Britain of food and raw materials before the Americans could start to play a significant role in the war. As a result, 1917 would see two extraordinary developments: direct American involvement in the affairs of Europe and a full-scale war on shipping conducted by submarines armed with torpedoes – a weapons system that had not existed 20 years previously.

THE POTENTIAL OF THE AEROPLANE

Another new weapon, which had been developed even more recently, was the aeroplane. Unlike the submarine, however, the aeroplane did not realize its full potential during the course of the war. When the war broke out, little over a decade had passed since the first powered flight, by the Wright brothers, of a heavier-than-air machine.

The first operational aircraft of the war were, typically, powered by engines of 100 hp or less, capable of a maximum speed of about 130 kph (80 mph) at sea level. They were unarmed, and most would have been incapable of carrying anything heavier than a rifle. Their role was exclusively reconnaissance, yet within four years almost every aspect of aerial warfare as waged in the 20th century had been developed.

The potential of air warfare was not unforeseen. It had inspired visions of universal destruction by aerial bombardment, such as H.G. Wells's *The War in the Air* (1908), in which civilization is destroyed by the bombs of airships. Germany had great faith in the power of its airships to undermine the morale of its enemies. One of its first actions in 1914 was to send Zeppelins flying over London and a number of British ports. As bombers, however, they proved too vulnerable, and Germany, like the other powers, turned instead to building huge long-distance aircraft that could bomb industrial targets and civilian populations deep inside enemy territory. By the end of the war the future development of aerial warfare was clear. Heavy bombers would deliver ever larger payloads, while fast, lightweight fighters armed with machine-guns would do battle for control of the skies.

A new kind of warfare
Germany's principal fighting force at sea proved to be not its magnificent dreadnoughts and battlecruisers, but its U-boats as they waged a war on merchant shipping.

The shape of things to come
Air power played a limited role in the war, but by 1918 it was possible to imagine how future wars would be fought. These giant British Handley Page aircraft were the forerunners of the heavy bombers of the Second World War.

Opening Moves at Sea

I N THE OPENING PHASE OF HOSTILITIES the British navy set about clearing the seas of enemy trade and carrying the war to enemy home waters and overseas possessions. Britain's geographical position astride Germany's lines of communication with the outside world ensured that German oceanic trade declined rapidly. In the first six months of the war the Allies detained, sank or captured 383 German and Austro-Hungarian steamers. Another 788 ships sought safety in neutral ports. Overall, Germany and Austria-Hungary were deprived of the use of 61 per cent of their merchant fleets.

RAIDERS ON THE HIGH SEAS

German ships that were either at sea when war broke out or sailed soon after included one battlecruiser and 14 cruisers and armed merchant cruisers. These posed a threat to Allied shipping and so were pursued, not always successfully. Two of the ships, the battlecruiser *Goeben* and the light cruiser *Breslau*, first bombarded two French North African ports, then evaded superior British forces before escaping into the Dardanelles. The arrival of the two ships at Constantinople on August 10, 1914 set the seal on the secret treaty concluded by Germany and Turkey on August 2.

Germany's Far Eastern Squadron, commanded by Admiral Graf Maximilian von Spee, found itself in the Caroline Islands at the start of the war. After Japan entered the war, the squadron could not hope to survive in the northern Pacific, so attempted to return home as a formation, except for the light cruiser *Emden*, which was despatched for a short but eventful career as a commerce-raider in the Indian Ocean. She was eventually destroyed by the Australian cruiser *Sydney* in November. That same month another successful German raider, the light cruiser *Karlsruhe*, which operated off the coast of Brazil, was destroyed in an accidental explosion.

The Far Eastern Squadron also met with some success. On November 1 it met and destroyed a hastily assembled force of three British cruisers and a converted merchantman off Coronel in Chile. However, within hours of this defeat, two British

Double German threat
The German dreadnought *Ostfriesland* and Zeppelin *L31* take part in a pre-war exercise in the North Sea. Zeppelins were intended to play a key role in naval reconnaissance, as were airships in the British navy, but often proved ineffective as a result of strong winds or poor visibility.

imposed a blockade on Germany's fleet and merchant shipping. This was enforced by the fleet which patrolled the waters between Scotland and Norway and another small force guarding the Strait of Dover. The blockade also involved the mining of German waters plus the use of submarines for reconnaissance and attacks on enemy units. The Germans, in their turn, mined British waters, sent out submarines and conducted defensive patrols with light forces in the Heligoland Bight.

HELIGOLAND BIGHT

The first sea battle of the war resulted from two British destroyer flotillas attempting to surprise and overwhelm a German torpedo-boat patrol in the Heligoland Bight on August 28. The would-be attackers found that their intended prey was supported by superior forces.

In the event only the timely and somewhat fortuitous intervention of Admiral Beatty's First Battlecruiser Squadron saved the British from serious embarrassment. An ill-planned affair on the British side, the Heligoland Bight action, with three German light cruisers and one torpedo-boat sunk, was nevertheless a clear victory. It was quickly offset, however, by the sinking by German submarines of a light cruiser off the Firth of Forth on September 6 and of three armoured cruisers off the Dutch coast on the 22nd. One more British light cruiser was sunk in the North Sea in October, in which month the dreadnought *Audacious* was lost off the north coast of Ireland in a minefield laid by the *Berlin*, a liner converted into a mine-layer. These German successes had the effect of forcing the British to pull back their patrols from the northern North Sea to the Scotland–Iceland gap. In spite of this, the blockade remained intact and the Germans suffered similar losses. In 1914 no fewer than ten German cruisers were lost in the North Sea and the Baltic.

battlecruisers were sent from home waters to form the nucleus of a new squadron in the South Atlantic. Arriving at Port Stanley one day before von Spee's squadron, the British force sank all but one of the German cruisers off the Falklands on December 8. The *Dresden* escaped to lead a furtive existence until trapped and scuttled at Mas a Fuera in the Juan Fernandez Islands off Chile in March 1915. With the *Königsberg* remaining in the Rufigi delta in East Africa where she had taken shelter, and the *Kronprinz Wilhelm*, last of the armed merchant cruisers, putting into Newport News, Virginia, in April 1915, the raider threat to Allied commerce effectively came to an end. Five cruisers and three auxiliaries had accounted for 47 Allied ships.

BLOCKADE AND THE NORTH SEA

The Falklands action was the second time that German cruisers had been defeated by the superior firepower of British battlecruisers. The first was in the action fought off Heligoland in August 1914. At the outbreak of war, Britain had immediately

REINHARD SCHEER

A TORPEDO EXPERT and champion of submarine warfare, Reinhard Scheer (1863–1928) was a Vice-Admiral in command of Germany's Second Battle Squadron at the start of the First World War. In December 1914 he took command of the Third Battle Squadron, which comprised Germany's newest dreadnoughts. When Admiral Hugo von Pohl fell gravely ill in January 1916, Scheer succeeded him as commander-in-chief of the High Sea Fleet.

Scheer envisaged a more active role for the German navy, in which U-boats would work together with the surface fleet. He could claim a tactical victory in the Battle of Jutland, in 1916, with more British vessels sunk and the German ships managing to slip away undetected. After this the kaiser expressly forbade any further forays of this kind and Scheer had to acknowledge that he could not risk sending his surface fleet into the North Sea. He pressed instead for a return to unrestricted submarine warfare, a move that was eventually to bring the United States into the war.

Shortly before the end of the war Scheer planned a dramatic final assault on the British Grand Fleet but this was thwarted by the Kiel mutiny in November 1918, and he was dismissed soon afterwards. Following the armistice he was retired from the navy. He published his account of the war at sea in 1920.

Naval blockade

The first 18 months of the war at sea were relatively uneventful. The British laid mines, sent out patrols and intercepted neutral shipping, while the Germans centred their efforts for the most part on submarine activity. The North Sea saw only minor naval engagements until the two fleets met at the Battle of Jutland in 1916.

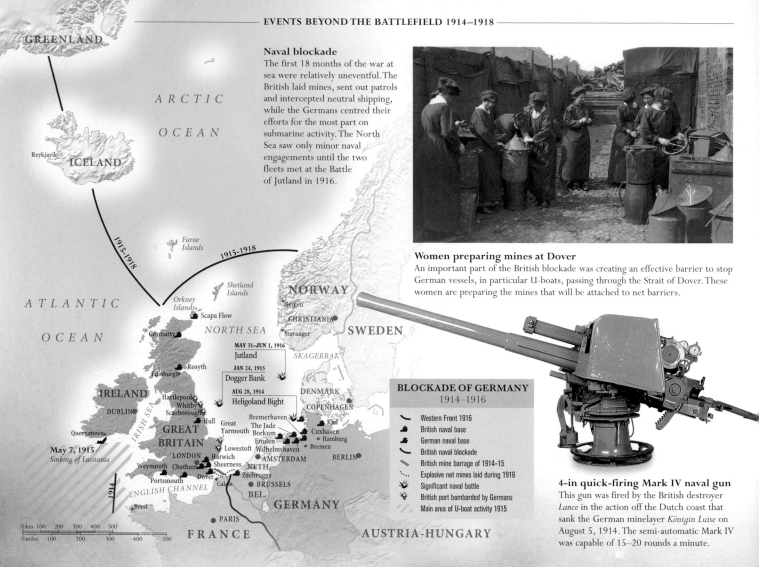

Women preparing mines at Dover
An important part of the British blockade was creating an effective barrier to stop German vessels, in particular U-boats, passing through the Strait of Dover. These women are preparing the mines that will be attached to net barriers.

BLOCKADE OF GERMANY
1914–1916

➴	Western Front 1916
⚓	British naval base
⚓	German naval base
➴	British naval blockade
▨	British mine barrage of 1914–15
⋯	Explosive net mines laid during 1916
✱	Significant naval battle
✹	British port bombarded by Germans
	Main area of U-boat activity 1915

4-in quick-firing Mark IV naval gun
This gun was fired by the British destroyer *Lance* in the action off the Dutch coast that sank the German minelayer *Königin Luise* on August 5, 1914. The semi-automatic Mark IV was capable of 15–20 rounds a minute.

EVENTS IN THE NORTH SEA

Before the war little thought had been given to the possibility of using submarines in an all-out campaign against enemy merchant shipping. In August 1914 Germany had only 28 U-boats in service. At first their main roles were mine-laying and using torpedoes against British warships, but in the first five months of war they did little to reduce British fleet strength. On October 20, 1914, however, *U17*, acting in accordance with

The stricken *Blücher* at Dogger Bank
German sailors cling to the hull of the German armoured cruiser as it capsizes in the action at Dogger Bank on January 24, 1915. Some 260 survivors were picked up by British ships.

international law, stopped, searched and then sank the British steamer *Glitra* off Norway.

In November the British blockade, plus the glimpse of the possibilities presented by the sinking of the *Glitra*, converted the German naval staff to the idea of waging an unrestricted submarine campaign against shipping. There were doubts as to whether the 29 U-boats available for operations at the end of 1914 could achieve anything significant. At the same time the civilian leadership hesitated to embark on a course of action that might add to the list of Germany's enemies. But with Germany

confronted by the prospect of protracted war on two fronts, caution, born of fear of alienating neutral states, was undermined by events.

In December 1914 German units bombarded Hartlepool, Scarborough and Whitby and only narrowly missed being intercepted by British battlecruisers. In January 1915, however, a German cruiser squadron conducting a reconnaissance off Dogger Bank was intercepted. Though on the British side the subsequent action was poorly conducted, the dramatic picture of the *Blücher* sinking gave the confident impression of British victory. The German naval high command was very conscious that its three battlecruisers had been lucky to escape and for the remainder of 1915 made no attempt to challenge British supremacy in the North Sea. On February 4, 1915 Germany announced that the waters around the British Isles constituted a war zone in which shipping was liable to be sunk without warning after February 18.

THE FIRST GERMAN U-BOAT CAMPAIGN

The first ten weeks of the campaign did not suggest that this was the answer to Germany's strategic problems. Between February 18 and April 30, 1915 U-boats accounted for just 39 merchantmen of 105,000 tons, mostly by gunfire or scuttling. In May the monthly total of British, Allied and neutral shipping sunk reached 120,000 tons, but a quarter of the figure represented the liner *Lusitania* on which 1,201 people, including 128 Americans, died (see page 197).

In spite of American protests, submarine operations continued and were responsible for 149,000 of the 185,000 tons of shipping sunk in August 1915. This was the peak of German achievement before 1917 and it was the first month in which losses exceeded new construction. On August 19 *U24* sank the liner *Arabic* off Ireland with the loss of 40 lives, three of them American. Subsequent American protests led to U-boats being ordered to spare passenger ships, to sink by gunfire rather than torpedo, and not to operate west of the British Isles. The German navy announced the end of its submarine campaign on September 18. This was a largely cosmetic gesture: U-boat activity was simply redirected to the Mediterranean and away from American shipping routes.

In 1915 U-boats sank 748,000 tons of shipping, and the German navy was now convinced that an unrestricted submarine campaign could drive Britain from the war. The U-Boats' success won over the military leadership, but the civilian

A COASTAL RAID

ON DECEMBER 16, 1914, hoping to lure the British Grand Fleet, or part of it, within range of their submarines and minefields, the Germans despatched four fast, modern battlecruisers and a heavy cruiser, accompanied by a number of smaller ships, to bombard ports on England's east coast. The raid had a secondary motive – to boost morale after the destruction of Graf von Spee's squadron at the Battle of the Falkland Islands eight days earlier. Soon after dawn the cruisers loomed out of the mist to fire over 2,000 shells at Scarborough, Whitby and Hartlepool. About 40 people were killed and hundreds injured – the first British civilian casualties of enemy action since the 17th century. Many buildings were damaged or destroyed, among them Whitby Abbey and West Hartlepool gasworks. A Whitby schoolgirl recalled running for shelter with "the deafening noise in our ears, the echo ringing even when the actual firing stopped for a moment". A "mantle of heavy smoke, yellow, unreal", hung over the town. The Admiralty's Room 40, where German wireless traffic was read, gave warning of the raid, but in drizzle and fog Admiral Beatty's squadron failed to engage, although a couple of British destroyers came briefly under fire. The raid was said to have stimulated British recruitment, and in the press the Germans became "the baby killers of Scarborough".

The shelling of Whitby Abbey
The Abbey Church on the cliffs above the port of Whitby was already a ruin when it was shelled, but pictures like this still made good anti-German propaganda.

government continued to oppose the idea. A restricted campaign in British home waters was authorized for April 1, 1916, but, even before it began, the torpedoing of the cross-channel ferry *Sussex* on March 24 spelt its end. On April 18 the United States threatened to sever diplomatic relations unless Germany curbed the activities of its submarines. The German government issued an order that U-boats conform to Prize Regulations,

stopping and warning ships before sinking them. As a result, on April 25 the High Sea Fleet recalled its submarines. The opening rounds of the campaign against shipping had ended in Britain's favour, but it was a hollow victory. British countermeasures had failed to curb mounting losses of merchant shipping and, between August 1914 and May 1916, Germany had lost only 34 U-boats. In addition, 100 new U-boats had been ordered in 1915.

German contact mines
At the outbreak of war, German mines were far more effective than British ones. The Germans set about minelaying as early as August 5, 1914, when the *Königin Luise* laid a field off the east coast of England.

Germany's Search for a Strategy

IN SPRING 1916, WITH GERMANY'S ARMIES unable to secure victory and the submarine offensive stalled, the battle fleet had to begin to justify the resources lavished on it over the previous decade. The new fleet commander, Scheer, began to adopt a more aggressive policy. The German battlecruisers under Hipper put to sea briefly on March 26, 1916 in response to an attempted British bombing raid on Zeppelin sheds in Belgium. This was followed by a sortie to bombard the ports of Great Yarmouth and Lowestoft on the east coast of England on April 25. On both occasions British forces, deployed as a result of timely intelligence, narrowly missed intercepting the German ships. It was again on the basis of intelligence warnings that the British were able to sail on May 30 in anticipation of an enemy move even before German warships had reached the open sea. On this occasion the Battlecruiser Squadron under Admiral Beatty was followed by the full might of the Grand Fleet under Admiral Jellicoe.

Boy hero of Jutland
Mortally wounded, with his ship ablaze around him, 16-year-old Jack Cornwall remained at his post manning a gun on the cruiser *Chester*. He was posthumously awarded the Victoria Cross.

THE BATTLE OF JUTLAND

Both sides sent their battlecruiser forces forward on exploratory sweeps with their main fleets in a covering role up to 110km (70 miles) astern. The German aim was to trap and overwhelm part of the British forces before the Grand Fleet could intervene in full strength. The smaller ships screening the battlecruisers made contact shortly after 2:00pm on May 31. This led to "The Run to the South" as Hipper sought to draw Beatty's force south on to the guns of Scheer's battleships. In the process, Hipper's ships managed to sink two of the British battlecruisers even before Beatty's force encountered the German battleships. Then the British began "The Run to the North" in an attempt to lead the High Sea Fleet into contact with Jellicoe's main battle force.

In poor light, for the only time in the war British and German battle fleets engaged each other in the course of two brief actions. In both, the High Sea Fleet found itself confronted by the entire strength of the Grand Fleet deployed made for the Ems or Heligoland. Thus during the night, Scheer's formation passed astern of Jellicoe's battleships. By dawn the Germans had cleared the battle zone. With no prospect of resuming the battle, the British fleet turned for home.

REACTIONS TO THE BATTLE

This bare record of events at Jutland gives no inkling of the controversy that followed the battle. Both sides were guilty of errors, and with national and personal reputations at stake, the outcome and detail of the battle were fiercely disputed. The British had suffered heavier losses: 14 ships sunk, including three battlecruisers, the *Queen Mary*, *Indefatigable* and *Invincible*, to the Germans' 11. Such statistics provided a basis for German claims to victory, but, whereas 32 British capital ships were ready for sea on June 2, the High Sea Fleet was unable to proceed to sea until August. Crucially, the battle left Germany's strategic position unchanged.

The eight months that followed Jutland were a twilight period in the war at sea. The one real battle fought in these months was within the German high command. The navy argued that, with the U-boat service having doubled in size since 1914, an unrestricted submarine campaign should be able to sink 600,000 tons a month. This, it calculated, would destroy 39 per cent of Britain's shipping within five months. It would also frighten off neutral shipping and so drive Britain from the war.

At first the politicians and generals questioned the accuracy of the navy's figures, fearing the reaction of the neutral states, in particular the Americans, to an unrestricted campaign against shipping. As the war entered its third year, however, the privations caused by the British blockade began to erode the policy of caution that seemed to offer no prospect of victory. At a conference held on August 30, 1916 Chancellor Bethmann left the final decision on the navy's demands to the army. This coincided with the dismissal of Falkenhayn from his position as commander-in-chief, so the decision had to be deferred. The new military leadership was prepared to sanction only the resumption of a

There was a terrific explosion aboard the ship, the magazines went. I saw the guns go up in the air just like matchsticks – 12-inch guns they were – bodies and everything. She was beginning to settle down. Within half a minute the ship turned right over and she was gone. I was 180 foot up and I was thrown well clear of the ship otherwise I would have been sucked under. I was practically unconscious, turning over really. At last I came on top of the water. When I came up there was another fellow named Jimmy Green and we got a piece of wood, he was on one end and I was on the other end. A couple of minutes afterwards some shells came over and Jim was minus his head so I was left on my lonesome.

SIGNALLER C. FALMER, *INDEFATIGABLE*

restricted campaign after October 6. All U-Boats were instructed to follow Prize Regulations: before sinking any merchantman, they had to stop and warn their quarry, then allow the crew to escape.

Victory souvenir
This silk scarf leaves no doubt that Jutland was a British victory, which in effect it was. The German fleet never again ventured out to fight in the North Sea.

Souvenir
OF THE
VICTORY OF JUTLAND

MAY 31ST 1916.

The might of the Royal Navy
The 4th Battle Squadron of the Grand Fleet, including the dreadnoughts *Iron Duke*, *Royal Oak*, *Superb* and *Canada*, steams across the North Sea. At Jutland the British had 28 dreadnoughts in the line compared to Germany's 16.

across its path, and the ships at the head of the German line were subjected to severe punishment. In both actions, however, the German line extricated itself from potential disaster by reversing course, and in neither case was this manoeuvre seen by or reported to Jellicoe. As night fell, Scheer, intent on avoiding a resumption of battle the following morning, set course for Horn's Reef off the Danish coast. Jellicoe, no less determined to avoid the lottery of a night action, steered a course that would ensure contact if the enemy

British battlecruisers going into action
The British battlecruisers *Lion*, and Admiral Beatty's flagship, *Princess Royal* and *Queen Mary* at Jutland. This was the last picture taken of the *Queen Mary* before she sank on the evening of May 31, ripped apart by a huge explosion.

In a period of just four months 516 merchantmen of 1,388,000 tons were sunk, and only eight U-boats were lost. To compound Allied problems, losses in the Mediterranean in the second half of 1916 were so heavy that shipping had to be diverted around the Cape. Meanwhile, a disastrous American harvest was forcing Britain to look to Australia for grain supplies in 1917. This would lead to a further reduction of available cargo space. Moreover, by the end of 1916, losses threatened to halt the vital British coal trade with France and Italy.

With only half the available U-boats committed to the attack on shipping, the implications of German success at sea were not lost on the Army's new leaders, Hindenburg and Ludendorff. They were ultimately won over by the argument that Germany had to achieve victory in 1917 rather than endure a fourth winter at war and that Britain would be defeated before the US could intervene on the battlefields of Europe. It was decided to unleash the U-boats on February 1 – the neutral states were not notified of the German intention until January 31. The resumption of unrestricted submarine warfare was

Coming up for air
A U-boat crew takes advantage of fine weather and a calm sea to come up on deck for a shower.

probably the most important single decision made in the course of the whole war. It all but guaranteed that the world's greatest industrial power would soon join the ranks of Germany's enemies.

UNRESTRICTED SUBMARINE WARFARE
Between February and June 1917 the German navy accounted for some 3,844,000 tons of shipping and achieved a rate of sinking that it had claimed would result in Britain's defeat in the summer of 1917. The effectiveness of the German campaign in its

initial stages has been attributed to its unrestricted character, the fact that U-boats were free to sink any ship without warning or regard for lives lost. In fact, the increase in merchantmen sunk after February 1917 was the result of the number of active submarines rather than the nature of their operations. By February 1917 U-boat strength had risen to 152, of which 111 were operational. The Germans were able to keep 50 at sea and 24 on station in their area of operations at any one time.

Another factor in the U-boats' success was the route they now followed when sailing to intercept shipping. During 1916 most U-boat sailings had been via northern Scotland, but operations in the Strait of Dover had revealed the ineffectiveness of British patrols and minefields there. On January 17, 1917, therefore, U-boats were ordered to sail through the Strait, thereby gaining immediate access to the heavy concentrations of shipping in the English Channel and the southwest approaches. This saved six days on passage, a major consideration for boats limited to a 25-day operational cycle, allowing the Germans to deploy many more U-boats for much longer periods.

THE SURVIVAL OF BRITISH TRADE
Britain's ability to survive the German onslaught has been generally attributed to the convoy system. This was initiated in February 1917 for the French coal trade and first used for oceanic trade in May. Over the 21 months of the German unrestricted campaign convoys did indeed reduce shipping losses and ensure Britain's survival. However, during the first five months of the campaign, when Britain came close to defeat, convoys saved no more than 80 ships – the difference between convoy losses and losses that might have been expected had these ships sailed independently.

> "Our armies might advance a mile a day and slay the Hun in thousands, but the real crux lies in whether we blockade the enemy to his knees or whether he does the same to us."
>
> ADMIRAL SIR DAVID BEATTY, JANUARY 1917

Sinking of the *Parkgate* by *U35*
The British freighter was sunk according to Prize Regulations. The Germans ordered the crew of the *Parkgate* into the ship's lifeboats and took the ship's documents from the captain. The ship was then sunk by gunfire.

THE U-BOAT THREAT

IN THE FIRST WORLD WAR, U-boats spent little of their time beneath the waves. Diving was a complicated manoeuvre generally reserved for firing a torpedo or for making an escape. To avoid burning up their air supply, submerged submarines ran on electric motors, powered by a series of huge rechargeable batteries, rather than the diesel engines used on the surface. This slowed them down and they could only dive for limited periods.

In 1914, the German navy was equipped with two basic types of submarine: small, coastal *UB1* class craft and longer-range "overseas" patrol boats of the *U5* and *U19* classes, known as the Mittel-U type. The former were capable of a top speed of just 7.5 knots and had two 450-mm (17-in) torpedo tubes and a crew of 14. The latter had a surface speed of 14 knots (8 knots when submerged) and they carried four torpedo tubes, one 51-mm (2-in) gun and a crew of 28. Wartime development resulted in the addition of the minelayer as a third category of submarine.

The improvement in the fleet was such that by the end of the war German coastal submarines were built to roughly the same specification as the patrol submarines of 1914. In the later stages of the war, patrol vessels were able to reach North American waters.

Torpedoes brought about some of the most notorious Allied shipping losses of the war, including the sinking of the Cunard liner *Lusitania* in 1915. However, they were expensive and against merchantmen the most practical method was sinking by gunfire or boarding the ship and placing charges to scuttle it. In response, the British used Q ships, well-armed ships disguised as merchantmen, to lure U-boats into making an attack. Following the resumption of unrestricted submarine warfare in 1917, the U-boats came close to breaking the Allies, but Britain was able to call on enough shipping, despite its increasing losses.

Propaganda poster
This German poster, dating from 1917, declares "The U-boats are out!"

In the torpedo room
Torpedo tubes were situated at either end of the U-boat. The crew had to work in incredibly cramped, hot conditions. Casualty rates for the service ran at 40 per cent, but there was never any shortage of volunteers.

The control room was abaft the crew's space, shut off by bulkheads forward and aft... A WC stood in one corner of the control room. It was screened by a curtain and, after seeing this arrangement, I understood why the officer I relieved had recommended the use of opium before all trips which were to last more than twelve hours.

JOHANNES SPIESS, WATCH OFFICER, *U9*. QUOTED IN *SUBMARINE BOATS*, R. CROMPTON-HALL

Loading torpedoes onto a U-boat
Although the most feared weapon in a U-boat's armoury, torpedoes were likely to fail with targets beyond 800 m (900 yds). Single hits might sink a cruiser, but rarely succeeded with a shallow-draught merchantman.

Submarine gun
A rapid-fire, high-velocity 10.5-cm (4.1-in) gun was mounted on the deck of all U-boats in the 560- and 900-ton classes. This one is from *U98*, which in the last year of the war sank three merchant ships.

An ideal convoy
A well-protected convoy sails with an escort of dazzle-painted warships and an RNAS (Royal Naval Air Service) airship. In the course of 1918 only two merchantmen were sunk by U-boats when their convoy had both sea and air escorts.

CONVOYS AND REDUCED SHIPPING LOSSES

~

BY THE END OF 1917 a total of 26,404 ships had sailed in convoys at a cost of 147 of their number. As a result the volume of British imports in 1917 increased from 1916 levels despite an 8 per cent loss of shipping capacity. The basic system that was to curb the U-boat threat was in place by November 1917 but it accounted for only half of all shipping movements. By October 1918 convoys accounted for 90 per cent of all sailings. In the course of 1918 U-boats sank a total of just 134 escorted merchantmen.

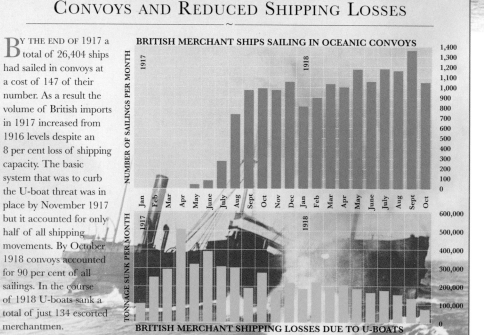

BRITISH MERCHANT SHIPS SAILING IN OCEANIC CONVOYS

NUMBER OF SAILINGS PER MONTH

1,400 / 1,300 / 1,200 / 1,100 / 1,000 / 900 / 800 / 700 / 600 / 500 / 400 / 300 / 200 / 100 / 0

1917 — Jan, Feb, Mar, Apr, May, June, July, Aug, Sept, Oct, Nov, Dec

1918 — Jan, Feb, Mar, Apr, May, June, July, Aug, Sept, Oct

TONNAGE SUNK PER MONTH

600,000 / 500,000 / 400,000 / 300,000 / 200,000 / 100,000 / 0

1917 / 1918

BRITISH MERCHANT SHIPPING LOSSES DUE TO U-BOATS

The key to British survival into autumn 1917 was neutral shipping. With the start of the unrestricted campaign, neutral shipping mainly confined itself to harbour in the hope that American pressure would force the Germans to moderate their new aggressive policy. Neutral sailings to and from British ports in February and March fell to 37 per cent of the January 1917 level. By July, however, neutral sailings had recovered to four-fifths of the January level. The neutrals obviously needed to continue to trade and Britain and the United States subjected them to intense political and economic pressure, while offering lucrative financial inducements to do so. These measures saw Britain through the critical months of 1917, but its long-term survival was ensured only by a comprehensive convoy system.

In the first 27 months of war, in which time no single month saw British losses exceed 150,000 tons, the Admiralty consistently refused to sanction the general introduction of convoys. It did so on the grounds that that there were not enough warships to provide escorts and that the sheer numbers of sailings to and from British ports, and the congestion caused by holding ships in harbour, rendered convoys impossible. In spite of these arguments, rising losses forced the Admiralty to accept the principle of sailing merchantmen under warship protection on three routes even before April 1917. A convoy system was introduced on the route to and from the Hook of Holland in July 1916 and on the Scandinavian route in January 1917. On February 10, at French insistence, the Admiralty also began sailing convoys of colliers to France at night.

Only three ships were lost in the first year of the Dutch "Beef Run", and losses on the French coal routes were reduced to just five out of a total of 2,583 sailings by escorted colliers in March and April 1917. The Admiralty nevertheless refused to consider the introduction of oceanic convoys even as losses rose alarmingly after February 1917. Prime minister Lloyd George was to claim that it was his intervention in April 1917 that forced the Admiralty to accept convoys; the Admiralty claimed that by then it had already come round to the idea.

CONVOYS PROVE THEIR WORTH

The first oceanic convoy of 17 merchantmen sailed from Gibraltar on May 10. It arrived in British waters without loss two days earlier than ships sailing independently might have been expected to do. On May 24 a convoy sailed from Hampton Roads, Virginia and arrived in Britain on June 10, just one straggler having been lost. In June four convoys arrived in British waters and July saw the start of regular convoy sailings from North America. In August regular convoys were instituted on the homeward South American and Gibraltar routes. Nonetheless the convoy system had its failings. Because homeward convoys were dispersed in the Channel and Irish Sea, unnecessary losses were incurred in home waters. In the first three months of oceanic convoys no attempt was made to escort outward shipping, and here losses continued on the scale of previous months. Losses of unescorted shipping also continued to be heavy.

Better reconnaissance and more effective use of mines and depth charges claimed 46 U-boats against the 42 commissioned between August 1917 and January 1918. In this six-month period both the number of U-boats at sea and sinkings per boat per month declined by 27 per cent. The German navy, however, still believed it was sinking merchantmen at a rate that would bring about Britain's defeat. In reality, less shipping was sunk in 1918 than in the first four months of the unrestricted campaign. The decline of the rate of sinkings through 1918 was primarily the result of the convoy system.

Dropping depth charges
It is estimated that a total of 29 German U-boats were lost to depth charges, most of them in 1918. Here the British torpedo boat destroyer *Tempest* prepares to drop depth charges in the North Sea.

The years 1917 and 1918 saw successive reductions in U-boat production from the peak levels of 1916. As a result, Germany entered 1918 with no more U-boats than in June 1917. In the course of 1918 Germany lost 69 U-boats. This was offset by the commissioning of 80 new boats, but the return per boat per month continued to decline. Moreover, after March 1918 new British minefields and patrols in the Strait of Dover forced U-boats to sail around the north of Scotland to and from their operational areas. While the number of U-boats at sea remained more or less the same as in 1917, this was achieved only by shortening periods of rest and refitting. Right up to the end of the war U-boats continued to inflict damage on Allied shipping, but the U-boat offensive never again came close to its goal of forcing Britain out of the war.

CAMOUFLAGING SHIPS

~

THE FIRST SUGGESTIONS FOR SHIP CAMOUFLAGE centred, naturally enough, on hiding the vessel in question against the backdrop of sea, sky and horizon. It was discovered that this technique could deceive conventional craft. Unfortunately a U-boat's periscope was still able to pick out a camouflaged ship as a silhouette. Then the new idea of dazzle-painting was proposed: not to hide the ship, but to create an optical illusion that made it very difficult to read its course accurately. By late 1917 the dazzle painting of the entire British merchant fleet, and some warships, was under way.

A dazzle-painted ship
The *Underwing*, a British Q ship, here typifies the use of angled black and white stripes to create a distorted perception.

Camouflaged convoy
The dazzle painting of individual merchant ships may have enhanced the success of the convoy system introduced in 1917.

Dazzle patterns
Artists at London's Royal Academy, led by Norman Wilkinson, who had first proposed the idea, created the dazzle designs. Dummy bridges and painted anchors were sometimes used, in addition to colour blocks.

Austro-Hungarian dreadnoughts at Pola
Pola, today the port of Pula in Croatia, was the main Austro-Hungarian naval base in the Adriatic. It was frequently the target of Italian raids by air and sea, although these inflicted only limited damage.

THE MEDITERRANEAN

Geography and superior numbers ensured that the Allies exercised command of the Mediterranean, although this never extended to the Dardanelles and the Adriatic. It was from these areas that the challenges to Allied naval power emerged. The challenge from the Adriatic proved the greater, once Germany had chosen to make its main U-boat effort in the Mediterranean from the ports of Austria-Hungary. In a sea that witnessed some 350 daily sailings of merchantmen, many carrying British, Dutch and French imports from the Far East, Germany's decision largely determined the course of the Mediterranean campaign.

Initially, the British and French had attempted a close blockade in the Adriatic but had been forced to withdraw their larger ships to Malta and Bizerta. After a brief flurry of raids and counter-raids following Italy's declaration of war on Austria-Hungary in 1915, the Adriatic became quieter, largely because of the vulnerability of large warships to submarine attack. The Allies then attempted to prevent U-boats sailing from the Adriatic to the Mediterranean by assembling a fleet of small fishing boats, mainly British drifters, to patrol the Straits of Otranto.

In the event the Straits were too deep to be mined and netted effectively and too wide to be patrolled properly. The Otranto barrage was described as "a large sieve through which

U-boats could pass with impunity". The barrage itself invited raids. On the night of May 14–15, 1917 three Austrian cruisers sailed through the barrage. They approached the drifters one by one, ordering the crews to abandon ship, then opening fire. Of the 47 drifters on duty, 14 were sunk and three seriously damaged. Not all such sorties succeeded. When the Austro-Hungarian navy sent a force to raid the barrage in June 1918, its four dreadnoughts also put to sea. One of these, the *Szent Istvan*, was torpedoed by an Italian motorboat on June 10.

The ease with which U-boats operated in this theatre was the result of the political infighting and lack of co-operation between the Allies. In 1916 the Mediterranean was divided into 18 separate Allied commands. Their patrols, which by 1916 involved 140 destroyers and sloops and some 200 armed trawlers, were so ineffective that in 1915 and 1916 only three U-boats were sunk, two by unknown causes. In August 1916 one boat, the *U35*,

Naval war in the Mediterranean
War in this theatre centred on the U-boats operating out of the Adriatic and the Dardanelles. The Allies tried, with very little success, to counter this threat by means of patrols and a barrage across the Straits of Otranto.

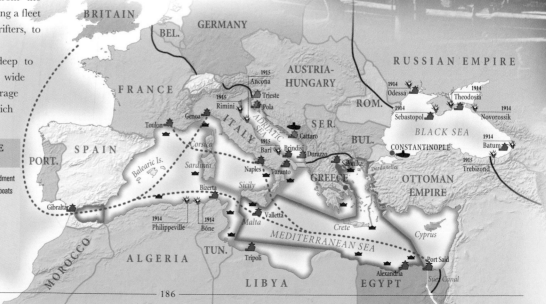

THE MEDITERRANEAN THEATRE
1914–1918

▬ Fronts at end of 1916	✹ Major naval bombardment
⛴ Allied naval base	⚓ Minefield laid by U-boats
⛴ Austro-Hungarian naval base	**ALLIED PATROL AREAS, ESTABLISHED 1916**
⚓ German U-boat base	▢ British
┈ Allied merchant shipping lanes	▢ French
▢ Otranto barrage	▢ Italian

accounted for two-thirds of worldwide Allied losses for that month in a single three-week cruise in which she did not fire a single torpedo. Losses reached a peak in April 1917, when there were 28 U-boats in the Mediterranean, with ten at sea on any one day. Not a single U-boat was sunk, while the Allies lost 94 ships. At worst, the voyage from Gibraltar to the Suez Canal could take a month.

As elsewhere, the counter to the U-boat in this theatre was the convoy system, first introduced by the Italian navy in spring 1917. Despite usually having no escort other than a single armed merchant cruiser, these Italian convoys immediately cut losses, as did the British introduction of convoys between Alexandria and Malta in May 1917. The first through convoy from Britain to Suez was run in October and the first homeward convoy in November. Shipping losses fell steadily between June 1917 and October 1918 when Germany recalled its U-boats as a result of the collapse of its allies. The

Drifters of the Otranto barrage at Taranto
Most of the drifters were British, each armed with a 6-pound gun and depth charges. They were supported by small Italian motor launches. In the course of the war only two U-boats were ever caught in the drifters' nets.

war in the Mediterranean ended with the Allied navies supporting military operations and occupying various ports to enforce armistice terms. On November 13, 1918 an Allied fleet sailed through the Dardanelles and anchored at Constantinople.

~

Although air power had only a minimal influence on the outcome of the war, the years 1914–18 were crucial in the development of the aircraft from a flimsy means of reconnaissance into a powerful weapon. By 1918, with fighters armed with machine-guns flying in huge squadrons and giant bombers capable of dropping 1,000-kg (2,200-lb) bombs, it was clear that the aeroplane would play a key role in any future war.

~

1914 AUGUST 20
German Zeppelins fly over London and British ports

1914 AUGUST 30
Paris bombed by German Taube

SEPTEMBER 3
French aerial reconnaissance spots crucial gap between German armies advancing to Marne

SEPTEMBER 5
Russian gunfire brings down Zeppelin at Lemberg. British planes begin night patrols over London

SEPTEMBER 16
First attack by sea-based aircraft: Japanese Farman bombs German warship at Tsingtao

SEPTEMBER 22
First British air raid on Germany. Zeppelin sheds at Düsseldorf and Cologne bombed by four Tabloids

DECEMBER 9
Warsaw bombed by Germans

1915 JANUARY 19
Beginning of Zeppelin campaign against Great Britain: Great Yarmouth bombed

1915 FEBRUARY
Frenchman Roland Garros uses fixed, forward-firing machine gun, with deflectors to protect propeller

MAY 31
First Zeppelin raid on London; 28 dead and 60 injured

JUNE 7
Zeppelin destroyed in flight by hand-launched bomb near Ghent

AUGUST 1
Start of "Fokker Scourge": German Fokker monoplanes dominate skies over Western Front

1916 FEBRUARY 18
Heavy bombing raid on Laibach by Italian Capronis in retaliation for earlier Austrian raid on Milan

1916 JULY 1
Anglo-French air supremacy on the Somme: 201 French and 185 British aircraft pitted against 129 German planes

OCTOBER 28
Oswald Boelke, whose superior tactics returned aerial dominance to Germans, killed in action

OCTOBER 8
German Airforce (*Luftstreitkrafte*) established (previous groups amalgamated)

1917 APRIL
"Bloody April", in which British aircrews suffer 50 per cent casualties in one month

1917 JUNE 13
"Diamond formation" Gotha bombers target London causing 158 deaths and 425 wounded: worst civilian casualties of war

1918 MARCH 21
Major German air offensive, to support Ludendorff offensive in northern France, but subsequently British regain air superiority

1918 APRIL 1
British RFC (Royal Flying Corps) and RNAS (Royal Naval Air Service) unite to form RAF

APRIL 21
Manfred von Richthofen, the "Red Baron", shot down and killed

MAY 13
British form force for strategic bombing raids

AUGUST 8
Amiens: British planes drop 1,563 bombs and fire 122,150 rounds in support of ground offensive

SEPTEMBER 12
1,476 Allied aircraft support American attack at St Mihiel

KEY
■ Western Front ■ Other events

War in the Air

B<small>Y THE OUTBREAK OF WAR</small>, all combatants had an air force of some sort. In spite of their particular interest in airships, the Germans had about 250 aircraft. Their organizational set-up and aircrew training were generally superior to that of the Allies. The Austrian air force was tiny by comparison, though the bird-like Taube ("Dove"), the chief German reconnaissance aircraft in the early months of the war, was of Austrian origin.

The French were outnumbered in aircraft by the Germans by about 3 to 2 and their command structure was less efficient, but in other, qualitative respects they were superior. Moreover, they had the largest manufacturing base, and were able to increase production quickly when war began. That was fortunate for Britain, which lagged behind both the French and Germans. The Royal Flying Corps was created in 1912, two years after the French equivalent, and deployed only about 60 aircraft at the front in August 1914. For the first year or two the British were heavily dependent on French engines and aircraft frames. However, Britain had the greater industrial base, and by the end of the war its aviation industry led the world.

The Russians had more aeroplanes than the British, and produced the giant four-engined Sikorsky Ilya Moroumetz, the world's first heavy bomber, in early 1915. But the confusing variety of Russian types made maintenance of their aircraft difficult. The same problem affected the French but they were quicker to realize the importance of

Knight of the air
A French pilot demonstrates the perils of flying in the First World War as he lets go of the controls to man the Lewis gun mounted on the upper wing of his aircraft.

standardization. Despite inept organization, Italy (the first nation to carry out aerial bombing – against the Turks in North Africa in 1911) produced some fine aviators and at least one outstanding designer, Gianni Caproni, whose bombers played a significant role in the campaigns on the Isonzo. His monstrous, three-engined, triplane bomber, the Ca 42, appeared in early 1918.

The first time I ever encountered a German plane in the air both the pilot, Harvey-Kelly, and myself were completely unarmed... The German observer did not appear to be shooting at us... We waved a hand to the enemy and proceeded with our task. The enemy did likewise. At the time this did not appear to me to be in any way ridiculous... But afterwards just for safety's sake I always carried a carbine with me in the air.

WILLIAM SHOLTO DOUGLAS ON HIS EARLY EXPERIENCES OF AERIAL RECONNAISSANCE IN FRANCE

Bristol BE2A

Strong, stable and easy to fly, the Bristol BE2 a was the most reliable of the reconnaissance planes brought over to France by the British Royal Flying Corps at the outbreak of war.

AERIAL RECONNAISSANCE

Reconnaissance in all its aspects, including artillery-spotting, was the most valuable task performed by aircraft throughout the the war. Army high commands failed, however, to anticipate that successful tactics would breed counter-tactics. Since reconnaissance proved so effective, the enemy naturally took steps to prevent it, while protecting its own reconnaissance operations. Nor did it take long to realize that if you can see the enemy, you can hit him, and so surveillance expanded into attack. The fighter, the bomber and the ground-attack aircraft were inevitable developments.

In spite of the pre-war predominance of monoplanes, the majority of aircraft throughout the war were biplanes, which were structurally more robust. Reconnaissance aircraft were generally two-seaters, and the observer was often senior to the pilot. Speed was unimportant and the main danger in the early months, apart from occasional ground fire, was engine failure. In the skies, opposing pilots allegedly exchanged salutes. They soon turned less friendly, taking shots at each other with rifles or revolvers, but there always remained among air crews respect and admiration for their opponents.

Mobile aerial reconnaissance rapidly proved its worth. As early as August 1914 British planes gave notice of the German outflanking movement at Mons, and German Taubes warned of the Russian advance at Tannenberg, enabling the outnumbered Germans to strengthen their forces at the vital point

to gain a sensational victory. Airborne French observers noted the gap between the advancing German First and Second armies on the Marne (September 3, 1914), prompting the successful Allied counterattack. The usefulness of aerial reconnaissance to the artillery, especially in correcting the gunners' range, was proved at the outset of trench warfare, on the Aisne in mid-September. The potential of reconnaissance aircraft increased as their role came to be better appreciated by army commanders, and they were fitted with two-way radios and effective automatic cameras, instead of relying on the observer's verbal reports and scribbled notes.

By 1915 the need to deny reconnaissance and artillery-spotting to the enemy had expanded the role of air forces. No longer "above the battle", aircraft became participants. The first fighters were existing aircraft armed with a machine-gun. But to attack enemy aircraft and observation balloons required different qualities, in particular speed and manoeuvrability, and the superior power-to-weight ratio of French rotary engines gave them the initial advantage.

AN EFFECTIVE FIGHTER

Another requirement was a fixed, forward-firing machine-gun that did not hit the propeller. Various solutions were tried. With a pusher-type aircraft, the engine and propeller were mounted behind, but this entailed some loss in performance. A French designer, Raymond Saulnier, devised an interrupter gear that enabled a pilot to fire through the propeller. This was adopted by the famous aviator Roland Garros with added metal plates to deflect bullets striking the propeller blades. When Garros was shot down and his plane captured intact, the mechanism was passed to the Fokker workshops, where an improved gearing system was devised that gave the Germans marked superiority.

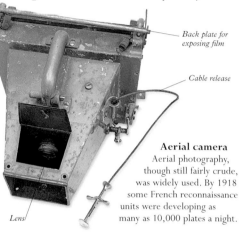

Back plate for exposing film

Cable release

Aerial camera

Aerial photography, though still fairly crude, was widely used. By 1918 some French reconnaissance units were developing as many as 10,000 plates a night.

Lens

FOKKER EINDECKER E III

~

Eindecker engine

The only surviving Eindecker is this one at the Science Museum, London. The photograph below is of a model.

DUTCH-BORN ENGINEER Anthony Fokker (1890–1939) produced about 40 types of aircraft for Germany during the war. He was adept at organizing production, most innovations originating with his design staff. The most striking of these was the interrupter gearing system that allowed a pilot to fire a machine-gun through the propeller. Fokker benefited from the capture of a French Morane with a crude device of this kind. Fitted to a Fokker Eindecker (monoplane), Fokker's improved interrupter achieved a pronounced superiority over Allied fighters and initiated the so-called "Fokker scourge" of 1915.

The Eindecker was an old pre-war machine that used wing-warping, governed by wires to control aircraft roll

The synchronized Spandau machine-gun fired through the propeller

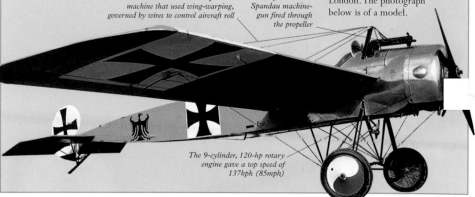

The 9-cylinder, 120-hp rotary engine gave a top speed of 137kph (85mph)

The so-called "Fokker Scourge" was partly neutralized by the adoption of formation flying (disliked by individualistic French pilots), by the creation of elite units like *Les Cigognes* ("The Storks"), and by adopting one type of aircraft, rather than a miscellany, for individual squadrons. It was finally overcome by better fighters – the British FE2 series, best of the pusher type, the new generation of Nieuports and later the tough and speedy Spad VII with its synchronized Vickers gun, which totally outclassed the Fokker Eindecker.

Tactics were developed largely on the wing by gifted pilots. Solo fighters soon learned the advantage of attacking from above and behind,

Manfred von Richthofen, the "Red Baron"
Richthofen stands in front of his trademark red Fokker triplane. He was credited with the destruction of a record 80 Allied aircraft between September 1916 and April 1918, when he was shot down over enemy lines.

preferably out of the sun. When operating in pairs, one approached from the side and opened fire early to distract attention from the other diving on the enemy from the rear. Some manoeuvres were associated with particular pilots, such as Max Immelmann. The "Immelmann Loop" required the attacking pilot to dive past the enemy, pull up into a near-vertical climb, turn sharply and dive a second time – not a tactic for the faint-hearted.

Immelmann's fellow-ace, Oswald Boelcke was even more influential. He was an early advocate of the 14-aircraft Jasta (short for Jagdstaffel, "hunter squadron"), commanding one of the first, which became operational in autumn 1916. Among his protégés was Manfred von Richthofen, most durable of German aces.

The brave and skilful fighter pilot rapidly became a cultural hero, a "knight of the air", perfect for national propaganda. His daring aerial exploits offered a welcome contrast to the anonymous industrial massacres going on below in the smoke and mud of Verdun and the Somme.

Aircrew were absurdly overworked, required to fly several patrols each day, for weeks and months. Allied pilots were pitched into the battle scandalously under-trained and inexperienced: 80 per cent of British casualties had flown less than 20 missions. The Germans were more careful, until heavy losses forced the sacrifice of standards. They were also better disciplined. By 1917, the day of the lonely hunter, such as Georges Guynemer, Albert Ball or Werner Voss, was over. Manfred von Richthofen, the most successful pilot of the war, was essentially an outstanding squadron leader.

CONTROL OF THE SKIES

The German Albatros biplanes regained fighter superiority for the Germans in late 1916 and retained it beyond "Bloody April" (1917), when British pilots' life expectancy dropped to 11 days. The Allies were able to win back control of the skies later in 1917, partly – and significantly – because German production was falling behind. French and British aircraft production in 1917 was double the German figure. To an extent the Germans compensated with their Jagdgeschwader or "Flying Circus" formations, made up of several Jastas and backed by extensive ground support and transport to move them quickly to where they were needed.

Several hundred US flyers had enlisted with the Allies at an early stage, but American impact on the air war was less than anticipated. In April 1917 the future USAAF, then a division of the Signal Corps, consisted of about 1,000 men and 250 aircraft, none fit for European combat. The US squadrons active on the Western Front in 1917–18 generally flew French aircraft.

Ironically, what was probably the best fighter of the war, the steel-framed 200-kph (125-mph) Fokker DVII, appeared when the battle was already lost and the Germans, bereft of vital materials, were hugely outnumbered by the Allies' SE5As, Sopwith Camels and Spads.

GEORGES GUYNEMER
~

FRANCE'S BEST LOVED ACE, Georges Guynemer (1894–1917) was mobbed by well-wishers in the streets of his home country. The young pilot had shot down 54 enemy aircraft by the time of his death at the age of 22. Guynemer was turned down five times by the French Air Force due to poor health before being accepted as a mechanic in 1914. He qualified as a pilot the following year. On July 19, 1915 he flew his first victorious mission above Soissons, bringing down a German plane after a fight lasting 10 minutes. First flying Nieuport 11s and later his trusty Spad VII, which he nicknamed Vieux Charles (Old Charles), he favoured the unconventional and risky frontal strike. He was shot down seven times. Perhaps because of his extraordinary knack for survival, the French public found it hard to believe he had perished when he failed to return from a flight over Poelcapelle on September 11, 1917. Neither his body nor his aircraft was ever found and it was never conclusively established that he had been shot down, as the Germans claimed.

FIGHTER PLANES

ADVANCES IN AIRCRAFT DESIGN were rapid: the fighters of 1918 were quite different from those of 1915. Air superiority changed sides often in the course of the war. The German Fokker Eindekker (see page 189) was superseded by French Nieuports and Spad VIIs over Verdun in 1916. Then the Albatros D series, with their in-line Mercedes and Daimler engines and twin machine-guns, regained fighter superiority for the Germans towards the end of 1916.

By 1917 the British aircraft industry was finally getting into its stride. The Royal Aircraft Factory's SE5 and SE5A were equipped with the outstanding Hispano-Suiza V8 engine, which also powered the French Spad XIII. The Sopwith Camel – in total "kills" the most successful fighter of the war – was operational from June 1917. The Sopwith Triplane (1916) proved marvellously manoeuvrable, but it was made for the RNAS (Royal Naval Air Service), not the RFC (Royal Flying Corps), and production was relatively small. The Germans reproduced its virtues in the Fokker Dr 1 triplane (late summer 1917), Richthofen's favourite. Right up to the end of the war both sides continued to come up with improved designs. In the end, however, superior performance was not enough; the advantage passed to the side with the greater industrial resources and greater number of planes.

Spad XIII
The sturdy single-seater with its twin synchronized Vickers guns was popular with all Allied pilots. It could reach a speed of 222 kph (138 mph) at 2,400 m (6,500 ft).

Albatros DIII
This powerful biplane, armed with twin Spandau machine-guns, served from January 1917 until the armistice. Its maximum speed at sea level was 175 kph (109 mph).

Back sight

Magazine held 97 rounds with a counter indicating cartridges remaining

Aircraft Lewis gun had no cooling system

Fore sight

ALTIMETER

Spade grip

Lewis gun used on Allied fighters
The Lewis gun was quickly adapted for use on fighters, either fixed above the upper wing of a biplane or mounted in the rear of a two-seater.

French pilot's kit
A pilot's clothing and equipment usually reflected his individual style. Essential elements were goggles and a fur-lined leather jacket, helmet and gloves to combat the intense cold.

GOGGLES

FLYING HELMET

Sopwith Camel
The Camel's idiosyncrasies, notably a viciously sharp right-hand turn, which could cause a spin, were an advantage in the hands of experienced pilots.

Main armament was synchronized Vickers machine-gun fired through propeller

130 hp Clerget rotary engine gave maximum speed at sea level of 190 kph (118 mph)

Fokker Dr 1
The triplane (1917) had a rapid rate of climb and was very manoeuvrable, but its top speed was only 165 kph (103 mph). Structural failures led to relatively few being built.

SE5A
This fast, reliable British plane could reach 221 kph (137.5 mph) at sea level. It had a nose-mounted Vickers plus a wing-mounted Lewis gun.

STRATEGIC DEVELOPMENTS

Although fighters became the dominant planes of the war, the only important roles for aircraft foreseen in 1914 were reconnaissance and bombing. Strategic bombing never became really effective in 1914–18, but its future potential became obvious.

The ineffectiveness of early bombers made the Germans' faith in Zeppelins understandable. For safety's sake they flew at night and maintained radio silence, which made navigation exceptionally difficult and bombing highly inaccurate. Secrecy was essential and, in spite of searchlights, they were frequently heard before they were seen. They carried out raids on Paris and other French cities, and – the most prestigious target – on London. However, they were becoming increasingly vulnerable and were withdrawn from a combat role after five were shot down over England in September 1916.

Specialized ground-attack aircraft were a late development. The Germans employed specialized two-seater aircraft in large formations called *Schlastas* (*Schlachtstaffeln*, "Battle flights"). They had a devastating effect at Cambrai (November 1917) and in the first German offensive of 1918, dropping bombs, strafing the enemy with machine-gun fire and at the same time providing information on the progress of the advance.

By 1918 air power was beginning to play an important role on the Western Front, where over 8,000 aircraft were in action. The size of units was

massively increased. The French, for example, operated a division of 700 mixed aircraft. With the development of ground attack, troop movements were seriously inhibited. The Germans often despatched 30-aircraft raids against targets behind enemy lines. The war was decided by events on the ground, but in 1918 events on the ground were dramatically affected by activities in the air.

In proportion to the numbers engaged, casualty rates were high. The rate among 22,000 British pilots was over 50 per cent, and German and

French rates were similar. More pilots were lost through accidents than in action. Fewer might have died if parachutes had been issued. They were provided for balloon observers but were considered impractical in aircraft, at first because they were too heavy. The Germans introduced them towards the end of the war, but the RFC command feared that parachutes would encourage aircrew to abandon their aircraft unnecessarily. The sight of an unharmed pilot jumping to his death rather than burn in his flaming aircraft was not easily forgotten.

ZEPPELINS – RIGID AIRSHIPS

~

ALL PARTICIPANTS HAD AIRSHIPS – essentially powered balloons – of some kind. They were normally used for surveillance and naval duties. The Germans' rigid-frame Zeppelins were the best and were considered ideal for long-range bombing. They could climb quickly to an altitude beyond most fighters and their range and bomb-carrying capacity were far greater than any aeroplane. But they were vulnerable to ground fire, totally dependent on weather conditions and, as fighters improved and tracer was introduced, the hazards of flying in a slow-moving target under a vast bag of inflammable gas became unpleasantly obvious. However, there was no doubting the endurance of Zeppelins. On a (failed) mission to carry supplies to the German forces in East Africa in 1917, the *L59* flew over 6,400 km (4,000 miles) in 95 hours.

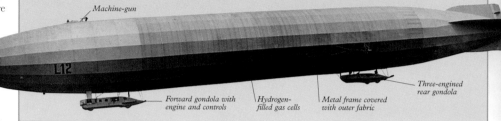

Machine-gun

L12

Forward gondola with engine and controls

Hydrogen-filled gas cells

Metal frame covered with outer fabric

Three-engined rear gondola

Anti-aircraft guns
All kinds of gun, from machine-guns to field artillery, were pressed into service to shoot at aircraft. Here British troops rush to man a gun in the Vimy Ridge sector of the Western Front.

HEAVY BOMBERS

THE FIRST BOMBERS WERE ADAPTATIONS of the heavier, two-seater, reconnaissance planes such as the Austrian Aviatik and the French Voisin, and the first bombs were artillery shells tossed hopefully out of the open cockpit. None of the early bombers were capable of delivering a significant bomb load and, although great progress was made during the next four years, the bomber remained a minor weapon, more valuable for its psychological impact than for the destruction it caused. The Royal Naval Air Service, operating from Belgian bases, mounted bombing raids on the Zeppelin base at Friedrichshafen as early as October–November 1914. The targets being large and inflammable, even 9-kg (20-lb) bombs were successful. By 1915 genuine bombers (all biplanes) were operational in Russia (Sikorskis), Italy (Capronis, the earliest and among the best bombers of the war) and Germany (twin-engined Gothas). The first British bomber, the Handley-Page O/100, first flew in December 1915. Bombing, however, remained a fringe operation until more specialized, more powerful and more numerous aircraft appeared in 1917. These included the R (Riesenflugzeug) planes, in particular the Zeppelin-Staaken series, which had two pilots sharing the cockpit, each holding a marine-type wheel (as used in airships), and engine pods containing compartments for in-flight mechanics. Strategic bombing of industrial targets was adopted in 1918 by the new Royal Air Force and advocated in France by Pétain. By that time bombers such as the Handley-Page O/400 could carry a bombload of around 900 kg (2,000 lb). Targets were industrial sites and railway stations. Air Marshal Trenchard told his pilots they need not be too careful of civilian lives, though in practice he concentrated on tactical rather than strategic bombing.

Handley Page O/400
With a span of 30.5 m (100 ft), the O/400's wings folded for storage. Powered by two 360 hp Rolls Royce Eagle V-12 engines, it had a top speed of 156 kph (97 mph).

Caproni Ca 3
Gabriele D'Annunzio, poet, patriot and right-wing man of action, sets off in a giant Caproni bomber to attack the Austro-Hungarian lines on the Isonzo front.

Zeppelin-Staaken RVI
This giant bomber had a range of eight hours and was used for night raids over London. It could carry a payload of 2,000 kg (4,400 lb).

British bombs
The two small bombs shown are a 9-kg (20-lb) Marten Hale high-explosive bomb (above) and a carcass incendiary bomb (below). The latter, usually dropped in large numbers, had perforated casing to allow the flames to spread.

Bomb damage
Territorials search the rubble of a London house bombed by a zeppelin. Over 500 British civilians were killed in zeppelin raids in the course of the war and a further 1,000 died in raids by aircraft.

The USA and the War

EVENTS IN THE USA

AUGUST 1914–JUNE 1917

~

However much the USA wished to stay out of the war, the declaration of neutrality and the observation of it proved to be two different things. Insistence on the right to trade and the right of free transit for neutral states inevitably brought the USA into conflict with Germany. After Germany's resumption of unrestricted submarine warfare in 1917, President Wilson was able to persuade Congress that the USA would have to enter the war.

~

1914 AUGUST 4
USA declares its neutrality

1914 DECEMBER 29
British government sends memorandum to USA in defence of its blockade policy

1915 FEBRUARY 6
British liner *Lusitania* arrives at Liverpool flying US flag; US government objects

1915 FEBRUARY 27
Dacia, steamer sailing from USA to Germany with cargo of cotton, seized by French

MAY 7
Lusitania torpedoed; 1,201 men, women and children drowned, including 128 US citizens

MAY 13
President Woodrow Wilson sends first of four diplomatic protests to Germany over sinking of *Lusitania*

AUGUST 19
Liner *Arabic* torpedoed and sunk. Further tension between USA and Germany

1916 JANUARY
President Wilson's adviser, Edward House, visits leading European statesmen to discuss peace options

1916 FEBRUARY
House Memorandum stating President Wilson will propose peace conference

JULY 30
Sabotage of munition ships causes massive explosions at Black Tom Island, Jersey City

NOVEMBER 7
Wilson re-elected on peace platform

DECEMBER 12
Germany advises USA of Central Powers' willingness to negotiate peace with the Allies

DECEMBER 18
Wilson invites warring sides to state their own terms for peace

DECEMBER 26
Central Powers call for meeting without stating their terms. Proposal rejected by Allies

1917 JANUARY 10
Allies name their terms for peace, in reply to Wilson's proposal of previous month

1917 JANUARY 19
Zimmermann telegram: German proposal for alliance with Mexico against USA; message intercepted by British and passed to USA

JANUARY 11
Kingsland, New Jersey: German saboteurs destroy munitions plant

JANUARY 29
Germany states its terms for peace to Wilson

JANUARY 22
Wilson's "peace without victory" speech to Senate

JANUARY 31
Germany tells USA it will resume unrestricted submarine warfare

FEBRUARY 3
Sinking of American grain ship *Housatonic*. USA severs diplomatic relations with Germany

FEBRUARY 25
Cunard liner *Laconia* sunk. Four Americans drowned. The "overt act" for which President Wilson was waiting

MARCH 12
Wilson orders arming of US merchantmen, despite failing to win approval from Congress

APRIL 6
US declares war on Germany

MAY 2
First US destroyer flotilla arrives at Queenstown in Ireland

MAY 18
Compulsory Service Act enacted in USA

JUNE 25
First contingent of US troops lands in France

KEY
- Events at sea
- Political and other events

THE ALMOST UNIVERSAL reaction of Americans to the outbreak of war in Europe was a determination to stay well out of it. Proclaiming US neutrality, President Wilson said that Americans should be impartial "in word and thought" as well as action, a characteristically high-minded but – in view of the strong cultural affinities with Britain and France – improbable aspiration.

Strict neutrality was impossible, and policies that were even-handed in principle turned out to favour the Allies in practice. At first loans to either side were barred, but this worked to the advantage of the Allies because they held substantial assets in the USA which they liquidated to buy goods. Then, when their credit was exhausted, the no-loans policy was abandoned for the sake of US export trade. Huge credits were extended, but loans to the Allies by 1917 were 75 times greater than loans to the Central Powers. An open-trade policy also favoured the Allies, as German ships could not cross the Atlantic.

The peace ticket
In the US presidential election of 1916 Wilson ran for re-election on a manifesto based on peace and prosperity.

Impartial spectators
President Wilson throws the ceremonial pitch to open the 1916 baseball season. For 32 months Wilson managed to keep the USA out of the conflict that had engulfed Europe.

In maintaining their blockade of Germany, the British published certain restrictions on trade. The confiscation of goods bound for a neutral port if likely to reach the enemy was not strictly within international law, but it had been practised by the USA in the Civil War. The British also extended the authorized ban on goods linked with war-making to all goods, including food. Ruthless enforcement brought protests from Washington – and soothing replies, plus compensation, from London.

More serious problems arose when Germany began a submarine blockade in February 1915. The Germans declared waters around Britain a war zone in which ships would be attacked on sight. One or two US ships were attacked in the following months and a few Americans killed, for which Germany promptly apologized. But the sinking of the *Lusitania*, with 128 Americans among the drowned, provoked a furious reaction.

THE SINKING OF THE LUSITANIA

~

BOUND FROM NEW YORK TO LIVERPOOL with 1,962 passengers and crew, the *Lusitania* was off southern Ireland on May 7, 1915. In spite of warnings (apparently unreceived) of submarine activity, Captain Turner was not following recommended tactics – full speed on a zig-zag course – but maintaining a straight course at reduced speed 20 km (12 miles) offshore. At 2:00 pm the liner was hit by a torpedo, fired without warning by the German submarine *U20*. The *Lusitania* sank in 18 minutes. Of the 1,201 passengers drowned 128 were US citizens, among them public figures who included the millionaire Alfred Vanderbilt. The Germans contended that the *Lusitania* was an armed merchant cruiser (a legitimate target), and carried Canadian troops and munitions. She was not armed, carried no troops, and the only munitions were 5,000 cases of cartridges, and probably some explosive fuses.

The *Lusitania* in New York harbour

When she was launched in 1907, the Cunard liner was, at 31,550 tons, the largest ship in the world. She was also one of the most luxurious and a great favourite on the transatlantic passenger route. Her turbine engines gave a speed of 25 knots, easily fast enough to outrun a U-boat.

Burying the dead

Some of the victims of the sinking are buried in a mass grave outside Queenstown (Cobh).

Life saver

This relic of the *Lusitania*, a lifebelt fitted with canvas breeches in which to place the legs, is preserved at the Imperial War Museum, London.

Grim memento

Germany issued an official apology for the sinking, but the German press was exultant: "With joyful pride we contemplate this latest deed of our navy." When a commemorative medal was struck, the British seized on this as a propaganda weapon, reproducing it in large numbers as an illustration of the enemy's baseness.

Heroic survivors

Two exhausted crew members from the *Lusitania* pose for the local Irish press after spending hours trying to help passengers to safety.

The sinking of the *Lusitania* in May 1915 seemed to have been a planned operation, not the result of an unauthorized decision by a U-boat commander (as the Germans explained it), since veiled warnings had been published in New York advising Americans against sailing in the delineated war zone. Moreover, there had been no warning. The Hague Convention of 1907 required a warship before attacking a merchant vessel to give warning, then, if she were suspected of carrying contraband, to carry out an inspection, and finally to make provision for saving crew and passengers.

The outrage helped to swing US opinion further against Germany, and in the long run towards participation in the war. Two more American citizens died when the British liner *Arabic* was torpedoed in the Atlantic on August 19. In reply to a fresh wave of protests, the German ambassador in Washington gave a somewhat vague undertaking that unrestricted submarine warfare would henceforth be suspended.

American pilot of the Escadrille Lafayette

Long before the US entered the war American volunteers were serving in Europe – fighting in the Foreign Legion, driving ambulances, or flying with the Escadrille Lafayette, the American air squadron with its Indian chief emblem.

The debate between American interventionists and isolationists intensified during 1916. The interventionists, led by former president Theodore Roosevelt, were growing stronger, but in spite of anti-German feeling, many Americans remained strongly anti-war: Midwestern farmers, who had never even seen the sea, cared little for the problems of Europe. Irish Americans' anti-British feelings were strengthened by the Easter Rising of 1916, and people of German, Austrian and Hungarian origin were naturally sympathetic to the Central Powers. Above all there was a strong peace lobby. Andrew Carnegie funded his Foundation for International Peace with $10 million.

The president appearing before Congress

Wilson asked Congress for a declaration of war on Germany on April 2, 1917. Four days later he received an overwelming vote of support for the war: 373 to 50 in the House of Representatives and 82 to 6 in the Senate.

Wilson had to face an acute moral dilemma. He was convinced that war was not only evil in itself but unreliable in its results. He was equally certain that in this war the Allies were in the right, and the Germans, to whose society and traditions he was by nature hostile, were in the wrong. Hence, after all his efforts to secure peace had failed, he was able to justify the war as the one way to "make the world safe for democracy". More practically, a German victory would be a disaster. Not only was the USA's traditional isolation dependent on Britain's command of the seas, but if the Allies were defeated their vast debts would never be repaid (the Germans later insisted this was the US motive for war).

Wilson won the presidential election of 1916 on the slogan, "He kept us out of war". Four months later, on April 2, 1917, he appeared before Congress to seek a declaration of war, determined to uphold American values by "force, force to the uttermost, force without stint or limit".

AMERICAN INDUSTRY

~

LIKE OTHER COUNTRIES, the USA faced a daunting task in converting to a war economy. This was aggravated by the size of the country and by traditions unsympathetic to federal controls. In 1914 the USA was the world's largest manufacturing state, and the stimulus of war provided incentives for investment and employment. In 1914–16 Britain, France and Russia depended heavily on US manufactures, food and credit. While some industries suffered as a result of the war, others, such as steel, shipbuilding and chemicals (in the absence of German competition), flourished. Agriculture, after a long recession, enjoyed vast increases in demand and hence prices – wheat rose from 70 cents a bushel in 1913 to $2.20 in 1917. The federal government's attitude towards free competition went into reverse. It took over communications and railways, controlled production and distribution of food and fuel, regulated labour and prices and (from February 1918) foreign trade. The war stimulated industrial changes already underway, such as standardization and assembly-line production. It also brought social change, for example the movement of Southern black workers to Northern cities.

Liberty Destroyer "139"
Keel Laid May 15th.
Will Be Launched
JUNE 1st.
14 DAYS OLD TO-DAY
SHE'S SOME BABY

John D. Rockefeller
The war brought great, though uneven, prosperity to the country. In 1916 it was announced that Rockefeller, founder of Standard Oil, had become the world's first billionaire.

Shipbuilding fever
Before the war, shipbuilding was not a major industry in the USA, but shipyards and their workers joined in the war effort with patriotic enthusiasm and competitions were staged between shipyards. The Mare Island shipyard set itself a challenge – to build a destroyer in 17 days. The ship, the *Ward*, fired the first shot of the Pacific War on December 7, 1941.

Civic pride
New York's skyline was the wonder of the modern world, with new skyscapers, such as the City Municipal Building (1913), springing up each year.

American oil wealth
Between 1859, when oil production started, and 1920, the USA was responsible for over 60 per cent of the world's petroleum production. Many prolific new fields were opened during the First World War.

American confidence
This poster advertises a film of an air trip to Panama. The USA prided itself on its modernity in contrast to Europe.

M.B.DUDLEY
GEO. F. COSBY Present
PANAMA AND THE **CANAL**
FROM AN
AEROPLANE
...IN SIX PARTS...
THE FEATURE FILM SENSATION OF THE CENTURY

The call to fight for Uncle Sam
When the USA declared war on Germany there was an initial flood of volunteers, but it was soon realized that conscription would be necessary. On May 18, 1917 the Selective Service Act was passed, allowing for a "selective draft". Eventually 11 million men were registered for military service and 4 million were actually called up.

Election slogans notwithstanding, Wilson had intimated during the election that US intervention might in the end be unavoidable. Many Americans agreed that the Allies were fighting a just war. Theodore Roosevelt wrote that if the Allies should seek US assistance it would be because they could fight no longer, "not because they regard us as having set a spiritual example to them by sitting idle, uttering cheap platitudes, and picking up their trade, while they have poured out their blood like water in support of the ideals in which, with all their hearts and souls, they believe."

GERMAN PROVOCATION

The Germans knew that the resumption of unrestricted submarine warfare would bring the US into the war. A German attempt to strengthen its position in such an event rendered the cause of neutrality a further blow when the Zimmermann telegram came to light in January 1917. This was sent by Zimmermann, a German foreign office minister, to the German ambassadors in Washington and Mexico City. It outlined a scheme to persuade Mexico to enter the war against the USA in return for German subsidies and a promise of the return of its lost territories in the American Southwest. It was intercepted and decoded by British Naval Intelligence, but by the time it was published in the press, Berlin had already announced the resumption of unrestricted submarine warfare on January 31. Eight US ships were sunk in February and March.

Although the Germans' main fear was the potential of US industrial production, it took time

to convert to a war economy and the Americans depended heavily on the European Allies for munitions and equipment throughout the war – no US aircraft made it to Europe before the armistice. But the Allies' most pressing need was for more troops, especially when collapsing Russian

WOODROW WILSON

~

SON of a Presbyterian minister, Wilson (1856–1924) had a brilliant academic career as a professor of history and politics, becoming president of Princeton in 1902. After serving as governor of New Jersey from 1910, he won the 1912 presidential election against the divided Republicans with 42 per cent of the vote. He secured a programme of progressive legislation, while pursuing mediation abroad. Instinctively opposed to war, he finally accepted US participation so as to promote American democratic and liberal values. To his dismay, the Senate refused to ratify the Versailles treaty. In October 1919 he suffered a disabling stroke.

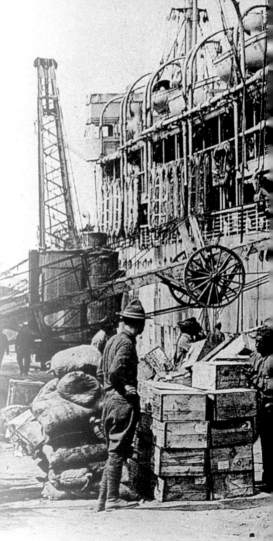

resistance allowed the Germans to reinforce the Western Front with troops from the East. Despite efforts to achieve "preparedness" for war during 1916, the USA was no better prepared in 1917 than Britain in 1914: the regular army numbered only 145,000. Once it had been decided to raise a large, independent army, conscription was introduced and 32 training camps set up. Initially, equipment was scarce and training rudimentary: six months' drill and rifle practice. However, it was obvious that the army would not be ready until 1918 (only 176,665 soldiers reached France by the end of the year). The US Navy was in slightly better shape, with six destroyers despatched immediately to Queenstown (Cobh) and 12 more operational within weeks, helping to patrol the waters around Britain.

The USA never became one of the "Allies", remaining an "Associated Power", and its military leaders, including General Pershing, the stiff-necked commander, were determined to keep the AEF (American Expeditionary Forces) under US command, so that "they could never be anything but an instrument of US policy".

A handful of US troops – the first ever to appear in Europe on active service – arrived in England on June 7, 1917 on their way to set up Pershing's headquarters in France. Landing on the French coast at dawn at a supposedly secret destination, they were greeted by cheering crowds.

Over there
US troops disembark in France in 1917. In some respects the Americans were well equipped – in motor transport, for example – but the tanks, guns and aeroplanes with which they fought were usually French.

DISILLUSION, MUTINY, AND REVOLUTION

1917

~

ALLIED HOPES THAT VICTORY MIGHT BE WON

IN 1917 COLLAPSED WITH THE FAILURE OF A MAJOR

FRENCH SPRING OFFENSIVE ON THE AISNE. MUTINY

IN A DEMORALIZED FRENCH ARMY SOON FOLLOWED.

THE BRITISH THEN LAUNCHED A CAMPAIGN IN

FLANDERS WHICH MANY VIEWED AS SO FUTILE THAT IT

CONTRIBUTED TO GROWING DISENCHANTMENT

WITH THE WAR IN BRITAIN AND FRANCE. SUCH

DISENCHANTMENT WAS EVEN GREATER IN RUSSIA

WHERE IT CULMINATED IN THE "OCTOBER

REVOLUTION" AND RUSSIA'S EXIT FROM THE WAR.

~

Australians at Château Wood, near Ypres
In October 1917 the Australians were involved in what, even at the time, was considered to be the most futile part of the Third Battle of Ypres: the struggle in the mud to capture the ruined village of Passchendaele.

FALSE HOPES

IN 1916, DESPITE SUFFERING HUGE CASUALTIES FOR LITTLE GAIN, THE ALLIES

WERE CONVINCED AT THE END OF THE YEAR – AS THEY HAD BEEN AT THE END OF 1915 –

THAT VICTORY WAS WITHIN REACH. AT THE CHANTILLY CONFERENCE IN NOVEMBER,

THE FRENCH PROPOSED, AND THE BRITISH ACCEPTED, A PROGRAMME THAT WAS

ALMOST IDENTICAL TO THE ONE THEY HAD ADOPTED THE YEAR BEFORE.

THE BRITISH AND FRENCH high commands believed that the Allies were now in a stronger position than a year earlier, and that the enemy was weaker. It was true that, despite the losses on the Somme, the British had more troops on the Western Front at the end of 1916 than at the beginning of the year. Both France and Russia, however, had serious problems with regard to manpower.

The French had only sufficient troops for one more offensive. France at this time had about 2,900,000 men on the Western Front, a total of some 110 infantry and seven cavalry divisions. But heavy losses in three successive years, plus the low birth rate in the decades before 1914, meant that the country had more or less exhausted its manpower reserves. Moreover, after its ordeal at Verdun, the morale of the army was uncertain.

The situation in Russia was even worse. In theory, Russia had a reserve of about 27,000,000 men of military age. However, a large number of exemptions, which included, most crucially, the whole of the Muslim population, meant that in reality this total was actually some 15 to 16 million.

Russia had already suffered perhaps as many as 7 million casualties, and by the end of 1916 it had an army of about 6,500,000 men – a total of about 150 infantry and 40 cavalry divisions. Just how serious Russia's lack of manpower was can be gauged from the fact that in the summer of 1916, the tsarist regime tried to impose conscription upon the Muslim population. Predictably, the result was widespread disturbances, which ironically but inevitably, had to be suppressed by the army.

By the end of 1916 the Russian military leadership knew that available reserves could soon not cover regular losses of some 200,000 men per month. Although Russian forces were as well supplied with weapons as at any time since September 1914, the Russian army was at the end of its strength. This situation could not be redeemed by success on the Italian, Salonika, Mesopotamia and Sinai fronts – not that success seemed very likely in any of these other theatres.

In the event, the shortage of manpower would not determine what happened on the battlefield in 1917 as much as other matters, the first of which was a change of personnel in the British government and in the French high command.

A Change of Command

On December 7, 1916 the British prime minister, Asquith, was ousted by Lloyd George, who was less than impressed by chief of staff Robertson and commander-in-chief Haig, and the way in which operations had been conducted in 1916. At this time, however, Lloyd George saw himself in office rather than in power, and hesitated to move directly against Robertson and Haig or to attempt to direct policy. Strategic policy had, in any case, been more or less settled by the decision at the end of 1915 to abandon the Gallipoli venture and by the defeats in the Balkans. The military high command, rather than the civil authorities, was now considered to be very much in charge of strategic policy.

In France, on December 12, Joffre was dismissed as commander of the French army. Throughout 1916 both the government and the National Assembly had become increasingly disenchanted with him, initially because of the situation at Verdun, and subsequently because of the failure on the Somme. But Joffre was not replaced by Foch or Pétain, as might have been expected, but by Nivelle, the French commander in the final successful stage of the Verdun campaign. Nivelle was certain that the tactics he had employed at Verdun would guarantee success over a wider front – namely, a massive bombardment of the German defensive positions, followed by a creeping barrage and a ferocious infantry attack. He envisaged a series of short assaults that could be halted if success was not immediate – not that he expected anything but total victory for his proposed offensive on the Aisne. This was to be carried out by the French, while supporting operations were conducted by the British and French between Arras and the Oise.

> *"The headlong pace of the advance was nowhere long maintained…The attack gained at most points, then slowed down, unable to follow the barrage which, progressing at the rate of a hundred yards in three minutes, was in many cases soon out of sight."*

GENERAL E. L. SPEARS, A BRITISH LIAISON OFFICER, DESCRIBING THE FRENCH ADVANCE ON THE FIRST DAY OF THE APRIL OFFENSIVE ON THE AISNE

French artillery practice
The offensive planned by Nivelle for the spring of 1917 relied on the effective deployment of artillery to achieve immediate success in breaking through the German lines.

ENDORSEMENT OF NIVELLE'S PROPOSALS

Nivelle's proposals were immediately endorsed by the British and French governments. Not only did they seem to offer the prospect of a victory without huge attritional cost, at a time when civilian morale was perceptibly beginning to falter, but they were also presented by a very unusual commander – suave, bilingual and highly articulate. The contrast with Haig, Joffre and Pétain could not have been more marked, and was certainly enough to ensure the support of Lloyd George. The British prime minister arranged for a conference to be held at Calais at the end of February 1917, ostensibly in order to resolve problems of transportation and lines of supply affecting the British and French armies, but in fact organized to place the British armies in France under Nivelle's direct command. The plan miscarried, and Lloyd George was forced to backtrack in the face of furious opposition from Robertson and Haig. In one respect, however, he and Nivelle were successful: the Nivelle proposal for the main effort on the Aisne and a secondary operation around Arras received approval, and the British armies were placed under the general direction of Nivelle. The problem was that this was to be about the sum of Nivelle's success.

GERMAN PREPARATIONS

The events of 1917 were also shaped by Germany's plans. At the strategic level, the new German military leaders – Ludendorff and Hindenburg – spent the autumn of 1916 considering Germany's military options. The most obvious point to take into account was that, on the Somme, the battle was now being fought on ground that marginally favoured the British and French; the Germans' marked tactical advantage in July 1916 had very largely disappeared. Thus, in the first weeks of 1917 the Germans began to make arrangements for the withdrawal of forces on the Western Front in March to what became known as the Hindenburg Line. In fact, the first defensive positions had been prepared as early as September 1916 but, by February 1917, a comprehensive defensive line from Neuville Vitasse, near Arras, to Cerny, east of Soissons,

had been prepared in depth. The forward defensive positions were up to 2,300 m (2,500 yds) deep, while the triple defensive lines extended over 7,300 m (8,000 yds). On the Aisne and Chemin des Dames, German arrangements were not on the scale of those of the Hindenburg Line. They were, however, sufficiently strong to ensure that Nivelle's formula was doomed to failure. The German positions could not be broken with a single blow.

Russian revolutionaries in March

Among the actions of mutinous troops in Petrograd was the seizure of a Rolls Royce used by the imperial family. The mutiny helped to persuade the tsar to abdicate.

"Do not trust the promises of the Bolsheviks! Their promise of an immediate peace is a lie! Their promise to provide bread is a fraud! Their promise to distribute the land is a fairy tale for children!"

RUSSIAN PRIME MINISTER KERENSKY IN A DECLARATION
MADE FOLLOWING THE LOSS OF RIGA IN SEPTEMBER, 1917

As spring arrived, doubts about Nivelle and his proposed offensive became widespread throughout the French military hierarchy, and there were fears that it would end disastrously. By this time, however, it was too late to halt proceedings that, in any case, Nivelle had promised he would end if the predicted victory did not happen straight away. He assured all doubters that his tactics would not just gain territory but would win the war – so raising expectations to a level where they could not be fulfilled. The result was to be a catastrophe that would further decrease what was left of the morale of the French troops and provoke the first serious mutiny of the war.

EVENTS AFTER NIVELLE'S FAILURE

Following the failure of the French offensive on the Aisne, the British took control of strategic policy on the Western Front. Haig was still devoted to the idea of an offensive that would win control of the Belgian coast, and to this end he launched a series of attacks in Flanders between June and November that would culminate in one of the most futile battles of the war: Passchendaele. Fought in particularly appalling conditions, and resulting in over 250,000 Allied casualties, it was regarded by Haig's contemporaries as the most notable example of his pointless sacrifice of men's lives.

The kaiser in Riga after victory over Russia
The capture of Riga by the Germans in September 1917 signalled the end of the war on the Eastern Front and promised the arrival of more German troops in the West.

As soldiers were dying in the mud around Passchendaele, the war on the Eastern Front was coming to an end. A revolution in March had forced the tsar to abdicate and had established a Provisional Government that was determined to maintain Russia's participation in the war despite mounting opposition. Following further Russian defeats, the Bolsheviks seized power on November 7 with a promise to take Russia out of the war.

Shortly after the Germans withdrew to their new Hindenburg Line defences, Nivelle launched a disastrous offensive that was to help provoke mutiny in the French army. Later in the year the British became embroiled in another terrible battle of attrition around Ypres. The only bright points for the Allies were the innovative tactics seen at Vimy Ridge, Messines and in the tank attack at Cambrai, which were not exploited.

MARCH 15
Germans begin withdrawal to Hindenburg Line

MARCH 20
Preliminary bombardment for Arras offensive begins

APRIL 9
British open offensive at Arras; Canadians storm Vimy Ridge

APRIL 14
Vimy Ridge offensive ends after failure to capitalize on initial gains

APRIL 15
Arras offensive comes to temporary halt

APRIL 16
French Nivelle Offensive starts in Aisne sector

APRIL 17
In Aisne sector first signs of mutiny in French army

APRIL 18
French take Chemin des Dames

APRIL 20
Nivelle admits that his offensive has failed

APRIL 23
British resume Arras offensive

MAY 9
Nivelle Offensive ends

MAY 15
Pétain replaces Nivelle as French commander-in-chief

MAY 16
Arras offensive ends

MAY 27
French troops refuse to obey orders to advance to Front as mutiny grows

JUNE 1
Further disorder in French army as infantry regiment takes over Missy-aux-Bois

JUNE 7
British capture Messines Ridge following detonation of mines in tunnels beneath German lines

JULY 31
Third Battle of Ypres begins

AUGUST 10
Renewed attack on Ypres salient, directed at Gheluvelt plateau

AUGUST 16
British again attempt to make headway on Gheluvelt plateau

SEPTEMBER 20
British Second Army launches attack astride Menin Road

SEPTEMBER 26
British launch assault around Polygon Wood

OCTOBER 4
British attack at Broodseinde

OCTOBER 9
British assault on Poelcappelle hampered by mud

OCTOBER 12
Australian and New Zealand troops make limited advance towards Passchendaele

OCTOBER 26
Canadian troops advance on Passchendaele

NOVEMBER 6
Allies capture Passchendaele

NOVEMBER 20
Battle of Cambrai begins; massed tank attack enables British to make significant gains

NOVEMBER 21
British capture Flesquières but suffer heavy losses elsewhere

NOVEMBER 22
Fontaine lost to German counterattack

NOVEMBER 27
Germans defeat last British attack on Fontaine

NOVEMBER 30
German counterattack eliminates a large part of Allied gains

DECEMBER 4
Battle of Cambrai ends

KEY
- Campaigns in Artois
- Nivelle Offensive April 16–May 9
- Campaigns in Flanders June 7–November 6
- Other events

Further Attrition on the Western Front

The rubble of Caulaincourt Château
During their withdrawal to the Hindenburg Line, the Germans practised a "scorched earth" policy and destroyed a number of impressive buildings. Here British soldiers are confronted by the evidence of this policy.

THE COLDEST WINTER of the century ended any possibility of an early offensive. As the British completed their preparations to launch a spring offensive at Arras, the Germans – between March 15 and April 5 – withdrew to the Hindenburg Line. Hindenburg and Ludendorff had decided on this withdrawal as a means of shortening the line by 40 km (25 miles), so reducing the number of troops needed to defend it. During the withdrawal, the Germans systematically destroyed all the roads, railways, bridges and buildings in their way, thus presenting the Allies with a devastated wasteland to cross before coming up against a purpose-built defensive position of intimidating strength.

THE BATTLE OF ARRAS

The main British effort at Arras was to be made by 20 divisions of the Third Army under Allenby. It was to be supported to the north by nine divisions, including the Canadian Corps, of the First Army, and to the south by seven divisions, including the I ANZAC Corps, of the Fifth Army.

BRITISH AND CANADIAN SUCCESSES

After a five-day preliminary bombardment, the offensive opened, in sleet and snow, on Easter Monday, April 9. At first both the British and Canadians were successful. On its right flank the Third Army captured Neuville Vitasse, while in the centre it pushed forward over a distance of between 3 and 5 km (2 and 3 miles) and captured a German gun park. On its left flank, the Allies broke through the German defences to secure Fampoux, their final-phase objective, in an advance of 5.5 km (3.5 miles), the greatest single advance registered in one day on the Western Front since November 1914.

The Canadians advanced rapidly towards Vimy Ridge. During the morning of April 9 the 1st and

THE CANADIANS

At the outbreak of war the Canadian government pledged formations for the British imperial cause. Between August 1914 and January 1917 five Canadian divisions were raised, though the last was used only for British home defence. Throughout 1916 numbers stayed at around 300,000, and Canada experienced increasing difficulty in maintaining its formations. Conscription came into force on October 13, 1917, but with very mixed results: there was widespread rioting in Quebec in March 1918 as a result of the arrest of a French Canadian who had refused to be conscripted. Ultimately some 628,000 Canadians enlisted, mostly voluntarily, of whom 365,000 – including 46,000 conscripts – served overseas. The total number of casualties was around 210,000.

The Canadian effort on the Western Front, where the Canadian 1st Division arrived in February 1915, is always associated with the offensive on Vimy Ridge in April 1917 and more generally with the Third Battle of Ypres (Passchendaele). At Vimy Ridge, in an episode etched into the Canadian national psyche, all four divisions of the Canadian Corps, working together for the first time, stormed a position thought impregnable and took it virtually in a morning. Canadian troops were at Ypres in April 1915 and Amiens in August 1918, but perhaps their greatest achievement was during the Hundred Days – between late August and October 1918 – when they breached the defences of the German Hindenburg Line. Their actions compounded a formidable reputation for professionalism, steadfastness and reliability; theirs was a full contribution to Allied victory.

INFANTRY CAP

ROSS BAYONET

PENKNIFE

Uniform and equipment
The Canadian "pattern service dress" was based on the British khaki uniform of 1902. The standard Canadian rifle, the Ross Mark III, was heavier than the British Lee Enfield. It was fitted with an unusual short, wide bayonet.

Canadians firing a captured German 105-mm howitzer
Men of the Canadian Field Artillery turn a German gun on its former owners. When the Canadian Corps stormed Vimy Ridge in April 1917, they captured some 4,000 prisoners and large amounts of equipment, including over 50 artillery pieces.

2nd Divisions secured Thélus and Farbus, some 3,660 m (4,000 yds) from their start line and the main objective. The 3rd Division, after taking La Folie Farm, was checked. On its left, however, the 4th Division secured Hill 145, the highest point on Vimy Ridge, in the late afternoon.

The taking of Vimy Ridge, coming after the many failures to capture it in previous years, was a major accomplishment. It was one of the greatest single day's achievements in the history of the Western Front and rightly became an important part of the Canadian military legend. The Canadians, however, were to suffer over 11,000 casualties in less than one week during their attempt to build on their success of the first day.

PROGRESS AFTER THE FIRST DAY
All the Allied forces lost momentum after the first day. Last-minute plans had been made for the Fifth Army's operations to include a massed armour attack. The tanks, however, were not ready for offensive operations on April 10, and when the next day just four crossed the start line, they did so late and behind the infantry they were supposed to lead and protect. The offensive was a complete failure, and at Bullecourt the Australians lost more troops than on any other day of the war.

Canadian artillery supply column
A Canadian artillery unit uses mules to transport ammunition along a relatively good road. During the Third Battle of Ypres, both supplies and mules were often swallowed up by bottomless mud.

On April 11 the Third Army secured Monchy Le Preux, but its attempts to move its artillery across the muddy battlefield, and send reserves and cavalry through the breaches that had been made in the German defensive line on April 9, foundered. There were the same basic problems that had plagued all previous offensives: those of command, movement and co-ordination.

Adding to the problems that now beset the British offensive was the recovery of the German defence. On April 9 the Germans had too many formations in forward defensive positions and held reserve formations too far from the battle zone to be able to counterattack quickly. By April 11, however,

the Germans had brought up reinforcements and reconstituted their defence. The British – after the capture of 112 guns and over 7,000 prisoners in two days at what was regarded as the comparatively modest cost of around 8,220 casualties – were beginning to feel more confident. This confidence, however, soon disappeared when their attempt to move forward on April 11 resulted in major losses.

As snow blizzards intensified and it became clear that the British troops were suffering from the intense cold as well as fatigue, the offensive was maintained only to distract attention from preparations for the French offensive effort in Champagne. It was halted on April 15.

THE NIVELLE OFFENSIVE

On April 16, after a number of delays because of bad weather, Nivelle launched his long-planned offensive along a 40-km (25-mile) front on the Aisne River after a two-week preliminary bombardment. For the main attack, east of Soissons, Nivelle had mustered two armies – the Fifth and Sixth – with some 3,810 guns, plus 128 tanks which were to be used by the French for the first time. He also had a third army in reserve and a fourth earmarked for a support and deception role east of Reims.

Nivelle's plan was for 20 French divisions to carry out a rapid assault behind a creeping barrage and capture the heights above the Aisne before breaking through the German lines on the Chemin des Dames road. Despite the failure of the French artillery to cut the German wire or to carry out an effective creeping barrage, the French made some impressive initial gains. On April 16 the Fifth Army penetrated up to 5 km (3 miles) and took Juvincourt, and on April 17 the Sixth Army secured the area around Fort Condé. From the start, however, the French effort was plagued by problems and it soon began to go disastrously wrong.

On the first two days, French artillery support was minimal, and the French tanks – which were better suited to break-out rather than breakthrough battles across open ground – were shot to pieces

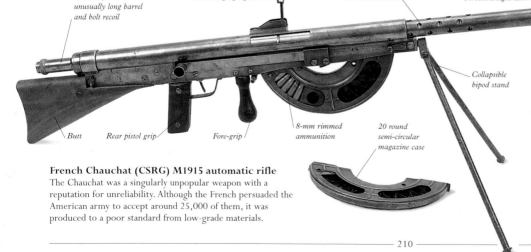

Receiver for unusually long barrel and bolt recoil

Rear ranging sight

Air-cooled barrel

Foreward sight

Collapsible bipod stand

Butt

Rear pistol grip

Fore-grip

8-mm rimmed ammunition

20 round semi-circular magazine case

French Chauchat (CSRG) M1915 automatic rifle
The Chauchat was a singularly unpopular weapon with a reputation for unreliability. Although the French persuaded the American army to accept around 25,000 of them, it was produced to a poor standard from low-grade materials.

French infantry advances along Aisne front
Nivelle's Chemin des Dames offensive, launched amid such high hopes but against an enemy forewarned of French intentions, would push the French army beyond breaking point and ruin Nivelle's reputation and career.

THE END OF THE OFFENSIVE

A shortage of ammunition imposed a halt on French operations on April 20, the day after the French president, Poincaré, had tried to halt the offensive. Nivelle's ambitions were now reduced to securing the Chemin des Dames, which had been reached on the third day. On April 23 Poincaré banned all further offensive operations, in effect spelling the end of both Nivelle as commander of the French armies on the Western Front and of his offensive. What he had promised – a major breakthrough in 24 hours – had not materialized. Instead of achieving an overall advance of 9 km (6 miles), they had made a general advance of just 500 m (600 yds). In the first ten days the number of casualties had reached almost six figures, instead of Nivelle's estimate of 15,000, and French medical support had all but collapsed.

By the time the last attacks in this offensive ended on May 9, the French had suffered 187,000 casualties. The Germans, despite their success in withstanding the offensive, had fared little better, suffering 167,000 casualties. The contrast between the promises of success and the offensive's failure amid heavy casualties proved particularly corrosive to the morale of the French army.

before they could have any impact. Furthermore, the French air force was unable to contest German superiority in the air, with obvious repercussions in such matters as artillery spotting. The Germans, who had advance notice of what the French were intending after acquiring detailed operational plans in routine raids, had strengthened their defences so that they were four lines deep in places. The artillery was sited beyond the range of French fire, which meant that it was able to shred the French infantry after it had secured the first defensive line during the first two days of the offensive.

TYPES OF BARRAGE

~

IN THE FIRST MONTHS OF THE WAR, artillery bombardments generally began with concentrated fire upon enemy defensive positions, followed by fire directed at other targets in the rear once the infantry assault began. In effect, this simplistic arrangement meant that infantry attacks were unsupported by direct fire. The development of trench systems spelt the need for heavier bombardments in order to ensure the destruction of defensive positions, and this meant larger guns and howitzers, and mortars with heavier shells. The loss of surprise was accepted as the price to be paid for what was hoped would be the neutralization of the enemy defensive positions. The hurricane barrage – a short, intense bombardment – was an anomaly in that it was used by the British in 1915 simply because they lacked the number of guns and shells for a protracted bombardment. In March 1918 the Germans used a hurricane barrage that was notable for its employment of gas. If an area could be saturated for more than 30 minutes, then defending troops would have to change their respirator filters, with obvious results.

The creeping barrage was different, involving as it did fire moving ahead of the infantry at a set rate, thus ensuring the suppression of the defence until the attacking infantry was all but upon the enemy positions. Employed in October 1916 to real effect during the Battle of Verdun, it was refined with a rate of advance set at 45 m (50 yds) a minute. Its success depended upon careful timing on the part of both guns and infantry, and upon the ability of the latter to move across No Man's Land at a rate that ensured it stayed close behind, and under the protection of, the curtain of fire. The fundamental weakness of the arrangement was that inadequate means of communication meant that the infantry were unable to summon fire on new positions or call a halt to bombardments. Inevitably, there were many casualties from friendly fire. It has been estimated that the French army's dead from its own artillery reached six figures over the course of the war.

French 270-mm howitzer
Once the war became a static affair, both sides sought to breach their opponents' defences with ever larger guns – larger even than the old French 270-mm howitzer. In fact, it was better co-ordination between infantry and artillery that would prove to be the key to success.

MUTINY IN THE FRENCH ARMY

The French infantry had been promised certain victory, not another pointless attritional battle. Coming after Verdun, failure on the Aisne temporarily broke the will of the French to launch another offensive. The number of desertions had increased significantly since the beginning of 1917, and in April – as the failure of the Nivelle Offensive caused disillusionment and anger within the army – there were the first signs of mutiny.

Faced with the need to restore order, the French authorities turned to Pétain, appointing him as chief of staff on April 29, and then as Nivelle's replacement in the position of commander-in-chief on May 15. Pétain had a reputation within the army for being more economical with men's lives than other generals, and having empathy with his troops, but ironically, the worst of the troubles that were to afflict the French army took place after this date. Up to 30,000 soldiers had abandoned the front along the Chemin des Dames when, on May 27, troops in four towns refused to obey officers' orders to advance to the front and seized some buildings. Two days later, several hundred troops already at the front refused to move into front-line trenches. On June 1 a French infantry regiment took over the town of Missy-aux-Bois, and for a week there was chaos as an increasing number of French soldiers refused to return to the trenches. Generally, however, such incidents were rare.

Signs of unrest were normally short-lived and focused upon two matters – the seemingly pointless offensives and the often appalling conditions in which the soldiers were expected to live, whether in or out of the line. Contrary to the impression conveyed by the word "mutiny", only on one occasion was there a refusal to take part in combat. In fact, 44 divisions were wholly unaffected, and of the 68 that were affected, 17 had just single incidents. Amongst the remainder, there was a total

French troops at Fleury

French infantry move up to the line in the Verdun sector. During the mutiny most troops were prepared to defend the line against German attack, but they refused to take part in any further futile offensives.

In some regiments in the French Army, the poor infantry officers said, "Well, you promised us that once we'd attacked we'd be relieved, and yet we stay here in the lines. It is always us that are killed"...And we, as cavalrymen, were on the front line, so we knew when there was bad feeling among the soldiers. This was not in all the regiments, but in those that had attacked too often, or when there were heavy casualties, they were somewhat discouraged. They refused to obey their officers. I saw poor officers walking here and there sadly and men not saluting them.

PRIVATE ROBERT POUSTIS, FRENCH CAVALRYMAN,
ON THE MUTINY AMONG THE INFANTRY

Spring offensives

Following the withdrawal of the Germans to the Hindenburg Line, the British Arras offensive took place along a 20-km (13-mile) front either side of the city where the German positions had not changed. After some initial success, the offensive achieved little. The French Nivelle Offensive, which began a week later, was a disastrous failure within a few days.

THE WESTERN FRONT
Jan–May, 1917

- Western Front Jan 1917
- German withdrawal to Hindenburg Line Mar 15–Apr 5
- Hindenburg Line Apr 5
- British Arras offensive
- French Nivelle Offensive
- Major railway

Apr 9
Canadians of the 1st Army succeed in taking Vimy Ridge

Apr 9
British subsidiary attack commences in Arras area. Offensive temporarily halted Apr 15

Apr 12
Attack by Australians at Bullecourt

Apr 16
French attack in Chemin des Dames area (Nivelle Offensive). Main offensive ends Apr 20 after heavy French losses and limited gains

1ST ARMY
3RD ARMY
5TH ARMY
6TH ARMY
1ST ARMY
2ND ARMY
7TH ARMY
3RD ARMY
6TH ARMY
5TH ARMY

Ostend, Bruges, Nieuport, Dunkerque, Calais, FLANDERS, Yser, Ypres, Saint-Omer, Boulogne-sur-Mer, Hazebrouck, Lille, Scheldt, Lys, Neuve Chapelle, Festubert, BELGIUM, Mons, Vimy, Arras, Bullecourt, Cambrai, Le Cateau, Sambre, Bapaume, Somme, Amiens, Chaulnes, St Quentin, Vervins, Montdidier, Noyon, Aillette, Laon, Compiègne, Craonne, Soissons, Chantilly, Reims, Vesle, Meaux, Epernay, Marne, PARIS

0 km 10 20 30 40 50
0 miles 10 20 30 40 50

Don't strike
A poster calls on French workers not to
strike. There was much industrial unrest
in France during the mutiny, and Pétain
saw it as a malaise that affected the army.

of 250 incidents in 152 regiments, mostly infantry.
Not one officer was murdered and there was only a
single incident of a general being manhandled. In
the vast majority of cases, French units refused to
involve themselves in costly, hopeless offensives but
declared a willingness to man the line.

Poor living conditions
The living conditions of the common
French soldier were improved as part
of Pétain's campaign to rebuild the
army's morale. An end to costly
offensives and greater emphasis on
defence in depth were also promised.

PÉTAIN'S RESPONSE

Pétain responded by ordering mass arrests. It appears
that 3,335 soldiers were court-martialled and 449
were condemned to death. Of these, 27 were actually
shot; the remainder were imprisoned. A total of
about 24,000 soldiers were punished at unit level.
Unrest rumbled on until October, but the crisis had
passed by mid-June after it became clear that Pétain
also intended not just to punish but to change tactics
and improve conditions. From now on there would
be limited attacks, in which the infantry operated in
small groups rather than *en masse*, and there would be
greater emphasis on defence in depth, with the front-
line trenches only thinly held and troops in the front
line being relieved by reserves on a more regular
basis. Troops would have seven days' leave every four
months, and more trains would be run to take them
on leave. Rest areas would be improved through the
provision of more beds, and food would be much
improved through the regular delivery of fresh
vegetables and the establishment of regimental
co-operatives offering extra, cheap provisions. There
would not, however, be any increase in pay.

Pétain personally visited 90 divisions to explain
these improvements. He also brought a temporary
halt to all offensives. He would not feel ready to
launch another until August, when an attack at
Verdun would drive the Germans back to the
positions they had occupied before their advance in
February 1916. Thus in June the immediate burden
of the Allied cause fell upon Britain.

MUTINY AND DESERTION

~

FOR MOST OF THE WAR, indiscipline was not a serious problem in any of the armies on the Western
Front. On the whole, the morale of the British, French and German armies did not crack, because
the soldiers were committed to their governments' war aims and respected their officers. Major though
they were, the French mutinies lasted for little more than two months, and German troops only rose up
against their commanders during the last stages of the conflict. Between 1914 and 1918 some 3,080
British soldiers were sentenced to death by court martial, mainly for desertion. Instead of being shot,
most were shipped off to British colonies. Far from being "cowards", a high proportion of the
307 men who were not reprieved were victims of "shell shock".

The incidence of desertion is hard to assess, partly because no army could
admit to dwindling numbers. It is clear that away from the Western Front it
became a major problem in the later years of the war. In 1916, for example,
Czechs and Ruthenes deserted *en masse* in the Austro-Hungarian armies resisting
the Russian Brusilov Offensive, and in the course of 1917 tens of thousands of
Russians deserted. By December 1917 at least 300,000 of Turkey's
poorly treated soldiers had also deserted. These deserters
roamed the countryside, living off the
land and turning into robber bands.

Court martial in session
Although military justice could be draconian, only
27 French soldiers were executed after the mutiny of 1917.
Others were imprisoned or sentenced to forced labour.

TUNNEL WARFARE

~

DIGGING TUNNELS TOWARDS AND UNDER the enemy's trenches (sapping), and then detonating one or more mines to create a breach in the enemy's defences, became an increasingly important tactic in trench warfare from the end of 1914. The Germans were the first to try it when they tunnelled towards a small section of the Western Front in Belgium in December and used ten small mines – each weighing between 23 and 137 kg (50 and 300 lbs) – to blow up an entire Indian brigade. It was only then that both the French and the BEF began to consider establishing their own effective tunnelling forces. Without them their men in the trenches would live in fear of being blown to pieces by an unseen foe – and no similar threat could be turned on the Germans.

In 1914 the French army had *sapeurs-mineurs* with some training but only archaic equipment, while the BEF had no mining specialists at all. At the end of the year the British created brigade mining sections, made up of men with no experience, tools or listening equipment, to work out where the German tunnels were. From February 1915 these men were joined by special tunnelling companies made up largely of coal miners.

Whatever the men's experience of working underground, it could not prepare them for the terror of being in a tunnelling party under No Man's Land. Each side would be listening out for the other, ready to blow a "camouflet" – a small charge that could entomb the enemy's miners without damaging one's own tunnel. Sometimes the two sides dug into each other's tunnels, resulting in bitter hand-to-hand fighting in which shovels and picks were employed as weapons. Other hazards included gas that could asphyxiate or ignite, shortage of oxygen, and having to work up to 12 hours at a time in 30 cm (1 ft) or more of water in bitterly cold conditions.

Throughout 1915 the Germans dominated the underground war. However, in 1916 the British and French tunnellers began to pose a serious threat, and by early 1917 they had gained the ascendancy. Great improvements had been made in their equipment: they now had sophisticated listening devices, such as the geophone; silent air and water pumps; and ammonal explosive charges in place of the more volatile gunpowder and guncotton.

FRENCH SAPPER'S ELECTRIC TORCH

German explosive
Westfalit was the standard explosive in German mines. Sixty tons were detonated in one mine at Vauquois in the Argonne on May 14, 1916.

British breathing apparatus
It was often essential for miners to use special apparatus to help them breathe in an environment where foul air or potentially fatal fumes could build up rapidly. The bags on this equipment contained compressed oxygen, which was released through the air tubes. Straps held the mouthpiece in place.

Skull cap

tubes

Gas tank

Regulator

Underground activity
It took a year for miners to dig the network of tunnels under Messines Ridge in what was the most successful, and spectacular, use of mines in the war. The explosion on June 7, 1917 was heard in London, 210 km (130 miles) away. 10,000 German soldiers disappeared off the face of the earth.

British detonator
The detonator sent a small electric charge to a primary explosive which discharged the high-explosive mine. The high explosives favoured by the British were amotal (TNT and ammonium nitrate) and ammonal (TNT, ammonium nitrate and powdered aluminium).

Germans detonating mines
The detonation of mines had to be synchronized with some precision. Blow the mine too early and the enemy could reoccupy the ground, too late and you risked friendly troops being caught in the blast.

> "...the noise of the guns deadened all sound from the mine, except that we could hear, even above this crescendo, the screams of the imprisoned Germans in the crater."

BRITISH OFFICER ANTHONY EDEN ON THE EFFECTS
OF A MINE EXPLOSION ON THE MESSINES RIDGE

RESUMPTION OF THE ARRAS OFFENSIVE

On April 23, to support French operations on the Chemin des Dames, the British resumed their offensive at Arras, on the Scarpe River. By the last week of April it was clear that the French offensive had failed, that Nivelle's days were numbered, and that the offensive capacity of the French armies had been impaired. Yet Haig was determined that the offensive should continue and ignored protests from Allenby about heavy casualties for very little gain.

The offensive was only finally called off in late May, the British and French high commands agreeing on a series of limited offensives over the following months. On June 2, however, Haig learned that the unrest within the French army made the offensive scheduled for the 10th at Malmaison impossible.

The French army's difficulties in spring 1917 left the British to determine strategic policy for the remainder of the year. Haig's initial reaction was to assume the defensive, but Russia's disarray, the danger of the Central Powers concentrating their attention on Italy, and the risk that a German attack on the Western Front might expose French weakness, finally made him decide on offensive action. He had long sought an offensive in Flanders, and in spring 1917 he received support for this from an Admiralty convinced that the war at sea would be lost if the U-boats were not denied the use of Belgian ports. Consequently, as a first step to gaining control of the Belgian coast, Haig gave the go-ahead for a long-planned attack designed to clear the Messines Ridge, at the southern end of the Ypres salient.

MESSINES RIDGE OFFENSIVE

The 76-m (250-ft) high Messines Ridge, with its German trenches and fortifications, dominated British positions to the south of Ypres. In the early hours of June 7 there were a number of enormous explosions – so loud they could be heard in southeast England – when 19 of the 21 mines placed in tunnels 15 to 30 m (50 to 100 ft) below the German lines on the ridge were detonated. The tunnels, one of which was 610 m (2,000 ft) long, had been dug by British, Canadian and Australian tunnellers over a 12-month period.

Arras town hall in ruins, May 1917
Although initial progress in the British offensive at Arras was promising, the battle degenerated into yet another one of attrition. The British lost more than 150,000 men, but the Germans also suffered some 100,000 casualties.

Australians at work below Messines Ridge
Members of the 1st Australian Tunnelling Company were among the tunnellers who excavated under the ridge and packed 21 chambers with 600 tons of explosive. Many Australian tunnellers had acquired their expertise while working in gold-mines.

Irish troops at Messines
Irish troops survey the unrecognizable ruins of the village of Wytschaete. The village was captured by men of the 16th Irish Division and the 36th Ulster Division on the first day of the Battle of Messines.

The effect was devastating. About 10,000 German soldiers were killed or buried alive. A British artillery barrage – involving over 2,250 guns – added to the terror. Many of the Germans were too stunned by the explosions to resist the British Second Army. Around 7,500 were taken prisoner.

By 7:00 am Messines itself had been captured; by 3:00 pm the whole ridge had been taken and Allied troops were moving down the eastern slopes. They quickly dug in and on the following day withstood all attempts by the Germans to counterattack. By June 11 the Germans had begun an orderly withdrawal and were establishing a new front line further east, convinced that there would be follow-up attacks and that they might have to give up ground north of the Lys. Haig, however, did not have the necessary forces in place to build on the success at Messines. Instead, he made preparations for a major offensive at Ypres later in the summer.

THE THIRD BATTLE OF YPRES

The British, with support from the French, began their major assault on the Ypres salient on July 31. In the weeks after the capture of Messines Ridge, the German Fourth Army had concentrated on strengthening its positions, and it now had three defensive lines, each some 1,800 m (2,000 yds) deep. It planned to hold the first line lightly, with reserve formations in the third. The artillery was positioned behind Gheluvelt where, on a reverse slope, it could enjoy considerable immunity from British gunfire.

As early as the 27th the British had succeeded in occupying a number of German forward positions that had been evacuated during preliminary bombardments. The main attack on the 31st, however, met with mixed success. The two flanking armies, the French First Army in the north and the British Second Army in the south, registered major gains. In fact, as on the Somme in 1916, the French achieved considerably more success than the attacks they were supposed to support – the attacks of the Fifth Army. The Fifth Army generally secured the first German line and in some places broke through it, but on the right it made very little progress. Furthermore, most of the 22 tanks committed to the attack became stuck in the heavily cratered ground. It was not until the British high command had considered the results of this first day's fighting that it began to realize the importance of the Gheluvelt position to the German defence. By this point, however, the rains that were to turn the battlefield into a swamp had begun.

After a three-day struggle the British secured control of the first German line, more than had been achieved by any other offensive on the salient, though far less than the progress envisaged by Haig. When, however, the main attack was resumed on August 10 – this time directed specifically against the Gheluvelt position – the German defensive measures proved to be extremely effective. Their losses were held to a minimum by the organization of a counter-barrage to isolate attacking units and the launching of counterattacks by local reserves.

A renewed British offensive on the 16th was no more successful than that of the 10th. On the 22nd a series of attacks yielded such disappointing results, with over 3,000 men lost for the gain of just 800 m (880 yds) on the Menin Road, that Haig had to accept that the offensive was not going to break the front. Instead, all that could be aimed for was the gradual wearing down of German defences.

THE SECOND PHASE

Other First World War battles lasted longer and claimed more casualties than the Third Battle of Ypres. But it was this battle, and in particular, the phase that focused on capturing the small village of Passchendaele, that gained particular notoriety in Britain. Not only was the battle fought in appalling conditions, but even by the standards of the First World War, it was particularly futile. No amount of

JOHN MONASH
~

GENERALLY REGARDED as one of the most brilliant generals on the Western Front, the Australian Monash (1865–1931) was only commissioned to join the Australian Imperial Force (AIF) after the outbreak of the war – previously he had served in the reserves. He insisted on doing everything possible to protect the lives of his men and developed new tactics such as the joint advance of tanks and infantry in order to achieve this.

Having commanded an infantry brigade sent to Egypt in 1915 as part of the ANZAC (Australian-New Zealand Army Corps) force, Monash later served at Gallipoli. Towards the end of 1916, he was transferred to France to lead the Third Division, which went on to serve with distinction at Messines and Passchendaele. Taking over from William Birdwood, in May 1918, as commander of the Australian army on the Western Front, Monash demonstrated remarkable leadership. This was apparent in his counterattacks during the German push of 1918, notably at the battle of Hamel in July and in the Australian advance of August 8, 1918, described as the "black day of the German army". He also led Australian forces in the capture of Mont St Quentin in September and the autumn offensive on the Hindenburg Line.

THE AUSTRALIANS

~

T HE GALLIPOLI CAMPAIGN of 1915 produced an upsurge of recruitment in
Australia, but meant that I ANZAC Corps (the 1st and 2nd Australian
Divisions and the New Zealand Infantry Division) did not arrive in France until
March–April 1916. II Corps, consisting of the 4th and 5th Divisions, arrived in
France in June; the 3rd Division was raised after the arrival of its constituent
units in Britain in July 1916. Australian horse units did not proceed to France,
but remained in the Middle East where they fought in the Sinai and Palestine.

In action the Australians quickly acquired a reputation as the elite in the
British imperial army, and also for insubordination, bloody-mindedness and
"resolute lack of military etiquette". No doubt the latter was partly a reaction
against the class distinctions they found in British civil and military life. For their
part, the Australians came to resent their use at the cutting edge of the British
effort. I Australian Corps, formed in November 1917, sustained 25,588
casualties between August 8 and October 5, 1918 and, after a series of incidents
tantamount to a refusal to undertake offensive operations, the formation was
withdrawn from operations. Unable to replace losses, which meant that
divisions were some 3,000 men under strength by the end of 1917, the
Australians were obliged to break up three battalions in May 1918 and eight in
September, when in effect two divisions were reduced to reserve status.

The increasing manpower problems of Australian formations after July 1916
provoked the bitterly divisive conscription issue within Australia. Referenda that
would have resulted in the national application of conscription were
defeated on October 28, 1916 and December
20, 1917. Nonetheless, with some 2,300,000
men of military age, Australia enlisted 416,809
men and despatched some 322,000 troops
overseas in the course of the war: the Australian
Imperial Force had a strength of some 200,000
men in February 1918. Australian casualties
totalled some 280,000 with almost 60,000 killed.

Australian soldier with a wounded German
Australian troops were invariably among the wounded
themselves. They suffered a higher proportion of
casualties than any other nationality in the war.

Calling up more volunteers
Throughout the war there was a vigorous
campaign in Australia to attract volunteers.
Of the large number who responded, the
great majority served as front-line troops.

Band of the 5th Australian infantry brigade
The brigade entered Bapaume in March 1917 during
the Allied advance across territory abandoned by the
Germans as they withdrew to the Hindenburg Line.

rationalization on the part of Haig and his apologists could ever disguise this fact. Haig resolutely ignored the warning made on August 16 by Gough, commander of the Fifth Army, that "tactical success was not possible under these conditions" and that it was now time for the attack to be abandoned. He preferred to believe that the morale of the Germans was steadily deteriorating and would finally be broken by the prolonged pounding of their lines.

Towards the end of August, Plumer, commander of the Second Army, was put in charge of operations in place of Gough. Haig still hoped for a breakthrough, but he accepted Plumer's very deliberate formula – four set-piece attacks, conducted with an overwhelming preponderance of firepower and for very limited objectives, with some six days between each attack.

ASTRIDE THE MENIN ROAD

Plumer's first two attacks were very similar: both were on very narrow frontages by formations attacking after artillery bombardments more severe than any before. Plumer, by limiting objectives to less than 1.5km (1 mile), sought to shatter an enemy defence now concentrated forward after the loss of its first line, and to destroy German counterattacks by forcing them to come within the range of the British artillery. In both operations, along a 13-km (8-mile) front astride the Menin Road on September 20, and an 8-km (5-mile) front around Polygon Wood on the 26th, forward German positions were pulverized and immediate counter-attacks broken. However, while most objectives were

Scene near Zonnebeke in September
In the vicinity of Polygon Wood, dead Germans lie at the entrance to a dug-out that has been destroyed by British artillery. This area was at the centre of a British attack in September, when losses on both sides were high.

secured, the average gain on both days only amounted to around 900 m (1,000 yds). Moreover, on the Menin Road, Australian and British forces incurred some 22,000 casualties and at Polygon Wood about 17,000 casualties. German losses were about the same as those incurred by the Allies.

Haig continued to be hopeful that the German line could be broken, and a further attack was planned for October 4, in which corps of the Fifth Army were to attack Broodseinde Ridge. The attack, carried out with no preliminary bombard-ment but with simultaneous artillery and infantry assaults, inflicted some 26,000 German casualties on what was the first of the "Black Days" recorded by Ludendorff. British losses, however, were scarcely fewer. They were also unable to exploit their initial

gains of just 640 m (700 yds), which despite being so limited were paraded as a great victory. Preparations were made for yet further major attacks.

DEATH IN THE MUD

At this time the rains returned to Flanders. In August, daily rain, combined with the smashing of the local drainage system by British operations, had created a marsh. This had drained itself during the abnormally dry September, when dust clouds were a regular sight, but as the rains began to fall in October the dust turned into liquid mud.

Despite this, and despite a considerable rise in desertion and sickness that was evidence of a decline in morale among British troops, Haig was determined to proceed with attacks due to be launched on October 9 and 12. Thus began what was without doubt the worst and most futile part of the Third Battle of Ypres.

The attack of October 9 at Poelcapelle made virtually no gains while the mud smothered both men and guns. New Zealand troops suffered particularly badly. Even the habitual optimism of Haig's staff wilted in the aftermath of this day. On the 12th, in the first of the two "Battles of Passchendaele", Australian and New Zealand troops were sacrificed in an advance of just 90 m (100 yds) towards the village. An attack on the 26th, the first involving Canadians, did scarcely any better; another on the 30th, with the Germans deliberately thinning their front, came to within 450 m (500 yds) of the village.

The final attack was conducted on November 6 at a time when the Italian disaster at Caporetto (see page 235) and the Allied creation of a war council pointed to the curbing of Haig's freedom of action. Canadian and Australian troops were among those who succeeded in taking the ruins of Passchendaele. The following day Haig's chief of staff visited the salient for the first time.

Sheltering in holes in the mud
These Canadian machine-gunners were among the men who had to endure the miseries of fighting in the mud at Ypres. While holes in the mud might provide shelter, they could also become death-traps in which men drowned.

THIRD BATTLE OF YPRES

JULY 31 – NOVEMBER 6, 1917

The Third Battle of Ypres was to become notorious for the particularly appalling conditions in which it was fought. In the first main offensive, launched on July 31, some small gains were made over three days before heavy rain brought operations to a halt. The offensive was renewed on August 10, and again on the 16th, but little progress was made. Accepting that there would be no immediate breakthrough, the British then decided on a series of set-piece attacks – to begin on September 20 – in which prolonged pounding would gradually wear down the Germans. The battle culminated in a terrible struggle in the mud to capture the village of Passchendaele – finally accomplished on November 6.

KEY

- British front line
- French front line
- British advance
- French advance
- Road
- Railway

British troops at Langemarck
Langemarck was captured on August 16. According to the original battle-plan, the date should have been August 2 or 3.

Aug 16
Langemarck is taken in renewed offensive, but there is little progress on the right

Aug 10
Following a halt in the fighting, British launch offensive against Langemarck-Gheluvelt line

Aug 22
The British Fifth Army is halted on the Menin Road

The first offensives
July 31–August 22
The French 1st Army and British 2nd Army met with more immediate success than the army they were supporting – the British Fifth. However, after three days, control of the German first line had been secured.

3:50 am July 31
Offensive launched. Gains are made on Bixschoote, Pilkem and St Julien ridges to north of Ypres

Nov 6
Canadians launch a final offensive against Passchendaele and capture it the same day

Oct 12
Assault lauched on Passchendaele. It is unsuccessful, as is a second assault on the 26th

Sept 26
5th Army advances towards Zonnebeke

Oct 4
2nd Army launches attack at Broodseinde and captures ridge

Sept 26
An attack secures half of Polygon Wood

Sept 20
Renewed offensive launched against Gheluvelt plateau on Menin Road

The build-up to Passchendaele
September 20–November 6
The first of a series of set-piece attacks against the Germans was launched on September 20 on the Menin Road. Further attacks then followed, at intervals of five or six days, on Polygon Wood, Broodseinde Ridge and Poelcapelle, before the attempt to take Passchendaele began on October 12.

Oct 9
An attack in the Poelcappelle region sees virtually no gains, as rains once again engulf men and guns

Official casualty figures for the Third Battle of Ypres suggest that the British suffered 245,000, the French 8,000, and the Germans 260,000. However, most of the 380,000 casualties suffered by the British in the second half of 1917 were incurred at Ypres. A particularly appalling statistic is that in the final stages of the battle, up to one in four British dead may have drowned in the mud.

> We were never hit, by the grace of God, for the deep mud was our salvation, that mud which we cursed and in which we stuck and staggered, slipped and slid, tugging our boots out of it each time we made a fresh step. Jerry's shells showered us with filth, they disturbed the riddled and broken corpses, they re-shredded the putrid flesh into scraps. It was easy to go "missing", if you got hit, the chances were you slipped into some yawning shell-hole full of greyly opaque water concealing unmentionable things and you drowned there.
>
> GUNNER LIEUTENANT R.G. DIXON, 14TH BATTERY,
> ROYAL GARRISON ARTILLERY

THE BATTLE OF CAMBRAI

The failure to make any real gains at Ypres put pressure on the British generals to produce a victory, any victory, on the Western Front in the autumn of 1917. In June, August and again in early September, the Tank Corps had proposed that it should lead a limited offensive over ground of its own choice. However, the fighting in Flanders meant that it was October before the proposed offensive was approved. The need to distract German attention from the Italian front provided an additional motive for launching an attack in front of Cambrai, a major rail centre, where the German defences on the Western Front were at their strongest.

The Tank Corps calculated that the depth and nature of the German trench system in this sector pointed to it being relatively lightly manned by an enemy that would not be expecting an attack. The element of surprise would be enhanced by the lack of preliminary artillery bombardment and the first use of tanks *en masse*.

The majority of tanks would be used in groups of three and would carry fascines (large bundles of brushwood) to drop into trenches and provide crossing points. Once each of the Germans' three main trench positions had been crossed, the tanks and accompanying infantry would clear the trenches. Cavalry would be held in reserve for the exploitation of any breach that might be made. Vague plans were devised for the crossing of the Sensée and driving northward in order to roll up the

British troops at work in the Flanders mud
Men of the 2nd Monmouthshire Regiment repair a plank road near Hooge during the Third Battle of Ypres. In the background an injured man is carried away on a stretcher.

German position, but, in a welcome break with past practice, the operation was to be halted after two days unless the situation justified otherwise.

Under a cloak of secrecy, the British Third Army assembled a total of 474 tanks, 1,003 guns and mortars and six of its 19 infantry divisions in a sector held by seven under-strength divisions of the German Second Army. Only on the eve of the British attack was security compromised and then not seriously: the Germans were not convinced by the information they received of the impending attack. In any case, the information came too late for them to act upon it effectively.

INITIAL SUCCESS
After slowly reaching their start lines, at 6:20 am on the morning of November 20, 381 fighting tanks began to advance towards a 9-km (6-mile) stretch of the German first line.

MEDICAL SERVICES AT THE FRONT

F OR THE MEDICAL PROFESSION, the First World War was an intensive learning experience – a huge laboratory and clinical trial – which directly involved thousands more medical staff than any previous war. Far fewer soldiers fell to "invisible enemies" such as typhoid than in the past. Yet despite medical advances, one in three casualties died in the First World War, compared to one in seven in the Second.

In their battle against germs and infections, the British army's "khaki doctors" drew on recent experience in the South African War of 1899–1902 and rose to the challenges of trench warfare. "Trench foot" was treated by purifying water with chlorine, fumigating clothes and ensuring regular bathing during rotations out of line. Injections averted tetanus and, for gas gangrene infections, there was "Dakin's solution", an antiseptic fluid developed by a British chemist and a French-American surgeon.

Wounds from shellfire were often fatal unless treated immediately, but once soldiers on the Western Front reached a field hospital they had a good chance of survival. Casualties were carried to regimental first aid posts, and then advanced dressing stations behind the front line. From there, they went by road to casualty clearing stations, then by rail to the stationary base hospitals. British troops with seriously disabling "blighty wounds" were evacuated to the UK, although fewer soldiers were evacuated after 1916. By 1917 casualty clearing stations had been developed into proper field hospitals, where American surgery teams played a key role.

The huge casualties and duration of hostilities forced governments and aid organizations to co-ordinate a vast range of medical services. Thousands of buildings were requisitioned. Army doctors worked with administrators, surgeons and specialists, and nursing became a major field of war work.

Wounded soldiers waiting for transport
Many men on both sides dreamed of a serious, but not fatal, wound that would get them sent home for treatment in a hospital far away from the front line.

AMPUTATION TOOLS

Vital tools
The tools for treating injuries did not include antibiotics, which meant that even minor wounds could result in limbs being amputated.

MEDICAL ORDERLY'S POUCH

MORPHINE AMPOULES

STERILIZING EQUIPMENT

Front-line treatment
American stretcher-bearers apply a field dressing before taking the casualty to a regimental aid post.

Dressing station
The condition of wounded men was checked on arrival at a dressing station. It would often take some time to then move the men on to the casualty clearing station, out of range of enemy artillery.

Horse-drawn ambulances
Critically injured men had to endure a slow and bumpy ride when taken by ambulance to the casualty clearing stations.

British Mark IV tank
The tank that fought at Cambrai in 1917 was not
very different from the Mark I of 1916, but it did
have a better radiator, a silencer and tracks with
better grip. It dispensed with the rear wheels.

THE TANK: NEW DEVELOPMENTS

~

THE NATURE OF TRENCH WARFARE required both a main battle tank to
breach the enemy's defences, and a light tank capable of exploiting a
breakthrough. The British improved their Mark I battle tank, leading to the
Mark IV and then the Mark V. The Mark V was slightly longer with better
trench-crossing capability and was the first main battle tank with a single driver.

The French heavy tanks were of limited use. Of the 132 Schneiders
committed on April 16, 1917, 57 were destroyed and many others damaged
beyond repair; of the 16 St Chamond tanks used in May 1917, 15 ditched as
a result of limited trench-crossing capabilities. The German A7V was equally
unsuccessful with only 15 built. The Germans preferred captured Mark IVs.

The French decided to concentrate on their Renault FT 17 light tank,
building over 4,000 by the end the war. Its performance was unremarkable, but
its single gun in a rotating turret was pioneering. The British light tank, the
Medium A or Whippet, was unusual in having engine and fuel tanks at the
front, and its turret with three fixed machine-guns in the rear.

All early tanks had problems that limited their effectiveness. The main
battle tanks lacked the speed and range to penetrate deeply,
while light tanks could not negotiate heavily-cratered
ground or survive enemy fire. Both had limited
visibility and lacked the radios necessary to
communicate with one another or
supporting arms. Heat and
lack of ventilation left
the crews exhausted.

Renault FT 17 Tank
The most successful French
tank of the war, the Renault
also served with the American
forces. Here a Renault
operates with US infantry
during the summer of 1918.

pistol grip

Preparing for battle
These British Mark IV tanks awaiting rail
transport to the front to take part in the Cambrai
attack are equipped with fascines. These large
wooden bundles were dropped into an enemy
trench, enabling the
tank to get across.

German failure
Germany's only war-
time tank was the A7V
Sturmpanzerwagen. With
a 57-mm (2.2-in) main
armament, six machine-
guns and a crew of 18,
it was slow, unstable and
not capable of crossing
heavily cratered or
rough ground. "Wotan",
shown here, took part
in the German spring
1918 offensive.

Whippet or Medium A
With a twin 45 bhp engine, the
Whippet was capable of
a speed of 13.4 kph (8.3 mph),
positively sprinting when
compared to the slow pace of
other First World War tanks.

Head protection

Tank crews used many purpose-built and adapted items of head gear to protect themselves from the splinters of hot metal created by bullets hitting the tank.

Riveted leather helmet

Slatted eye-protectors

Chain mail visor

LEATHER TANK CREW HELMET

Chain mail eye guard

ADAPTED BRITISH HELMET

Front sight

Anti-tank rifle

Spiked bipod support

The Germans developed this new weapon to try to neutralize the tank. Known as the "elephant gun", it fired single 13.3-mm rounds that penetrated armour up to 30 mm (1.18 in) thick.

Ditched Mark IV tank at Cambrai

British troops survey a tank that failed to cross a German trench 1 km (half a mile) west of Ribecourt on November 20. Such sights were common at Cambrai.

The tanks terrified the Germans, who were powerless to stop them smashing through the barbed wire in front of their trenches. By the end of just one day, the Third Army had penetrated 8 km (5 miles), destroying the equivalent of two German divisions and capturing 120 guns and 7,500 prisoners. There was jubilation back in Britain, where church bells rang for the first time since 1914 and the newspapers proclaimed the greatest British victory of the war.

Although successful, the operation had been marred by the failure to capture Flesquières in the centre, less than halfway between the starting point and Cambrai. One infantry division had not adopted tank corps procedures, leaving armour and infantry exposed to needless losses. The village was captured on the 21st, but that same day the British suffered heavy losses in securing Anneux, Cantaing and Fontaine, and they failed to capitalize on a temporary 5-km (3.5-mile) breach in the German line around Fontaine. Tank losses were also heavy: by November 23 only 92 would still be operational.

GERMAN RESISTANCE

British losses on the 21st were partly due to the arrival of a fresh German division from the Eastern Front. German counterattacks at Noyelles and Nine Wood marked the beginning of the British struggle to retain their gains. On the 22nd the Germans took Fontaine, and British attempts to recapture the village over the next two days failed. The tanks were able to fight their way into Fontaine, but they were at a disadvantage in the narrow streets, where the Germans found they could be halted by throwing bundles of grenades underneath them. On the 23rd the British took Bourlon Wood, with heavy losses. They failed, however, to take Bourlon village, and their positions in the wood soon became untenable.

By the 26th the British had few tanks available and the German reinforcement of the Cambrai sector was all but complete. On the 27th the Germans defeated the last British attack on Fontaine and decided to undertake offensive operations. They intended to eliminate the entire British salient by striking directly into the original British positions on the right.

GERMAN COUNTERATTACK

On November 30 the German attack ripped open the 29th Infantry Division's line around Gouzeaucourt. A British collapse was only averted by German confusion following initial success, and the timely intervention of a few British tanks. The battle ended on the night of the 4th, with an ordered withdrawal by the British. On reaching their new line they still retained the area around Flesquières. They had, however, ceded their other gains and had even lost fresh ground to the south.

Both sides had suffered about 45,000 casualties. The outcome of the battle – particularly disappointing for the British after the success of the first day – was partly due to the unreliability of the tanks and the lack of adequate reserves to consolidate the gains that had been made.

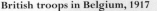

British troops in Belgium, 1917
Almost all the British troops in Belgium in 1917 were in the
Ypres salient, where from July they fought in what became
known as the Battle of Passchendaele. Rain and mud helped
to turn the battlefield into what many saw as a "living hell".

REVOLUTION AND THE WAR IN RUSSIA

MARCH – DECEMBER 1917

1917 saw the efforts of succeeding Russian governments to maintain the war effort finally unravel. The Provisional Government that took power in the wake of the "February Revolution" remained committed to the war. However, the failure of the Kerensky Offensive and the increasing disintegration of the Russian army allowed the Bolsheviks under Lenin to seize power and sue for an armistice with Germany.

MARCH 8
March in Petrograd on International Women's Day grows into mass demonstration: start of "February Revolution"

MARCH 12
Troops mutiny and join demonstrators in Petrograd

MARCH 14
Provisional Government proclaimed, with liberal Prince Lvov as prime minister

MARCH 15
Tsar Nicholas II abdicates

MARCH 22
Provisional Government recognized by several foreign nations, including Great Britain, France, Italy and USA

APRIL 16
Lenin returns from exile in Switzerland, his safe rail passage organized by Germans

MAY 16
Kerensky becomes war minister

MAY 19
Provisional Government issues declaration stating its intention not to seek separate peace for Russia

JUNE 21
Kerensky reviews new Women's "Death Battalion" in Petrograd

JUNE 29
Kerensky Offensive begins with two-day preliminary bombardment

JULY 16
"July Days" uprising, backed by Bolsheviks, begins in Petrograd

JULY 19
"July Days" uprising put down; Lenin flees to Finland

JULY 19
Germans advance 15 km (10 miles) on first day of counterattack

JULY 21
Kerensky becomes prime minister

AUGUST 1
General Kornilov replaces Brusilov as commander-in-chief

AUGUST 3
Austro-Hungarian forces reach Czernowitz

AUGUST 6
Mackensen's Danube Army begins successful counter-offensive in Moldavia

SEPTEMBER 1
German Riga offensive begins

SEPTEMBER 8
Kerensky dismisses Kornilov, who then marches on Petrograd

SEPTEMBER 5
Fall of Riga

SEPTEMBER 14
Kerensky proclaims socialist republic. Kornilov surrenders in suburbs of Petrograd

OCTOBER 8
Kerensky gives moderate socialists a majority in new coalition government

NOVEMBER 5
Kerensky attempts to arrest Bolshevik leaders, sparking off planned "October Revolution"

NOVEMBER 6/7
Kerensky flees Petrograd. Bolshevik coup sees Lenin heading government and Trotsky as foreign minister

NOVEMBER 26
Bolshevik government requests armistice

DECEMBER 15
Armistice signed between Russia and Germany

KEY

■ Events in Russia Mar 8–Dec 15   ■ Main offensives on the Eastern Front Jun 29–Sept 5

Russia and the Eastern Front

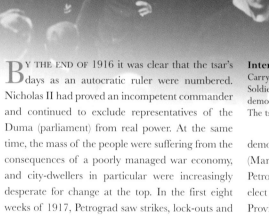

BY THE END OF 1916 it was clear that the tsar's days as an autocratic ruler were numbered. Nicholas II had proved an incompetent commander and continued to exclude representatives of the Duma (parliament) from real power. At the same time, the mass of the people were suffering from the consequences of a poorly managed war economy, and city-dwellers in particular were increasingly desperate for change at the top. In the first eight weeks of 1917, Petrograd saw strikes, lock-outs and queues for inadequate supplies of flour.

THE FEBRUARY REVOLUTION

On March 8 (February 23 by the old Russian calendar) a march by women in honour of International Women's Day grew into a mass demonstration against the continuation of war and Russia's autocratic government. Petrograd's military commander tried to use the army to restore order but the troops sided with the protestors, and anti-tsarist revolutionaries took over the railway stations, telephones and artillery supplies.

This "February Revolution" united the workers', peasants' and soldiers' deputies of the Petrograd Soviet (council) with the politicians of the Duma, who elected a Provisional Government (provisional in that it was to precede the adoption of a

International Women's Day demonstration
Carrying a banner that reads "Comrades, Women and Soldiers, support our demands", women march in the demonstration that triggered the "February Revolution". The tsar abdicated, but Russia stayed in the war.

democratic constitution and election). On March 14 (March 1 by the old Russian calendar), the Petrograd Soviet called on every military unit to elect a soviet of its own. On the following day the Provisional Government issued an eight-point programme calling for the appointment of elected officials in local government and the replacement of the imperial state police by a people's militia. That same day, Nicholas II was compelled to abdicate.

The Provisional Government was immediately recognized by the Allies, concerned to keep Russia in the war. It remained committed to the war, believing that a compromise peace could not be obtained

Lenin addresses a crowd
The driving force of the Bolshevik Party, Lenin was helped by the Germans to return home from exile.

THE EASTER RISING

~

THE IMPACT OF THE WAR on civilians caused unrest on the home fronts of the combatant states. Outside imperial Russia, however, this did not develop into armed insurrection before 1918. The one exception was Ireland where, in April 1916, a group of radical nationalists staged an uprising against British rule and proclaimed an independent Irish republic.

They seized key buildings in Dublin on April 24, and in the six-day battle that followed the city centre was extensively damaged. This "Easter Rising" was crushed by around 8,000 British troops stationed in Ireland. The nationalists numbered no more than 3,000 men and women, and initially they did not receive much public support. However, the execution of 15 of their leaders increased sympathy for their cause. (Eamon de Valera, later premier and president of the Republic of Ireland, escaped execution as, technically, he was an American citizen). In all but the northeast of the country, support grew for

Easter Rising aftermath
British troops patrol outside the battle-scarred General Post Office building on Sackville Street after its recapture on April 28. This had served as the rebels' Dublin headquarters.

independence, as opposed to the more limited "home rule" promised by a 1914 Act of Parliament but shelved for the duration of the war.

Despite this growth in nationalism, thousands of Irishmen enlisted in the British Army; their contribution has only recently been acknowledged. After the execution of the rising's leaders, one Irish soldier commented: "These men will go down in history as heroes and martyrs and I will go down – if I go down at all – as a bloody British officer".

British forces in Dublin, 1916
During the six days of fighting to suppress the rising, 116 British soldiers were killed.

German rifle shipped to the Irish
The 20,000 German-supplied rifles that the Irish nationalist Roger Casement attempted to ship to the rebels were captured, as was Casement himself.

with enemy forces occupying considerable areas of imperial Russia's territory. Moreover, the Russian army began 1917 better equipped than at any stage since September 1914. Russia's new leaders hoped that war weariness would be balanced by a new spirit of democratic patriotism.

BOLSHEVIK ACTIVITY

The eagerness of the Provisional Government to stay in the war was not shared by the Bolshevik Party (later known as the Communist Party), whose leader was the Zurich-based exile

Vladimir Lenin. With regard to the war, Lenin believed that the defeat of Russia would facilitate a further, more radical revolution. After the February Revolution, some Bolsheviks, including Stalin, had returned from exile in Siberia to Petrograd and Moscow. The Germans could see some benefit in Lenin also returning to Russia, and through intermediaries they made an offer that allowed him to cross German territory in a "sealed" train. A single-carriage train carried Lenin and 31 of his comrades back to Russia via Frankfurt, Berlin and Stockholm, and on April 16 he arrived at the Finland Station in Petrograd.

Since February, soviets of workers, soldiers and sailors had sprung up all over Russia, and the Bolshevik Party had grown into a mass movement. Many of the activists were stunned when Lenin scarcely acknowledged the achievements of the February Revolution, instead proclaiming his uncompromising "April Theses" against the "imperialist" war and the "capitalist" Provisional

Government. Translated into the slogan "Land, Peace and Bread!", the Bolsheviks' anti-war stance won great support among the Russian soldiers, mostly peasants who only wanted to stay alive and get home to benefit from the Provisional Government's promised land reforms.

And now the people take their revenge. There are fires everywhere in Petrograd, in all prisons, all police headquarters. If they set fire to the Palace of Justice it is because in the eyes of the people it was a fortress for the police, in the same way as the Bastille was the symbol of tyranny for the people of Paris.

MARYLIE MARKOVICH ON EVENTS IN PETROGRAD, FEBRUARY 1917

THE KERENSKY OFFENSIVE

It was against this background that the Provisional Government pressed ahead with plans to launch an offensive in July – the Kerensky Offensive. Alexander Kerensky, who had made his mark in the pre-war Duma as a moderate socialist, was appointed war minister in the Provisional Government of Prince Lvov on May 16. He then set about planning a "revolutionary offensive" with the aim of recapturing Lemberg (Lvov). The main effort, by the Seventh Army to the north of the Dniester River, was to be supported by the Eleventh Army in an attack directed

"War until Victory"
The Provisional Government believed that the war should continue in defence of Russia – a policy promoted in this poster.

against Zloczow (Zolochiv). Over a front of some 64 km (40 miles), the Russians concentrated 370 heavy, 158 medium and over 800 light guns. Unfortunately, this unprecedented number of guns meant that the tactics used in the Brusilov Offensive of 1916 – taking the opposition by surprise by attacking after a light bombardment – were rejected in favour of saturation bombardment.

From the outset, two major problems threatened to turn the offensive into a disaster. First, in revolutionary Russia no plan of campaign could remain secret. By the end of May the Germans had detailed knowledge of the plan, giving them time to prepare defensive positions in depth. Second, Russian preparations were woefully inadequate. Co-operation between artillery and infantry was minimal, reserves were kept too far from the front, the rear areas were congested with unused cavalry divisions, and commanders, staffs and formations changed constantly. There were also increasingly deep divisions within the army that rendered it, according to one onlooker, a debating society rather than a military organization.

The "Women's Death Battalion", July 1917
The Russian Orthodox patriarch blesses a women's battalion in Moscow before it departs for the front. The battalion was formed by Maria Bochkareva at a time when large numbers of men were deserting the Russian army.

OPENING STAGES OF THE OFFENSIVE

A two-day preliminary bombardment was followed, on July 1, by infantry attacks. The Germans withdrew to their second defensive line and the attacking Russians were generally cut to pieces. In a few places they succeeded in breaking into the third German line, and there was fierce fighting around Bresany (Bereshany) and Lysonia, the two strongest German positions. The Russians, however, were exhausted and were subsequently overwhelmed.

The Eleventh Army was able to register some gains against the Austro-Hungarians. South of the Dniester, an ill-prepared Austro-Hungarian Third Army was defeated and obliged to withdraw 50 km (30 miles) to Lomnica, the Russian Eighth Army securing Halicz (Galich) on July 12. But these counted for little alongside the failure elsewhere; by July 6 the main Russian effort had ended.

GERMAN COUNTER-OFFENSIVE

The problems that beset the attack now combined with the arrival of eight German divisions in Galicia. With these forces the Germans launched a counter-offensive on July 19. Tarnopol (Ternopil) was taken on July 26 and Czernowitz on August 3. General Kornilov – appointed as commander-in-chief in place of Brusilov on August 1 – attempted to reconstitute the Russian defence with the aid of draconian discipline that resulted in thousands of summary executions. The Russian army was, however, on the brink of disintegration.

THE RIGA OFFENSIVE

On September 1 Hutier's German Eighth Army attacked Kornilov's Twelfth Army around Riga, on the Baltic. The German plan was to cross the Dvina above the port and advance to the north and east – thus threatening Petrograd – while turning west to eliminate the Riga salient. After a brief bombardment, in which gas and smoke shells were fired at Russian positions on the north bank, three German divisions crossed the river on pontoon bridges.

The Kaiser's retinue in German-occupied Riga
The Riga Offensive effectively ended the war between Germany and Russia, although the Germans subsequently pursued the Russian Twelfth Army along the Dvina River.

HUTIER TACTICS
~

Oskar von Hutier
Von Hutier's innovative tactics were first used during the Riga offensive at the beginning of September 1917. They proved so successful that they were replicated at Caporetto in Italy and again in the German offensives on the Western Front in the spring of 1918.

OSKAR VON HUTIER WAS A CORPS COMMANDER on the Eastern Front from April 1915 and became commander of the Eighth Army in front of Riga in 1917. In September 1917 this army routed the Russian Twelfth Army in a matter of hours – a result of Russian demoralization and weakness, and the German employment of tactics that bore the name of the army commander.

The Hutier, or Infiltration, Tactics, involved the use of infantry companies, with high firepower provided by light machine-guns, flamethrowers and mortars, moving behind short but overwhelming artillery barrages. Their aim was to get into enemy rear areas, specifically the artillery positions. Gas and smoke shells were to be used to engulf the main points of enemy resistance, which were to be bypassed and left to a follow-up infantry attack to eliminate.

After Riga, the Hutier format was employed in October 1917 at Caporetto and in the counterattack at Cambrai on the Western Front, where Hutier was given command of the Eighteenth Army. This formation was to register major gains in the March 1918 offensive and modest initial gains in June 1918: thereafter it was forced onto the defensive. Hutier Tactics were distilled in *Der Angriff im Stellungskrieg* (Attack in static warfare), published in 1918, setting out the idea that infantry should determine the pace of advance and stressing the importance of surprise and use of the *Feuerwalze* (creeping barrage).

Russian trench during German gas attack
"Hutier Tactics" involved bypassing major enemy strongpoints, which were to be dealt with by later waves of troops. Smoke and gas shells were used to suppress these positions during the initial assault.

Bolshevik propaganda poster
The army, bourgeoisie, clergy and landowners were all opposed to the Bolshevik-led "October Revolution". In this poster they are caricatured proclaiming "Down with the soviet".

They turned west to capture Riga, which the Russians evacuated on the 2nd as they began a rapid retreat. The Germans occupied the port on the 5th and for the next three weeks pursued the remnants of the Russian army along the Dvina. They abandoned their plans to advance on Petrograd as it became clear that the Russian Provisional Government – led by Kerensky as prime minister since July 20 – was on the brink of collapse.

THE OCTOBER REVOLUTION

The Provisional Government had maintained the imperial government's fiscal and taxation policies and both inflation and the amount of money in circulation doubled between March (February) and November (October). As real wages fell and food shortages continued, the Provisional Government had lost the good will of workers in the cities. In the "July Days" uprising of July 16–19, armed workers, sailors and soldiers had tried, and failed, to seize power in Petrograd. Lenin had been forced into hiding, eventually taking refuge in Finland.

Architect of the Red Army
Leon Trotsky was the Commissar for War during the Russian Civil War that followed the October Revolution. He proved an inspired military organizer and played a key role in securing victory for the Bolsheviks over the forces of the opposing "Whites".

Demonstration in front of the Winter Palace
Economic hardships, war-weariness and lack of confidence in the government only served to increase popular demonstrations in Petrograd and elsewhere.

On September 8 the Provisional Government dismissed Kornilov, who marched on Petrograd with the aim of establishing a law-and-order dictatorship. He reached the suburbs five days later, but armed workers blocked his way. Alexeev, the

new commander-in-chief, persuaded him to surrender on September 14, but governmental authority was hopelessly compromised.

In early October, Lenin slipped back into Petrograd, convinced the time was ripe for a Bolshevik coup. Kerensky knew of the threat posed by the Bolsheviks but could not take decisive measures against them as they were in control of the crucial Military-Revolutionary Committee of the Petrograd Soviet. Led by Leon Trotsky, this now served as a committee for the overthrow of the Provisional Government. On the evening of November 6/7 (October 24/25), it put its plans into effect, and by November 8 a Bolshevik-controlled government had been set up. In the words of Lenin:

> "The task for which the people have been struggling has been assured – the immediate offer of a democratic peace, the abolition of the landed property of the landlords, worker control over production, and the creation of a Soviet Government."

Lenin was the leader of the new government and Trotsky was in charge of foreign affairs.

ARMISTICE WITH GERMANY
On November 26 the Bolshevik government asked for an armistice, and within days negotiations had begun at Brest-Litovsk. They were concluded on December 15, 1917; peace talks began a week later. Russia ceased to be a military factor in the war, allowing the German high command to draw upon some 80 divisions in the east as reinforcements for the Western Front. For the next three years, however, Russia was to be devastated by the civil war – between the "Reds" (Bolsheviks) and the "Whites" (anti-Bolsheviks) – which cost more lives than all the Eastern Front battles.

THE BOLSHEVIK COUP

O
N THE EVENING OF November 6/7, the Military-Revolutionary Committee's forces picketed key government buildings in Petrograd, and took control of the telegraph offices and railway stations. They also set up roadblocks on the bridges and around the Winter Palace, where the Provisional Government was in session. None of these actions was resisted, and the streets of Petrograd remained calm. That same night, Lenin joined the other Bolshevik leaders at the Smolny Convent, once a girls' school and now the headquarters of the Petrograd Soviet. On the following day, the revolutionary forces surrounded the Winter Palace, where the politicians of the Provisional Government were waiting, in vain, to be rescued. Very early next morning, the palace fell to the Bolsheviks but, contrary to later accounts, it was never "stormed". From the cruiser *Aurora*, which was moored on the Neva River across from the Winter Palace, Bolshevik sailors fired one blank salvo, and Kerensky was able to slip out of the building by a side entrance and leave the city by car. It was not a coincidence that a Congress of Soviets from all over Russia was due to open on the very next day. Packed with Bolshevik delegates from the provinces, it enabled the leaders of the October Revolution to neutralize opposition from other socialists and radicals, and to clinch the transfer of power from the Provisional Government to the Bolshevik-controlled Soviet of People's Commissars.

Ransacked room in the Winter Palace in Petrograd
The Provisional Government meeting in the Winter Palace in Petrograd made practically no attempt to resist the Bolshevik coup, Kerensky fled the city while other ministers were taken prisoner.

Seizing key sites
The evening they launched their coup, the Bolsheviks, orchestrated by Trotsky, seized key sites all across Petrograd, including the railway stations. Among them was the important Finland Station through which Lenin, who had been living in exile in Switzerland, returned to the city in April.

Red Guards
Red Guards man an armoured tram in Moscow. It took two days for them to overcome the resistance of the Bolsheviks' opponents in Moscow and gain control of the city.

BEYOND THE ISONZO
MARCH 1916 – DECEMBER 1917
~

By mid-March 1916 Italy's five Isonzo offensives, fought in some of the most extreme conditions of the entire war, had made limited progress against the Austro-Hungarians. But the Austro-Hungarian Trentino Offensive in May, followed by more assaults on the Isonzo front, undermined the Italian army's morale. It was rapidly pushed back 95 km (60 miles) by the Austro-German Caporetto Offensive in October 1917.
~

1916 MARCH 11
Fifth Battle of the Isonzo begins

1916 MARCH 16
Fifth Battle of the Isonzo ends due to bad weather

MAY 15
Austro-Hungarians launch Trentino Offensive

MAY 25
Austro-Hungarians push eastwards onto Asiago Plateau

JUNE 26
Trentino Offensive officially ends

JUNE 27
Italians retake Arsiero and Asiago in counterattack

JUNE 28
Major gas attack by Austro-Hungarians with 6,600 casualties

AUGUST 6
Sixth Battle of the Isonzo begins

AUGUST 16
Sixth Battle of the Isonzo ends after Italians have taken Gorizia

AUGUST 28
Italy declares war on Germany

SEPTEMBER 14
Seventh Battle of the Isonzo opens with nine hours of Italian shelling

SEPTEMBER 17
Seventh Battle of the Isonzo ends with minor Italian gains

OCTOBER 9
Eighth Battle of the Isonzo begins; 3-km (2-mile) advance by Italians

OCTOBER 12
Eighth Battle of the Isonzo ends

NOVEMBER 1
Ninth Battle of the Isonzo starts

NOVEMBER 4
Ninth Battle of the Isonzo ends; still no clear results

1917 JANUARY 17
Cadorna requests support of Allied troops for Isonzo front; not forthcoming due to commitments elsewhere

1917 JANUARY 5
Rome Conference of Allied military and political heads

MAY 12
Tenth Battle of the Isonzo starts

JUNE 5
Tenth Battle of the Isonzo ends with some Italian gains

JUNE 10
Italians launch local spoiling attack in the Trentino

JUNE 30
Action in the Trentino ends

AUGUST 18
Eleventh Battle of the Isonzo begins

SEPTEMBER 12
Eleventh Battle of the Isonzo ends after Italian 10-km (6-mile) advance

OCTOBER 24
Caporetto Offensive opens with Austro-German bombardment. Caporetto taken

NOVEMBER 8
Diaz succeeds Cadorna as Italian commander-in-chief

NOVEMBER 14
Italians successfully resist attacks on upper Piave; sporadic action follows

DECEMBER 30
Caporetto Offensive ends

KEY

■ Battles in the Trentino
May 15–Jun 29, 1916
and Jun 10–30, 1917

■ Battles of the Isonzo
Mar 11,1916–Sept 12, 1917

■ Caporetto Offensive
Oct 24–Dec 30, 1917

□ Other events

The Italian Front

War in the mountains
With all but a small section of the Italian frontier with Austria-Hungary in the mountains, specialist *Alpini* mountain troops were at a premium.

DURING THE FIRST 19 months of their involvement in the First World War, the Italians launched a series of offensives on the Isonzo and took part in operations in northern Albania and at Salonika. Only once in this period, in the spring of 1916, did Austria-Hungary initiate an offensive against Italy. The offensive was intended to raise morale among both troops and civilians. Deprived, however, of any support from Falkenhayn – who was concentrating on making preparations for the German offensive at Verdun in February – it soon became clear that his hopes for a quick, decisive victory would not be realized.

THE TRENTINO OFFENSIVE

The Austro-Hungarian attack was staged by the Third and Eleventh Armies. Sometimes called the "Asiago Offensive", it opened on May 15 in the Trentino, in a sector stretching through the mountains from west of Rovereto to west of Borgo. Up to now this had been the quiet sector, where the resident Italian First Army was known as "the convalescent corps" on

account of the importance attached to it by the Italian high command. Conrad's intention was to cut through the left flank of the First Army and advance towards Venice, thus cutting off the Italian forces on the Isonzo.

The Austro-Hungarians had gathered together 2,000 guns, and were able to open their offensive with a punishing barrage. The Italians, knowing that the attack was coming, resisted it heroically and fought in defence of one position after another, but they were slowly driven back. At the same time, the Austro-Hungarian forces were greatly hampered by the difficult, mountainous – sometimes snow-swept – terrain. Within five days their supply lines were being stretched to their limit and their artillery was no longer able to give them the support they so greatly needed.

Austrian mountain gun
Artillery used on the mountainous Italian Front had to be more portable than usual.

ITALIAN WITHDRAWAL AND COUNTERATTACK

On the 20th, when the Italians' appeals to Russia for assistance assumed a certain desperation, they took the decision to withdraw across most of the front. Though this withdrawal was completed by the 24th, the most threatening phase of the Trentino Offensive unfolded on the 25th, when Austro-Hungarian forces pushed forward towards Posina, while to the east they began the task of clearing the Asiago Plateau. By the 30th the Italians had withdrawn from both Asiago and Arsiero, and the Austro-Hungarians had established themselves within 6 km (4 miles) of the Sugana and in the rear of Italian positions around Borgo. They were not able to advance any further, however, the arrival of Italian Fifth Army reinforcements in effect spelling the end of the offensive. Though the Austro-Hungarians mounted further attacks in June, after the 12th their main effort was halted in readiness for the transfer of forces to Galicia where the Russian Brusilov Offensive (see pages 148–50) had been launched on June 4. The offensive officially ended on the 26th and the Italians reoccupied Arsiero and Asiago on the following day.

Nowhere had the Austro-Hungarian forces succeeded in advancing more than 19 km (12 miles), and while their losses were far lower than those of the Italians – 80,000 compared with 147,000 – they never posed any real threat of a breakthrough. The campaign had also worsened Austro-Hungarian relations with Falkenhayn, who had been angered by Conrad's disregard for his view that the Central Powers should concentrate on the Western Front and stay on the defensive against the Italians.

> As I descended the upper track two bandaged men were coming down on led mules. It was mid-August, and they were suffering from frostbite…For everywhere upon the icy pinnacles are observation posts directing the fire of the big guns on the slopes below…Snow and frost may cut them off absolutely for weeks from the rest of mankind. The sick and wounded must begin their journey down…in a giddy basket that swings down to the head of the mule track below.
>
> **HERBERT GEORGE (H. G.) WELLS,**
> **DESCRIBING THE ISONZO FRONT 1916**

MOUNTAIN TRANSPORT

WAR IN THE ALPS created supply problems unlike those faced in any other theatre. Unable to outflank the Austro-Hungarians in the traditional manner, Italian troops climbed higher and higher up the mountains in an attempt to dominate the enemy positions. The Austro-Hungarians replied in kind, with the result that tens of thousands of soldiers found themselves spending whole winters at heights of over 3,000 m (10,000 ft). All needed to be supplied with ammunition, food and fuel for cooking and heating. The Italians erected *teleferiche*, overhead cableways, that were driven by oil or electric motors. The largest were up to 8 km (5 miles) long and rose by as much as 1,500 m (5,000 ft) between the starting-point and the destination. Smaller ones could be dismantled and re-erected where required – some of these were driven by manpower. Even in the most isolated positions guns would be hauled up and the wounded evacuated on swinging cradles.

Fresh rations
Food and ammunition were the most important supplies to be delivered. In 1917 there were 530 motor-driven *teleferiche* supplying the Italian army.

Mountain artillery
In the mountains any peak or ridgeline was a potential gun emplacement, but moving even one gun into position required technical expertise and muscle.

BATTLES OF THE ISONZO

Between Italy's entry into the war and the Trentino Offensive, Italian forces had undertaken five offensives across the Isonzo. The fifth, from March 11 to 16, had barely carried the Italians beyond the enemy outpost line. Following the failure of the Trentino Offensive, however, the Italians were able, in the Sixth Battle of the Isonzo, to take the fortified town of Gorizia (Görz) on August 9, and then to clear part of the Carso (Karst). The Austro-Hungarian defence had been weakened by the diversion of forces to Galicia, but the Fifth Army continued to hold Tolmino, so ensuring that the northern sector remained closed to the Italian Second Army. The losses of the Austro-Hungarians were limited to the south, where they were pushed back to the their original last line of resistance.

The Italian Third Army's performance in a series of actions on the Isonzo after August – in the Seventh, Eighth and Ninth battles of Isonzo – was doggedly determined, but there was no escaping the fact that the new Habsburg defences in the Carso threatened to make 1917 as exhausting as 1916 had been. Furthermore, by the end of the year, the Italian state and army, which had no strong national and military traditions to draw on, had been severely weakened by its efforts.

ALLIED PLANS FOR 1917

Over the winter of 1916–1917 the Allies agreed to synchronize their offensive efforts in the spring, launching an Italian offensive at the same time as the Arras and Aisne offensives. This, however, was made impossible for the Italians by the lateness of the spring. In the following weeks, as spring gave way to summer, Italy was the first of the Allies to feel the effects of Russia's February Revolution. The arrival on the Isonzo of Austro-Hungarian forces

Austro-Hungarian river crossing
The pursuit of the Italians following the breakthrough at Caporetto was delayed by supply problems. Here Austro-Hungarian troops transport supplies across the Tagliamento on a bridge that has been only partially repaired.

that had been transferred from the Eastern Front convinced the Italian high command of the need to retain the initiative for the remainder of 1917. Accordingly, it decided to launch two offensives south of Tolmino, with the main effort being made by the Third Army on the Carso. In fact, in both offensives – the Tenth and Eleventh Battles of the Isonzo – it was the Second Army, to the north of Gorizia (Görz), that made the major gains.

In the tenth battle, launched on May 12, the Second Army secured most of the mountains that barred the way to the Bainsizza Plateau. The Third Army, however, lost some of its gains in the area around Kostanjevica on the Carso to an Austro-Hungarian counterattack in the first days of June.

ACTION IN THE TRENTINO

On June 30 the Italians launched a local offensive in the Trentino. This was intended to eliminate the positions won by Austro-Hungarian forces in 1916, from which they could threaten Venice and the areas to the rear of the Italian armies on the Isonzo. The pattern of the Isonzo offensives, however, repeated itself, with a series of hard-fought and costly battles for individual peaks bringing few Italian gains. Furthermore, most of the gains were quickly eliminated by a major Austro-Hungarian effort, which inflicted significant and morale-sapping losses on the Italians.

ELEVENTH BATTLE OF THE ISONZO

In the Eleventh Battle of the Isonzo, the Italian Third Army broke through the Austro-Hungarian front on August 21, and then cleared most of the Bainsizza Plateau. To the south, the Second Army failed to make any immediate major gains but broke two of the strongest enemy positions on the front. On August 21 the Italians cleared Monte Santo and on September 4 they succeeded in gaining the upper hand on Monte San Gabriele.

Such success cost the Italian army 155,000 casualties and exhausted it. The battle, however, convinced the Austro-Hungarians, reduced to their last defensive positions, that they could not face a twelfth battle of the Isonzo. Consequently, they sought the assistance of the Germans. Their request came at a time when Berlin, with some six divisions available for operations away from the Western Front, was contemplating a campaign in Moldavia to drive Romania from the war once and for all. Deciding, instead, to make a virtue of necessity, the German high command insisted upon command of an operation in which the Austro-Hungarian army was to play the supporting role.

THE CAPORETTO OFFENSIVE

Gathering some 15 divisions in the Fourteenth Army, the Germans planned to strike in the Tolmino area, where their ally had retained a bridgehead over the Isonzo, and to force an Italian withdrawal to the Tagliamento by threatening

A desperate defence
On the second day of the Caporetto offensive, Italian troops tried, unsuccessfully, to stem the Austro-German advance at Cividale to buy time to allow the Italian Third Army to retreat. The odds were overwhelming and these Italian troops paid the ultimate price.

the rear of the Italian Second and Third Armies. Some of the German staff thought that greater success might be possible and that a simultaneous effort should be made in the Trentino. However, the Central Powers lacked sufficient forces to make this second effort, and the armies committed to the offensive lacked the cavalry and motor transport to exploit success to the full.

What neither the German nor the Austro-Hungarian staffs could know was how far the battles on the Isonzo had completed the demoralization of the Italian army. Its awareness of failure and the futility of its sacrifices, of the little regard in which it was held by friend and foe alike, the example of the Russian revolution and the seething discontent within Italian society, had sapped the will of the Italian army. It was an army in which the treatment of the rank and file was at best abysmal and in which relations between regimental officers and staff were usually worse. Consequently, despite receiving detailed plans from deserting enemy officers and some six weeks' notice, the Italians did very little to strengthen defences in the Tolmino sector. The deployment of the Italian armies, with

Italian prisoners in Udine
On the eve of Caporetto the morale of the Italian army was very low. The Italians taken prisoner at Udine on October 29 were among almost 295,000 who surrendered to Austro-German forces during the offensive.

the bulk of Second and Third Armies beyond the Isonzo, invited a defeat that was to be turned into a debacle by the refusal of many formations to fight.

AN AUSTRO-GERMAN ROUT

After a two-day delay caused by bad weather, the offensive began, on October 24, with a four-hour bombardment. A large number of gas shells was fired as it was known that the Italians had only primitive protection against gas. Two Italian corps were then annihilated as the Germans advanced 19 km (12 miles) from Tolmino and Plezzo, crossing the Isonzo and taking the town of Caporetto. Within three days the Italian Second Army abandoned all its mountain positions. On the 25th

the Italians fought to hold Cividale to allow the Third Army time to withdraw to the Tagliamento. Cividale fell on the 27th, Gorizia (Görz) on the 28th, and Udine – headquarters of Cadorna – on the 29th.

Because of movement and supply problems, the Austro-Hungarian forces did not start to push back the Italians from the Tagliamento until November 2. It took another five days to cross the Livenza. Two divisions in the Trentino then joined the offensive, securing Asiago on the 9th, but the pace of the Austro-German offensive was slackening because of lengthening supply lines and a lack of reserves. The fall of Belluno on the 10th was among the last of the Italian losses.

On the 14th the Italians repulsed a series of attacks on the upper Piave. For the moment, and behind a river that in 1916 Cadorna had selected as the army's last line of resistance in the event of an emergency, the Italian army was safe and had the time to recover from its 96-km (60-mile) retreat. It had lost about 10,000 killed, 30,000 wounded and 295,000 prisoners, and at one stage had not been able to account for more than 400,000 troops. Its recovery was to be slow.

Collapse at Caporetto
In the weeks leading up to the Caporetto Offensive, the deployment of Italian troops in defensive positions was an inadequate response to the massing of German as well as Austro-Hungarian forces on the Isonzo front. The Italians were pushed back to the Piave before being able to stand their ground in mid-November. French and British divisions arrived in December to help strengthen front-line positions against future attacks.

THE CAPORETTO OFFENSIVE
Oct 24–Nov 12, 1917

- Italian front line Oct 24
- Italian front line Nov 1
- Italian front line Nov 12
- Movements of Austro-Hungarian forces
- Movements of German forces
- **SEPT 24** Date of capture of town by Central Powers
- - - - Major railway
- The Allies (and allied states)
- Central Powers (and allied states)

0 km 20 40 60 80 100
0 miles 20 40 60 80 100

AUSTRIA-HUNGARY

ITALY

Isarco
Bressanone
10TH ARMY
CARNIC ALPS

Bolzano
DOLOMITES
Pieve
Maggio

Nov
Austrian forces in Trentino join attack

Oct 24
German 14th Army advances, and the Italian front quickly collapses

Plezzo

14TH ARMY

2:00 am, Oct 24
Central Powers open hostilities with a sustained bombardment and gas attack

TRENTINO
11TH ARMY

4TH ARMY

Nov 4
Rapid advance of Austro-German forces, causing Cadorno to order retreat to Piave River

NOV 2
Cornino

Tarcento
Caporetto
Tolmino
2ND ARMY

OCT 27
Cividale

Isonzo
BAINSIZZA PLATEAU

Strigno
NOV 10
Belluno

OCT 29
Udine

Mt Santo
Isonzo

Trento
Borgo
Val Sugana
Feltre

Aviano
Nov 9
Germans continue pursuit, crossing the Livenza

OCT 28
Gorizia
Mt San Gabriele

Rovereto
NOV 7
Vittorio Veneto
Sacile

3RD ARMY

5TH ARMY

NOV 9
Asiago
Conegliano
CARSO (KARST)

Mt Pasubio
Posina Arsiero

Montefalcone

Portogruaro

Livenza
Trieste

Vicenza

Piave

Nov 12
Minor fighting continues for several weeks along Piave River. French and British reinforcements begin to arrive

Mestre

Padua
Venice

Gulf of Venice

The Middle East

MESOPOTAMIA AND PALESTINE

JANUARY 9 – DECEMBER 11, 1917

~

After the disappointments of 1916, the British needed results. Kut and Baghdad fell to Maude early in the year. In Palestine, however, Murray's failures at Gaza led to his replacement by Allenby, who reinvigorated British efforts. In July the Arabs seized Aqaba, resulting in enhanced British support for the Arab Revolt. In October, Allenby succeeded in driving the Turks out of Gaza and Beersheba, to seize Jerusalem in December.

~

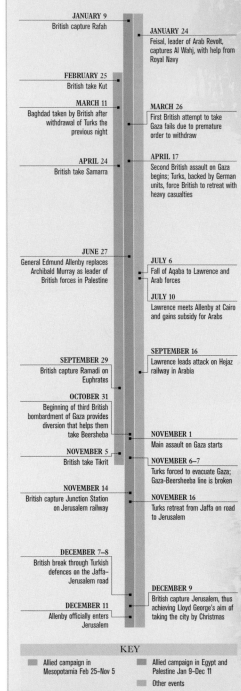

JANUARY 9
British capture Rafah

JANUARY 24
Feisal, leader of Arab Revolt, captures Al Wahj, with help from Royal Navy

FEBRUARY 25
British take Kut

MARCH 11
Baghdad taken by British after withdrawal of Turks the previous night

MARCH 26
First British attempt to take Gaza fails due to premature order to withdraw

APRIL 24
British take Samarra

APRIL 17
Second British assault on Gaza begins; Turks, backed by German units, force British to retreat with heavy casualties

JUNE 27
General Edmund Allenby replaces Archibald Murray as leader of British forces in Palestine

JULY 6
Fall of Aqaba to Lawrence and Arab forces

JULY 10
Lawrence meets Allenby at Cairo and gains subsidy for Arabs

SEPTEMBER 16
Lawrence leads attack on Hejaz railway in Arabia

SEPTEMBER 29
British capture Ramadi on Euphrates

OCTOBER 31
Beginning of third British bombardment of Gaza provides diversion that helps them take Beersheba

NOVEMBER 1
Main assault on Gaza starts

NOVEMBER 5
British take Tikrit

NOVEMBER 6–7
Turks forced to evacuate Gaza; Gaza-Beersheba line is broken

NOVEMBER 14
British capture Junction Station on Jerusalem railway

NOVEMBER 16
Turks retreat from Jaffa on road to Jerusalem

DECEMBER 7–8
British break through Turkish defences on the Jaffa–Jerusalem road

DECEMBER 9
British capture Jerusalem, thus achieving Lloyd George's aim of taking the city by Christmas

DECEMBER 11
Allenby officially enters Jerusalem

KEY

■ Allied campaign in Mesopotamia Feb 25–Nov 5
■ Allied campaign in Egypt and Palestine Jan 9–Dec 11
■ Other events

Beersheba
Turkish cavalry pass through this key town on their way to southern Palestine in April 1917.

AFTER THE SURRENDER of the British forces under General Townshend in Kut in April 1916, imperial prestige seemed to demand Britain's prompt recapture of the town. This did not, however, accord with the ideas of William Robertson, chief of the imperial general staff, who favoured a defensive posture. He was reluctant to commit more troops, and he considered that the purpose of the British presence was essentially to protect the Persian oil fields and guard the Shatt al-Arab waterway, not to embark on further conquest.

Robertson's appointee as the commander in Mesopotamia, General Maude, proved to have more ambitious aims. Having spent most of 1916 in preparation, building up supplies and raising morale, in December Maude began to extend his front farther up the Tigris, where he was supported by the naval guns of eight new gunboats plus a number of armed river steamers.

Advancing across the Sinai
British troops march to El Arish in February 1917 during preparations for the First Battle of Gaza.

ADVANCE THROUGH MESOPOTAMIA

The Turkish Sixth Army, commanded by Halil Pasha, who had accepted Townshend's surrender, was heavily outnumbered – ultimately by as much as four to one – and had severe logistical problems. As well as lacking equipment, weapons and essential draft animals, the Turks suffered from a shortage of food and clothing. Maude's advance was very cautious, but he did not want to provoke an order from London to bring operations to a halt. Although the British and Indian troops had better supplies than the Turks, but they did not find conditions comfortable and many fell victim to disease. Maude himself was to die of cholera before the end of 1917.

By mid-February 1917 the Turks around Kut were in a vulnerable position, and the town fell on February 25. Maude was then authorized to advance on Baghdad, and his forces reached the city two weeks later. It fell without resistance on March 11, the Turks – outnumbered and outflanked – having withdrawn the previous night. The British continued to advance, taking Samarra in April and Ramadi and Tikrit in the autumn. The demands of the Palestine campaign, however, increasingly inhibited operations in Mesopotamia.

THE ARAB REVOLT

The main, and eventually decisive, British effort against the Ottoman Empire in the Middle East came in Palestine. Here they were aided by the Arab Revolt against the Turks, proclaimed by Sherif Hussein Ibn Ali of Mecca – later king of the Hejaz (Al Hijaz) – in June 1916. The British had been encouraging Hussein to revolt for some time, and had supplied him with rifles.

The revolt was timed to coincide with the advance across the Sinai peninsula of Archibald Murray's Egyptian Expeditionary Force (EEF). Substantial British forces had been kept in Egypt since the Turkish attack on Suez. Owing, however, to demands from elsewhere, Murray had recently had to give up one division, and his remaining forces, which included the ANZAC Mounted Division, lacked adequate supplies of artillery and munitions. Initial progress was slow, though chiefly

because the troops were building roads, a railway and a vital water pipeline as they went. On December 20, 1916, the EEF took El Arish, clearing the Sinai peninsula of all Turkish forces.

Meanwhile, attempts were being made to revive the Arab Revolt, which had languished after the surrender to Hussein of the Turkish governor of the Hejaz in September. In October a British fact-finding mission arrived from Cairo. Its members included a young officer who had already made a reputation in military intelligence: T. E. Lawrence. A speaker of Arabic, and with some knowledge of Turkish and Arab customs, Lawrence had already written a memo on the Arab Revolt in which he

accurately forecast the future strategy of disrupting the Hejaz railway. He believed that the most promising leader – with whom he would form a close relationship – was Hussein's third son, Feisal, who was currently trying to hold together a band of largely untrained tribesmen based inland from the port of Yenbo (Yanbu).

Desert artillery
Although primarily used on the North West Frontier in India, the British 10-pounder mountain gun saw extensive service in the Mesopotamia and Palestine campaigns.

> "It was never easy for us to keep our movements secret, as we lived by preaching to the local people, and the unconvinced would tell the Turks."
>
> T. E. LAWRENCE ON CROSSING THE DESERT WITH ARABS WHO WERE
> IN REVOLT AGAINST THE TURKS IN JUNE 1917

The retaking of Kut
In March 1917 Allied troops retook Kut, scene of the humiliating surrender of General Charles Townshend's British force in April 1916.

Having become Feisal's official British adviser in November, Lawrence assisted Feisal in his defence of Yenbo against a Turkish attack. The Turks succeeded in breaking up Feisal's forces and in December they drove him back to the port. Faced, however, by the presence of five British warships a short distance offshore, the Turks withdrew.

CAPTURE OF AL WAJH

The failure of the Turks to capture Yenbo persuaded more tribesmen to join Feisal's forces and revived the Arab Revolt. With encouragement from Lawrence, Feisal captured the port of Al Wajh from the Turks in January 1917. The port then served as a base for attacks on Turkish positions throughout northern Arabia, forcing the Turks to mount a defensive campaign. In July Feisal captured Aqaba, on the northeastern tip of the Red Sea. This was to become his main base as later in the year he moved northwards into Palestine, where he recruited more followers and launched raids on the Turkish railway.

THE CAMPAIGN IN PALESTINE

Southern Palestine has a natural southern boundary – the hills between Gaza, near the coast, and Beersheba, 40 km (25 miles) inland. For Murray's EEF (five divisions plus other units), advancing along the coast in March 1917, Gaza became the objective. The town was surrounded by gardens and fields interlaced with cactus barriers, presenting formidable natural defenceworks as well as shelter for machine-guns. But the most crucial problem facing the EEF, as so often in desert warfare, was water. Only one day's supplies could be carried, and it was therefore essential to capture Gaza, where supplies were plentiful, within a day. If it were not captured before nightfall, total withdrawal would be necessary.

THOMAS EDWARD LAWRENCE

LEGEND AND MILITARY HISTORY meet in the exotic, robed figure of "Lawrence of Arabia" (1888–1935), the Welsh-born archaeologist who adopted Arab customs when campaigning in the desert during the First World War. A leader of the Arab Revolt against the Turks, he operated in tandem with Allenby's army, but ultimately felt that the Allies had ignored their promises to the Arab people.

Lawrence had been working on archaeological digs in the Middle East for several years when, in 1915, his knowledge of the local language and people led to his appointment as an intelligence officer. He was sent to establish cordial relations with Feisal Ibn Hussein and assisted him at the defence of Yenbo in November 1916. He was also instrumental in Feisal's capture of Aqaba in July 1917. He then turned his attentions to Palestine, where he took part with Feisal in guerrilla attacks and raids on the Turkish railway.

In 1918 Lawrence persuaded Feisal to support the British advance through Syria to Damascus, and Arab forces entered the city with the British on October 1. At the Paris Peace Conference in 1919, where Lawrence acted as Feisal's adviser, he viewed the placing of Syria under a French mandate as a particular betrayal. He subsequently wrote a number of accounts of his wartime experiences. *The Seven Pillars of Wisdom* is the most famous.

Martini-Henry
This 1870s-vintage British rifle was typical of the outdated firearms supplied as part of the support for the Arab Revolt.

Arab flintlock pistol
Although antique and largely worn for show, it is possible that weapons such as this did see service.

Sea fog delayed the start on March 26, but by dusk British troops were within the town. The defending Turkish troops were taken by surprise, and the German commander decided that he had no alternative but to surrender. At this point,

however, the British commanders based some distance away received reports of approaching Turkish relief and – to the astonishment of the local commanders – gave the order to withdraw.

The second battle of Gaza started on April 17. The situation was now entirely different. The advantage of surprise had been lost, the Turks defending Gaza had been reinforced (though still outnumbered), and they had added a labyrinth of trenches to the cactus hedges. Murray was given a few battered tanks and some gas shells (both proved virtually useless) but not the two extra divisions that he believed necessary. Water supplies were still inadequate. Murray ordered the new British attack without adequate reconnaissance, and after two days the Turkish defences were undented, British casualties were heavy (over 6,000), and a "temporary" cessation of fighting was ordered. The failure heralded considerable changes.

Arab irregulars enter Yenbo
In December 1916 Arab troops under the command of Feisal were forced to withdraw to Yenbo by the Turks. They subsequently engaged in guerrilla warfare.

COPING WITH THE DESERT

OR THE ALLIED FORCES CAMPAIGNING in the Near and Middle Eastern areas of the Ottoman Empire, the natural environment presented an extra, deadly enemy. To cope with the searing heat, soldiers were issued with sun helmets and spine pads (to protect their backs from the sun), but clean water was always in short supply. Water was crucial to the survival, as well as the success, of armies in the desert. To keep going for just one day, the Allied troops in Syria and Palestine required some 1,800,000 litres (400,000 gallons) of water. It was needed for animals – horses and mules – as well as men because many desert "roads" were not negotiable by motorized vehicles.

Extreme heat and poor sanitation meant that the Allied forces were dogged by a host of infectious diseases. Dysentery was the biggest killer, but whole regiments were also afflicted by malaria, yellow fever and typhoid. Until their rations were supplemented to include Vitamin C, Indian troops were also vulnerable to scurvy. In the last six months of 1916, more than 11,000 Indian soldiers succumbed to this "disease of deficiency".

In the desert, the conscript soldiers of the Turkish army also suffered, with seven times as many men dying of disease – dysentery, malaria, typhoid and syphilis – as died of wounds during the war. During the entire war the Turkish army employed no more than 2,500 doctors to treat its soldiers. Technically, there was no overall shortage of food in the Ottoman Empire, but getting it to the armies in the field was a problem. Sea transport was impossible because of the British blockade, and the limited, overburdened railway system could not cope. At one stage, Turkish troops in Palestine were surviving on rations of 350 grams (12.5 oz) of bread a day. They were badly equipped, and so often without footwear that to this day the war is referred to in Syria as "the barefoot war".

Water
This engraved silver bottle was used to carry the most precious commodity in the Mesopotamian campaign: water.

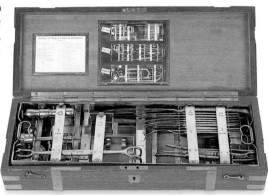

Surgeon's instrument set
Issued by the Indian Army, this instrument set contains forceps, clamps, scalpels and saws to deal with the effects of wounds. Disease, however, generally posed a greater threat than combat to the soldiers who fought in the desert.

Camel ambulance
Australian medical orderlies prepare to load a casualty on to a cacolet on a camel's back at Rafa. The camel's swaying motion must have been excruciating for a soldier suffering anything but the most minor of wounds.

THE ARRIVAL OF ALLENBY

In late June Murray was replaced by Allenby. A South African War veteran, Allenby gave the appearance of being a conventional, old-fashioned cavalry officer. But he also had an inclination towards the unorthodox and was tolerant of unconventional warriors, as his relations with Lawrence and the Arabs were to demonstrate. With the British prime minister Lloyd George now asking for Jerusalem as "a Christmas present", Allenby received the reinforcements that Murray had been denied. There were still, however, problems with transport – dependent on mules – and water.

Allenby decided on Beersheba as the objective. An element of surprise was necessary if it was to be taken before the Turks could destroy the wells, and to this end efforts were made to convince the Turks that, while diversionary action might be expected at Beersheba, the main attack would be on Gaza. Having heard from Lawrence about the achievements of the Arabs, Allenby requested that they should cut the railway at Der'a (Dar'a) at the beginning of November to coincide with his intended attack. This was a risky operation involving a 560-km (350-mile) ride through the desert and then settled territory, making surprise problematic. In fact, there may have been a traitor in the group, for the Turks gained advance warning. The raid failed, although Lawrence's band did succeed in cutting the line farther south.

Meanwhile, the Turks set about improving their defences prior to the arrival of the Turkish-German Yilderim ("Thunderbolt") Force under the command of Falkenhayn. Based on two Turkish divisions, but with largely German officers, the force had been intended for action in Mesopotamia before the success of the British in Palestine.

The Sakultutan Pass
While Allenby pressed on towards Jerusalem, Allied forces also advanced through Mesopotamia. On December 3 and 4 they occupied the Sakultutan Pass, a main Turkish supply route across the Jabal Hamrin, northeast of Baghdad.

CAPTURE OF BEERSHEBA AND GAZA
Allenby's campaign to take Beersheba began with an intensive bombardment of Gaza to reinforce the notion that the main blow would fall there, while troops moved east towards Beersheba under cover of night. On October 31 Allenby launched an attack with 40,000 men and over 100 guns on a front about 5 km (3 miles)

Turkish military band in Damascus
The Turkish army was driven back through Palestine and Mesopotamia during 1917, but despite shortages of food, clothes and weapons, it continued to be a reliable fighting force which was not easily defeated. It was to stay in control of Damascus until October 1918.

wide. The infantry advanced, cutting their way through barbed wire while under Turkish artillery fire. Meanwhile, after a hazardous night-time ride of nearly 50 km (30 miles), the ANZAC division attacked from the north and east where the Turks had not laid barbed wire. Sheer speed across the ground kept their casualties down and, when faced with concentrated rifle and machine-gun fire, they dismounted and fought their way forward on foot. They then galloped through two lines of trenches and into Beersheba, creating havoc among the defenders and taking 1,400 prisoners while suffering fewer than 200 casualties themselves.

The seizure of Beersheba forced the Turks to begin moving forces from Gaza in order to reseal the front. As they did so, the Allied forces launched their main assault on Gaza on November 1; by the night of November 6/7 the Turks were in retreat. The Gaza-Beersheba line was now broken, and the way to Jerusalem lay open for the Allies.

ADVANCE TO JERUSALEM

With Lawrence and the Arabs forming a detached flanking force on the right, in the desert, Allenby's forces advanced across the plain beyond Gaza, covering 80 km (50 miles) in 17 days and taking some 10,000 prisoners. Allenby then had to decide whether to pause and consolidate, or make a dash for "Jerusalem by Christmas". He decided on the latter and resumed the advance on November 18, despite the arrival of the winter rains, which for the moment created greater difficulties than the Turks. The camels in particular suffered.

On November 27 Falkenhayn, whose Yilderim Force had only begun to arrive in late October, launched a counterattack against a weak point in the Allied forces – a comparatively small cavalry force guarding British supply lines. The Turks made some impression, but their efforts soon petered out as Allenby called upon his reserves.

The Allied advance continued along the Jaffa-Jerusalem road during a pause in the rains that allowed the supporting artillery to move up. Although rain and mist soon returned, an attack on the night of

December 7/8 on the outskirts of Jerusalem, took the Turks by surprise. The EEF broke through their defences, pushing them back 7 km (4 miles) before pausing to wait for more troops to arrive from Bethlehem. Both sides were under orders to spare Jerusalem from fighting, and on the morning of December 9, Allenby's troops discovered that the Turks just to the north of the city had taken advantage of the lull in the fighting to withdraw during the night. Four centuries of Ottoman rule over the city had ended, and Lloyd George had his Christmas present.

Allenby enters Jerusalem

Allenby made his official entry into the city through the Jaffa Gate on December 11. The Turks, for whom the loss of the city was a terrible blow to morale, had begun to retreat towards Nablus and Jericho on the night of the 8th/9th.

Gurkha Lewis gunner

The Gurkhas had a reputation for being particularly determined fighters. It was one they lived up to in the fierce encounters that took place between Allied and Turkish troops in both Palestine and Mesopotamia.

THE CAUCASUS FRONT

Throughout 1917 the Turks had focused on the Mesopotamian and Palestine fronts, and paid little attention to the Caucasus front. Following the "February Revolution" the Russian army in the region had not been able to contemplate anything other than defensive action, and after the "October Revolution" the Russians had withdrawn altogether. This had left the way open for a revival of nationalist Armenian activity, and in the following months an estimated 50,000 non-Armenians were killed. In September the Armenians, Azerbaijani and Georgians established the joint republic of Transcaucasia, but there were deep divisions between the three nationalities, resulting in a very confused situation at the end of the year. It would not be difficult for the Turks to gain control again in spring 1918.

Allied advance from Gaza

After launching a surprise attack on Beersheba on October 31 and then capturing Gaza at their third attempt, EEF forces advanced northwards both up the coast and east of Sheria and drove the Turks from Jerusalem on December 9.

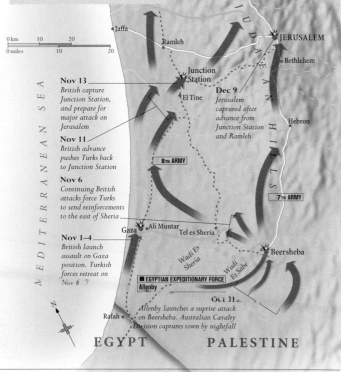

CAMPAIGNS IN PALESTINE
Oct 31–Dec 9, 1917

- Turkish defensive positions Oct 31
- Turkish positions Nov 13
- Turkish positions Dec 7
- Turkish outposts
- Allied offensives
- Major battle
- Railway
- Railway built by British 1917
- Main road

Nov 13
British capture Junction Station, and prepare for major attack on Jerusalem

Nov 11
British advance pushes Turks back to Junction Station

Nov 6
Continuing British attacks force Turks to send reinforcements to the east of Sheria

Nov 1–4
British launch assault on Gaza position. Turkish forces retreat on Nov 6–7

Dec 9
Jerusalem captured after advance from Junction Station and Ramleh

Oct 31
Allenby launches a surprise attack on Beersheba. Australian Cavalry Division captures town by nightfall

MEDITERRANEAN SEA

Jaffa
Ramleh
Junction Station
El Tine
JERUSALEM
Bethlehem
Hebron
JUDAEAN HILLS
8TH ARMY
7TH ARMY
Gaza
Ali Muntar
Tel es Sheria
Wadi Es Sheria
Wadi Es Sebe
Beersheba
EGYPTIAN EXPEDITIONARY FORCE
Allenby
Rafah

EGYPT   PALESTINE

0 km 10 20
0 miles 10 20

WAR POETS AND NOVELISTS

~

FOR MANY OF THE YOUNG MEN who donned uniforms in 1914, the war was a noble adventure, a chance to emulate the chivalrous knights of old. The brutal reality of the conflict – more hellish than any previously imagined hell – transformed this early idealism into an intense disenchantment, which found expression in a body of powerful literature.

The Western Front was especially conducive to poetry. Soldier-poets found themselves, as never before, in the very thick, or stalemate, of battle. In poems jotted down on the backs of envelopes and letters, they immortalized the tribulations of their comrades and the desolate landscape of corpses, churned mud, gaping shell-holes, barbed wire, splintered trees and smashed buildings.

Writing home from his first tour of duty on the Somme, 24-year-old Wilfred Owen wrote of "everything unnatural, broken, blasted, the distortion of the dead, whose unburiable bodies sit outside the dug-outs all day, all night, the most execrable sights on earth". His poems, not published until after his death, raged against the human cost of the war. Yet after being invalided home, he chose to return to the front line and was killed a week before the signing of the Armistice. Another casualty was Isaac Rosenberg. A frail and diminutive young man, he enlisted partly in the hope that his army separation allowance would benefit his mother, and was killed on a night patrol at the beginning of April 1918.

Like other English soldier-poets, notably Siegfried Sassoon and Robert Graves, Owen and Rosenberg expressed the gulf of understanding between the brotherhood of "those who were there" and civilians at home. A similar theme – intense suffering alleviated by comradeship – runs through *Le Feu (Under Fire)*, the war novel written by French writer Henri Barbusse, which contains many harrowing passages. In some cases, the bond of shared suffering was so strong it extended to the "enemy" on the other side of No Man's Land. This attitude pervades *All Quiet on the Western Front (Im Westen nichts Neues)*, a novel written by twice-wounded German veteran Erich Maria Remarque. First published in 1929, Remarque's pacifist message led to his work being publicly burned by the Nazis, and cost him his German citizenship. Elsewhere, *All Quiet on the Western Front* was a huge success, contributing to a retrospective perception of the war as a tragic catastrophe.

However, not all of writers were anti-war. While poets such as Owen and Sassoon were deeply critical of the war machine, and heedless politicians and generals, they did not consider the war itself to be futile. They would not have taken issue with the last verse of *In Flanders Fields*, in which the dead call upon the living to "take up our quarrel with the foe".

First published anonymously in 1915, *In Flanders Fields* was written by John McCrae, a Canadian doctor tending to Allied soldiers near Ypres. It remains one of the most famous and popular poems of the war.

> The darkness crumbles away –
> It is the same old druid Time as ever.
> Only a live thing leaps my hand –
> A queer sardonic rat –
> As I pull the parapet's poppy to stick behind my ear.
> Droll rat, they would shoot you if they knew
> Your cosmopolitan sympathies.
> Now you have touched this English hand
> You will do the same to a German –
> Soon, no doubt, if it be your pleasure
> To cross the sleeping green between.

EXTRACT FROM *BREAK OF DAY IN THE TRENCHES* **BY ISAAC ROSENBERG, WRITTEN JUNE 1916**

A self-portrait by Rosenberg
Isaac Rosenberg grew up in the poor Jewish communities in London's East End in the early years of the 20th century. His poor health, and particularly his weak chest, was ill-suited to the cold and wet conditions of trench life.

APOLLINAIRE

~

BORN WILHELM DE KOSTROWITZKY in 1880, Guillaume Apollinaire was the most influential avant-garde poet in early 20th-century France. A close friend of Picasso and a champion of Cubism, he wrote classical, lyrical poems and also bold, provocative, modernist works. In many of these he sculpted his words into graphic images on the page. After receiving a commission in the infantry in 1915, he was badly gassed, and then, in March 1916, suffered a serious shrapnel wound to the head that put him out of action for the rest of the war. He died in the influenza epidemic as it swept through Europe, in November 1918.

> In Flanders fields the poppies blow
> Between the crosses, row on row,
> That mark our place; and in the sky
> The larks, still bravely singing, fly
> Scarce heard amid the guns below.
>
> We are the Dead. Short days ago
> We lived, felt dawn, saw sunset glow,
> Loved and were loved, and now we lie
> In Flanders fields.
>
> Take up our quarrel with the foe:
> To you from failing hands we throw
> The torch; be yours to hold it high.
> If ye break faith with us who die
> We shall not sleep, though poppies grow
> In Flanders fields.

EXTRACT FROM *IN FLANDERS FIELDS* **BY JOHN McCRAE, FIRST PUBLISHED IN 1915**

Pressed poppy
The poppy became a powerful image of the soldiers' sacrifice.

Bent double, like old beggars under sacks,
Knock-kneed, coughing like hags, we cursed through sludge,
Till on the haunting flares we turned our backs
And towards our distant rest began to trudge.
Men marched asleep. Many had lost their boots
But limped on, blood-shot. All went lame; all blind;
Drunk with fatigue; deaf even to the hoots
Of tired, outstripped Five-Nines that dropped behind.

Gas! Gas! Quick, boys! – An ecstasy of fumbling,
Fitting the clumsy helmets just in time;
But someone still was yelling out and stumbling,
And flound'ring like a man in fire or lime…
Dim, through the misty panes and thick green light,
As under a green sea, I saw him drowning.
In all my dreams, before my helpless sight,
He plunges at me, guttering, choking drowning.

EXTRACT FROM WILFRED OWEN'S POEM, *DULCE ET DECORUM EST,*
DRAFTED IN OCTOBER 1917

Wilfred Owen
Not a pacifist, Owen was a courageous officer, liked and respected by his men. He won the Military Cross in October 1918.

Alan Seeger
When war broke out, Alan Seeger, although a US citizen, quickly volunteered for the French Foreign Legion. Seeger was killed on the Somme on July 4, 1916 and the statue in Paris commemorating the American volunteers is modelled on him.

Siegfried Sassoon
Before the war Sassoon was something of an idle country dilettante, but the war transformed him and he wrote emotionally about the realities of the conflict. Unlike many of his contemporaries, he survived the war to write several volumes of memoirs.

Scene of desolation
The impression made on young, idealistic and articulate men by the horror and suffering that characterized the Western Front produced a body of powerful literature and poetry protesting at the loss of a generation.

God knows 'twere better to be deep
Pillowed in silk and scented down,
Where love throbs out in blissful sleep,
Pulse nigh to pulse, and breath to breath,
Where hushed awakenings are dear…
But I've a rendezvous with Death
At midnight in some flaming town,
When Spring trips north again this year,
And I to my pledged word am true,
I shall not fail that rendezvous.

EXTRACT FROM *RENDEZVOUS WITH DEATH*
BY ALAN SEEGER, WRITTEN 1916

Ribs are scattered over the ground like the bars of old broken cages along with bits of blackened leather and battered drinking mugs and mess tins… Sometimes from elongated humps in the ground – for all the unburied dead end up by becoming part of the soil – a scrap of cloth pokes out to indicate that here some human being was destroyed.

EXTRACT FROM
LE FEU

Comrade, I did not want to kill you… You were only an idea to me before, an abstraction that lived in my mind and called forth its appropriate response. It was that abstraction I stabbed… Forgive me, comrade. We always see it too late. Why do they never tell us that you are poor devils like us, that your mothers are just as anxious as ours, and that we have the same fear of death, and the same dying and the same agony – Forgive me, comrade; how could you be my enemy? If we threw away these rifles and this uniform you could be my brother just like Kat…

EXTRACT FROM *ALL QUIET ON THE WESTERN FRONT*
BY ERICH REMARQUE, PUBLISHED 1929

Erich Maria Remarque
Remarque's novel *All Quiet on the Western Front* depicted the horrors of the war from the point of view of the ordinary German soldier and remains probably the most famous novel about the war.

Cet ouvrage est publié en deux volumes, à **1 fr. 75** chacun

Select - Collection

HENRI BARBUSSE

Le Feu

Tome 1

ERNEST
FLAMMARION
ÉDITEUR

Le Feu
Henri Barbusse's novel, describing the experiences of a group of French soldiers with stark realism, was published in Paris in 1916.

THE LAST GREAT BATTLES
1918

~

WITH THE ARRIVAL OF LARGE NUMBERS OF
AMERICAN TROOPS IMMINENT, THE GERMANS KNEW AT
THE BEGINNING OF 1918 THAT THEY HAD TO SECURE
VICTORY AGAINST THE BRITISH AND FRENCH IN
THE SPRING. IN MARCH THEY LAUNCHED A SERIES OF
FIVE OFFENSIVES ON THE WESTERN FRONT, BUT
ALTHOUGH SOME MAJOR ADVANCES WERE MADE, THERE
WAS NO DECISIVE BREAKTHROUGH. BY JULY THE ALLIES
WERE READY TO COUNTERATTACK. MEANWHILE,
GERMANY'S ALLIES WERE STRUGGLING TO AVOID
A COLLAPSE ON OTHER FRONTS.

~

American soldiers in action
"Doughboys", as the American soldiers were
known, head out on a trench raid carrying hand
grenades in canvas bags. The arrival of the Americans
spelt the end of German hopes for victory in the war.

A RACE AGAINST TIME

AT THE END OF 1917, PEACE APPEARED TO BE FARTHER AWAY THAN AT ANY TIME SINCE JUNE 1914. THE BRITISH ARMIES ON THE WESTERN FRONT WERE EXHAUSTED AND THE FRENCH ARMIES HAD STILL NOT FULLY RECOVERED FROM THE EFFECTS OF THE SPRING NIVELLE OFFENSIVE. FACING THEM WERE GERMAN ARMIES THAT WOULD SHORTLY ENJOY THE ADVANTAGE OF SUPERIORITY OF NUMBERS AND HOLD THE INITIATIVE FOR THE FIRST TIME SINCE THE OPENING WEEKS OF THE WAR.

FOLLOWING THE SIGNING of the armistice with Russia in December 1917, Germany had regained the position it had secured for itself in the period before the war – that of the strongest single power in Europe, with such advantages of size, position, population and industrial capacity that it could not be defeated by the other European powers. The entry of the United States into the war had, however, changed the balance of power. The question in the minds of all the combatants at the end of the year was whether Germany would be able to defeat Britain and France before the Americans could arrive in time to tip the scales decisively against it.

GERMAN STRATEGY FOR 1918

On November 11, 1917 Ludendorff and selected chiefs of staff met at Mons to determine German military strategy for 1918 – or, more accurately, to determine when and against which enemy to mount an attack in the spring. Without the means to conduct a general offensive on the Western Front, the German high command took the decision to mount a series of massive, closely-phased attacks that would either break the Allies' front conclusively or break their will to resist. Either way, the result would be a defeat that no number of American troops arriving in Europe could reverse.

The Germans also decided to focus on the strongest of their enemies, Britain, and to launch the initial attack on the Arras–St Quentin sector against the British Third and Fifth Armies. They calculated that a British defeat in northern France, where the British armies lacked space in which to manoeuvre and could be divided from the French armies, would seriously affect the French. On the other hand, victory over the French, in sectors of the Western Front where there was space for them to retreat without grave strategic risk, would not

necessarily affect British capacity to pursue the war. It is true that Germany's best chance of securing victory probably did lie in defeating Britain. But the vulnerability of the British armies on the Western Front was greatest in the north – where the ability of the armies to manoeuvre was more limited than in Picardy and where the Channel ports might be secured. In any event, an assault on the Arras-St Quentin sector required an advance to the southwest if the British armies were to be divided from the French, but to the northwest if the British armies were to be rolled up from the south. An offensive against the British armies in Picardy would also involve a German advance across the Somme battlefield and the area left devastated by the Germans themselves in the course of their withdrawal to the Hindenburg Line in 1917.

Despite the obvious problems, the German high command believed it had little choice in the matter. Ludendorff would have preferred to strike at the northern British armies, but it was vital to take the state of the ground into consideration. Having seen the difficulties created by the mud at Ypres in 1917, the Germans concluded that a March offensive was possible over the ground of Picardy, whereas the ground in Flanders would not be sufficiently dry before April. With time at a premium, the Germans committed themselves to a battle across the most devastated part of the front against an enemy they considered tactically less skilled and less able to respond effectively to events than the French.

FLAWS IN THE GERMANS' PLANS

The Germans planned to have a thin fighting line, into which reserves would be fed under the direction of the formations leading the attack. The fighting line itself would be firepower-heavy, and include artillery withdrawn from parent units in order to give direct support to the infantry. Special

"storm battalions" would be trained to operate in small groups that could exploit gaps and bypass resistance to break through the enemy rear positions after the initial assault. The assault would employ a detailed fire plan that had been used to great effect against the Russians at Riga in September 1917.

The preparations of the Germans for the offensive were impressive but not flawless. The assault was primarily dependent upon manpower and had no means other than men for the break-out

"Reinforcements were brought up from somewhere but it was hopeless. The Fifth Army was well whacked, with a German division facing one battalion of our lads. Hopelessly outnumbered."

BRITISH LANCE-CORPORAL SHARPE DESCRIBING THE IMMEDIATE EFFECTS OF THE FIRST GERMAN OFFENSIVE, LAUNCHED ON MARCH 21, 1918

phase that would follow any breakthrough. This was because Germany had been unable to maintain large cavalry forces on the Western Front and had failed to provide itself with light tank formations. It was also the case that unless the initial offensive in Ludendorff's planned series resulted in a decisive victory, the Germans would be forced to occupy conquered ground with fewer troops than were available beforehand. Each successive attack would inevitably worsen the Germans' problems. If the Allied forces were able to weather the initial assault, they would be able to reconstitute the line with the growing numbers of American troops.

In preparing for the 1918 offensive Ludendorff stated a willingness to accept the loss of a million men as the price of victory. Leaving aside all moral considerations, such a price was beyond German means in 1918. The "storm battalions" could only be raised by combing line units for their best officers and men. The price of this concentration of quality

German infantry staging an attack
This photograph was probably taken during training, but it gives a vivid impression of the assault faced by the British Fifth Army in the first of the German spring offensives.

in elite formations was the degrading of the combat performance of all other divisions. This meant that the greater part of German losses would be sustained by the elite formations – the battalions least able to absorb losses – while the task of defence would be left to forces of lower quality. The only way of hiding this weakness was to retain the initiative – but this would involve continuous offensive action, which was beyond German means.

RELATIONS BETWEEN BRITAIN AND FRANCE

In preparing for the spring offensive, Ludendorff made the assumption that the German armies would be able to defeat the British without French intervention. This was not an unnatural assumption to make given how the war had been fought to date. In November 1917, however, an organization was created that would ensure the effective co-ordination of Anglo-French efforts after March 1918. The Passchendaele offensive in October had cost Haig whatever confidence his prime minister, Lloyd George, had ever had in him. Unable to dismiss his senior field commander, the premier sought ways of curbing Haig's freedom of action, one of which was the creation of a supreme war council. The council would have executive powers, so reducing Haig to a position of inferiority vis-à-vis its chairman, Foch.

The proposal that Foch should be chairman made the council wholly unacceptable to Haig and his faithful defender, Robertson, the Chief of the Imperial General Staff who, in February, was replaced by the francophile Wilson. In March 1918 Haig sought to avoid Foch's council by a bilateral personal arrangement with Pétain, under which the two national commanders undertook to support each other should the need arise.

Australian victims of a gas attack, May 1918
Gas played a significant role in the Germans' preliminary bombardments in 1918, often being employed against the Allied forces' second line of resistance.

American troops landing at Le Havre, July 1918
The American troops, whose numbers began to swell rapidly from May, were much admired by the other Allied forces for their physique and initial enthusiasm for battle.

ON THE BRINK OF DEFEAT

The arguments over the role of Foch and the nebulous arrangements in which Haig placed his trust would have mattered little if the British had not become in urgent need of French support in March. Haig was to be converted to the principle of co-ordination of effort as a result of defeats in March that arose at least in part from mistaken British assumptions. The most significant of these was the failure to anticipate the nature of the German offensive. To the British high command, used to measuring its advances in terms of yards per month, it seemed impossible that the Germans would break the line and so achieve what had been beyond the Allies for more than three years. At the end of 1917 the British had adopted the defensive tactics employed so effectively by the Germans, and had then assumed that the Germans would be no more successful than the Allies in restoring mobility to the battlefield. Compounding this error was the fact that the part of the British line on which Ludendorff proposed to unleash his armies was the weakest. The British Fifth Army was the worst commanded and administered of the four British armies on the Western Front, but it had the longest and least prepared sector to defend, and only 11 battalions in the front line compared to the Third Army's 21. Furthermore, up to five days before the German offensive began, Haig's headquarters insisted that it would not be subjected to attack.

As February gave way to March, and as the significance of all other fronts lessened, the British armies on the Western Front stood on the edge of their greatest defeat of the war in the first of the German spring offensives: the Michael Offensive. Whether or not the defeat would be fatal to the Allied cause would only become apparent as each offensive planned by Ludendorff failed to achieve a conclusive breakthrough before the arrival of significant numbers of American troops. By July the Allies would be ready to launch the first of many counter-offensives against the Germans.

"Our lines are falling back. There are too many fresh English and American regiments over there. There's too much corned beef and white wheat bread. Too many new guns. Too many aeroplanes."

ERICH MARIA REMARQUE DESCRIBING, IN HIS NOVEL, *ALL QUIET ON THE WESTERN FRONT*, THE SITUATION THAT CONFRONTED THE GERMAN FORCES IN THE AUTUMN OF 1918

PEACE TALKS AND THE RUSSIAN CIVIL WAR
DECEMBER 9, 1917 – DECEMBER 31, 1918

~

An armistice between Russia and Germany led to nearly three months of negotiations before treaty terms were agreed. The Bolsheviks fought for control of Russia, but lost large swathes of territory in the west, including the Ukraine. By the end of 1918 White Russians, supporters of the tsar, were on the ascendant. In May 1918 Romania agreed a treaty with the Central Powers that greatly advantaged Germany.

~

1917 DECEMBER 9
Armistice signed by Romania and Central Powers

1917 DECEMBER 15
28-day armistice signed by Russia and Germany

DECEMBER 22
Brest-Litovsk peace talks start

DECEMBER 22
First major battle of Russian Civil War begins in Rostov, following its capture by Red Guards

DECEMBER 26
Bolsheviks temporarily break off negotiations because of German demands

1918 JANUARY 9
Kornilov and Alexeev issue White Volunteer Army manifesto, outlining policy of resistance against Reds and Germans

1918 JANUARY 24
Lenin's policy of seeking immediate peace rejected in favour of Trotsky's "no war, no peace"

FEBRUARY 6
Germany gives ultimatum to Romania regarding peace talks

FEBRUARY 10
Trotsky quits Brest-Litovsk talks for fourth time

FEBRUARY 14
Red Army formed

FEBRUARY 18
Germany resumes war with Russia

FEBRUARY 23
German negotiators arrive in Bucharest; peace terms for Romania become harsher

FEBRUARY 24
Russian Soviets accept German terms

FEBRUARY 27
Germany issues ultimatum to Romania insisting its peace terms are accepted

MARCH 3
Treaty of Brest-Litovsk signed

MARCH 5
Romania and Central Powers sign preliminary peace at Buftea

APRIL 13
Kornilov killed and is succeeded by Denikin as leader of White Volunteer Army in southern Russia

MAY 7
Treaty of Bucharest signed by Romania and Central Powers

MAY 14
Czech Tsarist POWs seize town of Chelyabinsk

MAY 24
British squadron lands at Murmansk

JUNE 29
Czech forces capture Vladivostok, having taken a number of towns along the Trans-Siberian Railway

JULY 31
Allied forces take Archangelsk in northern Russia

AUGUST 3
British and Japanese troops land at Vladivostok

AUGUST 30
Assassination attempt on Lenin marks beginning of "Red Terror"

OCTOBER 1
Ironside arrives in Archangelsk to take up role as new Allied commander-in-chief

NOVEMBER 18
Kolchak installed as supreme leader of Whites

NOVEMBER 26
Allied troops land at Odessa in southern Russia

DECEMBER 25
White forces seize Perm; French land at Sebastopol

KEY

- ■ Treaty of Brest-Litovsk negotiations Dec 15, 1917–Mar 3, 1918
- ■ Treaty of Bucharest negotiations Dec 9, 1917–May 7, 1918
- ■ Russian Civil War Dec 22, 1917–Dec 31, 1918

Treaties and Civil War

Germans standing by dead countrymen
German troops were killed in February 1918 by Bolshevik forces when, with treaty talks in deadlock, they began to advance through Latvia towards Petrograd.

FOLLOWING THE SIGNING of an armistice by Russia and Germany on December 15, 1917, formal peace negotiations between the two countries began at Brest-Litovsk on the 22nd. Trotsky, the Bolshevik commissar for foreign affairs, put forward proposals based on no indemnities, no annexation, and self-determination for subject peoples. Negotiations were long and angry, and in February, when Trotsky rejected the punishing German demands, the Germans renewed the fighting. Lenin, almost alone, recognized that a "breathing spell" was vital for the revolution, and he eventually forced his opinion through the Soviet Central Committee by threatening resignation. The treaty was duly signed on March 3, 1918.

THE TREATY OF BREST-LITOVSK

The terms of the treaty were harsh, stripping Russia of large swathes of its former empire, and leaving Poland and the Baltic states and, in effect Finland and the Ukraine, in German hands. In reality, these lands were already outside Bolshevik control. The Central Powers had agreed to recognize an independent Ukraine on January 9, 1918, signing a peace treaty with the new state a month later. Their

Armistice and treaty lines
Between December 1917 and March 1918 the Russian Empire lost control of a large area to the east of the armistice line. As a result of the treaty, it lost 32 per cent of its arable land and 69 per cent of its industry.

troops had thereby been able to advance deep into Ukraine, putting further pressure on Russia to sign the treaty. The Bolsheviks also agreed to pay financial "compensation" for war losses.

The Turks gained some territory and the promise of control of Baku and its oilfields.

TREATY OF BREST-LITOVSK
March 3, 1918

— Armistice line Dec 15, 1917
— Line set by Treaty of Brest-Litovsk Mar 3, 1918

Austria-Hungary gained nothing, while minor concessions in Ruthenia, eastern Galicia and Bukovina were granted to the Ukraine, thus permanently alienating the Poles from the "peace".

THE TREATY OF BUCHAREST

The collapse of the Russian armies in late 1917 had prompted Romania to sign an armistice with Germany on December 9. Treaty negotiations were complicated by the territorial demands of the other Central Powers, and the Treaty of Bucharest, signed on May 7, 1918, awarded some territory to Austria-Hungary and Bulgaria. Romania was made economically servile, with its agricultural surpluses and oil resources placed at Germany's disposal.

Occupying territories and enforcing these treaty provisions was to prove costly to the Germans who, despite keeping about 40 divisions in the east, were still unable to exploit the resources fully. Neither treaty lasted long, the Allies annulling them, as promised, when victory was achieved.

CIVIL WAR IN RUSSIA

One effect of Brest-Litovsk was to end the coalition government of the Bolsheviks and the Social Revolutionaries, who voted against the treaty. An assassination attempt by the Social Revolutionaries against Lenin on August 30 marked the beginning of the "Red Terror". The Bolsheviks moved their government to Moscow and adopted the title "Russian Communist Party (Bolshevik)".

By May, when the Treaty of Bucharest was signed, Russia was in chaos, embroiled in a civil war in which the Bolsheviks had to fight many different enemies, some of whom were as willing to fight each other as the Bolsheviks. They ranged from socialists who supported the February Revolution, but not the Bolsheviks' October Revolution, to former tsarist generals.

Considerable numbers of these counter-revolutionaries ("White Russians") gathered in Siberia, under the leadership of Admiral Kolchak,

Czech Legion
Czech soldiers were on their way through Siberia to Vladivostok when fighting broke out between them and the Bosheviks. They seized part of the Trans-Siberian Railway and controlled it through the use of heavily armoured trains.

who made his headquarters at Omsk. They had support from the Allies and also from an unexpectedly influential group, the Czech Legion. During the war some 30,000 deserters from the Austro-Hungarian army had fought for tsarist Russia. They now transferred their allegiance to White Russia. As a trained force, they were more than a match for the Bolsheviks who, by the end of July, had lost most of Siberia and the Urals, with the Czechs controlling the Trans-Siberian Railway.

ALLIED INVOLVEMENT

In the summer, the counter-revolution received further support when Allied forces landed in the north and later at Vladivostok. Their motives were confused and, in spite of the view of both Wilson and Lloyd George that the government of Russia was the business of the Russians, the Allies soon became involved with the White Russian forces. By the end of 1918 a largely British force,

Workers unite
A 1917 poster calls on workers to unite with the Red Army to fight the tsar's forces in Petrograd. Faced with the need to consolidate their control in Russia, the new leadership agreed to an armistice with the Central Powers, but balked at the peace terms offered.

supplemented by Latvians, Finns, Estonians, and even Australians and Italians, held substantial territory in the north. Vladivostok was occupied by US and Japanese forces (the latter seeking territorial gains); the French were in Odessa and Sebastopol, and Allied troops were co-operating in the east with Kolchak.

At the end of 1917, the Don Cossacks in the south had rebelled. In 1918 a number of tsarist generals, including Kornilov, Denikin and Wrangel, led further risings in the south. The counter-revolutionary movement encouraged the separatist tendencies of the peoples recently liberated from tsarist rule, who were also encouraged by the Allies' espousal of the principle of self-determination. In Finland, civil war between communists and their opponents erupted, and revolt in the Ukraine was only prevented by the German presence. With White Russian forces advancing from all sides, by the end of 1918 the Bolsheviks' situation looked hopeless.

"Michael", the first of the offensives planned by Ludendorff for 1918, broke the British Fifth Army on the Somme, but was only a partial success because it then failed to take Arras. This set a pattern for the next two offensives, both of which met with initial success but subsequently failed to achieve their main objective. By the time of the last two offensives, in June and July, there were obvious signs of German exhaustion.

MARCH 21
Ludendorff launches Michael Offensive: 65 divisions attack on 100-km (60-mile) front over the old Somme battlefields. Massive bombardment aided by mist

MARCH 23
Péronne captured as Germans make rapid advance; British 5th Army virtually destroyed. First long-distance shelling of Paris

MARCH 27
German 18th Army under Hutier takes Montdidier

MARCH 28
Failure of strong German attack (Mars Offensive) against Arras

APRIL 4
Michael Offensive peters out and line stabilizes

APRIL 9
German Georgette Offensive begins in Flanders. Four German divisions attack one Portuguese division, which immediately breaks. British again forced to retreat

APRIL 12
Voluntary British withdrawal of 2nd Army south of Ypres

APRIL 17
Renewal of Georgette Offensive

APRIL 24
German offensive at Villers-Bretonneux uses 13 tanks

APRIL 25
Germans take Kemmel Hill, south of Ypres

APRIL 29
Georgette Offensive comes to a halt

MAY 10
German gas attack on French and Americans in Meuse-Argonne sector

MAY 27
Blücher-Yorck Offensive begins. Achieves breakthrough against Allied positions on the Aisne

MAY 29
Germans occupy Soissons

MAY 30
Germans reach Marne

JUNE
Influenza epidemic reaches Western Front; German troops especially badly hit

JUNE 3
American action at Château Thierry helps halt Blücher-Yorck Offensive

JUNE 6
American counterattack in Battle of Belleau Wood

JUNE 9
Gneisenau Offensive makes limited gains

JUNE 13
Gneisenau Offensive ends

JUNE 25
Battle of Belleau Wood ends in success for Americans

JULY 15
Marne–Reims Offensive, the last by Germans, begins with attack on Marne by 52 divisions

JULY 17
Marne–Reims Offensive halted after only two days

KEY

■ Michael Offensive Mar 21–Apr 4	■ Gneisenau Offensive Jun 9–13
■ Georgette Offensive Apr 9–29	■ Marne–Reims Offensive Jul 15–17
■ Blücher-Yorck Offensive May 27– Jun 4	■ Other events

The German Spring Offensives

German infantry preparing to attack
Soldiers cross the Aisne-Oise Canal in preparation for an attack on the first morning of the Michael Offensive. The offensive was spearheaded by "stormtroopers", specially trained infantry whose role was to advance rapidly through any gaps that been created in the enemy line.

T HE WITHDRAWAL OF RUSSIA from the war enabled Germany to send troops from the Eastern Front to the Western Front, giving them a slight superiority in numbers. It was essential to take advantage of this before the Americans entered the line in significant numbers, and Ludendorff set about planning successive attacks that would drive a wedge between the British and French armies and destroy the British. The first of the attacks was codenamed Michael, after Germany's patron saint.

THE MICHAEL OFFENSIVE

The Michael Offensive – also known as the *Kaiserschlacht* (Kaiser's battle) – was directed by the German Second, Seventeenth and Eighteenth Armies against the British Third and Fifth Armies on the Somme (see map page 254). In the initial assault, launched on March 21, the Germans were supported by 6,473 guns – almost half the number of German guns on the Western Front – plus more than 3,500 mortars and 730 aircraft. To meet this powerful force, the British, who were stretched out along a 95-km (60-mile) front, had just 2,500 guns, 1,400 mortars and 579 aircraft.

When the men in the British Fifth Army were woken by the Germans' preliminary bombardment in the early hours of the morning, they immediately felt that it was more intense than any they had experienced before. It was, in the words of Gough, the Fifth Army commander, "a bombardment so sustained and steady that it at once gave me the impression of some crushing, smashing power". Before midday the Fifth Army was in retreat, overwhelmed by the German artillery and then what appeared to be inexhaustible

A stormtrooper's equipment
The shock troops of the 1918 offensives already resembled the German stormtroopers of the Second World War. Armed with lightweight submachine-guns and stick grenades, some even wore a *Totenkopf* (Death's Head) badge.

STICK GRENADE

DEATH'S HEAD BADGE

Air-cooled barrel

32-round "snail drum" magazine

MP 18/1 SUBMACHINE-GUN

numbers of advancing German troops. On the first day alone German forces took about 25,500 hectares (98.5 square miles) of British-held territory, which was about the total amount of German-held territory reconquered by the British during the whole of the 140 days of the Somme offensive in 1916. Over the next two days, they reached the line of the Somme between Péronne and St Simon. Without in-depth defensive positions, the British Fifth Army was literally ripped to pieces. At the end of the third day, for example, the XIX Corps could only muster 50 men from the eight battalions that had held the original forward positions astride the upper Somme and St Quentin Canal on March 21.

The Germans continued to advance across the old Somme battlefield, taking Albert, on the Ancre, on March 26 and Montdidier on the 27th. In doing so they briefly divided the British and French armies. The French had already made divisions available to help the British Fifth Army. Faced, however, with the need to maintain formations in order to cover routes to the south, they concluded that they could not make more divisions available to support their ally.

ERICH LUDENDORFF
~

I N AUGUST 1914 ERICH LUDENDORFF (1865–1937) demonstrated his dynamic leadership skills at Liège. Subsequently serving as chief of staff to Hindenburg, commander of the German Eighth Army on the Eastern Front, he helped secure victories at Tannenberg and the Masurian Lakes.

The offensives in Galicia and Poland in 1915 provided Ludendorff with more success, but Falkenhayn rejected his plans for securing a decisive victory on the Eastern Front. In August 1916 he became quartermaster general of the German army when Hindenburg replaced Falkenhayn as chief of staff. He was an ardent supporter of unrestricted submarine warfare, which ultimately led to the entry of the USA into the war.

As the driving force behind Hindenburg, Ludendorff had by 1917 gained control over Germany's economic and political life as well as its army. He negotiated the Brest-Litovsk and Bucharest treaties in 1917 and planned the spring offensives of 1918 against the Allies. After August 8, 1918, when the Germans were defeated at Amiens, he admitted that outright victory could not be won. He refused, however, to accept the terms of the armistice in October and was forced to resign.

GERMAN HALT AT ARRAS

In the first few days of Michael, many British troops had felt that defeat was not far away. But impressive as the initial success of Michael had been, not everything had gone the Germans' way. The German forces involved in the advance to Montdidier were now exhausted and their success had been in the sector where it had not been anticipated. The Germans had planned for their main success to be

around Arras, from where they were to advance against the British armies to the north. The forces on the upper Somme had been intended to have only a covering role, and when it became clear that they needed the support of fresh formations, the German high command was unable to provide them. Checked in front of Arras on March 28, the Germans allowed Michael to run down even as their Fourth and Sixth Armies were reinforced in readiness for the next offensive, Georgette. This was to be directed against the British First and Second Armies along the Lys in Flanders.

British gun in action
British troops attempted to withstand the German advance during the Michael Offensive, but they were soon overwhelmed. The Germans reached the British gun-line on the first day, capturing 383 guns from the Fifth Army and 150 from the Third.

THE GEORGETTE OFFENSIVE

Georgette opened on April 9, and – with nine German divisions initially directed against four comparatively inexperienced Portuguese brigades – it resulted in immediate and major German gains. An advance of 6 km (4 miles) brought the German Sixth Army to the Lys River on the first day. Neuve Chapelle, Messines and Armentières were then captured in quick succession. But despite gains that by April 17 had forced the British to abandon the Passchendaele ridge and to withdraw almost into Ypres itself, the German Sixth Army had failed to achieve major, still less decisive, strategic success. It had broken open the front between Béthune and Armentières in the first two days, but had then failed to secure the crucial road junction at Hazebrouck before British, Australian and French divisions could arrive from the south.

The Germans continued to attack, capturing Kemmel Hill on the 25th and the neighbouring Scherpenberg Hill – from French forces – on the 29th. More significantly, however, they failed in their attempt to revive the offensive in front of Amiens when, on April 24, the first tank battle of the war was fought in Villers Bretonneux. The Germans succeeded in capturing the village, but it was retaken in a night attack on April 24/25 and the battle then died. On April 29 the Georgette attack as a whole was abandoned.

THE IMPORTANCE OF FRENCH SUPPORT

The fact that the British had survived both Michael and Georgette had much to do with the support they had received from the French. As British troops had reeled before the two onslaughts, the French had fed divisions into the path of the Germans,

> *Things were so sudden, so hopelessly unexpected, and those who should have given warning had none themselves. Even in our first position, people would come weeping to us to know if they should go or stay, and we couldn't tell them. They looked to us for help and we couldn't give them it, they looked to us to stay the attack while they collected their few belongings and we couldn't do it.*

BRITISH MAJOR "JOHN" LYNE DESCRIBING THE EFFECT OF THE GEORGETTE OFFENSIVE ON THE LOCAL POPULATION IN THE VICINITY OF ARMENTIÈRES

Refugees from Armentières
The Germans entered Armentières on April 10. It had been occupied by them once before, in 1914, but it had quickly been recaptured by the British. The Georgette Offensive reduced the town to ruins.

German offensives
With the aim of defeating the British before the French, the first German offensive in 1918 was launched on the Somme. It resulted in the capture of Montdidier, but not Arras as planned, so failing, like the four offensives that followed, to win the war.

THE WESTERN FRONT
Mar 21– Jun 4, 1918

— German front line Mar 21

– – – German front line Jun 4

➡ German offensive

💥 Tank battle

Apr 9
Georgette Offensive opens. Germans enjoy an unopposed 5-km (3-mile) advance on the first morning

Mar 21
Michael Offensive opens. Within days British 5th Army is destroyed although 3rd Army is able to hold its main positions

May 27
Blücher-Yorck Offensive opens. Germans advance to a maximum depth of 65 km (40 miles) within 5 days

Nicuport
BELGIAN King Albert
BELGIUM
Dunkerque
Calais
English Channel
FLANDERS
2ND ARMY Plumer
Ypres
Kemmel
Lys
Scheldt
Armentières
Hazebrouck
Lille
Neuve Chapelle
6TH ARMY Quast
Béthune
1ST ARMY Horne
FRANCE
Souchez
17TH ARMY O. von Below
Arras
3RD ARMY Byng
2ND ARMY Marwitz
Bapaume
Cambrai
Albert
Amiens
Somme
Péronne
APR 24 Villers Bretonneux
18TH ARMY Hutier
St Quentin
Vervins
5TH ARMY Gough
Montdidier
La Fère
7TH ARMY Böhn
Noyon
Laon
Craonne
1ST ARMY F. von Below
Rethel
Compiègne
Oise
Aisne
Soissons
Reims
6TH ARMY Duchene
Vesle
5TH ARMY Micheler
Chantilly
Château Thierry
Marne
Epernay
Meaux
PARIS

0 km 10 20 30 40 50
0 miles 10 20 30 40 50

taking over British sectors in order to free British divisions, and allowing six badly depleted British divisions to move into quiet sectors of the French line. It was a terrible irony that as a result of this policy, British divisions were sent to the Chemin des Dames and the Aisne, sectors to which the Germans turned their attention following their failure to defeat the British on the Somme and Lys.

BLÜCHER-YORCK OFFENSIVE

If the German plan of campaign for spring 1918 was to succeed, individual offensives had to be halted early enough for assault forces and reserves to be redeployed even as Allied reserves were being committed to threatened sectors. There was also a

Propaganda poster
Although the German offensives in March and April had not quite gone according to plan, they had inflicted great damage on the Allies – as this German poster proudly proclaimed.

need for each offensive to follow hard on the heels of its predecessor in order to exploit advantages of numbers and timing. These conditions were not met with Michael and Georgette. Michael was initially so successful that the German high command persisted with it, so delaying the start of Georgette, while the employment of 46 divisions in Flanders during the Georgette offensive meant a delay of one

A casualty at Hazebrouck
The British successfully resisted the German advance on Hazebrouck. They were helped by the fact that German troops, deprived of alcohol by the Allied blockade, had found huge depots of wine and spirits and had got drunk.

month in moving formations into position for the third offensive: Blücher-Yorck. Yet this offensive, launched on May 27, was perhaps the most successful of the German efforts in 1918.

REASONS FOR SUCCESS

On the first day of Blücher-Yorck, divisions from the German Seventh Army achieved advances of 19 km (12 miles) and in one sector there was an advance of 65 km (40 miles) within five days. There were a number of reasons for this success. The First and Seventh Armies had gathered some 41 divisions and 3,719 guns for the attack, with the result that the initial bombardment was to represent the peak of German artillery achievement in 1918. Adding to the effectiveness of the bombardment was the French failure to prepare in-depth defences in the 40-km (25-mile) sector of attack, on the eastern Chemin des Dames. This failure was compounded by the refusal of the commander of the French Sixth Army, Duchêne, to conduct an in-depth defensive battle. He preferred to man front-line defensive positions in strength, and Pétain chose not to over-rule him.

As a result of the need to release troops to the reserve, the over-extended French Sixth Army had lengthened its front to 88 km (55 miles) until, by late May, its front-line divisions were holding sectors of some 7,300 m (8,000 yds). Compounding this weakness was the fact that four British divisions savaged in the earlier fighting were in the line, a result of the policy of moving exhausted formations into quiet sectors in order to release French reserves. Three of the divisions were in the sector immediately west of Reims, directly in the path of the main German effort.

Pétain had originally suspected that the main German attack in 1918 would fall on this sector, but after March 21 it had been concluded that this was now unlikely to happen. It was not until the final two days before Blücher-Yorck that German intentions became clear, by which time it was too late to remedy Allied defensive shortcomings. With the greater part of Allied infantry and artillery massed in forward positions and thus exposed to the full force of the initial German bombardment, four Allied divisions were destroyed and another four ruined within hours of the start of the Blücher-Yorck Offensive on May 27. By mid-morning the Germans had crossed the Aisne. The piecemeal commitment of reserves by Duchêne on May 27 and 28 only ensured that they were lost.

REVISION OF THE GERMAN PLAN

At this point the Germans abandoned their initial intention – to force the commitment of Allied reserves in this sector preparatory to a renewed effort north of the Somme. Instead, they decided to

FERDINAND FOCH

THE UNDENIABLE CONTRIBUTION to French wartime tactics by Ferdinand Foch (1851–1929) began well before the First World War at the Ecole de Guerre, where his influential lectures stressed the importance of offensive thinking.

Commander of the elite XX Corps from 1913, Foch launched successful counterattacks to protect Nancy and at the first battle of Marne in 1914. Although he had not yet had the chance to show his true offensive spirit, these defensive victories led to his appointment as leader of the French Northern Army Group on the Western Front. However, after two failed offensives at Arras in 1915 and his involvement in the first battle of the Somme, the value of which he had been sceptical about, Foch was sidelined in December 1916.

When Pétain took over from Nivelle as commander-in-chief in May 1917, Foch became chief of staff and really made his mark in the battles of 1918. Serving as Allied Supreme Commander on the Western Front from April that year, his armies the German offensives and recovered most of occupied France and part of Belgium before the end of the war.

expand Blücher-Yorck and drive on to Paris, so provoking the decisive battle. That same day Fère-en-Tardenois was captured and the Ourcq crossed.

On May 29 the Germans took Soissons and pressed on to the Marne, where they entered Château Thierry, just 90 km (56 miles) from Paris. They had taken some 65,000 prisoners and 800 guns, but by this time their advance was slowing down. On May 31 the Allies brought the German drive on Reims to a halt, and after minor actions over the next three days, the German Seventh Army cancelled plans to renew the offensive.

THE PEAK OF GERMAN SUCCESS

The Michael, Georgette and Blücher-Yorck offensives represented the peak of German success in 1918. Georgette very literally left the British armies in northern France and Belgium with no further room for

Prisoners at Laon
These French prisoners were among the 55,000 captured by the Germans between May 27 and June 4. At the end of the three spring offensives, over 355,00 Allied troops were either prisoners or missing.

withdrawal. Indeed, the situation in which the British armies found themselves on the Lys provoked Haig to issue a proclamation on April 11 which included the words: "With our backs to the wall and believing in the justice of our cause, each one of us must fight to the end." Against this, however, was the fact that while the German drive that secured Montdidier had separated the British and French armies, it had done so only briefly. It thus represented a failure for the German high command which had intended the separation to be permanent, laying the ground for the German defeat of first the British and then the French.

The disintegration of the British Fifth Army within three days of being attacked in the Michael Offensive had helped to convert Haig to the merits of a single French commander-in-chief who would ensure that the British received French support. Consequently, at the Doullens conference on March 26, the British and French military had decided that their separate efforts should be co-ordinated by Foch, the French chief of staff since 1917. This decision was to be of considerable benefit to the Allied effort in the future.

Also of great significance for the future was the fact that the Michael, Georgette and Blücher-Yorck offensives had exacted a toll that the German army could not afford. While, for example, the Michael attack cost the British 178,000 casualties and the French 77,000, it cost the Germans 239,000 casualties, of whom some 81,200 were from the Seventeenth Army opposite Arras. The Georgette Offensive cost the Allies around 118,00 casualties compared with German losses of 95,000. German casualties were high – during Michael some 11,000 a day – even if they were not as high as those of the

THE PARIS GUN

FROM AUGUST 29, 1914, the Germans made 30 air raids on Paris. On March 8, 1918 they dropped more than 90 bombs on the city, causing 200,000 people to flee. Consequently, Parisians were already living in some fear when, on March 23, the Germans began the first of four long-range bombardments using a weapon that they called "Wilhelm's Gun" in honour of the kaiser. Made by boring out a 38.1-cm (15-in) naval gun and inserting an inner tube, 30 m (98 ft) long and 21 cm (8.27 in) wide, the gun had a life expectancy of only 60 rounds because the powder charge was so powerful. The gun was fired at an elevation of 50° and, with a muzzle velocity of some 1,645 m (5,400 ft) per second, the 120-kg (264-lb) shell rose to a height of 38 km (24 miles). The maximum range was about 132 km (82 miles).

The first bombardment, which lasted until May 1, was from three emplacements at Crépy, near Laon; the last (August 5–9) was from the Bois de Corbie, further to the west. The Germans claimed to have fired a total of 367 shells in all, though the Parisians recorded only 320 hits on the city. With a light shell travelling a vast distance through unpredictable atmospheric conditions, what was hit was a matter of chance. The most destructive shell was one that hit a church on March 29, killing 88 people and wounding another 68. The gun was so inaccurate that it could only be used against a target the size of a city.

The Paris Gun in action
The Paris Gun did not stop the city and the government from functioning. It did, however, kill 256 and injure 620, and it increased fear among a population already subjected to air raids at night.

Bomb damage in Paris
Shortly before the first bombardment by the Paris Gun, the city was subjected to an air raid in which a number of buildings, including the War Ministry, pictured here, were destroyed.

Allies. Furthermore, they were suffered by the divisions who could least afford them – those that contained the highly trained stormtroopers.

German forces now held an extended front with lines of communication reaching back across a wasteland. (During the retreat of the Fifth Army, 248 bridges had been destroyed, and 300 locomotives and 20,000 burnt-out rail wagons abandoned.) Even more ominously for the Germans, Allied losses were being covered by the arrival of American forces. During May the number of American troops in France rose from 430,000 to 650,000 – and this was just the beginning of American deployment in strength.

INVOLVEMENT OF THE AMERICANS

The fact that the spring offensives had so far been conducted against little more than one-sixth of the total number of Allied divisions on the Western Front meant that Allied reserves could now be

A German casualty near the Aisne
The Germans had no difficulty in advancing across the Aisne on the first morning of the Blücher-Yorck offensive. However, as in the previous two spring offensives, they suffered high casualties.

"There has grown a wonderful mutual admiration and understanding between our boys and the Yanks. I'm sure the Yanks are going to prove excellent fighting troops."

AUSTRALIAN LIEUTENANT EDWIN TRUNDLE WRITING TO HIS WIFE IN JUNE

effectively redeployed. By the first days of June 1918 Allied forces were arriving on the Marne, and the French Fifth and Tenth Armies were taking over the Sixth Army's flank positions. American troops were also arriving to aid the Allied effort.

Pershing, commander of the American forces in France, had been determined that his forces should fight as one army rather than be divided up between the armies of the Allies. He had, however, been prepared to listen to the pleas of the British and French commanders for American support before it was too late. On May 28–29 the US Ist Infantry Division, in the first wartime attack of the American Expeditionary Force, had retaken the

village of Cantigny and held it against German counterattacks. More significantly, on June 3 the US 3rd Infantry Division was involved in action to the east of Château Thierry, where they blew up a bridge to prevent the Germans crossing the Marne. They also held the line on the Paris–Metz road.

Three days later, the US 2nd Infantry Division became engaged in the Battle of Belleau Wood, northwest of Château Thierry. It was to last for three weeks and cost the lives of 5,000 Americans, but it resulted in a victory that for the Germans was an ominous sign of things to come. The Americans were inexperienced but enthusiastic, and seeing them buoyed the spirits of the Allied troops.

American troops in Château Thierry
The Germans captured Château Thierry on May 30 and stayed in control of the town until forced to abandon it by an Allied advance on July 21. On both occasions, American troops were involved in the fighting that took place either nearby or within the town itself.

THE GNEISENAU OFFENSIVE

The German high command should, perhaps, have sought an armistice at the end of the Blücher-Yorck Offensive. If German armies at full strength could not win with their first attack, then successive offensives, conducted with declining strength, would not bring Germany victory. Whether Germany's enemies would have been prepared to concede an armistice is, of course, another matter.

As it was, even before Blücher–Yorck had run its course, the German high command prepared for their next offensive – Gneisenau. It was to be launched against the Montdidier–Noyon bulge with the aim of clearing Blücher–Yorck's right flank and perhaps opening the road to Paris. The defences in this sector were not well-prepared, but fortunately for the French Third Army, the haste with which the Germans attempted to redeploy formations meant that Gneisenau was the least organized of their spring attacks.

Forewarned of German intentions, the French were able to gather reserves and artillery for the counterattack. This did not, however, prevent three divisions of the French Third Army being destroyed in the opening hours of the German Eighteenth Army's attack on June 9. After an orderly withdrawal of its remaining forces, the French Third Army – with support from the Tenth – launched a counterattack on the 11th. This partially forestalled the German attack on June 12, with the result that the German advance was limited to a maximum depth of approximately 9 km (6 miles) across a 30-km (20-mile) front.

THE MARNE–REIMS OFFENSIVE

The failure of Gneisenau led the German high command on June 14 to begin preparations for a fifth offensive, despite very obvious signs of German exhaustion. Each of the German offensives was marked by widespread looting and drunkenness, and in June 1918 measures were introduced to curb the rising tide of desertions and, more seriously, the outbreak of an influenza epidemic. All armies were affected, but the Central Powers, weakened by blockade, were less able to resist than their enemies.

The German plan was to attack either side of Reims and across the Marne, so pinning down Allied reserves before launching a greater offensive in Flanders. The offensive had, however, been widely discussed throughout Europe in June, which meant that when it opened on July 15 it faced an alert defence prepared in depth in strong natural positions. Reserves concentrated against the exposed flank of the German Marne salient added to the Germans' difficulties.

Out-thought and out-fought both strategically and tactically, the Germans made only the most modest of gains outside the sector to the east of

Black Americans constructing trenches
Some 200,000 Black American troops were sent to France, where many worked as labourers. Black soldiers and officers were segregated in the US standing army and they continued to be segregated during the war, although the French were more inclined to treat them as equals.

Château Thierry, where the French Fifth and Sixth Armies met. Even in this sector the German advance was grinding to a halt by the evening of the 16th. As the French fed fresh troops into position in the forested Mont des Reims, the German high command conceded failure.

German offensives in June and July
Launched against the Montdidier–Noyon bulge on June 9, the Gneisenau Offensive destroyed three French divisions before grinding to a halt just four days later after a minor advance. The Marne–Reims Offensive launched on July 15 was no more successful.

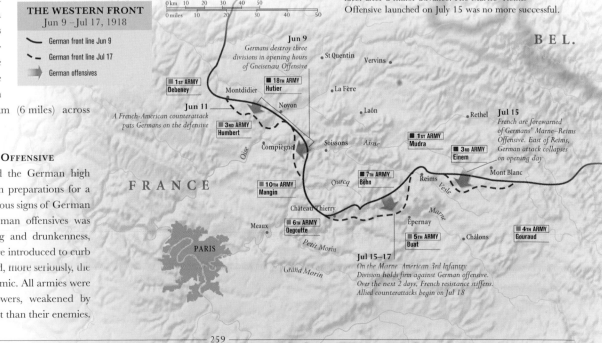

THE WESTERN FRONT
Jun 9 – Jul 17, 1918

— German front line Jun 9
- - - German front line Jul 17
➤ German offensives

Jun 9
Germans destroy three divisions in opening hours of Gneisenau Offensive

Jun 11
A French-American counterattack puts Germans on the defensive

Jul 15
French are forewarned of Germans' Marne–Reims Offensive. East of Reims, German attack collapses on opening day

Jul 15–17
On the Marne, American 3rd Infantry Division holds firm against German offensive. Over the next 2 days, French resistance stiffens. Allied counterattacks begin on Jul 18

St Quentin
Vervins
BEL.
1st ARMY Debeney
Montdidier
18th ARMY Hutier
La Fère
Noyon
Laôn
Rethel
3rd ARMY Humbert
Compiègne
Soissons
Aisne
1st ARMY Mudra
3rd ARMY Einem
Mont Blanc
FRANCE
10th ARMY Mangin
Ourcq
7th ARMY Böhn
Reims
Vesle
Château Thierry
Marne
Meaux
6th ARMY Degoutte
Épernay
Petit Morin
5th ARMY Buat
Châlons
4th ARMY Gouraud
PARIS
Grand Morin

0 km 10 20 30 40 50
0 miles 10 20 30 40 50

THE WAR IN ART

~

AMONG THE MILLIONS OF SOLDIERS who served in the First World War were thousands of artists. They included the German artist, Franz Marc, who died at Verdun in 1916, and the Italian Futurist, Umberto Boccioni, who died in a cavalry exercise. The British army even had an officer training unit, the Artists' Rifles, which attracted architects, surveyors and draughtsmen as well as sculptors and painters. One way or another, artists in uniform found ways of being useful, and expressing their war experiences. The English artist Stanley Spencer even painted signs for the sergeants' and the "men's" toilets.

From a fear that they might reveal strategy and new technology to the enemy, British soldiers were forbidden to draw while they were in the trenches. Even so, many of them evaded the regulations, concealing their sketchbooks. In 1916 the British government began to appreciate the propaganda value of authentic, "eyewitness" images, and around 100 artists were eventually licensed to record their impressions of the war. Other nations, on both sides, made arrangements similar to these.

French trench newspaper
Many artists drew cartoons to illustrate the morale-boosting trench newspapers produced by both sides on the Western Front.

Despite their official status, war artists were often obstructed by on-the-spot military commanders, irritated by the tendency of artists to "sit down and look at a place for a long time". Nor did their work always present the image of war the government desired. After Passchendaele, British war artists were banned from depicting the dead of either side.

Even once the fighting was over, the war was not necessarily finished for the artist, whose experiences might take several years to emerge, as with Otto Dix's powerful cycle of etchings, *War* (1924). After serving as a medical orderly, Max Beckmann had a nervous breakdown. In 1916 he began painting *Resurrection*, in which wounded soldiers emerge from the dark night of war into a frail and uncertain daylight. Stanley Spencer also chose this theme as the climactic scene in a series painted for the Burghclere memorial chapel in England. The dead soldiers come back to life, but there is neither joy nor sorrow on their faces.

War artist at work
War artists, such as Australian James Quinn, would record their visual impressions in the field, using them later as the basis for their final work.

Sir Stanley Spencer:
Travoys Arriving with Wounded at a Dressing Station at Smol, Macedonia
Stanley Spencer's experience of the effects of war, first as a hospital orderly in Britain, and then as a soldier in Macedonia, led him to portray in his paintings the acts of compassion shown by one human being to another. In this painting, the stretcher-bearers reach out to try and protect their wounded charges, as men and beasts gather round the lighted window of the dressing station in a scene reminiscent of the Nativity.

Egon Schiele:
Russian Officer
The Austrian Expressionist Egon Schiele was refused a post as an official war artist, but this did not stop him painting portraits of the Russian prisoners in his charge. His admiration for their stoicism in captivity is evident. He later admitted to feeling more in sympathy with the enemy countries, where he considered there to be "more thinking people", than in his own country, which was suffocating in the stultifying atmosphere of the decaying Habsburg monarchy.

Fernand Léger:
Soldier Smoking a Pipe
The French artist Léger served as an engineer, and his visual appreciation of the durable materials of war machinery is shown in the mechanical construction of this soldier. Other paintings by Léger, however, portray the terrible damage inflicted by war on human flesh.

Otto Dix:
Setting Sun (Ypern) 1918
Otto Dix enlisted in 1914 from a desire to experience humans in their "unleashed state". This painting shows the violence of war engulfing even the natural world, with the setting sun exploding like a bomb above cowering soldiers.

Wartime sketchbook
This watercolour portrait is from the sketchbook of Alexandre Zinoviev, a Russian, later a well-known stage designer, who joined the French Foreign Legion in 1914.

John Nash:
Over the Top
John Nash saw action in France before being appointed as a war artist in 1918. This painting depicts his worst experience as a soldier in an action he described as "pure murder". In December 1917 his company was ordered to carry out a diversionary attack in daylight in the snow, making them an easy target for German machine-gunners.

JULY 18
Allied counter-offensive begins with French advance to clear Marne salient

AUGUST 1
French forces occupy Soissons

AUGUST 3
Germans complete withdrawal from Marne salient

AUGUST 6
Franco-American force reaches Vesle River, thus straightening out Soissons-Reims salient

AUGUST 8
Launch of British offensive, with French in support, at Amiens (the "black day of the German army")

AUGUST 10
French forces occupy Montdidier

AUGUST 18
Start of French offensive that results in capture of Aisne Heights on 20th

AUGUST 18
British offensive in Flanders begins

AUGUST 21
British renew offensive on Somme

AUGUST 22
British forces capture Albert

AUGUST 27
French forces occupy Roye

AUGUST 28
Canadians smash through Hindenburg Line to reach Wotan position on 30th

AUGUST 29
New Zealand forces occupy Bapaume

AUGUST 30
Austro-Hungarian intention to sue for peace communicated to Germany

SEPTEMBER 2
Australian forces occupy Péronne; Canadian forces break through Wotan position

SEPTEMBER 5
German General Headquarters moved from Avesnes to Spa

SEPTEMBER 6
Germans complete withdrawal from Lys salient

SEPTEMBER 12
Launch of offensive on St Mihiel salient by Americans with some French support

SEPTEMBER 15
Start of Austro-Hungarian peace initiative and Allied offensive at Salonika

SEPTEMBER 16
Elimination of St Mihiel offensive salient completed in first victory by independent American army

SEPTEMBER 26
American and French forces begin Argonne offensive

SEPTEMBER 27
Start of British offensive between Lens and Epehy

SEPTEMBER 28
British, Belgians and French launch offensive: Fourth Battle of Ypres

SEPTEMBER 29
British offensive opens with Battle of St Quentin Canal

SEPTEMBER 29
Ludendorff calls for immediate armistice

KEY

■ Action in Champagne-Marne sector Jul 18–Aug 20	■ Action in Flanders Aug 18–Oct 3
■ Action in Somme sector Aug 8–Oct 3	■ Action in Meuse-Argonne sector Sept 12–29
	■ Other events

Beginning of the Allied Advance

German prisoners near Amiens
On August 8 the British and French launched an attack to the east of Amiens, in the Somme sector, against six German divisions that were outnumbered 6 to 1. The British alone took 13,000 prisoners on the first day.

BETWEEN JULY 18 AND NOVEMBER 11, 1918 the Allied armies conducted a series of offensives, each with limited aims, which eliminated the Germans' spring gains, took the war into territories that for years had lain well behind the front lines, and broke the German will to resist. In these four months the Allies out-fought, at both the strategic and tactical level, the Germans on ground they had held since September 1914. The key to the success of the Allies was their ability to mount a series of closely-phased offensives, each with marked local numerical superiority and for limited objectives. Taken together, they imposed an ultimately intolerable pressure on the Germans.

In fact, an Allied counterattack had taken place before July 18. On July 4, the Australian corps had mounted a small operation at Hamel, near Amiens, with the support of American infantry companies. Aiding the attack were 60 new Mark V tanks plus aircraft that parachuted supplies to forward units. The Allied forces advanced across a 5,500-m

(6,000-yd) front, and in a 90-minute attack they took Hamel. They also captured over 1,500 prisoners, two field guns and 171 machine-guns, for the loss of fewer than 1,000 casualties.

ATTACK ON THE MARNE SALIENT
On July 18 three French armies – with five American divisions – opened a campaign to recapture the Marne salient from the Germans. The inclusion of 225 Renault light tanks aided the Allies' initial attack on the vulnerable Soissons-Château Thierry road, where the Germans had failed to prepare their defensive positions properly. By marching late to their start-lines, the Allied forces took the Germans by surprise and by July 20 they had reached the Marne itself. They crossed the

river the following day. After this, however, progress was slow, partly because the land was so broken up. Fère-en-Tardenois was taken on July 27 and Soissons on August 1. On the 2nd/3rd the German Seventh and Ninth Armies completed a general withdrawal from the Marne salient. By August 4, when the offensive came to an end, the Allies had taken some 25,000 German prisoners in the course of advancing 50 km (30 miles).

OFFENSIVE AT AMIENS

On August 8 the British Fourth Army mounted an attack in front of Amiens with 456 tanks. In just one day the German front was broken over 24 km (15 miles) of its length to a maximum depth of 4 km (7 miles). Six weak German divisions were destroyed, with the British taking 13,000 prisoners

Wounded German prisoner
In many of the battles fought from July onwards, the German soldiers were not only outnumbered but had far less support from tanks and aircraft than the Allied troops. The toll of German prisoners steadily mounted.

and 400 guns. To the south the French First Army slowly advanced 5 km (3 miles) over a similar frontage before grinding to a halt.

The results achieved by the Fourth Army were little different from those registered on the first day at Cambrai in 1917. But in front of Amiens the

German defeat was marked by a collapse of formations which led Ludendorff to describe this as "the black day of the German army". Nonetheless, the German high command was able to respond quickly and effectively to this defeat. By midday on the second day, nine German divisions had been fed into the line. The British, with 145 tanks, advanced just 5 km (3 miles). On the third day of the offensive, when just 67 tanks remained in service, the only gains made were in the centre and to a depth of about 1.5 km (1 mile), at which point the British offensive was brought to an end.

PHOTOGRAPHY AND FILM

PHOTOGRAPHS WERE USED in training and propaganda, but photography in battle areas was severely restricted, and newspapers did not illustrate the actuality of trench warfare. Film, however, played an ever-increasing part in the effort to mobilize public support for the war effort. Newsreels, such as the French *Annales de la Guerre* and the official British record of the Somme in 1916, provided images of the front that were heavily censored or even staged. Cinema was immensely popular, and after 1916 films, commercial or state-funded, comedy or melodrama, took the lead in projecting the war as a contest between Good and Evil. Most commercial films were escapist, but others spread a moral message. Charlie Chaplin, in the outstanding *Shoulder Arms* (1918), was hugely popular, not least among Allied troops. Some films, such as D.W. Griffith's *Hearts of the World* (1918), encouraged an hysterical hatred of the enemy that complicated the task of the Versailles peacemakers. In Germany, a consortium of film companies, Universum Film AG (UFA), was set up as a state enterprise to make films under military control. Cinemas drew in the cold and hungry in 1917–18 as they received priority in coal and electricity supplies.

Hearts of the World
D.W. Griffith (wearing a bow-tie) during the shooting of *Hearts of the World* in France. His film attempted to bring the experience of battle and the reality of war into the movie theatre.

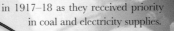

BOX OF SLIDES

FRENCH STEREOSCOPIC CAMERA

GLASS SLIDE WITH DOUBLE IMAGE

Stereoscopic camera
The war coincided with the arrival of affordable, easy-to-use cameras, thanks largely to Kodak. Particularly fashionable at the time was the stereoscopic camera, designed to mimic human vision. A special viewer was needed to appreciate the stereoscopic effect.

Attention now switched to the south where, on August 10, the French Third Army had occupied Montdidier, which had been abandoned as German forces withdrew from their most forward positions. This French effort continued, primarily around Lassigny, until the 16th. It was followed by an offensive by the Tenth Army on the 18th that resulted in the capture of the Aisne Heights on the 20th and the taking of some 8,000 prisoners in front of Noyon. As a result of what Ludendorff described as "another black day" of "heavy and irreplaceable losses", the French now threatened the German lines along the north bank of the Vesle.

BATTLE OF BAPAUME

Following diversionary attacks on the Lys, the British Third Army, with almost 200 tanks, attacked on August 21 along a 16-km (10-mile) sector between Albert and Arras. In the Battle of Bapaume that followed, Albert was retaken on the 22nd. The following day the British Fourth Army came to the support of the Third Army, and Bapaume was taken on the 29th. The battle came to an end on the 31st.

On the 26th the British First Army launched an offensive on the Arras-Cambrai road. With the weight of the offensive switched between different sectors,

Allied attacks in Flanders and France
From July 18 the Allies slowly pushed back the Germans all along the front line. The Germans reduced the length of the line in Flanders at the end of August in an attempt to halt the advance, but to no avail. They were more successful in the south, where they held up a French-US advance in the Argonne.

Australian formations were able to push across the Somme at Péronne on August 30 and secure the town on September 2. On the same day the Canadians, supported by two British divisions and 59 tanks, breached the German line, between Drocourt and Quéant, on an 8-km (5-mile) front.

With this latter success the British broke open the Hindenburg Line at one of its strongest points. In so doing, they not only carried the tide of battle into areas that had been under enemy control since August 1914 but made it impossible for the Germans to continue holding positions to the north. On August 31 German formations began to evacuate their positions on the Lys and around Kemmel Hill, so reducing the front line by 80 km (50 miles). Despite this reduction, the Germans were in no better position in September

Welcoming the Americans
A French poster welcomes the arrival of American troops. From the moment the United States declared war on Germany, in April 1917, the French looked forward to American troops joining them on the front line.

than in August to resist attack. The German armies had incurred 228,000 casualties and received only 130,000 replacements in the period between Amiens and Quéant. Consequently, in August, 21 German divisions were broken up and the Army Group Rupprecht's reserve was reduced from 36 to just nine divisions. In comparison, the Allies were in a position to clear the St Mihiel salient and move against the Hindenburg Line, to which the Germans had withdrawn in the spring of 1917.

ST MIHIEL OFFENSIVE
On August 30 the American First Army – activated on August 10 – was assigned the sector south of St Mihiel. With the aim of freeing the Paris-Verdun-Nancy railways, the Americans launched an attack on St Mihiel on September 12. One French corps was in the line and the French provided half of the gunners, but this was effectively the first action of an independent American army on the Western Front. Its objective was achieved with little difficulty, the Germans having started to evacuate their positions before the attack began. In the first two days of the offensive, the Americans took some 8,000 prisoners and a huge total of 443 guns.

THE WESTERN FRONT
Jul 18–Oct 3, 1918

ALLIED FRONT LINE JUL 18:
- Belgian sector
- British sector
- French sector
- American sector

ALLIED FRONT LINE SEPT 25:
- - - Belgian sector
- - - British sector
- - - French sector
- - - American sector

ALLIED ATTACKS:
- British offensives
- French offensives
- American offensives
- The Allies (and allied states)
- Central Powers (and allied states)
- Neutral states
- ⊡ Fortified town
- - - - Major railway

NETHERLANDS

BELGIUM

GERMANY

LUXEMBOURG

FRANCE

English Channel

Ostend
Bruges
Antwerp
Nieuport
Dunkerque
Ghent
BRUSSELS
Liège

Sept 28
4th Battle of Ypres
Ypres
BELGIAN
Albert
4TH ARMY
Armin
2ND ARMY
Plumer
FLANDERS
Hazebrouck
Lille
Mons
Namur
Charleroi

Sept 27
British 1st and 3rd Armies breach Hindenburg Line between Cambrai and St Quentin
Festubert
5TH ARMY
Birdwood
6TH ARMY
Quast
1ST ARMY
Horne
Arras
17TH ARMY
von Below
Maubeuge
Aulnoye

Aug 21
British 3rd Army opens offensive along a 16-km (10-mile) sector. British 4th Army resumes its advance
3RD ARMY
Byng
Quéant
Bapaume
Albert
Cambrai
Le Cateau
2ND ARMY
Marwitz
Amiens
Péronne
4TH ARMY
Rawlinson
St Quentin

Aug 8
4th Army opens first British offensive, supported by French to the south
Chaulnes
La Fère
18TH ARMY
Hutier
Mézières
Sedan
LUXEMBOURG
1ST ARMY
Debeney
Montdidier
9TH ARMY
Eben
Laon
7TH ARMY
Boehn
Longwy

Aug 20
Aisne Heights captured by French 10th Army
Noyon
3RD ARMY
Humbert
Soissons
Vesle
1ST ARMY
Eberhardt
3RD ARMY
Einem
5TH ARMY
Gallwitz
Thionville
Metz

Chantilly
10TH ARMY
Mangin
Fère-en-Tardenois
Reims
Mont Blanc
Argonne
Verdun
5TH ARMY
Berthelot
Château Thierry
4TH ARMY
Gouraud
St Menhould
1ST ARMY
Pershing
Troyon
19TH ARMY
Bothmer

Seine
PARIS
Jul 18
French launch counterattack to clear Marne salient

Aug 1
Soissons taken
Chalons
Marne
St Mihiel

Sept 26
Argonne offensive opens. Slow progress is made over difficult country by French and US forces
Bar le Duc

Sept 12
Americans begin attack on the St Mihiel salient. It is cleared by Sept 16
Nancy

0 km 20 40 60 80 100
0 miles 20 40 60 80 100

SHELL SHOCK

THE SUSTAINED PSYCHOLOGICAL and physical stress of soldiering in the trenches led to a new kind of war damage known as "shell shock". In dealing with victims of shell shock, army commanders and medical officers tended to be unsympathetic, partly because the condition ranged from frayed nerves to complete mental collapse. After 1918 there was a public debate in Britain about shell shock, and in 1922 a War Office Committee of Enquiry published its report on the phenomenon of shell shock, which was now termed "war neurosis". Although the report made it clear that loss of nerve or mental control would not be tolerated as an escape route by soldiers, it did acknowledge shell-shock victims as genuine casualties of 20th-century warfare. To prevent war neurosis, it recommended shorter tours of front-line duty, and more attention to the health and welfare of soldiers. It also recommended psychotherapy for the treatment of shell shock, which gave a boost to Sigmund Freud's revolutionary theories about repression and defence mechanisms.

Shell-shocked soldier
Faced with men displaying paralysis, muscular contractions and loss of sight that had no apparent physical basis, the military authorities saw cowards, "malingerers" and men who has simply failed to "get a grip".

Under fire
Men who deserted after repeatedly coming under fire may well have been suffering from shell shock.

ARGONNE OFFENSIVE

The American high command had wished to follow the clearing of the St Mihiel salient with an advance on Metz, aimed at severing the Strasbourg-Lille rail link. However, even before the St Mihiel offensive, it had been forced to accept a commitment in the Argonne as the price of ensuring its own distinctive national contribution to the common cause. Haig had drawn up a plan under which the Allies were to conduct complementary, converging offensives – the British from the Le Cateau area and the Americans against the Sedan-Mézières sector. Many American commanders at the time, and many American historians since, have portrayed this plan as the means of denying the Americans "the victory that would have won the war". The reality was that the war was not going to be won by

American troops in action
Many of the guns used by the Americans were supplied by the French, but here they are firing a US-made 356-mm (14-in) railway gun.

Salonika. On the 19th the British offensive in northern Palestine had begun and within three days it had destroyed the Turkish Seventh and Eighth Armies. On the 29th, as German positions on the Hindenburg Line crumbled, Bulgaria concluded an armistice.

REQUEST FOR AN ARMISTICE

In July, members of the German high command had urged a general withdrawal to the positions held before the Michael Offensive. This had been resisted in the belief that Germany could not abandon the gains of the previous four months without compromising its political and strategic position. Following the Allied attack at Amiens in August, the German high command, fearing that it faced an immediate collapse on the Western Front, had demanded that an armistice should be sought. This demand had been set aside with the slackening of Allied pressure. However, German losses of 230,000 men in September, coupled with a series of defeats towards the end of the month, destroyed any confidence that the German armies could still retain a coherent defensive position in the west. On September 28 Ludendorff suffered a seizure and collapsed, and on the 29th the German military authorities demanded that an approach for an armistice be made immediately.

a single victory, or the capture of a single town and railway, and that if German lateral communications were to be severed then both Luxembourg and Metz would have to be taken. But leaving aside these facts, whether the Americans could have taken Metz, the most strongly fortified city in Europe, is doubtful.

What cannot be doubted, however, is that the commitment of American forces to an offensive in the Argonne was both unnecessary and unfortunate. It was unnecessary because the British were to break the Hindenburg Line and could have done so without any supporting offensive. It was unfortunate because American formations were thus committed to an offensive on September 26 that was poorly organized and quickly descended into chaos as a result of the over-concentration of forces and the inadequacy of staff and transport arrangements. Fought over very difficult country and in almost continuous rain, the Argonne offensive took the form of a series of slow, bitterly-contested advances. The French Fourth and US First Armies had advanced to the outskirts of Sedan by November 11, but by this time the focus of events had shifted elsewhere.

CAMBRAI AND YPRES

The main focus of fighting on the Western Front in September was in front of Cambrai. Here, on September 27, the British First and Third Armies crossed the Canal du Nord and, with the Australians and US 2nd Corps in the line, breached the Hindenburg Line between Cambrai and St Quentin. The offensive was halted on October 5.

To the north, in a two-day action on September 28 and 29 known as the Fourth Battle of Ypres, the Belgians secured Dixmude and the British Second Army took Messines and its ridge, so threatening the German positions on the Belgian coast. On the second of these days, as Allied forces reached the outskirts of Cambrai, the various elements of German defeat came together. On September 15 Austria-Hungary had in effect sought a separate peace, while the Allies opened their offensive at

JOHN PERSHING

WITH HIS SERVICE EXPERIENCE IN CUBA, the Philippines and Mexico, "Black Jack" Pershing (1860–1948) was a natural choice to command the American Expeditionary Force. Arriving in France in mid-1917, he was determined not to allow his fresh soldiers to fight as reinforcements for the war-weary British and French armies. His position was made more difficult by the fact that he depended on the Allies for supplies.

When Ludendorff launched his Kaiserschlacht offensive in March 1918, Pershing relented somewhat, but American troops still only fought as full divisions. In September US forces were victorious in their first independent operation of the war, reducing the St Mihiel salient. Pershing then transferred his men straight to the Meuse-Argonne offensive, where progress was initially slow. Following reorganization in October, the second phase of the offensive, beginning on November 1, was much more successful.

During the course of American participation in the war, Pershing effectively set up the structure of a US national army. Returning home in 1919, he was awarded the unique rank of "General of the Armies".

THE AMERICANS

AFTER THE UNITED STATES ENTERED THE WAR, on April 6, 1917, their forces were eagerly awaited by the British and French, but it was over a year before American troops fought in any great number. In 1917 there were just 145,000 men in the regular army. With the introduction of conscription in May the numbers swelled considerably, but transporting them across the U-boat infested Atlantic, along with huge quantities of supplies, took months to achieve. By May 1918 there were 500,000 American troops in France, by mid-July twice that number, and by the end of the war over 2 million. Pershing sought to maintain unity of American command, but for many months American divisions were deployed to Allied armies. Not until August 1918 did the Americans secure separate status, with the raising of the First US Army.

The arrival of the American troops – physically and mentally fresh – raised the morale of the Allies, even though the US army still largely relied on them for guns, tanks and aircraft. American staff officers also lacked administrative experience; in the summer of 1918 thousands of American troops left their positions to seek rations from allied units. None of this should detract, however, from the American achievement. It was the certainty that American formations would arrive in strength during 1918 that prompted the German spring offensives, and it was the huge number of troops they provided that made the vital difference between defeat and victory for the Allies.

IDENTITY DISCS

CAMOUFLAGED HELMET

COMBINED KNIFE AND KNUCKLE-DUSTER

WIRE CUTTERS

BAYONET

US Army uniform
The American uniform had many distinctive features such as the light-coloured cotton ammunition pouches, which each held two clips of five rounds.

Americans in action
An American gun crew aims an anti-aircraft gun on the Western Front. Much of the heavier equipment used by the Americans was lent to them by the French.

Song of welcome
This sheet music for a stirring marching song, welcoming France's new allies, is dedicated to General Pershing.

Springfield rifle
The standard US rifle was the stubby 1903 model Springfield. Its .30-in calibre cartridges were known as .30-06.

SPRINGFIELD RIFLE

Grenade launcher

Rifle grenade

Shotgun cartridge

Cartridge belt

PUMP-ACTION SHOTGUN

Pump-action shotgun
This weapon was sometimes used by American soldiers for clearing trenches. Peppering the trench with a spray of shot allowed an attacker to disable more of the enemy than with a single bullet.

German prisoners after Amiens, August 1918
By the end of the Allied offensive launched at Amiens on
August 8, the Germans had lost 18,000 killed and wounded
and 30,000 had been taken prisoner. Never before in the
war had German troops surrendered in such numbers.

Apart from a failed offensive by the Austro-Hungarians on the Piave in June, the initiative rested with the Allies. In mid-September they launched offensives in Salonika and Palestine, and in October they fought their way across the Piave in a reversal of the action there in June. In all three regions they met with only limited resistance from opponents who had largely lost the resources, the energy and the conviction to fight.

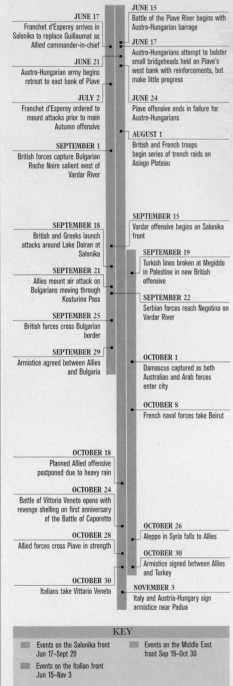

JUNE 17
Franchet d'Esperey arrives in Salonika to replace Guillaumat as Allied commander-in-chief

JUNE 15
Battle of the Piave River begins with Austro-Hungarian barrage

JUNE 17
Austro-Hungarians attempt to bolster small bridgeheads held on Piave's west bank with reinforcements, but make little progress

JUNE 21
Austro-Hungarian army begins retreat to east bank of Piave

JUNE 24
Piave offensive ends in failure for Austro-Hungarians

JULY 2
Franchet d'Esperey ordered to mount attacks prior to main Autumn offensive

AUGUST 1
British and French troops begin series of trench raids on Asiago Plateau

SEPTEMBER 1
British forces capture Bulgarian Roche Noire salient west of Vardar River

SEPTEMBER 15
Vardar offensive begins on Salonika front

SEPTEMBER 18
British and Greeks launch attacks around Lake Doiran at Salonika

SEPTEMBER 19
Turkish lines broken at Megiddo in Palestine in new British offensive

SEPTEMBER 21
Allies mount air attack on Bulgarians moving through Kosturino Pass

SEPTEMBER 22
Serbian forces reach Negotina on Vardar River

SEPTEMBER 25
British forces cross Bulgarian border

SEPTEMBER 29
Armistice agreed between Allies and Bulgaria

OCTOBER 1
Damascus captured as both Australian and Arab forces enter city

OCTOBER 8
French naval forces take Beirut

OCTOBER 18
Planned Allied offensive postponed due to heavy rain

OCTOBER 24
Battle of Vittorio Veneto opens with revenge shelling on first anniversary of the Battle of Caporetto

OCTOBER 26
Aleppo in Syria falls to Allies

OCTOBER 28
Allied forces cross Piave in strength

OCTOBER 30
Armistice signed between Allies and Turkey

OCTOBER 30
Italians take Vittorio Veneto

NOVEMBER 3
Italy and Austria-Hungary sign armistice near Padua

KEY

▮ Events on the Salonika front Jun 17–Sept 29	▮ Events on the Middle East front Sep 19–Oct 30
▮ Events on the Italian front Jun 15–Nov 3	

The Collapse of Germany's Allies

Moment of recoil
British troops fire a 2.75-in gun in the mountains above Salonika, as part of the September offensive that led to the defeat of Bulgaria and the liberation of Serbia.

GERMANY'S ALLIES were unable to summon up the same strength in terms of manpower and firepower as their much larger and more heavily industrialized senior partner. They did, however, serve a useful function, which was to draw British and French forces away from the main theatre of war – the Western Front.

DEFEAT OF BULGARIA

The campaign against Bulgaria had this effect. Between the end of 1915 and mid-1918 Salonika, in northern Greece, was referred to by the Germans as their "largest internment camp" because of the huge number of Allied troops stationed there.

For the Central Powers, especially Germany, an offensive against Salonika would have been a massive undertaking at the end of a long and inadequate line of communication, and any success would only have aggravated the conflicting territorial ambitions of Austria-Hungary, Bulgaria and Turkey in the region. For the Allies, on the other hand, there was a need to recover Serbia and to carry the war to Germany's partners. However, although there were 600,000 Allied troops in Salonika by mid-1917, priority was given to the Western Front and to the Middle East.

The Allies were also racked by national and personal differences and hampered by the ambiguous position of Greece towards their cause, but in 1917 certain of their problems eased. Growing and relentless Allied pressure on Greece bore fruit in June with the abdication of the pro-German king and the inauguration of the Venizelos administration. Greece declared war against the Central Powers on June 29, and Greek troops were added to the Allied forces.

In France, the new administration of Georges Clemenceau chose to recall Sarrail – a commander who had managed to alienate virtually all his subordinates. His replacement was Guillaumat, whose arrival in December ushered in a period of intense Allied activity, including the improvement of lines of communication and a slow recovery of morale. Careful plans were prepared for limited offensives, but the series of Allied crises on the Western Front meant that these had to be shelved and Guillaumat was in turn recalled, to be replaced by Franchet d'Esperey, in June 1918.

THE VARDAR OFFENSIVE

By mid-1918 the Allies held the advantage on the Salonika front. The new commander, fortified by the belief of his Serbian forces that the Bulgarians could be broken by a surprise attack through the mountains, sought official endorsement for a general offensive. Meanwhile, the French undertook the difficult task of secretly moving heavy artillery into the mountains, while the British undertook a local offensive in the Vardar valley to distract Bulgarian attention from what was happening to the west.

Final approval for an offensive was given on September 10, and the action opened with a heavy artillery bombardment on the night of September 14. At 5:30 am next morning, French, Serbian and Italian forces launched their assault. Within two days they had penetrated 10 km (6 miles) across a 30-km (19-mile) front; a day later the leading formations were 30 km (19 miles) beyond their start lines. With virtually no fresh forces to reconstitute the front, and Allied forces threatening to break into the Vardar valley, the Central Powers had reached crisis point. On the 18th and 19th, however, crack Bulgarian troops did manage to repulse British and Greek attacks around Lake Doiran, although the town of Doiran was taken by Greek forces.

With their defence to the west breaking, the Bulgarians proposed that their forces should disengage around Doiran in order to counterattack the Allied forces advancing in the Cherna valley. However, as incredulous Bulgarian soldiers obeyed orders to break contact around Doiran and move through the Kosturino Pass, they were subjected to

Inspecting the troops in Salonika
Franchet d'Esperey spent the summer of 1918 planning an offensive, and convincing his political masters and military superiors that it was viable.

Turkish cavalry
Turkey was threatened by the Allied action against Bulgaria, which was quite close to its European border.

overwhelming Allied air attack. Their cohesion crumbled, and so too did Bulgarian morale. By September 22 Serbian forces had reached Negotina on the Vardar, and three days later, as French colonial forces moved through the mountains on Skopje, British formations crossed the Bulgarian border. On September 28, Bulgaria, swept by anti-war riots and the proclamation of soviets in various cities, requested an armistice, and agreed to Allied terms the next day, with the armistice effective on September 30, 1918.

A British force continued eastwards through Thrace, seizing the bridgeheads over the Maritsa, in readiness for an offensive against Constantinople.

Advance in Salonika

Following the launch of the Allied offensive on September 15, the Serb forces in the centre made rapid progress into Serbia. In the west the Bulgarians collapsed, but they put up stronger opposition on the Vardar before being overwhelmed in the Kosturino Pass.

THE VARDAR OFFENSIVE
Sept 15–29, 1918

ALLIED ATTACKS:
- Serbian
- French
- British
- Central Powers front line Sept 14
- Central Powers front line Sept 29

- Town captured by Allies, with date
- The Allies (and allied states)
- Central Powers (and allied states)
- Major railway

SEPT 29 Skopje
French cavalry takes Skopje, and the Bulgarians sue for an armistice

SEPT 21 Kosturino
Bulgarian forces, moving through the Kosturino Pass, are subjected to an overwhelming Allied bombardment

SEPT 26 Strumitsa

SEPT 22
Serbian forces reach Negotina on the Vardar

Sept 18–19
British and Greek attacks to east of Lake Doiran are repulsed

Sept 15
Main offensive by French, Serbian and Italian forces begins

ADRIATIC SEA

ALBANIA

TIRANA

SERBIA

BULGARIA

RHODOPE MOUNTAINS

GREECE

THESSALY

GULF OF SALONIKA

Scutari
Drin
Lake Ohrid
Monastir
Durazzo
Valona
Kastoria
Veles
Negotina
Cherna
Vetrenk
Lake Ostrovo
Veria
Lake Doiran
Doiran
Salonika
Lake Langaza
Lake Bechik
Seres
Kavalla
Lake Tahinos
Struma

1ST ARMY
2ND ARMY
4TH ARMY
ARMY
11TH ARMY
2ND ARMY
1ST ARMY
ORIENT ARMY
ORIENT ARMY

This was made unnecessary by the Turkish acceptance of an armistice on October 30. French and Serbian forces, meanwhile, advanced to the north, reaching the Danube on October 19 and liberating Belgrade on November 1. With the signing of the Austro-Hungarian armistice on November 3, 1918, the Balkans campaign was over.

OPERATIONS IN THE MIDDLE EAST

After the British capture of Baghdad and Jerusalem in 1917, enforced inactivity characterized the situation in Mesopotamia and Palestine for much of 1918. Turkey, encouraged by the collapse of Russia, pursued extravagant territorial ambitions in Persia and Turkic Central Asia, while allowing its position in Arabia to all but collapse.

During 1918, Turkish forces in Mesopotamia were weakened by epidemics, desertions and a lack of reinforcements, which reduced the number of

> *The hill was about 2,500 feet high, very steep, and it was the heat of the day. There was very heavy machine-gun fire and some shelling. We captured a village en route and had to bomb the Turks out of a few houses. The hill was so steep and the men so done about three-quarters of the way men fell down and could not get up. If the Turks had counterattacked we should have had a bad time. I was so done myself that if a Turk had come for me I think I should have been too tired to shoot.*
>
> BRITISH LIEUTENANT-COLONEL H.J.H. DAVSON
> ON THE ACTION DURING THE BATTLE OF MEGIDDO

troops in the Kirkuk–Mosul area to about 20,000 by October 1918. The British, despite having 550,000 troops in Mesopotamia, were constrained by fears that German forces would advance through Persia and Afghanistan, and failed to make any significant moves until late October, when they finally launched a campaign that led to a Turkish surrender and the British occupation of Mosul.

PALESTINE AND SYRIA

Meanwhile, the Turkish Fourth, Seventh and Eighth armies holding the line in Palestine totalled around 32,000 infantry and 3,500 cavalry, but lacked overall strategy or mobility (despite the Seventh army being under the command of the future Turkish leader, Mustafa Kemal). They gathered no effective intelligence, and their line of communication from Damascus was in a state of collapse. They could only await defeat.

The intention of the British Egyptian Expeditionary Force under General Allenby to clear Turkish forces from Syria was, however, initially thwarted by the need to transfer five divisions to the Western Front in response to the German offensive of March 1918. In return, it gained Indian cavalry from France, and further Indian units were brought in from India and Mesopotamia. Training up these troops, however, and turning them into an effective fighting force took most of the summer.

The British had a number of advantages over the Turkish forces in Palestine. Apart from their numerical superiority (they had 57,000 infantry and 12,000 cavalry) and air supremacy, they also had a strategy. Part of Allenby's build-up to his main offensive in September was a series of decoy operations to the east of the Jordan that led the

Lawrence of Arabia
T.E. Lawrence standing surrounded by members of his bodyguard. He fulfilled an important role in liaising between British forces and sympathetic Arab leaders, and organizing action by Arab irregulars against the Turks.

Action and inaction in Mesopotamia
One of 3,000 Turkish soldiers taken prisoner near Kirkuk on April 29, 1918, after which British forces withdrew south to Kifri for five months of inactivity.

Turkish command to expect their railway supply line through Deraa to be the focus of any British attack. Instead, Allenby left that task to the Arabs, and made detailed preparations for an offensive from positions on the coastal plain, aiming to trap Turkish forces in the Judaean Hills, and leave a route to Damascus clear. He secretly amassed troops on this coastal sector, moving cavalry divisions westwards under cover of darkness, and using the RAF to keep Turkish reconnaissance planes away. By the opening of the offensive, Allenby had 35,000 infantry, 400 guns and 9,000 cavalry lined up on the coastal plain, facing an unsuspecting Turkish force of only 8,000 infantry and 130 guns.

THE BATTLE OF MEGIDDO

Defeat for the Turkish forces began to unfold at 4:30 am on September 19, 1918, and took only three days. In the coastal sector, the initial bombardment overcame the two corps of the Turkish Eighth Army, and by 7:30 am Indian and Australian cavalry had broken through the Turkish lines and headed northwards to block a Turkish retreat. The Turks were pursued by British infantry into the hills, where they engaged in fierce rear-guard actions. Meanwhile, the lead

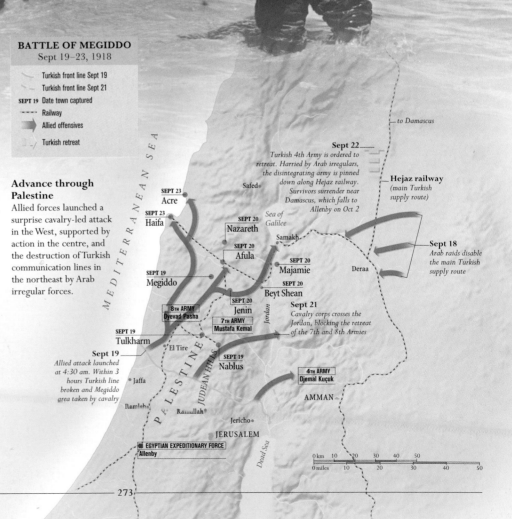

cavalry division advanced 110 km (70 miles) to Beisan in 34 hours at the cost of just 26 horses killed by exhaustion. Megiddo was in their control on the morning of the attack, and Afula, Nazareth, Majamie, Jenin and Beyt Shean by the end of the 20th. The British had now secured the upper Jordan and established themselves astride Turkish lines of communication and withdrawal, which became the target of a double attack – from the RAF and Arab irregulars operating east of the Jordan. The air campaign, which has been described as the most comprehensive disruption of command and supply in the First World War, has been subsequently obscured by the totality and speed of the Turkish collapse, and overshadowed by a post-war romantic view of the Arab Revolt.

THE ARAB CONTRIBUTION

The military contribution of the Arabs to the defeat of the Turks in northern Palestine was considerable. Before Allenby's offensive, Arab guerrilla forces attacked the railway around Deraa, cutting Turkish lines of communication. During the offensive they destroyed columns of the Turkish Fourth Army trying to withdraw to Damascus. Their involvement had great political significance, as indicated by the dispute over whether Australian or Arab forces were the first to enter Damascus on October 1.

BATTLE OF MEGIDDO
Sept 19–23, 1918

- Turkish front line Sept 19
- Turkish front line Sept 21
- **SEPT 19** Date town captured
- Railway
- Allied offensives
- Turkish retreat

Advance through Palestine

Allied forces launched a surprise cavalry-led attack in the West, supported by action in the centre, and the destruction of Turkish communication lines in the northeast by Arab irregular forces.

MEDITERRANEAN SEA

to Damascus

Sept 22
Turkish 4th Army is ordered to retreat. Harried by Arab irregulars, the disintegrating army is pinned down along Hejaz railway. Survivors surrender near Damascus, which falls to Allenby on Oct 2

Safed

Hejaz railway (main Turkish supply route)

Sea of Galilee

SEPT 23 Acre

SEPT 23 Haifa

SEPT 20 Nazareth

Samakh

SEPT 20 Afula

Sept 18
Arab raids disable the main Turkish supply route

SEPT 19 Megiddo

SEPT 20 Majamie

Deraa

8TH ARMY Dyevad Pasha

SEPT 20 Jenin

7TH ARMY Mustafa Kemal

SEPT 20 Beyt Shean

Sept 21
Cavalry corps crosses the Jordan, blocking the retreat of the 7th and 8th Armies

SEPT 19 Tulkharm

El Tire

Jordan

SEPT 19 Nablus

Sept 19
Allied attack launched at 4:30 am. Within 3 hours Turkish line broken and Megiddo area taken by cavalry

Jaffa

4TH ARMY Djemal Kuçuk

AMMAN

Ramleh

Ramallah

Jericho

EGYPTIAN EXPEDITIONARY FORCE Allenby

JERUSALEM

Dead Sea

0 km 10 20 30 40 50
0 miles 10 20 30 40 50

Austrian prisoners
Some Austrian soldiers at Montello failed to escape the Italian counterattack of June 18.

THE ITALIAN FRONT

Following Germany's redeployment of troops from Italy to the Western Front for its spring offensive, 53 Austro-Hungarian divisions faced 59 divisions under Italian command in the mountains east of Lake Garda and across the Piave River. While both Austria-Hungary and Italy might have preferred to await the outcome of the conflict between their senior partners on the Western Front, those partners were looking for complementary action on the Italian Front. Consequently, both Austria-Hungary and Italy planned offensives, although once the Italians realized the enemy was preparing to attack, they decided to stand on the defensive.

The Austro-Hungarian offensive was beset by difficulties. There was not enough food to feed the troops, some of whom were reaching starvation point. The army was short of horses, and there was a lack of spare parts for their locomotives and motor vehicles. There was also the question of what form the offensive should take. A concerted attack from the Trentino would have been the best plan, but it brought the risk of weakening the front by redeploying troops to just one sector. There were also the issues of how to exploit any advantage that might be gained by such an offensive and who should be called on to command it.

In the end, a compromise was reached: a simultaneous two-pronged attack by separate army groups – one in the mountains, and the other along the Piave. The plan was for the Eleventh Army to break through Italian lines and move towards Verona and Castelfranco, joining up with the Sixth and the Isonzo Armies, once they had crossed the Piave. Such an offensive, involving simultaneous attacks that were not mutually supporting, was bound to result in failure.

THE PIAVE OFFENSIVE

The Austro-Hungarian Eleventh Army opened its main offensive in the mountains on June 15 (following diversionary attacks to the west). Although some initial gains were made, these had been eliminated by the end of the first day, and late on the 16th the battle in this sector petered out.

In the Piave valley itself, things at first went a bit better for the Austro-Hungarians. The Sixth Army at Montello, and the Isonzo Army at the lower end of the river, made gains of 5 km (3 miles) on June 15, helped by smoke and fog. By the 16th they had five isolated bridgeheads over the Piave. By the 18th they had established a 19-km (12-mile) front across the river, but it was clear that success would be elusive for the Austro-Hungarians. Already, demands were being made on their reserves, the Piave River was in flood, and Italian aeroplanes were attacking their lines of communication.

The Austro-Hungarian high command hesitated to abandon its offensive, just as the Italian high command had hesitated in the first three days to mount counterattacks. On the 18th, however, the Italians committed themselves in the Montello sector. The Austro-Hungarians ordered a withdrawal behind the Piave, and an orderly evacuation took place on the nights of 21st/22nd and 22nd/23rd. The Italians, taken by surprise by the withdrawals, did not immediately attempt to pursue the Austro-Hungarian armies, although at the beginning of July troops were moved up to face the Austro-Hungarians across the river.

Aftermath of the fighting
The town of Nervasa was caught up in both the Austro-Hungarian attack and in the Italian counterattack in June 1918.

THE ITALIAN ARMY

IN 1915, ITALY WAS ABLE to put 900,000 officers and men into the field – organized into 35 infantry, four cavalry and 12 militia divisions, plus one elite light infantry division (the *Bersaglieri*) and 52 mountain battalions (the *Alpini*). The army's obvious weaknesses included lack of artillery and low levels of literacy among its infantry. However, in the course of the Isonzo offensives (1915–17) the army proved its toughness while fighting over some of the worst terrain in Europe, and its tenacity in the face of repeated failure. The autocratic chief of staff, Luigi di Cadorna, made impossible demands of his troops, and casualties in the course of the war amounted to 2,200,000, including 650,000 killed.

Much changed after the disaster of Caporetto in November 1917, during which the Italian army could not at one stage account for more than 400,000 officers and men. The final prisoner count was 270,000. Eleven British and French divisions moved into northern Italy to help stabilize the front. Cadorna was dismissed and replaced by Armando Diaz, while widespread reforms were introduced to rebuild the army. These included improvements in the pay, rations and leave arrangements

of ordinary soldiers, who also received free life insurance policies. The army managed to raise 25 new divisions by February 1918, and Italian industry replaced the 3,500 guns lost at Caporetto by mid-1918 .

Understandably, the new high command was content to remain on the defensive for a time, and it was not until the last weeks of the war that it authorized a major offensive. New tactics involved concentration on firepower rather than manpower, and defence in depth, based on strongpoints and counterattacks. In these, the assault battalions of the *Arditi* (Daring Ones), an elite founded in 1917, played an important role. They became the heroes of an adoring populace who, anxious to avoid defeat by a detested enemy, united behind the war effort.

IDENTITY TAGS

Bersaglieri hat
The Bersaglieri were an elite regiment of sharpshooters. Their usual form of transport was the bicycle.

Helmet, based on French Adrian helmet

HEAVY HELMET

Alpine fighters
Men of the *Alpini* were expected to be able to fight at high altitudes. The special corps had been founded in 1872, specifically to protect the mountainous northern borders of the new Kingdom of Italy. This inhospitable terrain called for special skills and demanded extraordinary powers of endurance. The First World War was the first time they had been called on to perform this duty.

FOLDING SHOVEL

Arditi badge

Italian uniform and weapons
Most Italian uniforms were grey-green in colour. Shown here is the superior quality tunic of the Arditi, who were also issued with a warm roll-neck sweater for mountain warfare. The standard rifle of the Italian army was the 6.5-mm Carcano (1891 model). The Carcano carbine had a retractable bayonet that folded back along the barrel when not in use.

BERETTA AUTOMATIC PISTOL

ARDITI UNIFORM

CARCANO CARBINE WITH FIXED BAYONET

Gun hole
An Italian patrol occupies a shallow gun hole with a Fiat-Revelli Model 1914 machine-gun, at Fossalta on the Piave River in June 1918.

The Italians had halted a major enemy offensive, with disastrous results for Austria-Hungary. In the wake of the failure, an increasing number of its Slav soldiers began to "vote with their feet", foreseeing the imminent defeat and collapse of the Empire.

BUILD-UP TO A FURTHER OFFENSIVE

During the summer of 1918, as victories over the Germans on the Western Front multiplied, widening differences emerged between Italy and its allies, who demanded that it capitalize on its victory over the Austro-Hungarians and launch an offensive across the Piave River. The Italian high command balked, citing, with good reason, the problems the enemy had encountered in crossing the river in its offensive in June, and the shortages faced by the Italian army. It was painfully aware that war had exhausted Italy's resources and had opened dangerous political and social divisions. It reasoned that Italy had strength left for only one offensive and that, given the likelihood of the war continuing into 1919, such action would be best deferred until the following year.

In September, however, the Allies broke out from their positions around Salonika and, as Bulgaria fell by the wayside, so Austria-Hungary began to fall apart. On October 6, two days after the German request for an armistice, the state of Yugoslavia was proclaimed by a provisional government that met in Zagreb, and on the 14th, a Czech provisional government was formed. On the 16th the Habsburg emperor put out a proclamation declaring Austria a federal empire. The Italian high command, fearing that unless Austro-Hungarian forces were driven back, Italy might lose territory in any peace settlement, felt forced to launch an offensive.

MONTE GRAPPA AND VITTORIO VENETO

The Italians planned a double attack: by the Fourth Army on Monte Grappa to the west, and by the Eighth Army on the Piave to the east. The aim was for the two armies to encircle and isolate the Austro-Hungarian Sixth Army. Three other armies – the Sixth, Tenth and Twelfth – which included British, French and American divisions, would support them. In the event, it was the supporting armies that broke through the enemy positions after the attacks by the Fourth and Eighth armies miscarried.

The British divisions of the Tenth Army established themselves across the Piave on the night

Allied advance in northeast Italy
The combined forces of Italian, British and French divisions succeeded in overcoming stiff initial resistance from Austro-Hungarian troops. Once through the enemy lines, the Allied forces advanced rapidly.

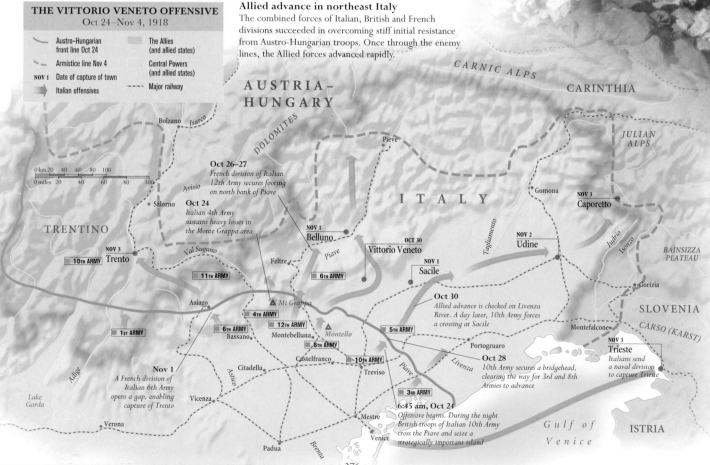

THE VITTORIO VENETO OFFENSIVE
Oct 24–Nov 4, 1918

- Austro–Hungarian front line Oct 24
- Armistice line Nov 4
- NOV 1 Date of capture of town
- Italian offensives
- The Allies (and allied states)
- Central Powers (and allied states)
- Major railway

Oct 26–27 French division of Italian 12th Army secures footing on north bank of Piave

Oct 24 Italian 4th Army sustains heavy losses in the Monte Grappa area

Oct 30 Allied advance is checked on Livenza River. A day later, 10th Army forces a crossing at Sacile

Oct 28 10th Army secures a bridgehead, clearing the way for 3rd and 8th Armies to advance

Nov 1 A French division of Italian 6th Army opens a gap, enabling capture of Trento

6:45 am, Oct 24 Offensive begins. During the night British troops of Italian 10th Army cross the Piave and seize a strategically important island

NOV 3 Trieste Italians send a naval division to capture Trieste

AUSTRIA-HUNGARY · CARNIC ALPS · CARINTHIA · JULIAN ALPS · DOLOMITES · ITALY · Pieve · Gomona · NOV 3 Caporetto · Tagliamento · NOV 2 Udine · Isonzo · BAINSIZZA PLATEAU · Gorizia · SLOVENIA · CARSO (KARST) · Montefalcone · ISTRIA · Gulf of Venice

Bolzano · Isarco · Avisio · Salorno · TRENTINO · NOV 3 10TH ARMY Trento · Val Sugano · 11TH ARMY · Asiago · 1ST ARMY · Adige · Lake Garda · Verona · Padua · Brenta · Astico · Vicenza · Citadella · Bassano · 6TH ARMY · 4TH ARMY · Mt Grappa · 12TH ARMY · Montebelluna · Montello · 8TH ARMY · Castelfranco · 10TH ARMY · Treviso · 3RD ARMY · Mestre · Venice · Piave · NOV 1 Belluno · Feltre · 6TH ARMY · OCT 30 Vittorio Veneto · NOV 1 Sacile · 5TH ARMY · Livenza · Portogruaro

Italian medical post on Monte Grappa
The mountainous terrain presented the problem of how to transport equipment and supplies, and how to bring back the wounded. Networks of cables were installed by both sides to provide lift systems.

of October 23/24 in advance of the main offensive, which began at dawn. The Eighth Army was able to secure shallow bridgeheads over a swollen Piave on the 26th. But it was the success of the Tenth and Twelfth Armies in securing the east bank of the Piave that enabled the Italians to cross the river on October 28 and take Vittorio Veneto on the 30th.

Meanwhile, a series of attacks carried out by the Italian Fourth Army on Monte Grappa failed to make any impression on a resolute Austro-Hungarian defence. On the 29th, Italian operations were halted in this sector as attention focused elsewhere. British and French divisions of the Sixth Army co-operated to break the Asiago position, thus ensuring the capture of Trento on November 3, just ahead of the arrival of lead elements of the Italian First Army. The main thrust of the offensive now began to unfold across the Venetian plain.

ITALIAN VICTORY

The Austro-Hungarians had fought tenaciously, but following the Allied crossing of the Piave, they were an army with days of existence left to it, fighting for a state that no longer existed. By November 1 the Italians had secured Sacile, and from this point the pace of the Allied advance quickened. Udine was secured on the 2nd, and the old battlefields on the Isonzo and at Caporetto on the 3rd. On the same day, Trieste was occupied by naval forces, and an armistice, effective the next day, was concluded.

The final battle of the Austro-Hungarian army cost it 30,000 dead and wounded and some 430,000 prisoners. At a price of some 38,000 casualties, Italy had secured the victory it needed to justify its territorial claims, and its right to be considered as a worthy partner of the Allies in their negotiations at the Paris Peace Conference in 1919.

Italian forces in Udine
The commander of the Savoy Cavalry (centre) leads the first patrol into the Piazza Contarena in the town of Udine on November 3 – the day after the Italians had succeeded in capturing it in their final advance.

THE CAUSES OF COLLAPSE

By late summer 1918 all three of Germany's allies had faced similar circumstances – dire hardship among their citizens, which a disastrous harvest and the onset of winter would only worsen, and a string of German military defeats that dashed any hopes of territorial gains. These, combined with factors specific to each of the countries, led to their collapse in the autumn of 1918.

THE COLLAPSE OF BULGARIA

Bulgaria had been the last of the Central Powers to enter the war and was the first to break ranks, with its separate armistice agreement made with the Allies on September 29, 1918. It would probably have preferred the war to end much sooner. By December 1915 it had gained all the Serb territory it had sought and, by December 1916, it had defeated Romania. Thereafter, the war had seemed pointless to many Bulgarians, and the social costs disproportionate. Even in 1914 living costs were high, and urban wages low. By July 1918 prices had inflated by 750 per cent. This had an impact on the morale of soldiers, who returned home on leave to find conditions even worse than in the army.

Turkish prisoners

For many Turks, conscripted reluctantly into an army that was often unable to feed and equip them properly for the terrain in which they were expected to fight, being taken prisoner was not necessarily an unwelcome option. By 1918, the army was down to 200,000 men.

Meanwhile, Bulgaria's motives for joining the war in 1915 had become largely irrelevant. They included resentment of the Russians for their support of Serbia in the Balkan Wars, and a distrust of the Allies, whom Bulgaria (correctly) suspected of having promised Constantinople to Russia in the event of victory over Turkey. The defeats inflicted on Russia, however, reduced the threat that it posed.

Bulgaria's desire for peace grew as it became apparent that it would receive little reward for its continued support of Germany. This was confirmed during the peace negotiations with Russia and Romania in Brest-Litovsk and Bucharest, when Bulgaria was not even awarded territories it had been forced to relinquish to Romania in 1913. Northern Dobruja was effectively placed under German military and economic occupation. The Bulgarian prime minister, Vasil Radoslavov, commented that his country had been treated more like a defeated enemy than as a victorious ally.

After 1916 Germany and Austria-Hungary had made increasing demands on Bulgarian agricultural resources, while Bulgarians in some regions starved. With the 1918 harvest threatening to be disastrous, and the resignation of the prime minister on June 20, Bulgaria had reached the end of the road.

THE COLLAPSE OF TURKEY

The First World War was in so many ways a war of exhaustion, and each year saw a poor and relatively undeveloped country such as Turkey lose ground. Although rural Turkey was largely self-sufficient, flour still had to be imported by sea to feed Constantinople and Trebizond. Military demands for manpower and draught animals reduced Turkey's agricultural output, and an economic blockade prevented supply ships from reaching Constantinople. Food shortages and the collapse of public health and sanitation programmes were producing 50 per cent infant mortality rates. Typhus, malaria and smallpox were widespread.

Russian territorial gains meant a flight of civilians to other provinces hopelessly ill-placed to support them. In 1918 there was a scramble the other way, when Russian armies abandoned their conquests, but with no harvest, famine and death were the inevitable results.

By 1918 the army was estimated to be at little more than one-sixth of its full strength. Estimates put the number of military casualties at over 1,500,000. Mass desertion seems to have been crucial in the saving of military lives and provided a further reason for signing an armistice with the British at Mudros on October 30.

THE COLLAPSE OF AUSTRIA-HUNGARY

Food shortages and the rising tide of socialism led to political unrest in Austria-Hungary. There was also a growing feeling among its ethnic minority groups – which included Bosnians, Czechs, Croats, Italians, Poles, Serbs, Slovaks, Slovenes and Romanians – that an allied victory would bring freedom from Austrian and Hungarian domination. The Czechs, Slovaks, Yugoslavs and Poles, in particular, were inspired by the promise made by the American President, Woodrow Wilson, in his Fourteen Points, of "the opportunity for autonomous development" for the nations of Austria-Hungary. The Habsburg Empire was disintegrating even as it signed an armistice on November 3, 1918.

GERMAN DOMINATION

One further factor was perhaps shared by all three of Germany's allies – a growing fear of, and resentment towards, Germany on account of its economic, industrial and financial strength, and its crass insensitivity toward its partners. By 1918, many people in Austria-Hungary and Bulgaria, in particular, wished for an end to the war as the means of escaping German domination.

FAMINE IN THE EMPIRE

~

WAR ON THREE FRONTS HAD, by the end of 1917, exhausted the resources of the Habsburg Empire. Acute shortages, poorly administered, ever-shrinking rations, *ersatz* (substitute) foods and rampant profiteering had brought famine, or near famine, to the towns and cities of Austria-Hungary. The arrangement whereby Austria, the industrialized core of the empire, traded goods with Hungary in exchange for food, had been disrupted by the war. Austria had little in the way of goods and by 1916 Hungary's harvest barely met its own needs. It sent just 100,000 tons of grain to Austria, compared with peacetime deliveries of 2,100,000 tons. Victory on the Eastern Front and the Treaty of Brest-Litovsk promised extra grain from the rich farmlands of the Ukraine, but this never materialized, and Austria-Hungary became increasingly dependent on its more powerful German partner.

Early in 1918 there were strikes in favour of peace, first in Austria and then in Hungary, where half a million workers registered political protest, inspired by the success of the Bolshevik revolution in Russia. Arms and munitions factories were affected, and output was reduced to pre-war levels. The army was called on to fire on striking workers, but as a means of restoring order on the home front it was unreliable, because its non-German units were more sympathetic to the Allies than to the Central Powers. Mutinies and desertions to the enemy increased. Loyal recruits from Vienna were only dissuaded from deserting by the grim realization that their daily rations of *ersatz* bread, thin broth and horsemeat were a feast by civilian standards.

Starvation
Thes two Viennese boys are clearly suffering from severe malnutrition. Austria could not produce enough grain to feed its population or obtain it from the Hungarians.

Food rationing
Bread is handed out in a Viennese street, with each person receiving only a fraction of a loaf. In January 1918 a cut in civilian flour rations led to widespread food riots.

American troops with German wounded
German prisoners receive attention at an American
field dressing station during the St Mihiel offensive of
September 12, 1918. The Americans successfully cleared
the St Mihiel salient in 36 hours, taking 8,000 prisoners.

Bitter fighting continued after the Germans had made a formal request to US President Wilson for an armistice to be negotiated on the basis of his Fourteen Points. While Wilson made, and the Germans resisted, a number of demands, the Allies launched another series of offensives, forcing the Germans into a general retreat. German army discipline had been broken by the time the Armistice was signed on November 11.

~

OCTOBER 4
Germans send request to US President Wilson for armistice on basis of Wilson's Fourteen Points

OCTOBER 8
Wilson demands withdrawal of Germans from occupied territories

OCTOBER 8
In Somme sector, Second Battle of Cambrai begins

OCTOBER 9
British forces enter Cambrai and begin advance to last line of trenches in Hindenburg Line

OCTOBER 10
Germans abandon Argonne as a result of American operations

OCTOBER 11
French and American armies advance to Sedan on Meuse

OCTOBER 13
French forces occupy Laon

OCTOBER 14
President Wilson makes a demand to Germans for end to all U-boat offensives

OCTOBER 14
British offensive around Ypres forces Germans to begin abandonment of Belgian coast

OCTOBER 17
British forces occupy Lille; Belgians reoccupy Ostend

OCTOBER 19
Belgians reoccupy Zeebruge and Bruges

OCTOBER 20
Germans make somewhat dismissive response to Wilson's latest demands

OCTOBER 23
Wilson refuses to negotiate for an armistice with existing German government

OCTOBER 25
State entry into Bruges of Belgian king and queen

OCTOBER 26
Ludendorff dismissed by Kaiser for appealing to army to ignore government and its armistice negotiations

OCTOBER 27
Emperor Karl informs Kaiser of the intention of Austria-Hungary to seek an armistice

OCTOBER 29
Start of mutiny in German navy

NOVEMBER 1
French–US offensive begins in Aisne-Meuse sector

NOVEMBER 3
Belgians advance to outskirts of Ghent

NOVEMBER 4
Start of final Allied offensive on Western Front

NOVEMBER 5
General retreat of Germans from the Meuse begins

NOVEMBER 8
German armistice negotiators arrive at Compiègne and are given armistice terms

NOVEMBER 8
Uprising in Munich and ten other major German cities

NOVEMBER 9
British capture Tournai; Belgian forces occupy Ghent

NOVEMBER 9
Ebert replaces Prince Max as Chancellor; Kaiser abdicates

NOVEMBER 10
In Meuse sector, French and American forces secure Mézières and Charleville and enter Sedan

NOVEMBER 10
Kaiser crosses border into Netherlands after losing support of army and navy

NOVEMBER 11
German armistice concluded

KEY

▇ German armistice negotiations Oct 4–Nov 11	▇ Final Allied offensives Oct 4–Nov 11
	▇ Other events Oct 4–Nov 11

The German Search for an Armistice

British troops in Lille
Lille was captured on October 17 without a single shot being fired after an offensive, launched on the 14th, forced the Germans to begin abandoning the Belgian coast.

FOLLOWING THE RECOGNITION by the German military authorities of the need for an armistice, a request for armistice discussions was sent via the Swiss to US President Wilson on October 4. In the weeks that followed, two sets of events moved in tandem: the events on the battlefield and the political events that were to flow from the request for an armistice – a request that had been made in order to avoid a military defeat that had yet to become comprehensive. Throughout this time the Allies sustained pressure on the German armies on the Western Front, inflicting losses that, coming on top of those of August and September, finally brought home to Germany's political and military leaderships the hopelessness of their country's position.

FURTHER ALLIED OFFENSIVES

In October, the Allies maintained the pattern of their earlier operations with successive offensives. On October 5 they broke through the last main positions on the Hindenburg Line, enabling them to carry war into areas that had not seen fighting since 1914. The British Third and Fourth Armies, after taking some 8,000 prisoners on October 8 alone, mounted an offensive that resulted in the recapture of Cambrai on the 9th and Le Cateau on the 10th. The extent of the German army's administrative disorder and the improvised nature of its defensive measures can be gauged by the fact that at Méricourt, Prémont and Sérain, the Germans lost 4,000 prisoners drawn from no fewer than 15 different divisions. By the 13th,

German forces were engaged in a general retreat across a front between St Quentin and the Argonne. On the 14th the British offensive around Courtrai forced the Germans to begin to abandon the Belgian coast and Lille. As a result, King Albert returned to Ostend on the 17th, and two days later Belgian troops entered Zeebrugge and Bruges.

A Decline in Pressure

From this point, pressure on the Germans slackened as Allied supply problems mounted. But as early as the 20th, British forces established themselves on the Scheldt, east of Lille, between Pecq and Lienfer and three days later, on the 23rd, the British Third and Fourth Armies mounted offensives between the Scheldt and Sambre. By this time German forces had abandoned their positions on the Aisne and were involved in a general withdrawal from all their positions west of the Meuse opposite the French and American armies. On November 1, with the French Fourth and US First and Second Armies resuming their offensives either side of Verdun, the Battle of the Sambre opened in Belgium. It was to end on the 11th with Belgian forces entering Ghent and British forces entering Mons. That same day,

the Germans agreed to accept the armistice terms that had been presented to them. The Americans, after an advance of 40 km (25 miles) since November 1, were on the heights overlooking Sedan, and the French were outside Mézières.

In the last three months of hostilities, the Allied armies captured some 363,000 prisoners and 6,400 guns, evidence that the cohesion and discipline of German armies was breaking down. The Allied forces, particularly the British, had inevitably suffered checks, and losses that were serious and ever less acceptable as victory came in sight. The checks, however, were temporary and tactical and at least partly caused by the very small number of tanks available for offensive operations. In any event, they were very quickly overturned by Allied success at the strategic level. There was no rupture of the German front in these weeks, just a persistent erosion of position and strength that the German forces could not prevent, still less reverse.

The German Home Front

The revelation of national military helplessness had come as a devastating shock to Germany's political leadership and civilian population in the first week

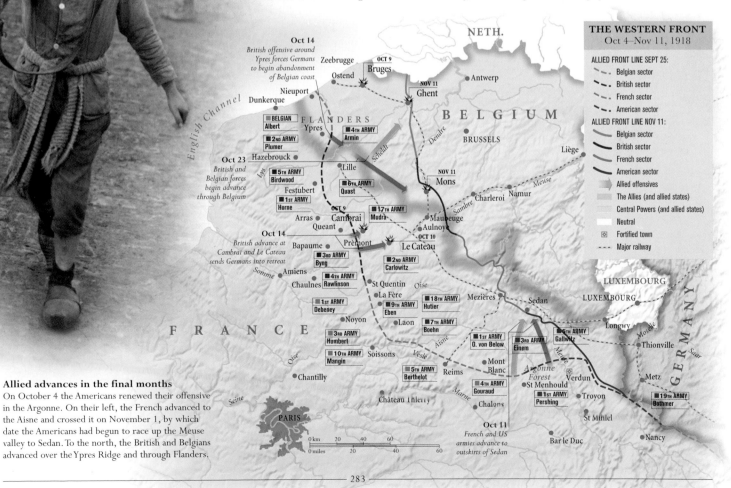

Allied advances in the final months
On October 4 the Americans renewed their offensive in the Argonne. On their left, the French advanced to the Aisne and crossed it on November 1, by which date the Americans had begun to race up the Meuse valley to Sedan. To the north, the British and Belgians advanced over the Ypres Ridge and through Flanders.

THE WESTERN FRONT
Oct 4–Nov 11, 1918

ALLIED FRONT LINE SEPT 25:
- Belgian sector
- British sector
- French sector
- American sector

ALLIED FRONT LINE NOV 11:
- Belgian sector
- British sector
- French sector
- American sector

- Allied offensives
- The Allies (and allied states)
- Central Powers (and allied states)
- Neutral
- Fortified town
- Major railway

Oct 14 British offensive around Ypres forces Germans to begin abandonment of Belgian coast

Oct 23 British and Belgian forces begin advance through Belgium

Oct 14 British advance at Cambrai and Le Cateau sends Germans into retreat

Oct 11 French and US armies advance to outskirts of Sedan

NETH.

Zeebrugge · Bruges · Antwerp
Ostend · Ghent · NOV 11
Nieuport · Dunkerque
BELGIAN Albert · FLANDERS · Ypres · 4TH ARMY Armin
2ND ARMY Plumer · BRUSSELS · Liège
Hazebrouck · Lille · 6TH ARMY Quast
5TH ARMY Birdwood · Charleroi · Namur
Festubert · 17TH ARMY Mudra · Maubeuge · Mons NOV 11
1ST ARMY Horne · Arras · Cambrai · Aulnoye OCT 10
Queant · Prémont · Le Cateau
Bapaume · 3RD ARMY Byng · 2ND ARMY Carlowitz
Amiens · Somme · St Quentin
Chaulnes · 4TH ARMY Rawlinson · La Fère · 18TH ARMY Hutier
1ST ARMY Debeney · 9TH ARMY Eben · Mézières · Sedan · LUXEMBOURG
Noyon · Laon · 7TH ARMY Boehn · Longwy
3RD ARMY Humbert · 1ST ARMY O. von Below · 3RD ARMY Einem · 6TH ARMY Gallwitz
10TH ARMY Mangin · Soissons · Thionville
Chantilly · Vesle · Mont Blanc · Argonne Forest · Verdun · Metz
5TH ARMY Berthelot · Reims · St Menhould
4TH ARMY Gouraud · 1ST ARMY Pershing · St Mihiel · 19TH ARMY Bothmer
Seine · Château Thierry · Marne · Chalons · Troyon
PARIS · Bar le Duc · Nancy

0 km 20 40 60
0 miles 20 40 60

of October. Until August the German civilian population had shown remarkably few signs of unrest, despite the hardships caused by the war. But from early autumn the problem of ensuring national solidarity had grown. During the spring offensives, trainloads of prisoners and German wounded had arrived on German railways, but the autumn fighting brought only more wounded. In August there was a further cut of food rations that were already barely adequate to sustain existence, while the worldwide influenza epidemic worsened throughout the summer. In the autumn the epidemic reached its peak in Germany, with 3,000 deaths occurring in October in the capital alone. (German civilian deaths from influenza were to number about 400,000 in 1918.)

On September 30 Chancellor Hertling was replaced by Prince Max of Baden, a cousin of the kaiser known for his liberal views. This could not, however, prevent the growth of unrest. On November 3, after warships of the High Sea Fleet were ordered to sea for one last climactic battle, crews at Kiel and Wilhelmshaven mutinied. Both cities were in revolutionary hands by the 7th, when Bavaria was declared an independent republic.

WILSON'S FOURTEEN POINTS

The request for armistice discussions that was sent to President Wilson on October 4 stated a German willingness to negotiate on the basis of Wilson's Fourteen Points. The president had first presented

Communication by telephone
Although wirelesses were beginning to appear on the battlefield in 1918, their use was by no means universal and there was still a heavy reliance on field telephones.

American troops advancing
Beginning with the first all-American minor action in June, American troops played an increasingly significant role in driving back the Germans. By the end of September their active participation had convinced the German high command of the need for an armistice.

the points to the American Congress in January 1918 as the foundation for a lasting peace, and had subsequently elaborated on them in a speech delivered in New York on September 27. In general, they embraced the principle of national self-determination. They called for the restoration of the Belgian state, the liberation of all French territory, and the return to France of Alsace and Lorraine. Elsewhere in Europe, Wilson envisaged an end to the Habsburg and Ottoman empires, and the creation of new national states in central and eastern Europe. These were to include an independent Poland with full access to the Baltic Sea.

Wilson, in his Fourteen Points, also urged the nations of western Europe to welcome Russia "into the society of free nations under institutions of her own choosing". Most importantly from the German point of view, he called for open diplomatic negotiations, the removal of economic barriers to trade, and "mutual guarantees of political independence and territorial integrity" to all states.

Wilson recognized that the British and French should play the leading role in drawing up the terms of an armistice. However, he succeeded in using his position to make a series of demands of Germany: the withdrawal of German forces from all occupied territories (October 8), an end to the U-boat offensive (October 14), and a recognition that peace could not be concluded with the existing German imperial and military authorities (October 23). He thus forced upon the German high command a piecemeal surrender that could not be reversed, and inextricably linked the armistice and peace treaty with the Fourteen Points.

GERMANY IN 1918

Since the severe winter of 1916–17 there had been a marked deterioration in the living conditions of Germany's civilian population. Those with insufficient funds to purchase food on the thriving black market had gone hungry: according to some estimates over 700,000 Germans died from malnutrition-related disease in the years 1914–18.

People living in towns and cities suffered most. In an attempt to eke out the meagre supplies of food, government scientists offered *ersatz* concoctions such as "meat" made of vegetable flour, barley and mushrooms. In a register of licensed *ersatz* goods set up by the government in 1918, over 11,000 had been listed by the end of the war.

Shortages of coal and soap meant that German civilians were not only hungry but cold, dirty and vulnerable to disease. At every turn, the complete failure of the authorities – state, military and local – to manage the war economy and keep up civilian morale was clearly visible.

While the Bolshevik Revolution in Russia of November 1917 enabled the German army to shift resources to the Western Front, it also gave a new, revolutionary dimension to civilian unrest. January 1918 saw a strike of more than 500,000 workers in Berlin and of about 1,000,000 in Germany as a whole, and the protests increasingly involved soldiers and sailors. By the end of August 1918, desertion from the German army had begun in earnest and was linked to the plundering of army food stocks and other stores.

By November there were 10,000 "Soldiers Councils", whose members were to be seen in all large German cities and towns, distributing flour, cocoa and tea to the civilian populations. Their efficiency contrasted favourably with the failures of the government, and helped to increase its unpopularity.

Starvation
Malnutrition left children and adults alike vulnerable to infectious diseases such as tuberculosis, influenza and pneumonia.

Food riots
Soldiers guard the remains of a looted butcher's shop in Invalidenstrasse, Berlin. The chemist's shop and bookshop either side of it were left untouched by the starving rioters, who were clearly only interested in food.

***Ersatz* products**
Substitutes used for coffee included dandelion roots and barley. Raspberry-leaf tea was also sold. Cotton was in short supply, so material was made from paper reinforced by woven fibres.

ERSATZ COFFEE

ERSATZ SOAP

ERSATZ TEA

ERSATZ CLOTH

Soup kitchens
Children are given food from a field kitchen set up to feed returning soldiers. By 1917 nearly a third of the population of Hamburg was surviving on "beggar's soup", doled out from such makeshift canteens.

> "On November 9 Germany, lacking any firm hand, bereft of all will, robbed of her princes, collapsed like a house of cards."
>
> GENERAL ERICH LUDENDORFF

Wilson's third demand, for a change of regime, caused Hindenburg and Ludendorff to call upon the army to ignore the government and its negotiations. For this act of insubordination, Ludendorff was forced to resign by the kaiser. Acceptance of the third demand was given on October 29 in a note that assured Wilson of the German government's credibility – although this was then undermined by the mutiny among the crews of the High Sea Fleet at Wilhelmshaven and Kiel. Meanwhile, Chancellor Prince Max was unconscious for 36 hours after taking a sleeping draught to alleviate the symptoms of influenza.

ARMISTICE NEGOTIATIONS

On November 5 Wilson informed the German government that negotiations could proceed on the basis of the Fourteen Points, and advised that an armistice would have to be secured from Foch. This was duly done, and at 2:30 am on the 7th the French radioed instructions for a German delegation to present itself at 8:00 pm that day. The delegation was taken by rail to Rethondes where, on the morning of the 8th, it was forced to ask formally for terms. Without access to radio and denied right of transit for 24 hours, the German delegation was unable to communicate the terms to German headquarters until the 10th.

On the previous day Prince Max had resigned as chancellor and had been replaced by the socialist

Ebert. The kaiser had been persuaded to abdicate. After authorizing acceptance of the armistice terms on the 10th, he took refuge in the technically neutral Netherlands, while his family remained in Berlin. Although the German high command judged the armistice terms to be punitive, it knew it had no alternative but to accept, and was authorized to sign by Prince Max (although no longer the chancellor) and by Hindenburg. When the German and Allied delegations met at 2:05 am on the 11th, the Germans were able to secure some minor concessions. This included a reduction in the amount of weapons and military equipment they had to surrender – on the grounds that they would need a certain military capability with which to maintain public order. With that the German delegation had to be content. The armistice, effective from 11:00 am, was signed at 5:10 am. The war, in effect, was finally over.

Armistice train
The armistice was drawn up and signed in a railway carriage *(above)* in a siding in the Forest of Compiègne, in northern France. The Allies were represented by Admiral Wemyss and Marshal Foch *(left)*. The German delegation, led by Erzberger, was given almost no room for negotiation and little opportunity to confer with the German government on the terms being offered.

ARMISTICE TERMS

The terms the Germans had signed amounted to total defeat. They were not only committed to evacuating all their troops from Belgium, France, Luxembourg and Alsace-Lorraine within 15 days, but also to withdrawing troops within Germany as far back as 40 km (25 miles) east of the Rhine, leaving all installations intact. The treaties of Brest-Litovsk and Bucharest, agreed between the Central Powers and the Russians and Romanians earlier in the year, were annulled and the Germans were ordered to make a start to the evacuations of the territories they had occupied in eastern Europe. They were also to allow the Allies right of access to Polish territories through Danzig on the Baltic Sea. German troops were also to cease fighting in East Africa (an order that took two days to reach them) and to evacuate the region.

Germany was to surrender almost all its artillery, machine-guns, mortars and aircraft, as well as 5,000 locomotives, 150,000 railway trucks, and 5,000 motorized trucks (along with sufficient spare parts for maintenance purposes). In addition, the Allies reserved the right to requisition further equipment and supplies from Germany, where necessary, with the cost to be borne by the German government.

The German airforce was to be assembled at one location and immobilized, and the naval fleet was to be interned and disarmed – a process that duly took place and involved a total of 114 German submarines being escorted into Harwich harbour in England between November 19 and 27.

All Allied prisoners of war were to be handed over by the Germans, and Allied nationals in occupied territories were to be repatriated. The Allies did not, however, state that they would reciprocate this arrangement. The Allied blockade of German ports, which was causing severe food shortages and hardship among German civilians and soldiers, was to continue, although the Allies agreed to "contemplate the provisioning of Germany... as shall be found necessary".

POLITICAL CHANGE

As Ebert took over as chancellor on November 10, the radical socialists Karl Liebknecht and Rosa Luxemburg held a rally at which they proposed a Russian-style soviet republic. To wrong-foot the

Exile for the kaiser

When it became clear that the kaiser no longer commanded the support of the army or navy, he left his headquarters in Belgium and crossed the border into the Netherlands. His abdication was announced by Prince Max on November 9, although the kaiser did not actually sign an official proclamation until November 28.

radicals, Ebert's followers declared Germany a socialist republic, and named the provisional government the Council of Peoples' Commissars.

A period of political unrest followed, during which Liebknecht and his communist followers, known as Spartacists, staged an uprising on January 6, 1919 and seized control of key government buildings. Their revolution was violently suppressed within a week by the right-wing *Freikorps* – private armies formed by senior German army officers.

SPANISH FLU
~

AFTER FOUR YEARS OF WAR, which saw massive movements of people between and across continents, the world was ripe for a pandemic. It took the form of a virulent strain of influenza that became known as "Spanish flu", possibly because, as a non-combatant state, the Spanish government saw no reason to suppress the news that the country was in the grip of an unusually severe kind of flu. It affected many non-combatant as well as combatant states.

The Spanish flu came in three waves, the first of which occurred in the spring of 1918, and began either in the USA or in American army camps in France. This first wave aroused little attention because it was a comparatively mild illness. Then, in August, a second, more virulent, wave struck at the same time in several localities thousands of miles apart: Freetown, the capital of Sierra Leone; Brest, the French port of disembarkation for American troops; and Boston in the USA. This highly infectious flu turned rapidly into pneumonia, against which medicine had no defence. It spread like wildfire among American soldiers at home and abroad. In all, 62,000 American service personnel died of the flu – more than were killed in battle.

The third wave, which happened in the spring of 1919, ravaged the war-strained, malnourished civilian populations of Europe. Despite frantic efforts to control and treat it, between 21 million and 25 million people died. Then, as mysteriously as it it had arrived, the Spanish flu disappeared.

Why catch their Influenza?

Repelling the germs

Mint throat lozenges – promoted here in an advertisement – were just one of the many anti-flu medicines available. All of them, however, proved to be totally ineffectual.

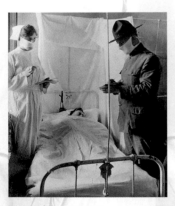

Caring for flu victims in the USA

Some of the American soldiers struck down by flu were nursed in large canvas tents in Lawrence, Massachussetts. Fresh air was thought to be beneficial.

Protective measures

Attempts were made to protect medical staff from infection by the use of gauze face masks, but many nurses and doctors contracted flu and died.

might be treated as an equal partner by the Allies at the Paris Peace Conference were dashed as the Germans were forced to wait on the sidelines until early April before being summoned to Paris to be dictated the terms of peace.

EUROPE AFTER THE ARMISTICE

What followed in the days, weeks and months after the signing of the armistice was very far from peace. While the institution of a republic in Germany was of huge significance, affecting as it did the most powerful single nation within Europe, events also occurred elsewhere – particularly in central and eastern Europe – that reflected profound political, economic and social changes. There was a vast movement of people during and after the German evacuation of Belgium, Alsace-Lorraine and Luxembourg in the west, and of Poland and the Ukraine in the east. The French occupied Strasbourg on November 25, and on December 9 the Allied armies moved into Germany, crossing the Rhine three days later. Meanwhile, Europe was gripped by an influenza epidemic that was to affect 100 million people worldwide

In Eastern Europe, Poland, proclaimed as a state on October 7, 1918 and formally constituted in the week after the armistice, held a general election in January 1919. Not included in this election was an

area in Galicia, around Lemberg, where there were clashes between Polish and Ukrainian forces in November 1918. In January 1919 Bolshevik forces occupied Vilna, an action that foreshadowed war betwcen Poland and Russia.

In the south, where a French army stood on the Danube for the first time in over 100 years, a kingdom of the Serbs, Croats and Slovenes was proclaimed on October 29 in Zagreb. It was formally established in the Serb city of Belgrade three days later. From the start, the new country was beset by border disputes with Italy, Romania and Bulgaria. Its main difficulties were, however, more basic: the land was ravaged by war and destruction and the peasantry by disease and starvation.

Elsewhere, countries such as Czechoslovakia, came into existence. Independence was declared from Austria by the Czechs on October 29, 1918, and from Hungary by Slovakia two days later. By January 1919, the integrated army of the newly united state had driven Polish forces from the disputed area of Teschen in Moravia.

All these developments were part of the legacy of what was, perhaps, the greatest single change within Europe as a result of the war: the collapse of the Habsburg Empire and the reconstitution of its territories on the basis of national self-determination. It was a change without parallel in Europe since 1453, when Constantinople had fallen to the Ottoman Turks. In the last days of the war, as Austria-Hungary collapsed, some 500,000 of its troops surrendered. Others abandoned their positions to march home across countries in chaos.

Surrender of the fleet
The German fleet, led by British warships, steams up the Firth of Forth on November 21. It was subsequently interned at Scapa Flow in the Orkney Islands, Scotland.

The election of an assembly to draw up a new German constitution went ahead on January 19, and included women voters for the first time. Parties that supported democracy received 75 per cent of the votes, and the elected assembly met in Weimar on February 6. The German provisional government, of which Ebert was now president, was, however, given little credit by the Allies for its overthrow of the old, autocratic order. Any hopes that a democratic and demilitarized Germany

Going home
Alsatians cross a bridge at Kehl, just east of Strasbourg, on their way back home in November 1918.

Hailing "Victory Day"
In England, as in the other Allied states, the celebration of victory lasted for just a few hours before people began to remember the reality of what had occurred over the previous four years.

ARMISTICE

O N 11 NOVEMBER AT 11 AM the guns on the Western Front at last fell silent. Within hours, church bells were pealing again in Britain, where it seemed that the entire population had come out into the streets to celebrate "Victory Day". Factories closed, pubs stayed open, and the flags of the Allied nations were unfurled under the dull November sky. In France, too, flags fluttered and huge crowds sang the "Marseillaise" but the celebrations were more muted than those of the Americans and the British, perhaps because the French people had suffered the highest proportion of deaths of any combatant nation, as well as the trauma of German occupation.

In Germany, news of the armistice was of minor significance, compared with reports of the kaiser's abdication and cities falling under revolutionary control. Among the German people, shielded from the events at the Western Front until the very last minute, there was bewilderment, and denial. They felt that because the armistice had been signed while their army still occupied parts of Belgium and France, they had not lost the war, but had been betrayed by their leaders. If the Allies had mounted victory parades in Berlin and Munich, the reality of defeat might have sunk in sooner. Instead, the terms of the armistice allowed German soldiers to march home, and be hailed as victors by the new German Chancellor, Friedrich Ebert. With the armistice began the myth of the "stab in the back", of which Adolf Hitler was to be the eventual beneficiary.

Celebrations
Among the crowds who celebrated on the streets of London were an American sailor, a Red Cross nurse and British soldiers, united in their enthusiasm for the peace.

German capitulation
The headlines on the front page of this French newspaper of November 11 announce the abdication of the kaiser and revolution in Germany, and look forward to the signing of the Armistice later in the day.

Le Petit Journal

L'ALLEMAGNE EN RÉVOLUTION
Le Kaiser a abdiqué, le Kronprinz renonce
UNE RÉGENCE ANNONCÉE — UN CHANCELIER SOCIALISTE : EBERT

On attend la capitulation

French victory postcard
The significance of the eleventh hour of the eleventh day of the eleventh month would never be forgotten.

Thanksgiving Day at Eagle Hut, London.
November 28th 1918.

Thanksgiving menu
The Thanksgiving dinner given for American military personnel in London on November 28, 1918 was an especially momentous event.

Cheering Australians
News of the armistice was received with joy and relief around the world. Crowds gathered to celebrate in Martin Place in central Sydney.

A NEW WORLD ORDER
1919–1923

~

THE PARIS PEACE CONFERENCE WAS
CONVENED AMID HIGH HOPES OF A EUROPE IN
WHICH OLD RIVALRIES AND RESENTMENTS WOULD BE
HEALED, BUT WHILE THE MAP OF EUROPE WAS
RADICALLY ALTERED BY THE TREATIES, MANY OF THE
UNDERLYING CAUSES OF THE WAR WERE NOT
ADDRESSED. THE HARDSHIP EXPERIENCED BY THE
PEOPLE OF CENTRAL AND EASTERN EUROPE, AND THE
EXAMPLE OF THE RUSSIAN REVOLUTION, LED TO
A PERIOD OF POLITICAL UPHEAVAL IN WHICH
EXTREMIST LEADERS GAINED POPULAR SUPPORT.

~

Wounded Red Army soldiers in 1919
Soldiers of the Red Army fought to consolidate the
hold of the Bolsheviks over Russia. They experienced
many setbacks, before eventually winning the war
against the counter-revoluntionary forces.

THE PEACE THAT FAILED

THERE WERE HOPES THAT A POST-WAR EUROPE COULD BE FOUNDED ON

THE PRINCIPLES OF NATIONAL SELF-DETERMINATION AND DEMOCRACY, AND

THAT FUTURE INTERNATIONAL CONFLICTS COULD BE SOLVED PEACEABLY

BY A LEAGUE OF NATIONS – ASPIRATIONS THAT HAD BEEN EXPRESSED BY

THE AMERICAN PRESIDENT WOODROW WILSON IN HIS "FOURTEEN POINTS".

WHEN PRESIDENT WILSON arrived in London in December 1918, on his way to Paris for the peace conference, he was greeted by many as though he were a divine messenger, bringing light to the Old World from the New. His proposals for a lasting peace, set out at the beginning of the year as his "Fourteen Points" (see page 284) and further elaborated in later speeches, had been the basis on which the German leadership had requested an armistice. He could thus be credited with playing a substantial role in bringing the war to its conclusion.

The Paris Peace Conference opened in January 1919 and was attended by representatives from 32 nations. A large number of commissions were set up to deal with different aspects of the settlement, which included separate treaties with each of the Central Powers, and a covenant establishing the League of Nations. The conference was unusual in not involving negotiations between opposing sides. The victors alone decided the terms, which the vanquished were then forced to accept. The main decisions were taken by the French prime minister, Clemenceau, the British prime minister Lloyd George, and the American president, Wilson. The Italian prime minister, Orlando, was somewhat sidelined, and the head of the Japanese delegation, Saionji, stood aside from the discussions when Japanese interests were not involved.

JUSTICE OR REVENGE?

There was strong public feeling in both Britain and France that Germany should make substantial financial reparations to compensate the Allies for the cost of the war. Lloyd George, a Liberal, was more moderate in his views, but his government depended on Conservative votes and he was thus a prisoner of vengeful public opinion. The Germans objected strongly to the demand for reparations, and to being made to a sign a "war guilt" clause. They had agreed to armistice talks on the basis of the principles embodied in the Fourteen Points, and they profoundly resented the way in which, in their view, the terms of both the Armistice and treaty contravened these principles. The Allies pointed out that the requirement for compensation had been included in a note Wilson sent to the Germans on November 5. Furthermore, they were, in effect, demanding no more than the Germans had exacted from the Russians and the Romanians in the treaties of 1918. In the event, agreement could not be reached on the amount of reparations to be paid by Germany, and the matter had to be left open.

The treaty stripped Germany of its overseas possessions in Africa, China and the Pacific, and imposed the added humiliation of the reduction of the German army to 100,000 officers and men, and the navy to nothing more than a coastal defence force; Germany was denied an air force.

"The German people, after all the frightful suffering of the last few years, lack all means of defending their honour by external action …The Government of the German Republic therefore declares that it is ready to accept and sign the conditions of peace imposed by the Allied and Associated Governments."

EXTRACT FROM THE STATEMENT ISSUED BY THE GERMAN GOVERNMENT
IN WHICH IT AGREED TO SIGN THE VERSAILLES TREATY

THE FUTURE SECURITY OF FRANCE

In a speech made in February 1918 Wilson had expounded the principle that territorial settlements should be made in the interest of the populations concerned, and not on the basis of claims by rival states. Set against this, however, was the Allies' concern for the long-term security of Belgium and France in the face of Germany's potential economic might. The return of Alsace-Lorraine (annexed by Germany in 1871) had been established by Wilson as the eighth of his Fourteen Points and was thus easily agreed upon. French demands for German territory in the Rhineland, indeed the division of Germany itself, were, though, seen by Wilson and Lloyd George as likely to ensure future conflict. A compromise was agreed in April that provided for a military occupation of the Rhineland by the

Allies extending 50 km (30 miles) to the east, lasting for 15 years, and for its permanent demilitarization. The Saarland would be under French control in order to provide compensation for the German wrecking of the coalfields of northern France, its ultimate fate to be decided by plebiscite.

These arrangements were incorporated into the Treaty of Versailles, which, despite misgivings by Wilson and Lloyd George about certain of its provisions, was presented to Count Brockdorff-Rantzau on May 7, 1919. After minor amendments it was reluctantly signed by the German delegation in the Hall of Mirrors on June 28. The treaty was subsequently ratified by the governments of all parties except the United States, whose Senate had no enthusiasm for becoming further involved in international affairs through the League of Nations. An Anglo-American guarantee to France, offered in return for the modification of French demands on the Rhineland, was thereby lost, and Clemenceau, widely blamed for having failed France in these matters, was defeated in the 1920 election.

Scuppered at Scapa Flow
The commander of the German fleet, anticipating that the Versailles Treaty would require him to hand over his ships, despatched an order on June 21, 1919 for the fleet to be sunk. A total of 74 ships were sent to the bottom.

"You may strip Germany of her colonies, reduce her armaments to a mere police force and her navy to that of a fifth-rate power; all the same, in the end if she feels she has been unjustly treated in the peace of 1919 she will find means of exacting retribution from her conquerors."

LLOYD GEORGE, *THE TRUTH ABOUT THE PEACE TREATIES*, 1938

THE CREATION OF STATES

The principle of national self-determination had been accepted, in some cases reluctantly, by all parties, but putting it into practice was not straightforward. The collapse of the empires of Austria-Hungary, Russia and Turkey left the whole of Eastern Europe virtually a blank slate. New nation states were created, and old ones enlarged (or shrunk), according to boundaries agreed by a series of commissions at the peace conference, but the integrity of the process was called into question by an evident bias against the Central Powers, and by the Allies' desire to create relatively strong states bordering on Bolshevik Russia. These matters were dealt with in individual treaties with Austria (Treaty of Saint-Germain), Hungary (Treaty of Trianon) and Bulgaria (Treaty of Neuilly).

Finland and the Baltic states were granted their independence, and Poland, which had ceased to exist in the late 18th century, was reconstructed. Territory of the former Habsburg Empire was divided between seven states, of which Austria was, ironically, the smallest. Although borders were dictated, as far as practicable, by ethnic groups, there were exceptions. Czechoslovakia and Romania gained territories in which many people were Magyar-speaking, and others (as in Sudetenland) that were largely German-speaking. Among the gains Italy acquired as reward for its war efforts were German-speaking areas in the Tyrol.

THE BREAK-UP OF THE OTTOMAN EMPIRE

The defeat of the Turks resulted in the disappearance of the Ottoman Empire. In August 1920, the last and in some ways the most difficult of the peace treaties was signed at Sèvres, although it was almost immediately overtaken by events and was never actually ratified.

The harsh treatment of Turkey in the Treaty of Sèvres was apparently designed to terminate its independence. The sultan surrendered all territory

already lost by the empire and gave up any claim to territories outside the boundaries of Turkey. Britain and France had already staked out territories for themselves in the Middle East, which they held under the legal form of a mandate from the League of Nations (a form of government also adopted for the former German colonies). Turkey handed over eastern Thrace, including Gallipoli, to the Greeks, who also occupied Smyrna (Izmir). An independent Armenia was projected, and provision was made for a self-governing Kurdish state that would incorporate parts of Anatolia and Mesopotamia (Iraq).

The peacemakers
The British prime minister, Lloyd George, the French prime minister, Clemenceau, and the American President, Wilson, arrive at Versailles in 1919.

ITALIAN RESENTMENT

It was not only Germany and its allies that considered themselves ill-treated by the peace settlement. Ever since its unification, Italy had exhibited, as Bismarck observed, a giant appetite for territory without possessing the requisite teeth. Italy's allies considered its contribution to the war effort small, which was true in terms of its effect, but ignored its high casualty rate. Italy's rewards from the peace settlement fell short of the claims it had made in the Treaty of London when it entered the war in 1915, which included, among other things, the Dalmatian coast. The Italians resented the secret wartime diplomacy of Britain and France, notably the Sykes–Picot Agreement of 1916, in which the British and French had divided up the Middle East to their mutual benefit. They also objected to the creation of the Slav state that was to become Yugoslavia, inhabited by many of the people Italy had been fighting.

The rejection of Italy's demand for Fiume on the Adriatic coast caused particular bitterness. The Italian delegation briefly withdrew from the peace talks, and in September 1919 the poet D'Annunzio seized it for Italy. His proto-fascist regime lasted a year before the Italian government suppressed it. In spite of this episode, and the widespread social unrest that appeared to threaten revolution in 1919–20, there was little real support for parties of the far right at this time, although over the next two years parliamentary democracy in Italy collapsed.

Under the terms of the Treaty of Sèvres, Turkey effectively ceased to be an independent state. Control of the straits between the Black Sea and the Mediterranean was given to an international commission. The army was reduced to a token force. Trade and financial affairs were to be controlled by a commission representing Britain, France and Italy, with each country being awarded a "sphere of influence" within Turkey.

Destruction of weapons
Under the terms of the Treaty of Versailles, Germany was forced to disarm. This included the destruction of its tanks – even this British model, captured during the war.

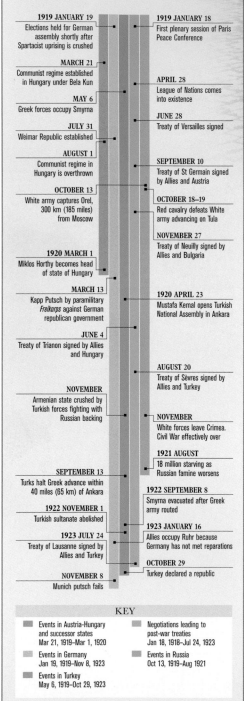

PEACE TALKS AND CONFLICT
1919 – 1923
~

The peace negotiations of 1919, which involved individual peace treaties being made with each of the defeated countries, did not take place in a world devoid of conflict. Several countries in Europe experienced short-lived periods of violent political upheaval, while the Bolsheviks battled with the White Russians for control of Russia. The Turks meanwhile proved that they would not submit to European domination.

~

1919 JANUARY 19
Elections held for German assembly shortly after Spartacist uprising is crushed

1919 JANUARY 18
First plenary session of Paris Peace Conference

MARCH 21
Communist regime established in Hungary under Bela Kun

APRIL 28
League of Nations comes into existence

MAY 6
Greek forces occupy Smyrna

JUNE 28
Treaty of Versailles signed

JULY 31
Weimar Republic established

AUGUST 1
Communist regime in Hungary is overthrown

SEPTEMBER 10
Treaty of St Germain signed by Allies and Austria

OCTOBER 13
White army captures Orel, 300 km (185 miles) from Moscow

OCTOBER 18–19
Red cavalry defeats White army advancing on Tula

NOVEMBER 27
Treaty of Neuilly signed by Allies and Bulgaria

1920 MARCH 1
Miklos Horthy becomes head of state of Hungary

MARCH 13
Kapp Putsch by paramilitary *Freikorps* against German republican government

1920 APRIL 23
Mustafa Kemal opens Turkish National Assembly in Ankara

JUNE 4
Treaty of Trianon signed by Allies and Hungary

AUGUST 20
Treaty of Sèvres signed by Allies and Turkey

NOVEMBER
Armenian state crushed by Turkish forces fighting with Russian backing

NOVEMBER
White forces leave Crimea. Civil War effectively over

1921 AUGUST
18 million starving as Russian famine worsens

SEPTEMBER 13
Turks halt Greek advance within 40 miles (65 km) of Ankara

1922 SEPTEMBER 8
Smyrna evacuated after Greek army routed

1922 NOVEMBER 1
Turkish sultanate abolished

1923 JANUARY 16
Allies occupy Ruhr because Germany has not met reparations

1923 JULY 24
Treaty of Lausanne signed by Allies and Turkey

OCTOBER 29
Turkey declared a republic

NOVEMBER 8
Munich putsch fails

KEY

Events in Austria-Hungary and successor states
Mar 21, 1919–Mar 1, 1920

Negotiations leading to post-war treaties
Jan 18, 1918–Jul 24, 1923

Events in Germany
Jan 19, 1919–Nov 8, 1923

Events in Russia
Oct 13, 1919–Aug 1921

Events in Turkey
May 6, 1919–Oct 29, 1923

Aftermath of the War

Hungarian Red Army troops
The dillusionment of defeat, and sympathy for Bolshevik Russia fuelled the revolution in Hungary, where Bela Kun was supported by a Hungarian Red Army.

T HE PRINCIPLE OF NATIONAL self-determination, espoused by the peacemakers, ensured the liquidation of what remained of the ancient, multi-ethnic Habsburg Empire – the Dual Monarchy of Austria-Hungary. As well as the Versailles Treaty, separate treaties were made with Austria at Saint-Germain-en-Laye and with Hungary at Trianon.

Austria was reduced to a state of only 6.5 million people, over a third of whom lived in Vienna. Except for the loss of the South Tyrol to Italy, the borders roughly outlined the German-speaking area, and the chief Austrian complaint was that union (*Anschluss*) with Germany was forbidden, in breach of the principle of national self-determination. There were doubts over whether a truncated Austrian state was economically viable, and the state was further weakened by tensions between the citizens of Vienna (who were primarily socialist in sympathy) and the agrarian population (who were primarily Catholic and conservative).

In Hungary there was acute indignation at the loss of more than 70 per cent of its pre-war area and nearly 65 per cent of its population. Just days before the war ended Hungary had declared its independence from Austria and instituted a democratic regime under Count Karolyi, in the hope of being treated as one of the newly independent nations, rather than as an enemy. The disillusion provoked by the peace process led to Karolyi's resignation, the setting up of a short-lived

communist republic led by Bela Kun, and a brief Romanian occupation of Budapest. Not until the reactionary regime of Admiral Horthy established itself was the Treaty of Trianon ratified.

SOUTH SLAVS, CZECHS AND SLOVAKS

Serbia, now part of the Kingdom of Serbs, Croats and Slovenes (renamed Yugoslavia in 1929), was represented at the peace conference, but the new kingdom was not officially recognized until May 1919, mainly because of objections by Italy, whose territorial ambitions it thwarted. The new nation's economic weakness, revolutionary ideas among workers and intellectuals, and hostility towards the Serbs among the other ethnic groups (especially the Croatians) created political problems. These were aggravated by religious differences – the Serbs being Greek Orthodox, the Croats and Slovenes Roman Catholic – and social tensions. The Serbian army and police established a reasonable degree of stability by 1920 under Nikola Pasic, but it seemed that the disintegration of the kingdom could only be prevented by a strong authoritarian regime.

In 1914 most Czechs and Slovaks had been sympathetic towards Russia. Thousands were interned or shot for disloyalty to Austria-Hungary.

TERMS OF THE PEACE SETTLEMENT

TREATIES WERE DRAWN UP at the Paris Peace Conference with each of the Central Powers. All were modelled on the Treaty of Versailles.

VERSAILLES (JUN 28, 1919) – WITH GERMANY

Alsace-Lorraine ceded to France and northern Schleswig to Denmark; large area in east ceded to Poland, including a "corridor" giving Poles access to Baltic; plebiscites in disputed regions, including the Saar (under temporary international control); Rhineland demilitarized; Danzig made a free city; international access guaranteed to Kiel Canal and stretches of Danube, Elbe, Niemen, Oder and Rhine; reparations to be made, although amount unspecified; all colonies ceded to Allies or League of Nations; army and navy reduced; air force banned. A covenant established the League of Nations.

SAINT-GERMAIN (SEPT 10, 1919) – WITH AUSTRIA

Recognized independence of Czechoslovakia, Poland, Hungary and Yugoslavia; all states to protect ethnic minorities; Trentino, South Tyrol, Trieste and Istria ceded to Italy, eastern Galicia to Poland; unification with Germany forbidden without League of Nations approval; armed forces circumscribed, the need for reparations acknowledged, although amount unspecified.

NEUILLY (NOV 27, 1919) – WITH BULGARIA

Independent Yugoslavia recognized; Aegean coast ceded to Greece; armed forces reduced; amount of reparations agreed (uniquely among the peace treaties); most of which was subsequently paid on time and without serious problems.

TRIANON (JUN 4, 1920) – WITH HUNGARY

Slovakia, Bratislava and part of Ruthenia ceded to Czechoslovakia; Croatia and Slovenia and part of Banat to Yugoslavia; Transylvania and most of Banat to Romania; Burgenland to Austria, Fiume to Italy; armed forces limited, reparations imposed.

SÈVRES (AUG 20, 1920) – WITH TURKEY

Ottoman Empire abolished; all non-Turkish territories removed; independence of the Hejaz, Yemen and Armenia recognized; Syria made a French mandate of the League of Nations; Mesopotamia and Palestine made British mandates; Dodecanese islands and Rhodes ceded to Italy, other Aegean islands and the region of Smyrna in Anatolia, pending a plebiscite, to Greece; the Dardanelles and the Bosphorus straits internationalized. The treaty was rejected by nationalists and was never ratified, although the mandates in the Middle East remained in force.

Protest in Berlin
Friedrich Naumann, leader of the German Democratic Party, expresses the outrage felt by many Germans at the harsh peace terms Germany was forced to accept.

LAUSANNE (JUL 24, 1923) – WITH TURKEY

This treaty superseded that of Sèvres (never ratified). Eastern Thrace, Smyrna, and control of the straits returned to Turkey; an exchange of populations with Greece agreed and implemented.

Lloyd George leaves the Trianon Palace
The British prime minister tried to tread a fine line between the desire for vengeance expressed by many in France and Britain, and his own more moderate views.

Masaryk, Benes and others lobbied in Allied capitals for Czecho-Slovak independence, and by September 1918 all the Allied nations had affirmed support for an independent state. An interim Czecho–Slovak government was set up in Paris in October, shortly before Austria's surrender, which led to a declaration of independence in Prague. An interim constitution established a democratic republic, with Masaryk as president. The hostility of the substantial German minority in the Sudetenland led to violence, and some Hungarians were forced out of former Hungarian territory in Slovakia. Under the constitution of 1920 Czechoslovakia became the most stable and prosperous of the new states – and the only one in which democracy survived until 1939.

POLAND REBORN

Poland was reconstituted from the lands of the three imperial powers that had partitioned it among themselves between 1772 and 1795 – Austria, Prussia and Russia. The Bolsheviks had renounced Russian claims on Poland at Brest-Litovsk, but angered the Poles by ceding Polish territory to Austria and to the short-lived republic of the

What honest man can sign such a capitulation? Would not the hand wither that put itself into such bonds? This treaty will make a corpse not just of Germany but of the right to self-determination, of faith in treaties. It will be the beginning of a general process of barbarization.

CHANCELLOR SCHEIDEMANN ON THE TERMS PRESENTED TO THE GERMAN DELEGATION AT VERSAILLES ON MAY 8, 1919

Ukraine. The Allies accepted a united, independent Poland in June 1918, and the Poles themselves drove the Germans out of Poznan.

The circumstances of the newly restored state, a democratic republic with Pilsudski as head of state, was unenviable. The peace terms left intractable territorial problems that were not resolved by plebiscites, with Danzig, becoming a free city under League of Nations protection. Frontier quarrels provoked armed conflict with the Germans, Czechs and Ukrainians,

arbitrated by the Council of the League, and war with Bolshevik Russia, which ended in March 1921.

These territorial disputes set back the immense task of the reconstruction of Poland. As a result of war, the country's industry was at a virtual standstill, communications were disordered, and the civil service non-existent. Polish agriculture was laid waste by famine and disease. New laws limiting land holdings were largely ignored by the nobility, who held on to their vast estates with the support of elements of the urban middle class, fearful of communist influence among workers and peasants.

The collapse of the Russian empire in 1918 gave Estonia, Latvia and Lithuania a chance to declare their independence, although they subsequently came into conflict with the Bolsheviks. During the early 1920s they made peace with Russia and were granted international recognition, although Lithuania lost its capital, Vilna (Vilnius), to the Poles.

A welcome fit for heroes
Front-line German soldiers returning to Berlin were greeted with much rejoicing. Having been largely kept in ignorance of the circumstances surrounding the armistice, many Germans did not realize that they would be expected to pay the price of defeat.

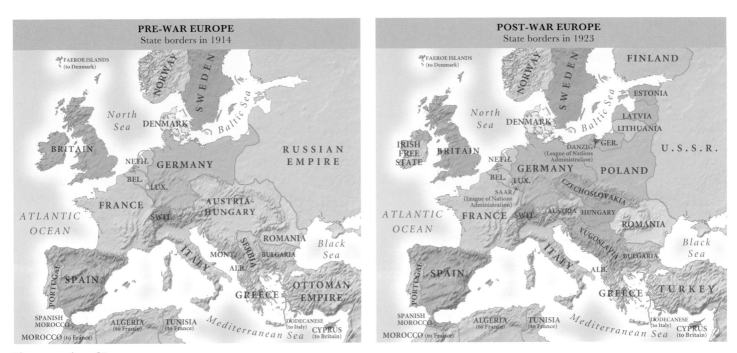

PRE-WAR EUROPE
State borders in 1914

POST-WAR EUROPE
State borders in 1923

The remapping of Europe
From the Baltic to the Aegean, European borders were redrawn. Seven new nation-states were created from land once ruled over by Austria-Hungary and Russia, and France regained Alsace-Lorraine from Germany.

GERMANY AFTER VERSAILLES
The Treaty of Versailles was presented to a German delegation led by Count Brockdorff-Rantzau on May 7, 1919. The Germans responded with an outcry of protest at the harsh terms that were being dicated to them. In the days that followed notes were exchanged but there was no face-to-face discussion. On June 16 the Allies threatened to renew hostilities if the Germans did not sign within a week. Seven days later they agreed that they would sign. The official ceremony took place in the Hall of Mirrors at Versailles on June 28.

Germany at the time of the ceremony was under a provisional government, while an elected National Assembly met in Weimar to work out a new, democratic constitution for the country. This was finalized in July 1919, and the Weimar Republic was born. Parliament was to consist of two houses, the more important of which was the Reichstag, to which ministers were responsible, and whose members were elected by univeral suffrage. The president, who was to be directly elected, would normally have only a ceremonial role, but in an

Spartacists on the march
Germany's provisional government faced many challenges including, in January 1919, a short-lived revolution in Berlin by the Spartacists, who made the mistake of thinking the country was ripe for communist revolution.

emergency had the right to dissolve the Reichstag and rule by decree. What exactly constituted an emergency situation was not defined.

POLITICAL AND ECONOMIC DIFFICULTIES
The Weimar Republic was dominated by problems connected with the Versailles Treaty, especially the payment of reparations and the reduction of the army. The generals blamed the politicians rather than themselves for defeat, and in the so-called Kapp Putsch of March 1920 the *Freikorps* – a voluntary paramilitary group formed from demobbed soliders – attempted to overthrow the

republican government. The coup failed thanks to a general strike in Berlin, but the campaign of political terrorism pursued by the *Freikorps* was to continue for the next three years.

Negotiations with the Allies over reparations were dogged by the wide divergence between Allied demands and Germany's estimate of its ability to pay. Both sides were divided within themselves, with Britain favouring more tolerant treatment of Germany than did France. The sum to be paid was eventually fixed by the Reparations Commission in 1921 at the equivalent of £6,600,000,000 ($28 billion), to be paid over 42 years.

On the German side, the Right argued for obstruction and non-compliance, the Centre and Centre-Left for a more willing attitude, in the hope of negotiating future reductions. The moderates were weakened in June 1922 when their leader, the extremely able foreign minister, Walter Rathenau, a Jew, became the most notable victim of a series of assassinations by rightists. Ironically, two months earlier he had concluded, as a concession to the hard-liners, the Treaty of Rapallo for economic collaboration with the Soviet Union, which included a secret clause permitting Germany to manufacture armaments in Russia, in defiance of the Versailles Treaty.

With Rathenau removed, the obstructionists gained the ascendancy and, in response to Germany's failure to make reparations on schedule, French and Belgian troops occupied the industrial region of the Ruhr in January 1923. Their intention was to divert the output of the mines to France. The miners went on strike, with the backing of the German government, which was then faced with the problem of how to prevent the miners and their families from starving.

A thorny welcome in the Ruhr
A cartoon by Erich Schilling in the satirical journal *Simplicissimus* draws attention to the fact that the French occupation of the Ruhr was not going smoothly, thanks to the non-cooperation of the miners.

RAMPANT INFLATION

Germany had largely paid for the war, not by taxation, but simply by printing money, and this policy was adopted again, with the mint's presses stretched to the limit. The result was a total collapse of the currency, which within eight months, at 4,200 billion marks to the dollar, was not worth the paper it was printed on.

Naturally, wages and salaries failed to keep pace, while pensions and investments became almost worthless. People survived by selling possessions and bartering for food and necessities (although some benefited from speculation). Worst affected were the middle classes, normally a conservative element, who were radicalized by this bitter experience. The Republican government was discredited, the country in chaos. Separatism became a powerful force once more, and extremist parties of both right and left gained power in several states.

Gustav Stresemann, once an extreme nationalist, admirer of the kaiser, supporter of the military, and in 1923 leader of a right-wing party in the Reichstag, took the lead in persuading the Germans of the futility of passive resistance in the Ruhr. In his brief period as chancellor of a national coalition from August 13 to November 23 he managed to stabilize the currency. Indeed, the situation was sufficiently improved to undermine popular support for Adolf Hitler's Munich putsch on November 9.

The destabilization of Germany was not in the interest of the rest of Europe and there were international moves to help resolve the country's economic problems. Under the Dawes Plan of April 1924 arrangements were agreed for Germany's payment of reparations, made possible by a substantial initial international loan.

Stresemann served as Foreign Minister from late 1924 until his early death in 1929, and was involved in negotiating the Locarno Pact of 1925 – a set of agreements guaranteeing peace in Europe. It led to Germany's acceptance into the League of Nations in 1926, to improved relations with its neighbours, and, in 1930, to the evacuation of Allied troops from the Rhineland, five years ahead of schedule.

Cartloads of money
German inflation in the early 1920s led to scenes such as this, in which money to pay employees' wages had to be wheeled from the bank in laundry baskets.

REVOLUTIONS IN EUROPE

THE RUSSIAN BOLSHEVIKS confidently anticipated the spread of communism throughout Europe in the wake of their own revolution, but although leftist uprisings broke out in Germany and elsewhere, the looked-for international revolution never occurred.

In Germany, the Spartacists, a group of radical socialists led by Karl Liebknecht and Rosa Luxemburg, founded the German Communist Party. In January 1919 they instigated an uprising in Berlin against the socialist-led provisional government, but it was violently suppressed within a week. Liebknecht and Luxemburg were shot by the right-wing *Freikorps*. Risings in Hamburg, the Ruhr and other areas were also suppressed.

On November 8, 1918 the Wittelsbach dynasty in Bavaria was overthrown in a coup led by Kurt Eisner – a socialist. He declared a republic, but his party failed in the elections of January 1919, and in February he was assassinated. The communists responded by taking control of Munich and instituting a "Red Terror". The local *Freikorps* recaptured Munich in May and imposed their own "White Terror".

In March 1919 the Hungarian president, Count Karolyi, resigned and handed power to a communist regime led by Bela Kun, a Russian Jew and Soviet agent. His promise to enlist Soviet assistance to regain land confiscated from Hungary by the Allies gained widespread support. His Red Army forces attacked the Czechs, but were forced to withdraw by the Allies. His increasingly dictatorial rule eroded popular support, and an invasion and advance to Budapest by the Romanian army caused him to flee in August. After the restoration of the monarchy by the Hungarian parliament, Miklos Horthy was elected regent in March 1920. He encouraged a purge of revolutionaries and Jews.

Revolutionary cheer
Crowds in Budapest, Hungary, on March 21, 1919 celebrate the new soviet regime, which the next day seized all private property and took control of banking and trade.

Rosa Luxemburg
Luxemburg, a Pole, studied in Switzerland, where she gained a doctorate. She was imprisoned for her revolutionary activities in Warsaw in 1905 and for her opposition to the war in Germany.

Bela Kun
A founder of the Hungarian Communist Party, Kun allied himself with the Russian Soviet government and, in his short period in power in 1919, used ruthless methods in his drive to rid Hungary of its capitalist system and establish a soviet state.

Lenin sweeps the world clean
The aim of the Bolsheviks in the early days of their revolution was not just to transform Russia into a communist state, but to rid the rest of the world of its ruling monarchs, capitalists and clerics. The dream was not realized, however, as the proletariat of the defeated states tended to favour nationalism over socialism.

ТОВ. ЛЕНИН ОЧИЩАЕТ ЗЕМЛЮ ОТ НЕЧИСТИ.

The Red Army advance into Poland
A detachment of Red Army cavalry enters Soldau, north-west of Warsaw, in its advance into Poland. Only splits within the Red Army leadership and the clever strategy of Pilsudski saved the Polish capital from invasion.

THE RUSSIAN CIVIL WAR

This brutal and destructive war cost an estimated 13 million lives, many of which were lost as a result of famine caused by the extensive disruption to food supplies that reduced production to one-seventh of 1914 levels. At the end of 1918 the Bolsheviks had been in danger of losing control of Russia. That they eventually won the civil war was partly thanks to the strength and unity of their leadership, but also to the divisions among their enemies.

The counter-revolutionary leaders of 1918 had included socialists and others opposed to the Bolsheviks, none of whom had any experience of military leadership. They were gradually pushed aside by the generals – members of the old, aristocratic, ruling class. Although the moderate socialists badly needed the military ability of the tsarist generals, and the generals

White Army gunners
Wrangel's White Russian Army in the Crimea in 1920 included survivors of Deniken's army, which had been decimated by the Bolsheviks earlier in the year. Wrangel himself was forced to withdraw in November in the face of the overwhelming strength of the Red Army.

in turn needed the popular support that the socialists commanded, the inevitable antagonism between them was ruinous to the counter-revolutionary cause. Most of the Russian people were peasants, on whom all parties relied for food and transport. They were far from natural allies of the Bolsheviks, but they came to see the Bolsheviks as representing "the people" against the reactionary White Russian generals.

Other factors contributed to the Bolshevik victory. They held a strong position in the centre of the country, and they were able to sustain the morale and discipline of their supporters at a time of near-total social breakdown. Trotsky's outstanding organization and leadership of the Red Army produced, from almost nothing, a force that was superior to any the ill-assorted counter-revolutionaries could raise. As for the intervention of the Allies in support of the White army, this may well have worked in the Bolsheviks' favour. While the number of Allied troops sent to Russia was too small to affect the result of the war, it was large enough for the Bolsheviks to be able to brand their White opponents as lackeys of the imperialists.

VICTORY IN THE NORTH, EAST AND SOUTH

For much of 1919 the survival of the Bolshevik regime hung in the balance, but by the end of the year, it had won victories on all fronts. In the north, the withdrawal of Allied forces in the autumn left the Whites weakened and demoralized. In the east, Kolchak's White forces had seemed set to continue their successes of the previous year, but they had been gravely weakened by a split with the moderate socialists in late 1918, which lost them popular support and resulted in the Czech soldiers fighting alongside them losing interest. Kolchak's successes at the beginning of 1919 proved misleading. Confronted by the full force of the Red Army on the Volga, his men were soon in rapid retreat back across Siberia. Omsk was lost in November, and in February 1920 Kolchak was captured and shot. By the end of the year communist rule was restored in Siberia, barring an eastern strip where Japanese forces remained in occupation until November 1922.

The greatest threat came from the forces of Denikin in the south. Advancing steadily from the region of the Caucasus, he conquered a huge swathe of territory north of the Black Sea, and by October he was less than 320 km (200 miles) from Moscow. There, he was brought to a halt when confronted for the first time by the Red Army in strength. He retreated to the northern Caucasus, where his army was destroyed early in 1920. Meanwhile, Yudenich had launched an attack from Estonia. In October, at the time when Denikin was threatening Moscow, Yudenich's forces were in the suburbs of the former capital, Petrograd. His defeat, however, coincided with that of Denikin, and within a few days the communists' near-disaster had turned into near-total victory. The only White Russian force remaining was that commanded by Wrangel in the Crimea.

WAR WITH POLAND

At this point another player entered the stage. Russia had not been represented at Versailles in 1919 and it was therefore difficult to fix its border with the newly recreated Poland. The proposed Curzon Line (similar to the current border) had not satisfied the Poles, and with Russia in disarray the opportunity to advance it eastwards was tempting. The Poles did not want to support the campaign of the counter-revolutionaries, who could be assumed to be more antagonistic than the Bolsheviks to an independent Poland, so they waited until the Red Army had largely ended the counter-revolutionary threat before invading the Ukraine in April 1920.

In less than two weeks the Poles were in Kiev, but the defeat of the White Russians had released more Red Army troops, and over the next three months the Poles were driven back to the walls of Warsaw. The threat of a Soviet presence deep

Revolutionaries
The role played by the peoples of the Caucasus Red Army in 1920 in the defeat of the White Russian forces is celebrated on this poster.

in Europe prompted the swift despatch of a French military mission under Weygand, but it was the strategic grasp of Pilsudski in his counter-attack against the Soviet lines of communication, and the exhaustion of the Bolshevik forces, that saved the Polish capital. It was the Red Army's turn to retreat. The matter was concluded at the Treaty of Riga in March 1921, when the Russo-Polish border was drawn along a line more generous to the Poles than the Curzon Line, although short of the boundary they aspired to. Ukraine, granted nominal independence in 1918, came once more under Russian domination as a part of the new Soviet Union.

The final campaign, undertaken by the Red Army after the armistice with the Poles, was their defeat in the Crimea of Wrangel's forces, who put up considerable resistance. By November 1920, however, the Bolsheviks had triumphed in the west, although Central Asia was not secured until 1923.

THE MIDDLE EAST

Even in the thick of war the British and French had discussed how to divide up the Ottoman Empire. Under the secret Sykes–Picot agreement of May 1916 France was to receive a substantial portion – not only present-day Lebanon and Syria, but areas of southern Turkey and northern Iraq. Britain was to have southern Mesopotamia and the ports of Haifa and Acre; Palestine was to be placed under international rule. An Arab state or confederation was mooted for the centre of the region – divided into French and British spheres of influence.

Polish troops off to war
Soldiers of the newly re-formed state of Poland march into action against the Bolsheviks in a drive to expand their country's eastern territory.

The Arabs, however, had expected to be awarded much more, following pledges made by the British in letters sent to the Sharif of Mecca in 1915–16, as an inducement for his support against the Turks. Balfour, in November 1917 had compounded the confusion, by writing to Lord Rothschild of his sympathy for the idea of establishing a Jewish national home in Palestine.

By the end of the war, however, Lloyd George had concluded that Britain's much greater involvement in fighting in the region entitled it to more territory than had been agreed by Sykes and Picot. Further negotiations took place, and although the British allowed the French to remain in control of Lebanon and Syria, they insisted on control of the oil-rich region of northern Mesopotamia (Iraq). Feisal became king of Syria, but was driven out by the French after attempting to expand his kingdom, and in 1921 was installed as king of Iraq by the British. The British also controlled Palestine, which dashed the hopes of those who had looked for an Arab Palestinian state within a federated Syria.

Following an agreement made at San Remo in April 1920, all these territories were governed under the legal form of a mandate from the League of Nations. Although this arrangement assumed that the counties would eventually become independent, it did little to appease Arab nationalist leaders, who had looked for more immediate rewards for their help in vanquishing the Turks.

TURKEY

The Treaty of Sèvres of 1919 allowed for a nominally independent Turkish government under the sultan, but for large "spheres of influence" in Anatolia for the British, French, Italians and Greeks. Events moved so swiftly in the region, however, that by the time the treaty was signed in August 1920, it was largely redundant.

In May 1919 the Greeks had occupied the port of Smyrna (Izmir), in an area of Turkey that was home to a large Greek population. The Allies, who had provided military protection for the Greeks, watched from their warships as Turkish residents were massacred. This incursion by the Greeks stirred up nationalist feelings already fermenting among the Turks. The successful general Mustafa Kemal, sent on a mission by the sultan to the east of the country, instead met resistance leaders at Amasia in June 1919, where they signed a protocol stating their determination to oppose both the Allies and the sultan. During the summer Kemal presided over meetings of resistance groups and decided that Ankara, in the middle of Anatolia, should be the

MUSTAFA KEMAL (ATATÜRK)

~

GIVEN THE NAME KEMAL ("Perfect") while at school, Mustafa Kemal Pasha (1881–1938) was an intuitive wartime leader. Although strongly opposed to Turkey siding with Germany, once war was declared in October 1914 he did more than any other general to defend his country against Russian, British and French invasions.

Kemal's first command was at Gallipoli in 1915, where he correctly predicted the Allied forces' landing places in both April and August, held the strategically important Sari Bair Ridge and provided the inspired leadership that enabled the Turks to hold back the Allies. Promoted to general, he then served in the Caucasus, before being transferred to Syria as commander of the Seventh Army. With Allenby's final offensive in Palestine in August 1918, Kemal retreated to the Turkish border rather than surrender, and held this position until the armistice.

After the war Kemal organized nationalist resistance to the Greek invasion, and negotiated improved terms for Turkey in the Treaty of Lausanne. He became the first president of the Turkish Republic in 1924, later taking the name Atatürk ("Father of the Turks").

Greek refugees in Smyrna
As Turkish troops closed in on Smyrna (Izmir) in September 1922, many of the Greeks who lived there, anticipating the massacre that was to take place, waited desperately on the quayside for ships to take them to safety. In the fighting that ensued the old town was almost completely destroyed by fire.

focus of the nationalist movement. On April 23, 1920 a Grand National Assembly declared its right to represent the nation, with Kemal as its president.

GRECO-TURKISH WAR

On June 20, 1920 the Greeks sent forces beyond the confines of Smyrna into the hinterland and, despite various setbacks, by August 1921 were threatening Ankara. In a three-week battle on the Sakarya River, Turkish forces, under Kemal's command, forced the Greeks to regroup east of Eskisehir. The following year the Greek army was routed, and in September 1922 the Turks retook Smyrna (Izmir), where they, in turn, massacred civilians.

The Greeks, in the Treaty of Sèvres, had also been

Turkish celebrations
Turks surround a huge Turkish flag, made to celebrate the retaking of Smyrna (Izmir). Animosity between the Greeks and Turks in the surrounding region was intensified by the war, and led to the relocation of around 1.5 million people.

awarded control of eastern Thrace – Turkey's foothold in Europe. Kemal pressed on to reclaim this area, reached the Dardanelles and entered into a stand-off with a small British force protecting the neutral zone on the eastern shore. The British prime minster, Lloyd George issued an ultimatum for the immediate withdrawal of Turkish forces, but the British commander deliberately omitted to pass it on. While diplomats discussed a possible resolution of the crisis, British and Turkish troops confronted each other over the barbed wire. Kemal, confident of being awarded his objective in any subsequent peace conference was, in fact, unwilling to attack. Lloyd George backed off, and shortly afterwards, having lost the Conservative support he relied on in Parliament, resigned as prime minister.

TREATY OF LAUSANNE

The Treaty of Sèvres was replaced by the Treaty of Lausanne, signed on July 24, 1923. In recognizing the boundaries of the modern Turkish state, it met almost all Turkey's demands. The losers under the new treaty were the minority populations in the region. Animosity between Greek and Turkish communities led to a "population swap" involving around 1.5 million Christian Greeks and Muslim Turks. The Kurds, under the Treaty of Sèvres, had been granted some degree of autonomy. All that was now forgotten. The Armenians, hundreds of thousands of whom had died in 1915–16 as a result of forced relocation by the Turks, had been granted an independent state under the first treaty. This had, however, been crushed by Kemal's forces in January 1921, with the Turks gaining further land from a supportive Russian Bolshevik government.

Kemal terminated the sultanate and converted the Ottoman Empire into the Turkish republic in October 1923. He became its first president – a post he held until his death in 1938.

THE MIDDLE EAST
State borders in 1914

THE MIDDLE EAST
State borders in 1923

Lines in the sand
The map of the Middle East was almost completely redrawn following the dissolution of the Ottoman Empire. Britain and France divided much of it between them, controlling "mandates" that gave them access to countries' raw materials (such as oil), while they guided them towards independence.

THE LEGACY OF THE WAR

The turmoil let loose in August 1914 did not end with the peace settlement, but only after two disturbed and threatening decades had culminated in a second world war – a legacy of the political extremism the first had helped to create. To prescient statesmen this was already apparent in 1919: "We shall have to fight another war all over again in 25 years," said Lloyd George at Versailles.

The unnecessary war of 1914–18 was, regardless of long-term effects, one of the greatest tragedies Europe had experienced since the Black Death. In human terms it was almost as destructive and cruel: maybe as many as 10 million men dead ("the lost generation"), and countless millions permanently damaged in body or soul, or emotionally destroyed by the decimation of families.

From a broad historical viewpoint the war could be seen to have brought some social benefits. Like most wars, it stimulated overdue changes, including the loosening of the stranglehold exerted by the class system. No one could suggest, though, that this made it worth fighting. The sacrifice of the cream of European youth left enduring scars. But for the war, and the failure of governments to prevent the disasters that followed, the names of Stalin, Mussolini and Hitler might now be unknown.

CULTURAL CHANGE

Cultural damage is less easily expressed in figures. Pre-1914 European culture, whatever its faults, was relatively liberal, tolerant, progressive, and confident that society – even human nature – could be improved. The mechanized abattoir of the trenches shattered these ideals. In the immediate aftermath of the war, many survivors and the bereaved wanted to put it from their minds, and the 1920s became a period in which people focused on trying to enjoy themselves. Ten years later, however, attitudes were changing. People began to visit the battlefields, with 15,000 people signing the visitors' book at the Menin Gate in August 1928, and towns such as Ypres becoming tourist centres.

Books on the war began to sell in huge numbers, led by Erich Maria Remarque's famous novel *All Quiet on the Western Front*. Published in 1929, it had

Reburying the dead

After the war there was the massive task of disinterring the corpses of the fallen and reburying them in dedicated war cemeteries, where the ranks of white crosses stand like soldiers on endless parade.

sold 4 million copies by 1931. Books, plays and films, whose influence on the popular conception of the war was more powerful than the events themselves, universally pictured it as a vast, horrible and pointless disaster, distressing those who clung to the idea that their sons and husbands had not died in vain. The political extremists of the 1930s promoted a different idea of the soldier, as agent of progress rather than exploited victim, but few even of their own people were truly convinced.

France and Britain went to war again in 1939 with the utmost unwillingness. The even greater slaughter of the Second World War, with the mass murder of civilians on an unimaginable scale, suppressed memories of the First, which passed swiftly from contemporary consciousness into faded history. It seemed, by comparison, a minor affair.

Attitudes changed again as a new generation grew up and the second war lost its immediacy. Something of the cynical wit, black humour and nihilistic politics of the 1920s was reflected in the culture of the 1960s, and people began to regard the First and Second World Wars as part of the same catastrophic conflict.

THE CONTINUING IMPACT

The First World War still engages contemporary writers, and its impact is keenly felt, not least by visitors to the vast cemeteries that are strung out across the main battlegrounds. Not all of the visitors have been directly affected by the war – some are the great-grandchildren of those who fought – but strong emotions sometimes break through the banal phrases in the visitor's books as people

struggle to express their feelings on being confronted by the evidence of such slaughter. The sounding of the Last Post every evening at the Menin Gate cannot fail to haunt the listener – whether it inspires thoughts of military glory or of the futility of death in battle.

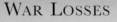

Temporary grave
This wooden cross was placed over the battlefield grave of a Frenchman, later reburied in an official war cemetery.

WAR LOSSES

~

ESTIMATES OF THE NUMBER of men killed in fighting during the First World War range from around 8.5 million to 10 million, with over 20 million wounded. These figures may well be under-estimates. The war was also directly responsible for a large number of civilian deaths – including around 2 million in both Russia and Turkey, 275,000 in Bulgaria, 500,000 in Romania and 600,000 in Serbia.

Allied Powers	Number mobilized	Military dead	Military wounded	Civilian dead
RUSSIA	12,000,000	1,800,000	4,950,000	2,000,000
FRANCE	8,660,000	1,390,000	4,330,000	40,000
BRITISH EMPIRE	8,780,000	900,000	2,090,000	1,000
ITALY	5,900,000	460,000	960,000	unknown
UNITED STATES	4,350,000	50,000	230,000	none
OTHERS	2,320,000	405,000	320,000	1,260,000

Central Powers	Number mobilized	Military dead	Military wounded	Civilian dead
GERMANY	13,400,000	2,040,000	5,690,000	700,000
AUSTRIA-HUNGARY	7,800,000	1,020,000	1,940,000	unknown
TURKEY	1,000,000	240,000	1,270,000	2,000,000
BULGARIA	1,200,000	80,000	150,000	275,000

Visiting a battlefield in France
A party of tourists visits the battlefield at Viel Amand after the war. This was the site of savage fighting between the Germans and the French in the Vosges mountains between 1915 and 1918.

GLOSSARY

~

ABBREVIATIONS

BEF
The British Expeditionary Force.

OHL
Oberste Heeresleitung, the German military high command.

Stavka
Shtab glavnogo/verkhovnogo komandovaniya, the Russian supreme military headquarters.

MILITARY ORGANIZATION
GENERAL TERMS:

unit
The basis of military organization. For administrative purposes "unit" usually meant a battalion, but a unit's size depended on circumstances. For tactical purposes in battle it could be much smaller.

formation
A number of units joined to form a single organization. The term was applied specifically when a military command had under its authority units of all the different "arms" – infantry, artillery and cavalry – as, for example, in a division.

establishment
The formally approved size, composition and equipment of a military unit or formation.

SPECIFIC TERMS:
Although there was a fundamental similarity in the way the armies of different countries were organized, there were differences in terminology. As the war progressed, changes were made to the organization, and in countries where manpower was a problem, the number of men at each level was reduced.

battalion
The standard organizational unit for infantry (about 1,000 men). The battalion was further broken down into companies, platoons and specialist sections such as machine-gun, mortar, pioneer and trench artillery sections.
The equivalent unit for cavalry was the regiment, and for artillery the battery.

battery
Unit of organization for artillery, normally consisting of six guns (France four, Russia eight). Three batteries constituted a group (named a brigade in the British army), and two or three groups a regiment.

regiment
Military formation for continental infantry comprising three battalions (3,000 men); in the Russian army it comprised four battalions (4,000). For British infantry, the formation of equivalent size was the brigade.
A cavalry regiment was a basic unit of between 500 and 1,000 men, which was further broken down into squadrons.

brigade
A military formation under one command. In continental armies it consisted of two infantry regiments (6,000 – 8,000 men); in the British army, four infantry battalions (4,000 men). This level of command was generally either reduced or discarded during the course of the war.

division
The smallest body of men fully organized for the conduct of war, complete with infantry, artillery, cavalry and other specialist troops, as well as the necessary administrative services (17,000 – 20,000 men at full strength). The infantry strength of a continental army division was normally two infantry brigades (12 battalions, although the Russian army had 16 battalions). British army divisions included three infantry brigades (12 battalions). The size and composition of a division changed during the course of the war.
The term was also used in the cavalry for a unit of 5,000 men, including two or three brigades of cavalry, batteries of horse artillery, a detachment of engineers, and sometimes light infantry.

corps
Military formation, usually consisting of two divisions (around 40,000 men).

army
Highest military grouping, found necessary only in time of war. Its size varied considerably, from three to six corps.

TYPES OF WARSHIP

dreadnought
Type of battleship, powered by turbines, with standardized heavy armament. It was named after HMS *Dreadnought* (authorized by the British government in 1905 and launched in 1906).

pre-dreadnought
Term applied to all battleships with mixed heavy and medium main armament. A few such warships were built after the launch of the superior HMS *Dreadnought* 1906, but only because they were so advanced in planning that cancellation was not a realistic possibility.

battlecruiser
Term that came to be applied to the class of warship that was initiated with the *Invincible* class (1905). It had a standardized heavy armament, but less armour and a higher speed than a dreadnought. Originally conceived of as fast battleships, battlecruisers were better suited to guarding sea routes and acting as an advance guard or scouting force than to fighting in line of battle.

cruiser
There were three types of cruiser: the armoured cruiser, the protected cruiser and the light cruiser. When *Invincible* class

battlecruisers first appeared in 1905 they were termed armoured cruisers. The older armoured cruisers, hopelessly outclassed in terms of firepower, speed and armour, were reduced to secondary duties. The British nonetheless had some at the Battle of Jutland.
The protected cruiser had some measure of armour, but was not intended to operate against powerful enemy formations. By 1914 it was being superseded by the light cruiser, which was fast enough to play a reconnaissance role, and had sufficient armament to deal with enemy destroyers.

destroyer
A class of fast, lightly armoured warship, originally called the torpedo-boat destroyer. It was developed in the 1890s to combat the torpedo boat, but took on many other functions. During the First World War it was armed with torpedoes and anti-submarine equipment.

WEAPONRY

carbine
Short rifle usually carried by cavalry.

howitzer
Short-barreled, high-angle artillery piece, normally a heavy or medium gun used for destroying fortifications, buildings and trench systems by means of high-trajectory, high-explosive shells.

limber
Simple trailer, consisting of two wheels, an axle and a pole, attached to the rear of a gun carriage for transporting ammunition.

mines
Explosives laid in tunnels excavated under enemy positions. Also explosive devices floating on or just below the surface of the sea.

mortar
High-angle, short-ranged artillery piece. Primarily a trench weapon, not a field piece.

shrapnel shell
A projectile containing a number of small bullets that exploded before impact.

tracer bullet
A small arms or machine-gun bullet with illuminant to allow sighting and correction of fire.

MILITARY TERMINOLOGY

bridgehead
Position occupied on the far side of a river, with communication ensured by either a captured or built bridge.

communications trench
The means of access between successive lines of trenches and forward defensive positions.

creeping barrage
A form of artillery bombardment intended to creep ahead of advancing infantry and thereby prevent the enemy re-occupying forward fire positions. It was first employed during the First World War, in 1916.

cuirassiers
Type of cavalry that wore a metal breast and back plate (a cuirass).

defence-in-depth
A concept that emerged in 1916 when the Germans abandoned the practice of defending from forward positions, at the point of first contact and within range of enemy artillery, in favour of defending from successive positions that stretched back 8–10 km (5–6 miles). This was too great a distance to be overcome in any single attack. As German defensive capacity increased, so did losses for both sides, as the real battlefield moved from No Man's Land into the defensive labyrinth. Neither the British nor the French, committed as they were to offensive operations, really adopted the principle of defence-in-depth.

enfilade
To fire from the flank of an enemy formation along its length. Enfilading fire caused heavy losses among advancing troops.

hurricane bombardment
Name given to intense bombardment of very short duration, minutes rather than hours or days. First employed in 1915.

mask
To position a force in order to prevent enemy movement, such as when a city is controlled from the outside by a force that intends not to take it but to neutralize it and prevent sorties from within by enemy formations.

sap
A deep, narrow trench used to approach or undermine an enemy position; the act of digging such a trench.

sapper
Term used for an engineer.

screen
A small force protecting a larger force.

scuttle
To deliberately sink a ship to prevent its surrender or capture.

turn the enemy's flank
To pass around the enemy's unsecured flank and take up a position behind or alongside it. Rather than a frontal attack, this was the recommended manoeuvre for surrounding and crushing an enemy formation.

uhlan
A lancer – a cavalryman armed with a lance.

INDEX

ACKNOWLEDGEMENTS

The publisher would like to thank the following for the their kind permission to reproduce the photographs:

ABBREVIATIONS KEY:

a = above, b = bottom, c = centre, l = left, r = right, t = top

Bundesarchiv: Bundesarchiv, Koblenz

Firepower: courtesy of Firepower, The Royal Artillery Museum, Royal Artillery Historiacal Trust

Hulton: Getty Images/Hulton Archive

TAA: the**art**archive, London

Ullstein: Ullstein Bild, Berlin

Verney: Collection Jean-Pierre Verney, Paris

front endpaper TAA

1 t Verney; b IWM

2–3 Hulton

4–5 Hulton

6–7 TAA

8–9 AKG

10–11 Imperial War Museum

12 bl Bundesarchiv

12–13 Heeresgeschichtlichen Museum, Vienna

14 t Hulton; b AKG

15 b TAA

16 t Ullstein; bl AKG; br Hulton

17 t Ullstein; b AKG

18 t and tl DK/Firepower; cr Hulton; bl DK; br DK/Firepower

19 tr TAA; b Deutsches Historisches Museum, Berlin

20 t Hulton; b Novosti

21 tr, cl, cr and b Imperial War Museum

22 t Hulton; b Roger Viollet

23 t and cr Endeavour Group; b TAA

24–25 Roger Viollet

26 Imperial War Museum

27 t and cr Imperial War Museum; b Heeresgeschichtlichen Museum, Vienna

28 TL Verney; tc Firepower; all other images Verney

28–29 b Bundesarchiv

29 tl Verney; tr Imperial War Museum; c Deutsches Historisches Museum, Berlin; br TAA

30 tr TAA; cl Verney; cr Robert Harding Picture Library

31 tl Verney; tr Roger Viollet

32 bl TAA

32–33 Roger Viollet

33 tr Hulton; tl AKG; tc, cl and cr TAA; br DK

34–35 Endeavour Group Uk/States Archives of Film, Photography and Documents, St Petersburg

36–37 Heeresgeschichtlichen Museum, Vienna

38 b Roger Viollet

38–39 Roger Viollet

40 TAA

41 background image TAA; bl John Foley; bc Imperial War Museum; br TAA

42 t Verney; bc TAA

43 b Robert Hunt Picture Library/Imperial War Museum

44–45 TAA

46–47 t TAA

47 tr Hulton; b Novosti

48 t Hulton; b Ullstein

49 t Ullstein; br Imperial War Museum

50 t Imperial War Museum; b Hulton

51 tr Corbis; c Roger Viollet

52 b TAA; t Roger Viollet

53 background image Roger Viollet; other images Verney

54 t Imperial War Museum; b TAA

55 tc and tr Firepower; b Robert Hunt Picture Library

56–57 b Hulton

57 t Hulton; b TAA

58–59 t Imperial War Museum; b Robert Hunt Picture Library

59 t, c and b IWM

60 tr Imperial War Museum; t and tl Verney; cl Firepower; c Verney; bl Imperial War Museum

60-61 background image Verney

61 bl Verney; tr and br Imperial War Museum

62 bl Robert Hunt Picture Library

63 t TAA; b Ullstein

64 Oesterreichisches Institut für Zeitgeschichte, Vienna

65 t TAA; c Imperial War Museum; b Novosti

66 t Robert Hunt Picture Library; b Bundesarchiv

67 t Imperial War Museum

68 tl Museo Storico della Guerra, Rovereto; c Weltkriegbucherie Stuttgart; b Robert Hunt Picture Library

69 background image Imperial War Museum; other images Verney

70–71 Roger Viollet

72–73 Oesterreichisches Institut für Zeitgeschichte, Vienna

74–75 Robert Hunt Picture Library/Imperial War Museum

75 b Hulton

76 TAA

77 tl Verney; cl Firepower; cr Verney; cb Imperial War Museum; bl and bc Roger Viollet; br Robert Hunt Picture Library

78 t, bl and br TAA

79 tr and tl TAA; cr Australian War Memorial; b TAA

80 t and br TAA

81 br TAA

82-83 TAA

84 t TAA; b Roger Viollet

85 br Novosti

86 t IMM; br Robert Hunt Picture Library

87 t Robert Hunt Picture Library; b Imperial War Museum

88-89 t Hulton

88 bl TAA; c Verney

89 b Hulton

90 t and b Imperial War Museum

91 t Imperial War Museum; bl Bildarchiv

92 t Robert Hunt Picture Library

93 t and c Robert Hunt Picture Library; b TAA

94 background image Roger Viollet; tl and bl Verney; br Roger Viollet

95 br Robert Hunt Picture Library; tl Imperial War Museum; tr Hulton; c TAA; bl Roger Viollet

96–97 TAA

98–99 TAA

100 t Oesterreichisches Institut für Zeitgeschichte, Vienna

100–101 Roger Viollet

102 TAA

103 bl Imperial War Museum; cr Firepower; br TAA

104 Roger Viollet

105 background image and tr Verney; bl Imperial War Museum; br TAA

106 al Verney; tc Imperial War Museum; tr Firepower

106–107 background image TAA

106 br Verney

107 tl and tr Verney; c TAA; cr and b Verney

108 t Verney

108–109 Robert Hunt Picture Library

109 t TAA

110 bl Verney

110–111 background image TAA

111 t, tl, cl, cr Imperial War Museum; bl Verney; br Corbis

112–113 Roger Viollet

114–115 Robert Hunt Picture Library

115 Oesterreichisches Institut fur Zeitgeschichte, Vienna

116 t Imperial War Museum

116–117 b Heeresgeschichtlichen Museums, Vienna

117 t Imperial War Museum

118 tl AKG; b Heeresgeschichtlichen Museums, Vienna

118–119 Imperial War Museum

119 b Heeresgeschichtlichen Museums, Vienna

120 l TAA

120–121 b TAA

122 t Verney; b Roger Viollet

123 t Hulton; b Roger Viollet

124 t Verney

124–125 b Roger Viollet

125 tl Verney; tr Imperial War Museum; cl and br Verney

126 t TAA; b Verney

127 t Hulton; tr Imperial War Museum; b TAA

128 background image and cl Imperial War Museum; b TAA

129 tl TAA; tr Hulton; bl Verney

130 background image and c IWM; br TAA

130–131 background image AKG

131 tl TAA; tr Verney; br Hulton

132–133 Corbis

134–135 TAA

136 l Imperial War Museum

136–137 TAA

137 tr TAA

138 Hulton

139 background image and cr TAA

140 bl and br Roger Viollet

141 bl Roger Viollet

142 tl Roger Viollet; tr TAA

142–143 b Roger Viollet

143 bl Austin Brown

144 bl Imperial War Museum; bc Firepower; c Verney; br IWM

144145 TAA

145 t Robert Hunt Picture Library; tc Verney; bc Firepower; bl TAA; br Imperial War Museum

146–147 Novosti

147 tl, cl Imperial War Museum; tr TAA; cr, bl and br Verney; b Firepower

148 t Novosti

148–149 b Novosti

149 tr IWM

150 Bildarchiv fur Preussischer Kulturbesitz

151 tr Roger Viollet; cl TAA; b Novosti; br TAA

152 t Robert Hunt Picture Library; b Imperial War Museum

153 t Imperial War Museum

154 t and bl Verney

154–155 TAA

155 tl TAA; tlc Verney; tc, tr and ctr TAA; cl, cr and bc Verney; bl and br TAA

156–157 Hulton

158 t and b TAA

159 Robert Hunt Picture Library

160 TAA

161 t IWM; b TAA

162 t and cr Imperial War Museum; bl Verney;

162–163 TAA

164 t and cl Tank Museum; b Imperial War Museum

164–165 background image Imperial War Museum

165 tl and tc Tank Museum; tr Imperial War Museum; bl and br Tank Museum

166-167 b TAA

167 t Imperial War Museum

168 tl Firepower and DK/Imperial War Museum; cl and b Firepower

168–169 background image Imperial War Museum

169 tl Imperial War Museum; tr Verney; cl and bl Firepower; cr and br DK/Imperial War Museum

170–171 Imperial War Museum

172–173 TAA

174–175 Imperial War Museum

175 Imperial War Museum

176–177 TAA

177 br TAA

178 t and c Imperial War Museum

178–179 b Imperial War Museum

179 t Imperial War Museum; b Roger Viollet

180 b Imperial War Museum

180–181 t TAA

181 b Imperial War Museum; br TAA

182 t Imperial War Museum; b Bundesarchiv

183 tr, background image and bl TAA; br Imperial War Museum

184 t Imperial War Museum; b TAA

185 t TAA; b and cb Imperial War Museum; cr TAA

186 t Heeresgeschichtlichen Museum, Vienna

186–187 Imperial War Museum

188 Verney

189 tl DK/IWM; tr Verney; cr Science and Society Picture Library; b Quadrant

190 t Corbis; b Verney

191 background image and tr Imperial War Museum; cl and cr Verney; bl DK/Imperial War Museum; bra TAA; br Philip Jarret

192 t Imperial War Museum; b TAA

193 tr, cr Imperial War Museum; c Museo Storico della Guerra, Rovereto; cl DK/Imperial War Museum; b TAA

194–195 Verney

196 t and b Corbis

197 background image Roger Viollet; cr Imperial War Museum; bl Verney; bc and br Hulton

198 t Hulton; b TRH Pictures

199 background image, tl, tr and c Hulton

200 tl Hulton; tc TAA; tr Culver Pictures

200–201 Roger Viollet

202–203 TAA

204–205 Roger Viollet

206 b Novosti

206 207 Ullstein

208–209 Robert Hunt Picture Library/IWM

209 tr Verney; bl and br TAA

210 b Verney

210-211 Roger Viollet

211 Roger Viollet

212 Roger Viollet

213 t TAA; tl and b Verney

214 background image Imperial War Museum; tl and tr Verney; bl DK/Imperial War Museum/Andy Crawford; br Verney

215 tl Corbis; bl TAA; br Imperial War Museum

216 t and b TAA

217 background image, tr and cl TAA

218 t Imperial War Museum; b TAA

219 t TAA

220 t Imperial War Museum

220–221 Imperial War Museum

221 tr Roger Viollet; cl and cr Verney; bc Roger Viollet

222 tl Tank Museum; tr Verney; bl Ullstein

223 tl DK/IWM; tr Imperial War Museum

222–223 c Firepower; cl Imperial War Museum; b Tank Museum

224–225 Hulton

226 t Novosti

226–227 b Hulton

227 tr and tc Imperial War Museum; c DK

228 t Novosti; b TAA

229 t Bildarchiv für Preussischer Kulturbesitz; c Robert Hunt Picture Library; b Novosti

230 tl Hulton; tr TAA; b TA

231 t, c and bl Novosti

232 t Museo Storico della Guerra, Rovereto; b Firepower

233 t Museo Storico della Guerra, Rovereto; c Robert Hunt Picture Library

234 t Heeresgeschichtlichen Museum, Vienna; b Ullstein

235 t Heeresgeschichtlichen Museum, Vienna

236 t and b Robert Hunt Picture Library

237 t Firepower; b Robert Hunt Picture Library

238 t IWM; c Verney; cr and b Imperial War Museum

239 tl Firepower; tr Imperial War Museum; b Australian War Memorial

240 t Ullstein; b Robert Hunt Picture Library

241 t Robert Hunt Picture Library; b TAA

242 tc and cl Imperial War Museum; b Bridgeman Art Library

242–243 background image TAA

243 tl and tr TAA; b Verney

244–245 Imperial War Museum

246–247 TAA

248 BL TAA

248–249 Imperial War Museum

250 Bildarchiv für Preussischer Kulturbesitz

251 t TAA; b Corbis

252 t Ullstein

252 bl Firepower; br Verney

253 t Hulton; b TAA

254–255 t TAA

255 bl Deutsches Historisches Museum, Berlin; br Imperial War Museum

256 t Imperial War Museum; B Deutsches Historisches Museum, Berlin

257 t Roger Viollet; cl Imperial War Museum; br Roger Viollet

258 t ECPA

259 t Imperial War Museum

260 tl Verney; b Imperial War Museum

260–261 t Australian War Memorial

261 tl Bridgeman Art Library © ADAGP, Paris and DACS, London 2003; tr Albertina, Vienna; c Stadtisches Galerie, Albstadt © DACS 2003; bl Imperial War Museum; br Verney

262 Imperial War Museum

263 t TAA; bl Verney; br Roger Viollet

264 Verney

265 tl and tr TAA; b Imperial War Museum

266 t TAA; b Verney

267 background image and other images Verney

268–269 Imperial War Museum

270 Robert Hunt Picture Library

271 t Robert Hunt Picture Library; bl Roger Viollet

272 b TAA

272–273 t Imperial War Museum

274 t Museo Storico della Guerra, Rovereto; b Robert Hunt Picture Library

275 background image Museo Storico della Guerra, Rovereto; br Museo Storico della Guerra, Rovereto; other images Verney

276–277 t Museo Storico della Guerra, Rovereto

277 b Robert Hunt Picture Library

278 Imperial War Museum

279 tl Imperial War Museum; c Hulton

280–281 Corbis

282–283 TAA

284 t and b Verney

285 tr Ullstein; cl and cr Imperial War Museum; b Ullstein

286 t TAA; c Imperial War Museum

287 t Imperial War Museum; c Advertising Archives; bl Culver; br Hulton

288 t TAA/Imperial War Museum; b Roger Viollet

289 background image John Frost Newspapers; c TAA; cr and bl Verney; bc TAA; br Verney

290–291 Endeavour Group

292–293 TAA

294–295 Hulton

295 Hulton

296 t Ullstein

297 t Bildarchiv für Preussischer Kulturbesitz; b Hulton

298 b Bildarchiv für Preussischer Kulturbesitz

299 b Bildarchiv für Preussischer Kulturbesitz

300 t Bildarchiv für Preussischer Kulturbesitz; b Ullstein

301 tr Corbis; cl AKG; bl and br David King Collection

302 t and b Roger Viollet

303 tr Corbis; b Roger Viollet

304 b Private collection

304–305 t Roger Viollet

305 b Hulton

306-307 Roger Viollet

307 tr Verney

308–309 Roger Viollet

DORLING KINDERSLEY PHOTOGRAPHY:

Peter Chadwick, Andy Crawford, Geoff Dann; Anthony Haughey

CREDITS FOR QUOTATIONS

Every effort has been made to gain permission from the relevant copyright holders to reproduce the extracts that appear in this book. The following have kindly given permission for extracts to be quoted in the book:

109 Extract from *Goodbye to All That* by Robert Graves. Used by permission of Carcanet Press Limited.

114; 150; 205 Extracts from *The First World War* by John Keegan published by Hutchinson. Used with permission of the Random House Group Limited.

135 Extract from *Storm of Steel* by Ernst Jünger, published by Penguin Books.

160; 212 Extracts from *Forgotten Voices of The Great War* by Max Arthur published by Ebury. Used by permission of the Random House Group Limited.

233 Extract from *War and the Future: Italy, France and Britain at War* by H. G. Wells. Used by permission of A P Watt Ltd on behalf of The Literary Executors of the Estate of H. G. Wells.

237 Extract from *Revolt in the Desert* by T. E. Lawrence, published by Wordsworth Editions Ltd.

242 Extract from *Break of Day in the Trenches* by Isaac Rosenberg, taken from The Complete Works of Isaac Rosenberg (1979), edited by Ian Parsons.

243 Extract from *Dulce et Decorum Est* by Wilfred Owen, taken from Complete Poems and Fragments of Wilfred Owen (1983), edited by John Galsworthy.

243 Extract from *Le Feu (Under Fire)* by Henri Barbusse, published by Penguin Books.

247; 254; 258 Extracts from *The Imperial War Museum Book of 1918* by Malcolm Brown, published by Macmillan, London, UK.

DORLING KINDERSLEY WOULD LIKE TO THANK:

Jean-Pierre Verney for all his help and advice. Les Smith and his staff at Firepower, the Royal Artillery Museum, Elizabeth Bowers and her staff at the Imperial War Museum. Tom Coulson at Encompass Graphics. Alex Reay and Phil Crowcroft at Advanced Illustration.

THE AUTHOR WOULD LIKE TO THANK:

Everybody at DK's History and Cartography department who worked on this book. He would also like to thank the following for their professional help and guidance in the making of the book: Tony Clayton, Michael Coles, Spencer Johnson, Terry Lilley, Adam Lynde, Gordon Angus Macinley, John Andreas Olsen, William O'Neil, Jack Sweetman, Tohmatsu Haruo, John Votaw and Steven Weingartner. He is also grateful for the invaluable support of his professional colleagues, Tim Bean, Patrick Burke, Nigel de Lee, Christopher Duffy and Paul Harris. Special thanks are also due to librarians Jennie Wraight, Iain MacKenzie, Andrew Orgill, Ken Franklin and John Pearce, for providing access to their libraries, collections and personal knowledge.